Customs & Excises in One Lesson

Customs & Excises in One Lesson

The Shortest and Surest Way to Understand Basic Customs & Excises

Christiaan Viljoen de Lange

Wolters Kluwer

Published by:
Kluwer Law International B.V.
PO Box 316
2400 AH Alphen aan den Rijn
The Netherlands
E-mail: lrs-sales@wolterskluwer.com
Website: www.wolterskluwer.com/en/solutions/kluwerlawinternational

Sold and distributed by:
Wolters Kluwer Legal & Regulatory U.S.
920 Links Avenue
Landisville, PA 17538
United States of America
E-mail: customer.service@wolterskluwer.com

ISBN 978-94-035-3702-3

e-Book: ISBN 978-94-035-3703-0
web-PDF: ISBN 978-94-035-3704-7

About the Author

Christiaan Viljoen de Lange is an experienced and seasoned Customs and Excises practitioner. He is passionate about the history and evolution of Customs and Excises, as well as the practical application of its provisions. Christiaan communicates and educates on the fundamentals and the simplification of Customs and Excises intricacies through various channels, including articles, chapters in books, conferences, courses, and lectures. He has actively participated in tariff and trade policy negotiations for the world's largest trade bloc and the world's oldest operational trade bloc. Christiaan has supported governments and businesses in tariff and trade applications, policy formulation, and strategy formulation by providing practical insights and rigorous economic analysis. He authored a definitive guide on trade remedies – dumping, countervailing (anti-subsidy), and safeguards in the world's oldest operational trade bloc. Christiaan has consulted with governments, non-governmental organisations (NGOs), blue-chip multinational companies and family-owned businesses internationally, in various jurisdictions, and on various projects. He has lectured on Economics, International Economics, Customs and Excises at universities. Christiaan holds an MCom (Economics), MPhil (Taxation), Master in Business Leadership (MBL), BCom Hons (Economics) and BCom (Economics), as well as various Customs and Excises qualifications and certifications.

Table of Contents

Overview

Customs and Excises continue to be shrouded in mystery, primarily due to the inconsistency in the use of its terminology, its application, and ignorance. The primary challenge is that its applied terminology is not unique or subject specific. As a consequence, it tends to be erroneously read, interpreted, and understood for its linguistic meaning rather than for its specific Customs and Excises meaning. Another more critical oversight is that Customs and Excises are inherently Economics, founded on its principles.

As the scope of Customs and Excises is so broad, it is not possible to consider it as a specialisation without defining the demarcated focus. The focus of this book is solely on the goods – the merchandise.

This book will provide you with a unique and innovative roadmap to easily navigate your way through the Customs and Excises cornerstones, concepts, methodologies, and procedures and to provide you with a Customs Optimisation Process, which was derived from the Lesson. This book challenges the fallacy that the Customs and Excises environment is not susceptible to a coherent summary.

Customs and Excises can be reduced to a single lesson and itself into a single sentence. *'The art of Customs and Excises consists of not merely accepting the terminology for its linguistic meaning; it consists of ensuring that the terminology, its context, its meaning, and its effective, efficient, and compliant application is fully understood, and appreciated, in both its reference and application.'*

For easier understanding, the book is presented in two parts:

Part I: The Lesson
Part II: The Lesson Applied
Section I The Cornerstones, Remedies, Duty, Tax, and Levy
Section II Special Customs Procedures/Regimes
Section III Trade Blocs – Economic Integration
Section IV Non-Tariff and Trade Barriers
Section V International Commercial Terms (Incoterms®)
Section VI Denied Party Screening, and Sanctions Screening

Section VII The Lesson's Roadmap, Timeline, Milestones, Elucidations of Trade Terms, Organisations, Agreements, Conventions, Resources, and In a Minute (I'm ™)

Including International Organisations, Selected Resources, Elucidation of Terms, Acronyms and Agreements and Conventions.

Each Section concludes with a *'Points of Interest'*.

The analysis of Customs and Excise topics is based on the Agreements, Conventions, Declarations, and Frameworks administered by the World Customs Organization (WCO), the World Trade Organization (WTO), and other key International Organisations.

This book intends to provide you with a roadmap to navigate the Customs and Excises environment, supplemented with diagrams that can be used independently or as a collective.

This book caters to Customs and Excises compliance practitioners, trade compliance practitioners, students and young professionals who are in the early stages of understanding the nuances of Customs and Excises. It also informs tax practitioners, in-house tax counsels, academics working in international organisations, the business community, advisory firms, and government officials interested in understanding the intricacies and the foundations of Customs and Excises.

Preface

This book identifies, accentuates, and articulates the inconsistency in the use of Customs and Excises terminology and the application of the methodology while proceeding, chapter by chapter, to develop a unique framework to collectively serve as a one-page roadmap for both the novice and the more experienced practitioner. The roadmap challenges the fallacy that the Customs and Excises environment is not susceptible to a coherent summarisation. The fallacy is in part attributable to the fact that although premised on fundamental Economic principles, the Customs and Excises environment tends not to be a domain inhabited by Economists, nor are the Economic fundamentals appreciated and even adhered to. Customs and Excise courses tend not to acknowledge the Economic foundation, thus neglecting to elucidate the fundamental economic principles.

The volume makes its claim to originality as it offers a unique reflection on not only the historical origin and perspective of the present-day cornerstones – codification, origination, and valorisation, remedies – anti-dumping, countervailing, and safeguards, duties, taxes, and levies, but also the PSST procedures/regimes, trade blocs – economic integration, non-tariff measures, non-tariff barriers, and trade barriers, international commercial terms, denied party screening, and sanctions screening. All of which are encapsulated into a diagrammatic observation – '*The Lesson's Roadmap*', the components of which could be considered in the '*Points of Interest*' section that provides practical schematics, encapsulating the essence of the section. To remedy and to challenge the inconsistency in the application and use of the terminology and methodology, insight and explanation are offered through the '*Acronyms and Elucidation of Trade Terms*', accentuating what is covered within the book. To encourage you to embark on further exploration, the more pertinent '*International Customs and Trade Organisations, Committees, Agreements, and Conventions*', with its objectives are referenced. If you wish to explore the historic evolution, the '*Customs and Excises Timeline and Milestone*' will chart the route. To ensure that your knowledge remains relevant, the '*Selected Resources*' is the final offering, which offers a treasure-trove of practical references.

If you are a novice or a more experienced Customs and Excises practitioner, it should nevertheless bear a continuous reminder that Customs and Excises are essentially Economics. It requires you to possess or attain a basic working knowledge of the Economic fundamental principles.

While this book has been composed as a unit, it can be read out of section and chapter sequence, although it is recommended that, when you read it for the first time, you should consider it in its sequence as it ultimately leads to the formulation of '*The Lesson's Roadmap*'.

I am most grateful to you for your investment and commitment, even if it is only out of pure curiosity to embark on your Customs and Excises journey or reevaluate it.

The most frustrating and challenging aspect of the Customs and Excises environment is the inconsistent and inaccurate use of terminology. Your constant challenge will be to ensure that you acquire and maintain an accurate understanding of its terminology, concepts, methodologies, and, most critically, the account for the context in which it is applied.

Acknowledgements

Even though only one name appears on the cover, its creation is no solo endeavour by any stretch of the imagination. The Highlander's mantra that '*There can be only one*' does not apply, just as it is not possible for there to be self-made millionaires, nor even remotely self-made billionaires. It is a collective effort, with many a faceless individual having contributed, both wittingly and unwittingly.

In pitching the idea for this book, I was extremely fortunate to have found editors in Simon Bellamy and Gwen de Vries, and a publisher who believed in the book's conceptualisation, even though they did not know me from a bar of soap. The single objective in authoring the book was to provide you with a working knowledge of Customs and Excises, contribute to and challenge, and do so as succinctly as possible.

The book you hold in your hands is a culmination of over 34 years of blood, toil, sweat, tears, and laughter, more often than not out of pure desperation. In the desperation of my desire to complete the book by the deadline, I found solace in the sage words of John Cleese (as Brian Stimpson in the film *Clockwise*), '*It is not the despair, I can take the despair. It is the hope that is what is killing me.*'

Customs and Excises is a specialisation for which one is seemingly unwittingly chosen or drawn, just like an unsolved mystery, a cold case. It is a specialisation filled with mystery, suspense, and intrigue, where, as with any good mystery, there are characters aplenty that know both a truthful fact and also hold certain unwavering untruths and have their beliefs in fallacies. The latter causes will challenge your resolve, but do not let it lead you to desperation, and frustration. On your journey, you will encounter many an Inspector Jacques Clouseau. Still, you should seek the equivalent of Agatha Christie's Hercule Poirot for sage guidance and counsel. I hope this book will serve as your companion and be a trusted reference as you journey to honing your skills to become a Customs and Excises maven, that seemingly unattainable level of proficiency that we all strive to achieve. As with karate, although attaining a black belt is an awe-inspiring accomplishment, it does not mean that you have reached the pinnacle of karate skills, as there are 10 levels of black belts or dan. The attainment of each ensuing dan, or advanced rank, requires years of intense and continuous training.

As you embark on your Customs and Excises journey or continue along its winding road, heed the profound words of Mark Twain, '*It ain't what you do not know that gets you into trouble. It is what you know for sure that just ain't so.*'

In making this book a reality, I acknowledge and confess that writing and its associated research is a selfish endeavour; let no one ever profess otherwise. All praise be to God. On a human level, I dedicate the fruits of my toil to my only constant, my wife, Callie; my son, Lochlan; and my lifelong mentor, Len Chalom. Thank you for your unwavering support and patience, particularly in writing this book, for which I had a burning desire. Although your sole Customs experience has been to pass through its borders on your travels, you still have plenty of a war story to share. As for your Excises experience, I could not possibly comment.

In the instance of the faceless many that I neglected in expressing my individual appreciation to, please take solace in the words of my former President, Nelson Mandela, '*I am what I am both as a result of people who respected me and helped me and of those who did not respect me and treated me badly.*'

Part I The Lesson

CHAPTER 1

The Lesson

Caveat Lector[1] – 'A Duty is a Tax that you Levy'[2]

'*Customs and Excises is Economics*', plain and simple. You have been done a great disservice if you were not attuned to this fact. Within the fray of Economics, the economist Henry Hazlitt attests that '*Economics is haunted by more fallacies than any other study known to man.*' The aforementioned could not be truer than for Customs and Excises, with the added dimension that it is professed by many to be an area of constant evolution and innovation if only this were true. As a case in point, the League of Nations (LN)[3] '*International Convention relating to the Simplification of Customs Formalities*' was registered with its Secretariat on 3 November 1923 and entered into force on 27 November 1924. Fast forward to our present day, and you would be hard-pressed to find anything remotely new in the '*International Convention on the Simplification and Harmonization of Customs Procedures (as amended)*', simply known as the Revised Kyoto Convention or RKC, which contends to be '*the blueprint for modern and efficient Customs procedures in the 21st century*'.

The core principles in Economics are the trilogy of scarcity, choice, and opportunity cost. Within these confines, the producers or manufacturers strive to maximise

1. *Caveat lector* is a Latin phrase which means '*let the reader beware*'. Due care should be taken to assess whether the content is accurate, reliable, and dependable.
2. Although '*duty*', '*tax*', and '*levy*' are three quite distinct concepts in the Customs and Excises environment, they tend to be used interchangeably, seemingly assumed to be synonyms. Out of frustration, early in my career, of not being provided with a clear and concise distinction between the three concepts, I questioned whether, '*A duty is tax that you levy?*' Do not be lured into a false sense of security, it is not a case of '*potato, patato*' or '*potayto, potahto*'; these are three distinct terms. There could be the assertion, in Europe, of a fourth concept – '*cess*', shortened for '*assess*'. Governments impose it for a specific purpose. The revenue collected from its imposition must be ringfenced; it must be used solely for the intended cause, which could be agreed to be the purpose of an excise duty, in its purest form. '*Cess*' is not further explored in the book.
3. The League of Nations (LN), founded at the Paris Peace Conference on 24 April 1919, was the forerunner of the United Nations (UN).

their profits. In contrast, consumers seek to maximise their utility or benefits. It is not concerned with the Authority, but it is the Customs Authority that impacts either the extent of the businesses' and consumers' interaction or the extent of their respective maximisation through its actions.

Consumers aim to address their needs and wants, as for desires, which are not an Economic concept, the latter being to acquire and consume non-essential goods, also known as luxury goods, and vanity goods. Suppose the goods are not available in a domestic market. In that case, it is imported, while goods which are not needed in a market or of which there is a surplus supply are for which a demand in a foreign market is supplied to the market, in other words, exported.

The primary challenge[4] in the Customs and Excises environment is that its applied terminology is not subject matter specific. As a consequence, the terminology tends to be erroneously read, interpreted, and understood for its linguistic meaning rather than for its particular Customs and Excises subject matter meaning. Consider the instance of a '*drawback*', which, contrary to its linguistic definition, is not a disadvantage but, to the contrary, renders a financial advantage or benefit in its Customs and Excises application. The challenge with gaining a working knowledge of the Customs and Excises terminology is partly due to the nature and extent of the subject matter coverage, its myriad of role-players, its institutions, its rules, regulations, conventions, agreements, and frameworks and the context in which it is applied.

There is no stronger exemplification of the indiscriminate and interchangeable use of Customs and Excises terminology than the phrase, '*A duty is a tax that you levy.*' As you embark on your journey or continue, never simply accept the word being used; actively question and interrogate its context, relevance, and meaning. Heed the words of William Shakespeare, an English playwright, who said: '*A rose by any other name would smell as sweet.*' In other words, it matters what something is, not what it is called.

Suffice it to say customs duty is simply not a '*tax*', a '*levy*', a '*charge*' (*surcharge*), or a '*toll*', as is evidenced when considering its origin. Its naming convention originates as a '*customary due*'. A '*due*', or present-day '*duty*', holds distinct and differing characteristics from a '*tax*', as it does from a '*levy*' and as a '*levy*' does from a '*tax*'. It is not helpful that customs and excise duties are classified as *indirect taxes,*[5] subdivided into '*sin taxes*'[6] and '*luxury taxes*'.[7] Then, although customs duty and import duty are used interchangeably, an import duty includes several duties payable on import, taxes,

4. As you approach 'The Lesson' do heed the words of Mark Twain, '*It ain't what you don't know that gets you into trouble. It's what you know for sure that just ain't so.*'
5. Indirect taxes are taxes that are levied on the consumption of goods, which implies that the consumer ultimately pays the tax, although the producer might collect it and pay it to the Customs and Excises Authority, Institution, or Agency. In the instance of Customs and Excises, it should really be '*indirect duties*'.
6. '*Sin taxes*' are taxes which are levied on goods which through its manufacture of use are considered to be harmful or costly to the society. In the instance of Customs and Excises, it should really be '*sin duties*'.
7. '*Luxury taxes*' or '*non-essential taxes*' are taxes imposed on goods which could well be considered vanity goods, which are not really needed and merely contribute to the depletion of the world's natural resources. In the instance of Customs and Excises it should really be '*luxury duties*'.

levies, and surcharges, including excise duty itself. A '*levy*' is imposed for a designated purpose, while a surcharge, as the word suggests, with the prefix '*sur*' meaning an '*over and above*' charge.

As for ancient times, the Romans did not distinguish between '*indirect taxes*' and '*direct taxes*' but rather between '*Tributa*' and '*Vectigalia*'.[8] '*Tributa*' meant '*land tax*', or '*poll tax*', which would qualify as modern-day direct taxes, and '*Vectigalia*', which meant other states' revenue, such as '*Portoria*',[9] which refers to customs duty and tolls, qualify as modern-day indirect taxes.

Although not associated with tax, the Rosetta Stone is a key artefact that significantly contributed to deciphering ancient Egyptian hieroglyphs. It is primarily a tax document explaining new tax laws decreed. In 196 BC, the Rosetta Stone, a fragment of a larger slab, was erected at an Egyptian temple during the reign of Ptolemy V, a Ptolemaic king of Macedonian Greek ancestry.[10]

Customs, not the institution but the duty, have been around for as long as humanity. It even has its own gods - in Greek mythology, Hermes - the protector and patron of trade who delivered messages and instructions between the gods and mortals. Hermes was the only Olympian god capable of crossing the borders between the living and the dead. In Roman mythology, Hermes was known as Mercury, a name originating from Latin '*merx*', from which the word '*merchandise*', which tends to simply be referred to as '*goods*', is derived, and the word '*merchant*'.

Then, for good measure, Customs the subject matter has its own Adam. In a twist of irony, Adam Smith is widely considered the father of Economics and the author of *An Inquiry into the Nature and Causes of the Wealth of Nations*, simply known as *The Wealth of Nations*, the seminal work in Economics, was not only the guardian for free trade but in his final years also served as the Commissioner of Customs, Edinburgh, Scotland. In *The Wealth of Nations*, published on 9 March 1776, coincidently also the year of the American Declaration of Independence, Smith writes, '*Customs had existed since time immemorial, but was unable to say precisely when they were first introduced.*'

Well, maybe not quite. Arguably, the most visible part of customs, the duty or customs duty, originates from the word '*customary due*' and was first applied in 609 BC in Egypt. The Romans called their customs duty equivalent '*Portorium*', but it had a much broader scope than present-day customs duty. It covered three elements. Customs duties were collected at the frontiers (what we know as borders) of provinces

---

8. '*Vectigalia*' consist of four principal taxes, namely: (i) '*Portoria*' - customs duty and tools; (ii) '*Vilesima Hereditatium*' - inheritance and legacy tax; (iii) '*Vicesima Libertatis*' - postage tax; and (iv) '*Centesima*' or '*Ducentesima Rerum Venalium*' - auction sales tax.
9. '*Portoria*', also known as a '*poll tax*'. In ancient Rome, income tax was not imposed, a tax was however imposed on goods entering of exiting Rome. The tax was an *ad valorem* tax, imposed on the value of the goods. It was abolished in 60 BC. '*Portoria*' should not be confused with '*Porto'rium*' which was a branch of the Roman state that collected revenues.
10. On 15 July 1799, the Rosetta Stone was found by a French officer, Pierre-François Bouchard, during the Napoleonic campaign in Egypt. The stone is built into an old wall near the town of Rashid (Rosetta) in the Nile Delta. On 14 September 1822, Jean-François Champollion, who dedicated his life to studying historical languages, discovered how to read Egyptian hieroglyphs using the Rosetta Stone and unlock the secrets of the ancient civilisation. In the process, he solves one of history's greatest mysteries.

or states for the account of the state (the central government). Then, '*Octroi*' was collected at the time of entry into or departure for a city or the territory of a city for the account of the city (the local government). And finally, a '*Toll*' was a passage tax paid for using a road or crossing over a bridge.

Although this is a significant landmark in Customs, the more significant dates are those that led to the refinement of Customs, which are acknowledged to be the cornerstones of Customs.

In contemplating the cornerstones, without being tempted to page forward, imagine that you are faced with a good of which you hold no prior knowledge. There might well be those who take issue and offer a contrary view, sighting that the Mesopotamians collected customs duty more than 3 500 years ago. These were, in fact, '*Tolls*' imposed on the movement of the goods themselves rather than on the goods being traded. The Egyptians, in contrast, imposed a customs duty on the goods being traded. This saw customs duty being employed as a fiscal measure, but that is not customs duty's sole application. It can also be utilised as a protective[11] measure to restrict the import of goods into a country or territory. It was first employed as such in 1664 by the French Finance Minister, Jean-Baptise Colbert.[12]

When faced with a new good, I contend that you would pose only three primary questions in your observation. You would want to know – *What is it? Where is it from?* (*Where it is made?*) *What is its price?* (or what is its worth?). These are no different from the questions that Customs and Excise Authorities pose in considering, assessing, and deliberating imported or domestically produced or manufactured goods. These questions have remained unchanged for centuries, and to this day, they are the questions that need to be answered to determine a good's Customs and Excises liability.

Customs Authorities, also known as Customs Institutions, Customs Administrations, Customs Service, or Customs Agencies,[13] have traditionally been assigned a three-pronged responsibility to collect, protect, and facilitate.[14] '*To collect*' implies that all duties, taxes, levies, and surcharges imposed on goods must be collected. '*To protect*' means security, and facilitation refers to trade facilitation. For security and trade facilitation, the World Customs Organization (WCO)'s Framework of Standards to Secure and Facilitate Global Trade, also known as the SAFE framework, was adopted at its June 2005 Council Sessions.[15] '*To facilitate*', or trade facilitation, there is an

11. A country's government's view of the role of their Customs Authority can, more often than not, be gleaned as its main administrative responsibility, be it as revenue authority, or a protective authority. A revenue authority if there is a strong reliance on the revenue collected on imports, and as a protective authority if the intention is to enforce import and export prohibitions, restrictions, controls, protective measures, and trade preferences, and agreements.
12. Comptroller-General of Finances under Louis XIV (the Sun King and creator of the Palace of Versailles). Colbert was responsible for the creation of commercial companies such as the East India Company in the 1660s and 1670s. He lent his name to Colbertism, a form of Mercantilistic policy, that encourages state intervention and protectionism.
13. Another example of the interchangeable nature and use of terminology. My continued challenge to you is to vigilantly pursue the purpose and distinction of the designations.
14. The traditional responsibility to Collect, Protect, and Facilitate, which some argue to have changed to a modern-day responsibility of Taxation, Security, and Trade Facilitation.
15. The SAFE Framework sets forth the principles and the standards and presents them for adoption as a minimal threshold of what should be done by WCO Members.

agreement, the World Trade Organization (WTO) Trade Facilitation Agreement (TFA),[16] the most recent of its Agreements, which entered into force on 22 February 2017. Trade facilitation, called *'the plumbing of business'*, intends to reduce all the transaction costs associated with the enforcement, regulation, and administration of trade policies.[17]

I would argue that their Customs Authorities have quadruple *'ion'* responsibilities, that of collection, protection, facilitation, and harmonisation. Should you cite enforcement, I would argue that it is at least accounted for in collection and protection, and then too in the facilitation and harmonisation. To articulate the addition of the explanation of facilitation and harmonisation is required. In addition to the earlier description, facilitation includes the implementation of measures leading to the simplification, standardisation and modernisation of the formalities, procedures, documents and operations inherent to international trade transactions. *'Harmonisation'* refers to the alignment of national formalities, procedures, documents, information, and operations to acceptable international commercial norms, practices and recommendations.

Returning to the consideration of the good, the *'What is it?'*, or the classification - tariff classification - dates back to 199 BC when the Roman Customs Administration first established it. The *'Where is it from?'* (*'Where is it made?'*), or the origin of the goods, dates back to between AD 907 and AD 911 when the Byzantine Empire first applied preferential duty for goods originating in Russia. The *'What is its price?'* (*'What is its worth?'*), or the valuation - customs valuation - dates back to 400 BC, with the Arthashastra, which established and defined the customs valuation practice. The three pillars could also be termed *'codification'* (tariff classification), *'origination'* (origin), and *'valorisation'* (customs valuation). The *'ion'* suffices, denoting the action that needs to be undertaken.

Contrary to popular belief, these concepts are by no stretch of the imagination modern in their conceptualisation. But that is not to say that the evolution is not continuing; take Value Added Tax (VAT), first introduced in France on 10 April 1954, and Transfer Pricing (TP), which saw the Organisation for Economic Co-operation and Development (OECD) publishing its first guidelines in 1976. In recent years, there has been persistent deliberation on the harmonisation of customs valuation, VAT, and TP, which imposes its own challenges on Customs and Excises Compliance.

The *'elements of taxation'* - classification, origin and valuation - as the European Commission (EC) references it, and which I prefer to call the *'cornerstones'*, are at the core of the interplay in the calculation of a good's duty liability. As for the imposition of the duty, tax, and levy (the types, not the rate), there is an array of types, the most prominent of which are *ad valorem* (according to value), specific (quantitative measure), and compound (combination of the two).

As a result of the adherence to the cornerstones, not only can the duty liability be calculated but so too the imposition of trade remedy duties (also known as trade

16. *'The Four Pillars of Trade Facilitation'* is defined by the Swedish National Board of Trade to be Transparency, Simplification, Harmonisation and Standardisation.
17. *'Development, Trade, and the WTO'* by Bernard Hoekman, Philip English, and Aaditya Mattoo.

defence duties) – dumping (first introduced in Canada in 1904), countervailing, or anti-subsidy (first introduced in the United States of America in 1897), and safeguards (considered to be bounties, as detailed by Adam Smith in *The Wealth of Nations*);[18] the applicability of import control, export control;[19] whether it is prohibited goods, and restricted goods; and its classification as Non-tariff Measures (NTMs)[20] and Non-tariff Barriers (NTBs).[21] For completeness, there is also an export duty, which can be imposed on exported goods, dating back to 1275 when it was first imposed in England. '*Export duty*' is still being imposed, predominantly in developing countries, but not to the same extent as customs duty. An '*export duty*' tends to be imposed on raw, primary, or unprocessed materials. That said, in recent years, the use of Voluntary Export Restraint (VER) has found more favour. The '*voluntary*' tends to be a contradiction in terms, as the action is more of a compulsory nature. It is reminiscent of the term '*free trade*', which is in its purest form but mere '*fair trade*'.[22]

Turning to the rate of customs duty or tariff, it suffices to say that it originates from the word '*Tarifa*',[23] a small Spanish town on the Strait of Gibraltar.[24] Tarifa is the town where two seas – the Mediterranean Sea (calm and warm) and the Atlantic Ocean (wild and rough),[25] and two continents – Africa and Europe – meet. Tarifa is also where legend has one of the Pillars of Hercules, the other being in Ceuta, a Spanish exclave in North Africa, marking the world's end, with the inscription '*Non plus ultra*', meaning '*Nothing further beyond*'. Tarifa has the distinction of being the town that both introduced tariffs to the world and also marked the end of the ancient world, not that tariffs today are the end of the world.

The Revised Kyoto Convention or RKC developed and administered by the WCO, which entered into force on 3 February 2006, promotes trade facilitation and effective controls through its legal provisions that detail the application of simple yet efficient procedures and defines '*customs duties*' as '*duties laid down in the Customs tariff* …'. It does not offer a definition of '*import duties*'. It does define '*export duties and taxes*' as '*Customs duties and all other duties, taxes or charges which are collected on or in connection with the exportation of goods, but not including any charges* … .' To further illustrate the challenge in terminology, a '*tariff*' has a trilogy of meanings. It could first be a list or a schedule that depicts the rates of duty payable on the importation or the exportation of the good. Second, it could refer to the actual duty being levied on the

18. *See* Chapter 5 '*Trade Remedies – Dumping, Countervailing, and Safeguards*'.
19. *See* Chapter 14 '*Import Controls and Export Controls*'.
20. *See* Chapter 15 '*Non-tariff Measures*'.
21. *See* Chapter 16 '*Non-tariff Barriers*'.
22. One of the WTO's '*Principles of the Trading System*' is '*Freer trade: gradually, through negotiation*'.
23. Tarifa situated at the southernmost point of the Iberian Peninsula, on the Costa de la Luz ('*coast of light*'), across the Strait of Gibraltar from Morocco, is nowadays famed as one of the world's most popular destinations for wind sports.
24. Legend has that Hercules made the Strait of Gibraltar. The Temple of Hercules Gaditanus, on the southern outskirts of Gadir-Gades, present-day Cádiz on the Spanish west coast, is said to have housed the remains of Hercules.
25. The main distinction between a sea and an ocean is size and location. Oceans are the largest and the deepest, while seas are smaller and often partially enclosed by land.

importation or the exportation of the good. Third, it could be the law that provides for the schedules of not only the tariff but also the customs provisions to mitigate the rate of customs duty. So it could, depending on the context, be the list or schedule, duty, and law.

The RKC promotes trade facilitation and effective controls through its legal provisions detailing simple yet efficient procedures. It also contains new and obligatory rules for its application, which all Contracting Parties must accept without reservation.[26]

With the potential customs duty liability, barriers to trade, and restrictions known, several mitigations could be considered for application based on the nature and customs treatment of the goods. Before considering the mitigations, the principle of customs duty exemption is nothing new. Diplomats in Greece, Rome, and the Indian Subcontinent were exempted from the payment of customs duty at least as long as 2,000 years ago.[27] The '*Lex Portorii Asiae*' (Customs Law of Asia) dealt with the customs dues of the Roman province of Asia and Bithynia (western Türkiye). It was enforced from 75 BC to AD 62 and contained a provision for import duty exemptions in Pergamene harbour (enforcing Augustus Caesar's decision) and also conceded the ambassadors (diplomats); and the exemption from customs due (import duty) for conveyances in the course of transit. Present-day '*transit*' is considered a '*Special Customs Procedure*' or '*Special Customs Regime*'.

Considering the '*Special Customs Procedures*' or '*Special Customs Regimes*' available to businesses, you could do so surreptitiously by being attentive to a whisper - PSST. Although it might not specifically be called by these names of categorisation (even though it is the international Customs intention for it to be) - Processing (P), Specific Use (S), Storage (S), and Transit (T), these are what I call Special Customs Procedures/Regimes (SCP), which are broadly applied: Processing - Inward Processing (IP) and Outward Processing (OP); Specific Use - Temporary Admission (TA) and End Use; Storage - Customs Warehousing (CW) and Free Zones (FZ); and Transit - Customs Transit and Transhipment. These SCP allow for the customs duty liability to be deferred or suspended, subject to specific Customs provisions that are underwritten by guarantees or security. This should not be confused with duty suspensions and tariff suspensions. Countries can introduce their own procedures, which are not considered SCP, such as Returned Goods Relief (RGR), which provides for the re-importing of goods that were previously exported. Another such procedure is Temporary Storage (TS) where imported goods are temporarily stored under Customs control before they are placed under an SCP, released to free circulation, also known as home use, or which are exported.

Then there is the terminology of '*drawback*', '*rebate*', and '*refund*' that is still in use, and which definition can cause confusion. The confusion is created by the fact that traditionally, a '*rebate*' allows for the reduction or waiving of the import duties, while a '*drawback*' for the recovery of import duty once a specified economic activity had

26. '*The Revised Kyoto Convention*' tends to also be written as '*The revised Kyoto Convention*'.
27. Le Portorium Chez Les Romains

been completed, and then a *'refund'* for the overpaid import duties to be recovered from the Customs Authorities.

An additional consideration to the application and use of SCP to reduce the customs duty liability is to employ trade preferences and trade agreements, the latter known as *'trade blocs'*. The aforementioned is not a spelling error, as *'trade blocs'* is its economic spelling. By now, you would have surmised and acknowledged that the core of Customs and Excises is Economics, which begs the question of why all involved in Customs and Excises do not have an economic grounding or, at the very least, a working knowledge of Economics. The training on offer tends to exclusively focus on the administrative aspects of Customs and Excises' processes and procedures while not focusing on the policy aspects, and, as a consequence, not acknowledging but rather ignoring the foundation of it all – Economics.

If you are under the impression that trade blocs are a modern invention, you might want to reconsider, as the oldest trade bloc dates back to the Hanseatic League that existed between the 12th and 17th centuries, which became modern-day Germany. If you associate *'free trade'* with the *'trade blocs'* and, consequently, are quite mesmerised by the word *'free'*, take heed of John Ruskin's profound words, *'There is no free lunch.'* To further counter your mesmerisation, consider just how *'free'* the following is, *'Free range eggs sold here!'* and *'Free advice, you get what you pay for!'*

'Free trade' implies many things but does not entirely mean *'free'*. The more pertinent question would be, *'free trade'* of what? Just exactly what is *'free'* to trade? If anything, it might instead indicate *'freer trade'* and possibly, at its pinnacle, *'fair trade'*. If you need reminding, one of the principles of the WTO is *'Freer trade: gradually, through negotiation'*. Maybe the *'r'* in *'freer'* has become silent in its pronunciation or silent to the ear.

Other than tariffs, there are NTMs and NTBs that restrict the movement of goods. Unfortunately, although these terms are technically different, they are more often than not used interchangeably. It does not help that there is no formal definition for NTBs. NTBs are, in fact, a subset of NTMs that are considered to have potentially trade-inhibiting effects. For its part, Rules of Origin (RoO)[28] and Commodity Codes, also known as Harmonized System (HS) Codes – used in tariff classification – are considered an NTB. To add another layer of complexity, certain NTMs are not actually barriers; instead, they can actually increase the volume of trade. There are additional barriers in the form of import control, export control, prohibited goods, and restricted goods. This is reminiscent of my father's wise words, *'If you are not confused, you do not have all the facts.'*

Although its fit is not always apparent in the Customs and Excises environment, the International Chamber of Commerce (ICC) International Commercial terms or Incoterms®[29] tend to also contribute to the confusion, particularly in the use of two of the Incoterms® CIF – abbreviated from Cost, Insurance, and Freight, and FOB – abbreviated from Free On Board. These three-letter acronyms also appear in Customs

28. *See* Chapter 3 *'Origination – Origin'*.
29. *See* Chapter 18 *'International Commercial Terms (Incoterms®)'*.

legislation, where they are used to denote the basis for the value for customs duty purposes (customs valuation). Incoterms® are *'delivery terms'*, which are not concerned with the transfer of title of the goods. Instead, it denotes the point and/or the place of delivery and, as a consequence, assists in identifying the costs that should be included or excluded in determining the customs valuation of the good.

The Customs cornerstones and procedures are founded and entrenched in International Conventions and International Agreements, which are by and large administered by the Customs Cooperation Council (CCC), better known as the WCO, and the WTO. Although the WCO and the WCO apply International Agreements and Conventions, the application and implementation are facilitated through national or country-specific legislation and regulation. The book intends not to consider and account for national regulation but to provide oversight and insight into international obligation and commitment.

The WTO succinctly summarised the principles of the trading system: (i) Trade without discrimination – Most-Favoured Nation (MFN):[30] treating other people equally. Yet, as its *'founding principle'*, there are exceptions to the MFN treatment. It is reminiscent of Groucho Marx's wise words, *'Those are my principles, and if you don't like them ... well, I have others.'* (ii) Freer trade: gradually, through negotiation – Lowering trade barriers is one of the most apparent means of encouraging trade. (iii) Predictability: through binding and transparency – sometimes, promising not to raise a trade barrier can be as important as lowering one. (iv) Promoting fair competition: the WTO is sometimes described as a *'free trade'* institution, but that is not entirely accurate. The system does allow tariffs and, in limited circumstances, other forms of protection. More accurately, it is a system of rules dedicated to open, fair and undistorted competition. (v) Encouraging development and economic reform.

Now, turning to a country's domestic economic activity, national duties, taxes, and levies are traditionally imposed on domestic manufacture and collected by Customs and Excise Authorities. Here, too, its application is no longer in line with its origin, as presently the duties, taxes, and levies tend also to be imposed on imported goods. The origin of the term *'Excises'* is also steeped in legend and history. Depending on your source of reference, it is as early as the Han dynasty, from 207 BC to AD 220, where *'Excises'* were levied[31] on tea, liquor, fish, and reeds used for fuel and thatching.[32] As for the origin of *'excise duty'*, it is derived either from the Dutch *'accijns'*, for which there is the argument that it originates from the Latin *'accensare'*, which means *'to tax'*, or from the Latin *'excisere'*, which means to *'to carve, to cut out'*. The latter reference is said to refer to the carvings on a stick intended for measuring quantities of beer or liquor. Within this context, it is argued that an *'excise tax'* was first imposed by Caesar Augustus, the first Roman Emperor, who reigned from 27 BC to AD 14 before Caesar Caligula abolished it in AD 38. Also not helpful is the conversation

30. The Most-Favoured Nation or MFN principle requires that countries should treat all their trade partners equally and as a consequence that no one country should receive an increased preference or be *'more favoured'*.
31. The reference to 'levied', not very helpful.
32. IMF document 'Excises' Ben JM Terra

about whether excise is a duty, a tax, or a levy. It was only in the mid-17th century that excise duty returned, being reintroduced by the Dutch (The Netherlands). Excise duties tend to be excluded from international trade agreements, including trade blocs, as it is considered a '*national competence*'. In recent literature, the term '*Excises*' has been conceived, which is defined as '*broadly speaking, the distinguishing features of excise taxation are selectivity in coverage, discrimination in intent, and some form of quantitative measurement in determining the tax liability*'.[33]

The modern-day application of excise duty is essentially as a fiscal measure (although they tend to be disguised as not being as such), in other words, to raise revenue. Its most effective application is on goods whose demand is perfectly inelastic. Thus, no matter the extent of the increase in the price of the good, the quantity demanded remains unchanged due to the imposition of the excise duty. In recent years, an added dimension to the application of excise duty is '*internalising the external costs*'. It simply means that the use of a good by the consumer and its production by the producer might impose a cost on the general public or the environment – a cost which is not accounted for in its price. Economists call this 'market failure' as the market's price mechanism fails to reflect its full societal cost of the good, in its production, or through its societal cost of its consumption. The resultant '*externality*' needs to be remedied by the government imposing an 'Excises' on the good's production and/or consumption. You might well be familiar with the '*polluter pays principle*'.[34] It is hard, if not near impossible, to argue against its application under this premise. Excise duty is also considered to be a '*consumption tax*'. It is known as a Pigouvian tax, which is imposed to discourage consumption. Both references to '*tax*' are not helpful, nor is its categorisation as an '*indirect tax*'.

The second argument, the weaker one, for the imposition of excise duty is that imposed on *luxury goods*, more aptly known as '*non-essential goods*'. An argument for its imposition is that non-essential goods deplete resources, attributing to its scarcity, one of the three cornerstones of Economics. The other two are choice and opportunity cost. The challenge in the justification of the imposition of an Excise duty is the definition of '*luxury goods*' or '*non-essential goods*'. In economics, there is a distinction between wants and needs, which is less helpful in the application of the distinction between being a luxury and being essential. Economics does not deal with desire.

Excise duty has become even blurrier in its application, with the term '*Excises*' created as a collective for imposing all forms of excise duties, taxes, and levies. In addition to its classification as '*sin taxes*' or '*luxury taxes*', '*Excises*' can alternatively be classified as either '*grey taxes*' or '*gloomy taxes*', which apply to tobacco products, alcohol, hydrocarbon fuels, petroleum, energy, and health (sugar, sugar-sweetened beverages);[35] or as '*green taxes*', which apply to Carbon dioxide (CO_2), deforestation,

33. The definition is attributable to Sijbren Cnossen.
34. The '*polluter pays principle*' advocates that those who cause pollution ('the externality') should bear the costs of its management, prevention, and remediation.
35. Excises tend to be imposed on these Categories (i) Alcohol: beer, wine – including sparkling, cider, perry, spirits, low alcohol beverages, other fermented beverages, and ethyl alcohol; (ii) Tobacco products: cigarettes, cigars, cigarillos, rolling tobacco, chewing tobacco, pipe tobacco, and fine cut tobacco; (iii) Fuel, gas, and oil: hydrocarbon fuels and oils, petroleum, biofuels,

plastic, climate change, and the environment. As Columbia University economics professor and Nobel Laureate Joseph Stiglitz so aptly wrote almost a decade ago, '*Not paying the cost of damage to the environment is a subsidy, just as not paying the full costs of workers would be.*'

It is important to remember that Customs and Excises exist within the confines of Economics, and specifically International Economics. As a consequence, you should be cognisant of the fact that, ultimately, consumers aim to maximise their utility and achieve the highest possible satisfaction from the use of a good, while producers want to maximise profits. These tend to be conflicting objectives.

It is imperative to remember that Customs and Excises are conducted within a rule-based system, which is evidenced by the Bretton Woods trilogy of institutions – the International Monetary Fund (IMF), the World Bank (WB), and the WTO. The WTO, which for all intents and purposes should have been the International Trade Organization (ITO) and introduced at the time of the IMF and the WB, was institutionalised with the incorporation of the General Agreement on Tariffs and Trade (GATT), concluding the triology. In addition to the various Agreements that the WTO administers and the Agreements and Conventions that the WCO administers, arguably the two most important ones from a facilitation perspective are the RKC and the WTO TFA. Both aim to simply cross-border trade, with the TFA founded on the principles of transparency, simplification, harmonisation, and standardisation. Customs and Excises processes and procedures must be evaluated against the RKC and the TFA.

Not traditionally considered to be part of the Trade Compliance[36] function are '*Denied Party Screening*' and '*Sanctions Screening*', but similarly to Customs and Excises, it also has its terminology challenge. '*Denied Party Screening*', also known as '*Denied Trade Screening*' or '*Sanctions Party Screening*', tend to be used interchangeably with '*Restricted Party Screening*'. Its trilogy of focus relates to client screening, party-based screening, transaction screening or transaction-based screening, and hybrid screening. '*Sanctions Screening*', in turn, relates to a financial institution's control in detecting, preventing, and managing the disruption of financial crime and, in particular, sanctions risk. '*Screening*', although it tends to be considered an evolving element of Trade Compliance, is arguably not in the true sense of a Customs and Excises Compliance activity as its compliance focus is not on the good but instead on the transacting parties.

As with Customs and Excises, sanctions too are steeped in history, its first recorded use dating to 432 BC, when the Athenian-led Delian League banned traders from Megara from its marketplaces. It was not until the 20th century that sanctions increased in prominence and use. The LN, the predecessor to the United Nations (UN), played a crucial role in forging country-based sanctions, which are a restrictive measure imposed by one country on another to limit or impede its trade and business relations. Its use was adopted following the enactment of the LN Covenant on 28 June

liquid petroleum gas or LPG, methane, gas oil, heavy oil, and kerosene; (iv) Energy: electricity, natural gas, coal and coke, and (v) Environment: Climate change, deforestation, and plastics.

36. Encompasses all the processes, rules, regulations, and laws that govern the treatment of goods entering and exiting a country.

1919, authorising the use of economic sanctions against countries which had committed military aggression against other states. The application of '*sanctions*' has become one of the most favoured tools for governments to respond to foreign policy challenges.

The whole of Customs and Excises can be reduced to a single lesson, which in itself can be reduced to a single sentence. '*The art of Customs and Excises consists of not merely accepting the terminology for its linguistic meaning; it consists of ensuring that the terminology, its context, its meaning, and its effective, efficient, and compliant application is fully understood, and appreciated, in both its reference and application.*'

Should you be more Customs and Excises savvy, this book intends not to serve as a technical reference but rather as a primer.[37] If you are less experienced, the book intends to provide a roadmap that charts the most prominent features in the Customs and Excises environment. No matter your experience, either you have the option of approaching this book the traditional way by sequentially following its pages or you could start with the end in mind by turning to the one-page schematic summary at the end of '*The Lesson's Roadmap*',[38] and to use it as a map of your progression.

As Stephen Covey, author of *The 7 Habits of Highly Effective People*, eloquently claims, '*To begin with the end in mind means to start with a clear understanding of your destination. It means knowing where you are going so that you better understand where you are now and so that the steps you take are always going in the right direction.*'

Once you have contemplated '*The Lesson's Roadmap*', you could turn to the one-page '*The Customs Optimisation Process [A Practical Approach Derived from the Lesson]*',[39] which provides a practical process that can be employed in assessing a business' Customs and Excises compliance.

37. A '*primer*' is either an article or a book that provides basic information on a particular subject.
38. '*The Lesson's Roadmap*' is in Chapter 20.
39. '*The Customs Optimisation Process [A Practical Approach Derived from the Lesson]*' is in Chapter 20.

PART II The Lesson Applied

Section I

The Cornerstones, Remedies, Duty, Tax, & Levy

While section II deals with the treatment of the good, the focus being on PSST – processing, specific use, storage, and transit – section I is concerned with the nature of the good.

The real challenge for an entrant entering the Customs and Excises environment is the identification of its core components – its cornerstones, of which there are three and only three. The substantiation and motivation of its identification will be eluded to. Once the cornerstones have been established, the progression is to trade remedies, or remedies for short, as the remedies employ the cornerstones in their consideration and application. It then concludes with the consideration of the measure that has to be imposed, be it a duty, a tax, or a levy. Although used interchangeably, they are distinctly different.

Since there tends to be disagreement on whether there are three or indeed four cornerstones, it is best to, in its consideration, account for the Customs Conventions and International Trade Agreements that specifically refer to the identity of the goods and whether these goods are imported goods which cross national borders or are manufactured within its national borders – locally (domestically) manufactured.

According to this measure, there is a single Convention that the CCC, better known as the WCO, administers, namely the International Convention on the Harmonized Commodity Description and Coding System, better known as the HS Convention. The latter relates to the codification – tariff classification of the goods, also known as classification, which constitutes the first cornerstone.

The WTO administers many Agreements; the two most pertinent to the nature of the goods and their movement are the Agreement on RoO and the Agreement on the Implementation of Article VII of the GATT 1994. The latter is better known as the Customs Valuation Agreement. This constitutes the second and third cornerstones, respectively, namely origination – origin – and valorisation – customs valuation, also known as valuation.

The three cornerstones – classification, origin, and valuation – are required when considering the imported goods' duty, tax, levy liability, or domestically manufactured goods. The cornerstones subsume a *'customs debt'*, which relates to the amount of import duty, and export duty that is due to a Customs Authority.[40] A *'customs duty'* differs from an *'import duty'* in that a customs duty is a subset of import duty. *'Customs debt'* is also relevant when the SCP, collectively called PSST in this book, is a consideration in the treatment of imported goods and domestically manufactured goods.

Once the cornerstones are accounted for, trade remedies are an essential consideration as they account for all three cornerstones to determine their applicability. Trade remedies include anti-dumping, or simply dumping, countervailing or anti-subsidy, and safeguards. The WTO also administers the Trade Remedy Agreements, namely the Agreement on the Implementation of Article VI of the GATT 1994, which is better known as the Anti-Dumping Agreement; the Agreement on Subsidies and Countervailing Measures; and the Agreement on Safeguards.

Dumping and countervailing remedies are called *'unfair trade remedies'*,[41] while a safeguard is *'fair trade remedy'*,[42] which are also incorrectly called *protective measures*. The imposed measures are *'corrective measures'* rather than *'protective measures'*, while they are essentially *'protective measures'* in the instance of safeguards.

The section concludes with a consideration of the types of duties, taxes, and levies which are imposed on the goods being imported and exported. The word *'import'* originates from the Latin word *'importare'*, which means to *'carry in'* or to *'bring in'*, while the word *'export'* originates from the Latin word *'exportare'*, which means to *'carry out'* or to *'send away'*.

This is where the real challenge in the application and use of Customs and Excises terminology starts. Although import duty tends to be used interchangeably with customs duty, import duty is a collective term, while customs duty is merely an element of import duty, as is excise duty. This adds to the confusion as excise duty originated as a duty on domestic manufacture and was never intended to be a duty on importation. *'Excise duty'* should not be confused with an *'export duty'*.[43]

40. The RKC Chapter 2 *'Definition'* defines *'Customs'* to mean the Government Service which is responsible for the administration of Customs law and the collection of duties and taxes, and which also has the responsibility for the application of other laws and regulations relating to the importation, exportation, movement or storage of goods.
41. *'Unfair trade remedies'* does not mean that the remedies are unfair but rather that the remedy intends to redress unfair trade practices.
42. 'Fair trade remedies' is a misnomer in that it does not remedy fair trade but rather to provide a country's domestic manufacturer(s) with protection in excess of the country's WTO bound rate, or ceiling rate.
43. The RKC Chapter 2 *'Definitions'* defines 'export duties and taxes' to mean Customs duties and all other duties, taxes or charges which are collected on or in connection with the exportation of goods but not including any charges which are limited in amount to the approximate cost of services rendered or collected by the Customs on behalf of another national authority.

Import duty includes customs duty, excise duty, anti-dumping duty, countervailing duty (also known as anti-subsidy duty), safeguards or safeguard measures, import VAT, charges (including surcharges), and levies.

A Customs Authority always has a financial interest in the movement of goods – entering and leaving its territory (crossing national borders) due to the duty, levy, and tax liability. As for the type of duty, tax, and levy that can imposed, it tends to primarily be an *ad valorem* duty, from Latin meaning '*according to the value*' of the good; specific duty, which is based on the quantity, weight, or volume of the good; and a compound duty based on a combination of both an *ad valorem* duty and a specific rate duty. The compound duty is not to be confused with a mixed duty, which also stipulates an *ad valorem* duty, and a specific duty. However, in the instance of a '*mixed duty*', both duties are calculated with the duty rendering the highest duty liability being applied. These are but the primary types of duty, tax, and levy; there are many more.

CHAPTER 2
Codification – Tariff Classification

Codification, known as tariff classification, abbreviated as classification, is the first cornerstone in the consideration of the good when it moves across a national border or as a good is manufactured. The concern is with its identification – '*What is it?*'. The expression, '*It is what it is*', might well not be so apparent in its identification. The nature, or essence of what the good is, must be considered on its own merits – its '*essential character*'.[44] In other words, the answer to the question, '*What is it really*'? This terminology is founded on the first of the six tariff classification methods, which account for around 90% of all classifications. It is important to remember that the classification is not concerned with the quality or even with the brand of the good.

Tariff classification is the process of assigning a specific code to a good, which then identifies the duties, taxes, levies, trade barriers, and trade restrictions applicable to the good, as well as whether the good qualifies for any preferential treatment. For the codification, an international standardise system is required to ensure consistency in use and application.

As a consequence, in the majority of instances, determining the classification of a good is not and should not be a complicated process and procedure. It is imperative to be mindful that the correct classification is a legal responsibility. To facilitate trade, a system must ensure the uniform and consistent identification and classification of goods.

As the terminology '*tariff classification*' suggests, the classification of the good is required in order to determine, associate, or allocate a tariff applicable to the good, also known as the rate of duty. The classification is not only restricted to the rate of duty but also used to determine whether the good is subject to prohibition or restriction.[45] Then,

---

44. The United States of America (US) Customs and Border Protection (CBP) defines '*essential character*' as '*the attribute which strongly marks and serves to distinguish what an article is – that which is indispensable to the structure, core, or condition of the article*'.
45. Imported goods and exported goods can be subject to Import Control, Export Control, be Prohibited Goods, be Restricted Goods, to Trade Remedies (*dumping, countervailing, and safeguards*), to NTMs, and to NTB, etc.

from a regulatory perspective, the classification facilitates the enforcement of laws and treaties, trade negotiations, and economic and business planning.

§2.01 HISTORY

The first reference to the classification of the goods dates back to 199 BC when the Roman Customs Administration established it. Our modern-day classification starts at the 9th International Statistical Congresses that were held between 1853 and 1876, where the idea of an attempt at an international statistical nomenclature was mooted. At the 1889 International Commercial Congress, the question was put, '*Would it not be in the interest of all nations to adopt in their Customs tariffs and their official statistics' comparable classifications and uniform vocabularies?*' The creation of a uniform vocabulary for goods proved a challenging endeavour. At the 1931 LN's Sub-Committee of Experts for the Unification of Customs Tariff Nomenclature, it completed its '*Draft Customs Nomenclature*', commonly referred to as the Geneva Nomenclature. The Nomenclature had 941 four-digit headings, organised into 86 Chapters grouped into 21 Sections. A revised version was issued in 1937, which was halted by World War II.

In 1948, the European customs group continued to work on the Geneva nomenclature, and in 1949, a preliminary draft containing headings and subheadings was issued. On 15 December 1950, the 1949 draft became the Brussels Convention on Nomenclature for the Classification of Goods in Customs Tariffs (Nomenclature) was released and came into force on 11 September 1959 following the adoption, on 1 July 1955, of a Protocol of Amendment establishing a revised version of the Nomenclature.

The Nomenclature was initially known as the Brussels Tariff Nomenclature or BTN, but in 1974 it was renamed the Customs Co-operation Council Nomenclature (CCCN). It comprised 1,241 headings (1,011 headings until 1987) divided among 96 Chapters (99 Chapters until 1987), themselves arranged in 21 Sections. Each heading was identified by two groups of two digits each: the first group represented the Chapter in which the heading appeared, while the second indicated its position in that Chapter. The CCCN was supported by the Explanatory Notes (EN) for official interpretation, Alphabetical Index listing, and a Compendium of Classification Opinion.

The CCCN was subsequently updated on 1 January 1965, 1 January 1972, 1 January 1978, and on 1 January 1988, the Harmonized Commodity Description and Coding System, generally referred to as the '*Harmonized System*' or simply 'HS', was introduced. Since 1 January 1988, every five years a revised HS iteration has been introduced. The most recent HS2022 was introduced on 1 January 2022, and the next was supposed to have been HS2027.

However, at the 72nd Session of the Harmonized System Committee (HSC), in which the ICC and the WTO participated as observers, which took place from 18 to 29 September 2023, the decision was made to extend the review cycle until 2028. Accordingly, the next edition of the HS – HS2028 – will be officially implemented on 1 January 2028. The reason for the decision was due to the exceptional circumstances of the COVID-19 pandemic and its effect on the negotiation cycle. This extension will not affect the length of the next cycle, which will remain a five-year cycle, resulting in HS2033.

§2.02 HARMONISED COMMODITY DESCRIPTION AND CODING SYSTEM (HS)

The HS, a multipurpose international product nomenclature consisting of 5,000 commodity groups, is used by more than 212 countries, territories, customs unions or economic unions and accounts for the classification of over 98% of goods. Although the nomenclature is for goods, it does strangely include electricity. It is, in essence, a numeric filing system of goods, as it identifies the good based on a collection of digits.

Tariff classification is governed by '*The International Convention on the Harmonized Commodity Description and Coding System*', widely held as the true '*language of international trade*' or the '*numeric language of international trade*' which is arranged in a legal and logical structure and is supported by well-defined rules to achieve a uniform and consistent classification. This does not imply that there are no disputes in the determination and use of a tariff classification, also known as commodity code. The main reason for the dispute originates from duty liability, as the Customs Authorities and traders hold different objectives. Traders want to maximise their utility or welfare, so they generally want to pay the least amount of duty, tax, and levy, thus deriving a large profit margin on sales. Consequently, they might seek to identify commodity codes that facilitate such. Customs Authorities, dependent on their focus on their trinity of obligations - collect, protect, and facilitate - might well seek the commodity code that renders the highest duty liability, thus maximising their financial return - revenue collection.

The HS Nomenclature transcends trade policy, RoO, monitoring of controlled goods, internal duty, tax and levy, freight tariffs, quota controls, and economic research and analysis is supported by:

- The Explanatory Notes (EN), although not part of the Convention, constitutes the official interpretation of the Nomenclature approved by the WCO:
  - EN provides technical descriptions of goods and practical indications for the classification and identification of products. Although the EN is not part of the HS Convention, it informs the official interpretation of the HS Nomenclature at the international level and serves as a reference.
- The Alphabetical Index lists all the goods referred to or described in the Nomenclature and the EN.
- The Compendium of Classification Opinions lists all the Classification Opinions that the WCO adopted.

§2.03 THE STRUCTURE OF THE HS

The HS Nomenclature is comprised of four tiers:

- Section I to XXI [1 to 21]
- Chapter 2-digit code Sector HS2
- Heading 4-digit code Sub-Sector HS4
- Subheading 6-digit code Product Level HS6.

Descending from the Section, the tariff classification becomes more specific.

§2.04 THE HS TIERS EXPLAINED

The HS code can be summarised as follows:

- + 6,500 tariff lines
- 21 Sections (International):
  - Roman numerals
  - Section/Section Title/Section Note
- 97 Chapters (International):
  - The first two digits of the commodity code
  - Chapter 77 *'Reserved for future use'*
  - Chapter/Chapter Title/Chapter Note.

Sections/Chapters/Chapter Description

I	1-5	Live animals; animal products
II	6-14	Vegetable products
III	15	Fats, oils and waxes
IV	16-24	Prepared foodstuffs, beverages, spirits, and tobacco
V	25-27	Mineral products
VI	28-38	Products of the chemical and allied industries
VII	39-40	Plastics and rubber
VIII	41-43	Raw hides and skins, leather, and fur skins
IX	44-46	Wood, wood charcoal, cork, straw, basket ware and wickerwork
X	47-49	Wood pulp, paper or paperboard
XI	50-63	Textiles and textile articles
XII	64-67	Footwear, headgear, umbrellas, and artificial flowers
XIII	68-70	Articles of stone, cement, ceramic products, and glass

XIV	71	Jewels, jewellery, and coins
XV	72-83	Base metals and articles thereof
	77	Reserved for future use
XVI	84-85	Machinery, mechanical appliances, and electrical equipment
XVII	86-89	Vehicles, aircraft, vessels, and transport equipment
XVIII	90-92	Optical instruments, photographic equipment, clocks and watches
XIX	93	Arms and ammunition
XX	94-96	Miscellaneous manufactured articles
XXI	97	Works of art, and Antiques.

Source: The World Customs Organization.

- *Headings (International – HS4):*
  - \+ 1,200 headings (International)
  - The first four digits and five digits of the commodity code
  - Heading Notes
- *Subheadings (International – HS6):*
  - \+ 5,300 subheadings (International)
  - The first six digits of the commodity code
  - Subheading Note
- *Subheadings (National/Country Specific – HS8, HS10, HS12):*
  - Depending on the country's requirement
  - More than 6 digits up to 12 digits
  - Additional Notes.

The WCO endeavours to get countries to use six digits for commodity codes for tariff classification purposes, although they acknowledge that countries could use more commodity code digits to account for permits, prohibitions and restrictions.

A national or country-specific tariff is considered a commodity code in excess of six digits and from Chapter 98 onwards. Chapter 99 has a national application, which can be used for goods or services.

§2.05 INTERNATIONAL TARIFF AND NATIONAL (COUNTRY-SPECIFIC) TARIFF

The table that follows offers a visual insight into the International Tariff, and National, also known as a Country-Specific, Tariff.

In the instance of truffles, in Chapter 7 and section II, the International Tariff classifies it up to 6 digits - 0709.59. A country could then classify it as 0709.59.10, or 8 digits, and even up to 12 digits. These are fresh or chilled truffles, in the instance of it being frozen, the International Tariff classifies it up to 6 digits - 0710.80, while the National Tariff can classify it up to 12 digits:

	International		National / Country Specific	
International				
SECTION	**I**	**LIVE ANIMALS; ANIMAL PRODUCTS**		
Chapter	01	LIVE ANIMALS		
Section	**II**	**VEGETABLE PRODUCTS**		
Chapter	7	EDIBLE VEGETABLES AND CERTAIN ROOTS AND TUBERS		
Tariff Heading	07.09	Other vegetables, fresh or chilled:		
Tariff Subheading	0709.5	Mushrooms and truffles:		
Tariff Subheading	0709.59	Other		
Tariff Subheading			*0709.59.10*	*Truffles*
Tariff Subheading			*0709.59.10.10*	*National / Country Specific*
Tariff Subheading			*0709.59.10.10.10*	*National / Country Specific*
Tariff Heading	07.10	Vegetables (uncooked or cooked by steaming or boiling in water), frozen:		
Tariff Subheading	0710.80	Other vegetables:		
Tariff Subheading			*0710.80.10*	*Truffles*
Tariff Subheading			*0710.80.10.10*	*National / Country Specific*
Tariff Subheading			*0710.80.10.10.10*	*National / Country Specific*
SECTION	**XXI**	**WORKS OF ART, COLLECTORS' PIECES AND ANTIQUES**		
Chapter	97	WORKS OF ART, COLLECTORS' PIECES AND ANTIQUES		
National				
SECTION	***XXII***	***NATIONAL / COUNTRY SPECIFIC***		
Chapter	*98*	*NATIONAL / COUNTRY SPECIFIC*		
Tariff Heading	*9801*	*National / Country Specific*		
Tariff Subheading	*9801.+*	*National / Country Specific*		
Tariff Subheading	*9801.++*	*National / Country Specific*		
Tariff Subheading	*9801.++.++*	*National / Country Specific*		
Tariff Subheading	*9801.++.++.++*	*National / Country Specific*		

Source: Author's own compilation.

As a rule of thumb, a Commodity Code that contains the number '9' towards the end of the Code, such as 19, 29, 90, and 99, refers to other in the 'Other', which simply means that there is not a specific Code for the good being classified, or that has been classified.

§2.06 THE CORE PRINCIPLES OF TARIFF CLASSIFICATION

A good can be classified by the following:

- Terms of the Heading
- Notes to Sections, Chapters, or Subheadings
- General Interpretative Rules (GIR)

This can be expounded into five parts: three with legal force and two with no legal force:

- Legal force:
  - Descriptions
  - Legal Notes
  - General Rules
- No legal force:
  - Explanatory Notes
  - Classification Opinions.

§2.07 GENERAL RULES OF CLASSIFICATION (GRI)

In order to determine the good's or most suitable tariff classification or correct commodity code, the importer or its intermediary (agent) must consider the General Rules of Classification or GRI in a hierarchical (sequential) order starting with GRI 1. The GRI is the set of rules that governs the interpretation of the six-digit commodity code.

There are six GRIs that describe how to classify the goods, which can be summarised as follows:

- GRI 1: Classify goods at a four-digit heading level based on the wording of the Sections, Chapters, and Sub-Chapters Notes.
- GRI 2(a): Incomplete or unfinished; Unassembled goods or disassembled goods:
  - Part One: Incomplete or unfinished goods
  - Part Two: Unassembled or disassembled goods
- GRI 2(b): Mixtures, as well as combinations of goods.
- GRI 3: Goods that are, prima facie, classifiable under two or more Headings:
  - GRI 3(a) Most specific/Something more specific
  - GRI 3(b) Essential character

  - GRI 3(c) Last tariff subheading in numerical order
- GRI 4: Most akin, as the goods cannot be classified according to GRIs 1, 2, and 3.
- GRI 5: The classification of packing containers:
  - GRI 5(a) Special containers (Case, Boxers, and similar containers)
  - GRI 5(b) Packing materials and packaging containers
- GRI 6: Classify goods at a six-digit subheading level based on the wording of the Sections, Chapters, and Sub-Chapters Notes. This is known as the Subheading Rule.

On consideration, you will notice that the six GRIs fall into two main groups – GRIs 1 and 6, which are respectively concerned with the four-digit heading level and the six-digit heading level, and GRIs 3, 4, and 5, which are concerned with the essence and character of the goods – what it is?

Most goods are generally classified by GRIs 1 to 3, which cover a wide range of descriptions. That said, GRI 4, goods most akin to, has gained in popularity due to the speed of technological enhancements and improvements, the differing technologies employed in its manufacture, and due to the fact that the HS is only revised every five years.

Ultimately, having a clear understanding of the GRI and its application will significantly increase the likelihood of determining the correct tariff classification of the goods.

§2.08 MULTIPURPOSE NOMENCLATURE

The multipurpose nature of the Nomenclature is evident in its application and use as:

- The basis for Customs tariffs:
  - Non-preferential and preferential rates of duty.
  - Whether trade remedies – dumping, countervailing, and safeguards – apply.
  - Whether import permits or export permits are required.
- The basis for the collection of international trade (Customs and Excises) statistics.
- The basis for RoO – preferential and non-preferential:
  - Most-Favoured Nation (MFN) status under Free Trade Agreements (FTA) and trade preferences.
- The basis for freight and transport tariffs.
- As a basis for trade negotiations, WTO schedules tariff concessions.
- For transport tariffs and statistics.
- For the monitoring of controlled goods:
  - Prohibited goods and restricted goods.
- Considering the process areas of Customs controls and procedures.

§2.09 STAGED CONSIGNMENT/STAGGERED CONSIGNMENTS/SPLIT CONSIGNMENTS/SPLIT SHIPMENTS

Although this goes by many names, it is an essential element in the movement of machinery and equipment under section XIV and Chapters 84[46] and 85.[47] A Customs Authority will consider the classification of the goods in the manner in which it is presented for clearance. In instances where a consignment consists of more than one shipment, it will arrive separately but needs to be considered a single consignment. An application needs to be made for the Customs Authority to consider the multiple shipments as a single consignment. These types of consignments tend to apply to goods which are too large to be transported as a single shipment. The various shipments contain goods which are in an unassembled or disassembled state.

§2.10 TARIFF ENGINEERING – REDUCING DUTY OBLIGATIONS

It is possible for importers and their intermediaries to design, assemble, or disassemble a good to take advantage of lower rates of duty. The importer or the manufacturer will consider the rates of customs duties on certain materials and stages of assembly and design the goods to be customs duty optimal.

This is the Customs equivalent of tax avoidance in that it attempts to lower the customs duty liability. Thus, in comparison to tax evasion, customs duty evasion in this context would imply the failure to pay customs duty or a deliberate underpayment of customs duty.

§2.11 BINDING TARIFF RULING/BINDING TARIFF DETERMINATION/BINDING TARIFF INFORMATION

For an importer and/or its intermediary to not only mitigate its customs duty liability risk but also to provide legal certainty, an application could be made to a Customs Authority to provide a written tariff ruling. In some instances, Customs Authorities also provide a verbal tariff ruling, which is rather an indicative indication of the customs duty liability rather than a definitive ruling.

§2.12 ADVANCE CLASSIFICATION RULING

In accordance with the RKC and the WCO Recommendation, importers and related parties can, in advance, request classification rulings from their Customs Authorities. From the WTO's Bali Ministerial decision on the Agreement on Trade Facilitation

46. Chapter 84 '*Nuclear reactors, boilers, machinery and mechanical appliances; parts thereof.*'
47. Chapter 85 '*Electrical machinery and equipment and parts thereof; sound recorders and reproducers, television image and sound recorders and reproducers, and parts and accessories of such articles.*'

(TFA), the WCO developed a single document covering procedures for issuing advance rulings on classification, RoO and customs valuation of the goods.

§2.13 ANOTHER CLASSIFICATION SYSTEM – STANDARD INTERNATIONAL TRADE CLASSIFICATION (SITC)

The SITC is a classification of goods used to classify the imports and the exports of a country to enable a comparison of different countries and years. The SITC, currently in a fourth revision,[48] is maintained by the United Nations (UN). While the SITC is to be for analytical purposes only, the HS is to be used for the collection and compilation of trade statistics:[49]

The grouping of the SITC reflects:
- The production materials
- The processing stage
- Market practices and uses of the products
- The importance of goods in world trade
- Technological changes.

The main categories are as follows:
- Food, drinks and tobacco, including live animals (sections 0 and 1)
- Raw materials (sections 2 and 4)
- Energy products (section 3)
- Chemicals, including pharmaceuticals and plastics (section 5)
- Machinery and transport equipment (section 7)
- Other manufactured goods (sections 6 and 8)
- Other goods (section 9).

§2.14 CUSTOMS LABORATORIES

These are a very important instrument for Customs Authorities as their traditional work is the chemical analysis to determine tariff classification and the level of duties, levies, and taxes. Modern customs laboratories play an important part in environmental protection,[50] endangered species protection, control of dangerous goods such as pesticides, persistent organic pollutants, chemical weapons, as well as narcotics and drug precursors.

The WCO has developed, for its Member, a '*restricted access*' handbook *The Customs Laboratory Guide* that includes the '*best practices*' covering a variety of

48. SITC Revision 4 was accepted by the United Nations Statistical Commission at its 37th session.
49. The following excerpt from the United Nations Statistics Division (UNSD), International Trade Statistics branch, '*For compiling international trade statistics on all merchandise entering international trade and to promote international comparability of international trade statistics.*'
50. The control of ozone depleting substances.

laboratory operations. The handbook is supported by the WCO-developed technical assistance and training programme.

CHAPTER 3

Origination - Origin

The second cornerstone in the movement of a good across a national border, or as a good is manufactured, is establishing its origin - '*Where it is from?*', '*Where is it made*'. In essence, it refers to the identification of the good's '*national source*' or its '*economic nationality*'. In the instance of the Rules of Origin (RoO),[51] the '*Made in ... where?*' are the criteria used to determine the national source of a good, otherwise, the criteria of conferring origin. Due to its intertwining nature, the origination - origin of a good is also considered to be both an NTM and an NTB.[52]

The determination of the origin is also an imperative as to whether a good:

- is subject to trade remedies - dumping or countervailing (anti-subsidy) measures;
  - [It excludes safeguards since it is a '*fair trade remedy*' imposed against all countries, with the possible exclusion of Least Developed Countries (LDCs)];
- qualifies for market access - MFN treatment (non-preferential treatment) or preferential treatment;
- is subject to government procurement;
- is subject to labelling and marking requirements; and
- is subject to the application of commercial policy instruments - import control, export control and whether the goods are prohibited, or restricted.

§3.01 HISTORY

The concern with the determination of the origin of the goods dates back to between AD 907 and AD 911 when the Byzantine Empire first applied a preferential rate of duty for goods originating in Russia.

51. Is referenced in the RKC Specific Annex K Chapter 1 '*Rules of Origin*'.
52. A NTB is a subset of the NTM.

In recent times, the GATT[53] allowed each contracting party to determine their own RoO and also permitted them to name several RoO, as there are no specific rules governing the determination or identification of the country of origin.

The WTO Agreement on RoO does not specify rules of implementation as it does for customs valuation, and the WCO HS Convention does but rather aims for long-term RoO harmonisation. The WTO has an interest in the RoO granting tariff preferences, but only to the extent that it does not create unnecessary obstacles to trade. Both the WTO and WCO focus on the harmonisation of the RoO.

The onus, at present, on WTO members is to ensure that their RoOs are transparent, not restrictive, distorting, or disrupting international trade and that the RoOs are administered in a consistent, uniform, impartial and reasonable manner. A third requirement is that the RoO be based on a positive statement, which confers origin to be stated rather than what does not.

§3.02 RULES OF ORIGIN (ROO)

RoO forms an essential part of trade rules, the specification criteria employed to define where a good was made, and its qualification for tariff and trade treatment. RoO is best defined in the RKC as '*the specific provisions, developed from principles established by national legislation or international agreements ("origin criteria"), applied by a country to determine the origin of goods*'.

Determining the origin of the good, which is complex, requires consideration of where the good has been grown, produced, or manufactured and might differ from the country from which they are bought or shipped. The origin of the goods might infer that the goods have a preferential tariff or a non-preferential tariff. Applying the preferential tariff is attributable to trade agreements and trade preferences such as the Generalised System of Preferences (GSP) or trade quotas.

To consider the qualification of a good for trade preferences, the origin of the composition of its materials/inputs must be known. It is an imperative to qualify whether these materials/inputs originate from a single country or from multiple countries. In order to substantiate its origin, additional trade documents, such as a Certificate of Origin (CoO) and Certificate of Authenticity, could also be required.

The RoO needs to be considered to determine a good's national source or economic nationality as it provides the criteria. An added importance of the RoO is that it impacts the duties and restrictions that would apply to the imported product.

It is imperative to be cognisant of the fact that origin is not simply conferred based on the last country of shipment.

53. The GATT should not be confused with the World Trade Organization (WTO). GATT was an international treaty, while the World Trade Organization (WTO) is a permanent body that was institutionalised on 1 January 1995 to administer the GATT Agreements. Another distinction is that while GATT applied to the trade in merchandise goods, the WTO covers the trade in services as well as trade-related aspects of intellectual property rights.

§3.03 TYPES OF RoO

There are two types of RoO for which certificates of proof of originating status are required:

- *non-preferential RoO*; and
- *preferential RoO*.

In the instance of the CoO, a certificate of non-preferential origin to receive the MFN treatment is typically issued by a Chamber of Commerce and Industry (CCI). These CoOs quite simply certify that these goods do not qualify for preferential treatment, but it does infer the country of origin. This is another instance where acronyms are not useful. A certificate of preferential origin, which allows for the goods to qualify for a preference, is normally issued by a Government Authority, but this authority could also be delegated.

Non-preferential origin rules are used in the instance of non-preferential commercial policy measures, such as MFN treatment, unfair trade remedies (anti-dumping duties and countervailing duties), the fair trade remedy (safeguards measure), origin marking, quantitative restrictions (QRs), and tariff quotas, to name but a few.

The origin is derived when, in the instance of a single country, the goods are '*wholly obtained*' or in the instance of more than one country where the goods underwent their last substantial (economically justified) processing, working, or manufacturing.

The Preferential RoO could best be summarised in the table below.

§3.04 PREFERENTIAL RoO – IN SUMMARY

In-Country Goods

The origin criteria commence with a twofold consideration:

- Wholly obtained goods.
- Sufficient worked or processed/substantial transformation:
  - *Ad Valorem* Rule/Value-Added Rule/Value Content Rule/Percentage Rule.
  - Tariff Shift Rule/Change of the Tariff Classification Rule/Specified Process Rule.
  - Specific Rules/Specified Product or Process/Technical Rules.

Out-of-Country Goods

The consideration of the type of Cumulation – combining materials without losing originating status:

- Bilateral cumulation
- Diagonal cumulation

- Regional cumulation
- Full cumulation
- Extended cumulation
- Multilateral cumulation
- Multilateral extended cumulation.

Exception to the Sufficiently Worked/Substantial Transformation Criterion

- Cumulation (Full Cumulation)
- *De minimis*
- Non-qualifying operations.

Source: Author's own compilation.

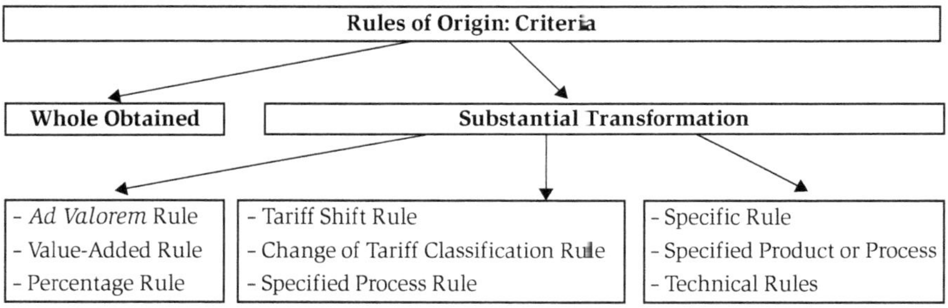

Source: Author's own compilation.

§3.05 PREFERENTIAL RoO – IN-COUNTRY GOODS

The origin criteria commence with a basic twofold consideration to determine whether the goods are *'wholly obtained'* or *'sufficiently/substantially worked for processed (transformed)'* in a country.

Wholly obtained goods, as the name suggests, are exclusively produced or originate in a country and do not contain or incorporate any material from another country(ies).

Sufficient worked or processed, also known as substantial transformation, requires the qualification with three major product-specific rules or criteria:

- *Ad Valorem Rule/Value-Added Rule/Value Content Rule/Percentage Rule:*
  - *25% Rule.*
  - Origin is based on *'value thresholds'* (*'local content'* or *'regional content'*).
  - When the value added of a good increases up to a specified level expressed by an *ad valorem* percentage:

  - The '*value-added criterion*' can be expressed in two ways: a maximum allowance for non-originating materials or a minimum requirement for domestic content.
- *Tariff Shift Rule/Change of the Tariff Classification Rule/Specified Process Rule:*
  - It requires that there is a change in the HS classification (commodity code) of each of the non-originating inputs or components to the commodity code of the final product.
  - The rule specifies a good's transformation during the manufacturing process.
- *Specific Rules/Specified Product or Process/Technical Rules:*
  - The origin is based on specific manufacturing steps or other specific processes which led to the production of a good.
  - As a '*technical requirement*', regardless of a change in its classification, a good is considered substantially transformed when the good has undergone specified manufacturing or processing operations.

Should the product-specific rules be met, goodwill is obtained or originating status is gained, dependent on the trade preference/agreement that could be the actual originating percentage or be considered 100% originating.

In preferential trade agreements, goods obtained in or where processing took place in a member country are considered to originate under a provision known as cumulation or accumulation. Simply meaning '*to combine into one*', cumulation allows for production sharing between the member countries.

There is also the '*roll-up rule*', also known as the '*absorption principle*', that allows originating materials to be considered originating even when used as input in a subsequent transformation. This means that non-originating materials that have acquired originating status through a previous process are treated as originating in the final product. The rule aims to encourage regional trade by allowing materials that have been process to an originating level in one stage of manufacture to be treated as originating in all subsequent stages of production.

§3.06 PREFERENTIAL RoO – OUT-COUNTRY GOODS

Cumulation is a deviation from the principle that goods must be produced entirely in the country of exportation, or have undergone sufficient working or processing there, in order to qualify as originating goods. It allows producers in one country to source components and inputs from other countries without losing the originating status of that component or input. Under cumulation, foreign components and inputs are not considered imported (non-originating) for purposes of '*substantial transformation*' requirements.

The seven types of cumulation are as follows:

- *Bilateral Cumulation:*
  - As the name suggests, '*bi*' meaning '*twice each*' allows for the materials from the two contracting parties to be considered as originating. This

cumulation may stipulate that the rules of '*sufficient worked or processed*' or '*substantial transformation*' be adhered to.

- *Diagonal Cumulation:*
  - It is essentially similar to bilateral cumulation, with the only difference being that it applies to more than two contracting parties.
- *Extended Cumulation:*
  - Allows materials from countries that do not necessarily have FTAs with each other to be considered as originating in the country of export, for purposes of preferential treatment. It provides more flexibility than traditional cumulation, which may require identical RoOs between all contracting countries.
- *Full Cumulation:*
  - This is the most preferential and flexible of the types of cumulation as it allows for components (inputs) that are not sufficiently worked or processed or originating in any of the contracting country to be considered originating.
- *Multilateral Cumulation:*
  - Materials or processing from multiple countries within an FTA are considered when determining the origin of a good. Essentially, it allows for a good to be treated as originating from one country within the FTA even if they were partially produced or sourced in other contracting countries.
- *Multilateral Extended Cumulation:*
  - An FTA provision where multiple countries can consider products originating in any of the contracting countries as if they originated in the final country of production, even if the countries do not all have identical RoO. This is a more flexible approach to RoO than other forms of cumulation that require similar RoO between all participating countries.
- *Regional Cumulation:*
  - A form or diagonal cumulation that is only applied to the GSP and in instances between members of a regional group of beneficiary countries. GSP, which is discussed under '*Trade Blocs*',[54] refers to tariff preferences on imported goods being extended by developed countries to developing countries.

54. Chapter 13, in section III.

§3.07 EXCEPTIONS – *DE MINIMIS* RULE OR TOLERANCE RULE

As a general rule of thumb, the *de minimis* rule, also known as the '*tolerance rule*', permits a specified percentage, generally between 10% and 15% of the value or volume of the final good, to be non-originating without the good losing its originating status. It is also possible that a trade agreement or preference might specify a specific percentage. An added specification could be stipulating a negative list of components that would be excluded from the *de minimis* or tolerance rule.

§3.08 EXCEPTIONS – NON-QUALIFYING OPERATIONS

There are operations conducted that do not confer origin:

- Insufficient Production:
  - Where the requirements or specifications of the RoO have not been met, this would be considered to constitute '*insufficient production*' and thus cannot confer origin. These activities are also called '*simple*' or '*simple assembly*'.
- Minimal Operations and Processes:
  - Agreements tend to identify and specify insufficient manufacturing operations to confer origin. These types of '*manufacture*' are labelling, packaging or assembly, to name but the most prominent.

§3.09 OTHER CONCEPTS RELATED TO ORIGIN

There are a number of considerations:

- Packing and packaging:
  - Similar to tariff classification, packaging is treated as part of the good if such items that are usually included as part of the cost of the goods are not invoiced separately, and classified with the good.
- Accessories, spare parts and tools:
  - It is the practice for RoO to disregard these costs if the parts are sold with the main good and correspond to the equipment.
- Direct consignment:
  - Goods must be transported directly from the last country of production to the importing country, with the underlying stipulation that the goods have not undergone any transformation during trans-shipment.[55]

55. '*Trans-shipment*' is considered to be the shipment of goods, first to an intermediate destination, then on to another destination, which could be its final destination.

§3.10 GEOGRAPHICAL INDICATIONS (GIs)

The place or region in which a good originates tends to be definitive of its character and associated with its quality and reputation. Consider, for instance, '*Rooibos*', '*Karoo*', *Champagne*', '*Tequila*', or '*Roquefort*', which are definitive of the geographical origin as it is a brand. A GI is an indicative sign used on goods to identify a product whose quality, reputation or other such characteristics relate to its geographical origin.

GI status gives consumers a guarantee of authenticity, quality and distinctiveness linked to origin while protecting producers from competitors trying to exploit their reputation and know-how developed to produce genuine high-quality products.

The Agreement on Trade-Related Aspects of Intellectual Property Rights (TRIPS)[56] contains a section on GIs. It enhances their protection and extends it to more countries than previous international agreements. The Agreement requires WTO Member countries to make patents available for any inventions, whether products or processes, in all fields of technology without discrimination, subject to the normal tests of novelty, inventiveness and industrial applicability. The WTO negotiations included establishing an international register for GIs and extending the protection currently granted to wines and spirits to all products.

§3.11 GENERALISED SYSTEM OF PREFERENCES (GSP)

Explained in '*Trade Blocs – Economic Integration*' as an exception to the WTO's MFN treatment is a system that applies RoO to determine whether a good qualifies for preferential tariff treatment. A GSP specifies the criteria a good must meet to be considered originating and as a consequence being eligible for the tariff preference.

The GSP tariff preference normally applies when:

- the good is originating in the GSP beneficiary country;
- the direct transport rule requires that the good eligible for preferential treatment is transported directly from the exporting country to the importing country without significant manipulation in a third country. The intention of the rule is to maintain the originating status of the goods and prevent the exploitation of the GSP by third non-beneficiary countries;
- the Certificate of Origin (CoO) is submitted that confirms the GSP beneficiary country as the originating country.

56. Article 22.1 of the TRIPS Agreement defines GIs as '*indications which identify a good as originating in the territory of a Member [of the World Trade Organization], or a region or locality in that territory, where a given quality, reputation or other characteristic of the good is essentially attributable to its geographical origin*'.

§3.12 ORIGIN ENGINEERING – REDUCING DUTY OBLIGATIONS

It is possible for importers and their intermediaries to source a good's inputs or raw materials from qualifying countries in order to take advantage of the final good qualifying for a tariff preference due to it meeting the origin requirements.

This is the Customs equivalent of tax avoidance in that it attempts to lower the customs duty liability. This is in comparison to tax evasion, customs duty evasion in this context, which would imply the failure to pay customs duty or a deliberate underpayment of customs duty.

§3.13 BINDING ORIGIN RULING/BINDING ORIGIN DETERMINATION/BINDING ORIGIN INFORMATION

For an importer and/or its intermediary to not only mitigate its customs duty liability risk but also to provide legal certainty, an application could be made to a Customs Authority to provide a written origin ruling. In some instances, Customs Authorities also provide a verbal binding ruling, which is rather an indicative indication of the customs duty liability than a definitive ruling.

These rulings or determinations are binding on both the holder and the Customs Authorities of the issuing country and are valid for as long as the described circumstances remain unchanged. The rulings or determinations are normally issued for a period of time, three to five years from the date of issue.

§3.14 ADVANCE BINDING RULING

In accordance with the Revised Kyoto Convention (RKC) and the WCO Recommendation, importers and related parties can, in advance, request origin rulings from their Customs Authorities. From the WTO's Bali Ministerial decision on the Agreement on Trade Facilitation (TFA), the WCO developed a single document covering procedures for issuing advance rulings on classification, RoO and customs valuation of the goods.

CHAPTER 4

Valorisation – Customs Valuation

The third and final cornerstone in the movement of a good across a national border, or as a good is manufactured, presupposes that its value needs to be established – '*What is its price?*' Before getting fixated on the word '*price*',[57] while the title mentions '*value*',[58] and being cognisant of the fact that internationally traded goods are sold, any Customs Authority's concern is with the '*economic value*'[59] of the good. This indicates the value that the buyer places on a good based on the benefit that the buyer derives from a good. The calculation of the value for customs duty purposes – valorisation – or '*customs valuation*' for short, must reflect the real economic value of imported goods and include all costs associated with the goods.[60] It follows that the question should be '*What is it worth?*' rather than '*What is its price?*'[61]

The determination of the customs valuation, which is a very complex and challenging process, defines the value of the good on which the rate of duty, levy, or tax will be applied. Under no circumstances can fictitious, arbitrary, or, as it is generically known in the industry, '*nominal values*' be used or ascribed to a good, even if the good has no commercial value.[62] A Customs Authority is not concerned about the commercial value of the good but its economic value. As it is most aptly described, the

57. The price, or the market value, of a good is determined by the supply factors and demand factors of the market price.
58. As the Irish poet and playwright Oscar Wilde observed '*We know the price of everything, and the value of nothing.*'
59. The economic value represents the maximum amount that the consumer is willing to pay for the good.
60. This represents the conflict in approach where the importer generally attempts to assign the lowest possible value to the imported good, while the Customs Authority the highest value.
61. In the words of Warren Buffett, the American business magnate, '*Price is what you pay for it, value is what you get.*'
62. The commercial value is considered to be the '*actual price*' at which a good is sold to either an unrelated party or a related party at arm's length. The assertion of '*arm's length*' is that both parties act in their own self-interest and as a consequence they are not subject to pressure from the other party. Under no circumstances may FAN customs values be used – fictitious, arbitrary, or nominal.

requirement is to '*valorise*' the goods, in other words, to ascribe an '*economic value*' to the goods.

Customs valuation forms the basis of the assessment for all goods which are liable for an *ad valorem* duty applied to the value of the good. Still, it does not apply to a specific duty that relates to a quantitative measure such as quantity, weight, and units.

There are essentially two bases for customs valuation, which should never be confused with the '*delivery terms*' that were devised by the International Chamber of Commerce (ICC) in its International Commercial Terms or Incoterms®.[63] A country's basis for customs valuation could either be on a Free on Board (FOB) basis or a Cost, Insurance and Freight (CIF) basis. The majority of countries favour CIF, with only a few countries favouring FOB.[64] Those countries favouring FOB base their self-identification on being '*long-haul destinations*'. As a consequence, the basis of calculation excludes the addition of international freight and international insurance from the value of the goods as its inclusion would substantially increase the customs value.

§4.01 HISTORY

The first reference to customs valuation is found on the Indian subcontinent around 400 BC, which was documented in the Arthashastra, establishing the practice of assigning a valuation to goods. The Arthashastra articulates the duties and functions of 28 administrative departments, which include, among others, agriculture, trade, shipping, prostitutes, infantry, and toll. In this context, the toll is understood to mean Customs.

The valuation practice described by the Arthashastra is for merchants, on the importation, to cry out thrice '*Who will purchase this quantity of merchandise for this amount of price?*' Should this result in a response '*I (we) will*', *then the merchant is* obligated to sell the goods at the expressed price. This principle is consistent with the present-day customs valuation practice, which – as its basic rule – considers the '*price paid or payable*'.[65]

Little is known about the evolution of customs valuation prior to the signature of the 1947 General Agreement on Tariff and Trade (GATT) Customs Valuation Agreement; other than that prior to 1947, for more than 60 years, a dual valuation system existed which was used to determine the value for customs duty purposes of imported goods. Accordingly, the customs value could either be the domestic value of the

63. *See* Chapter 18 '*International Commercial Terms (Incoterms®)*'. International Commercial Terms, abbreviated as Incoterms® – it is not plural – are '*delivery terms*' and as a consequence it is not concerned with the transfer of title of the goods. Its only concern relates to the interaction of three issues between the buyer and the seller – obligations, risks, and costs.

64. The countries that favour FOB as the basis of customs valuation are Australia, New Zealand, South Africa and the United States of America.

65. In essence to determine all the costs that are associated with the good. So, to prevent costs which were incurred at a later stage, but which is associated to the good to also be accounted for and included in the customs valuation of the good.

imported goods in the country of export or the FOB price. The valuation, which resulted in the highest customs duty, was applied.

After the end of the Second World War (World War II), deliberations at Bretton Woods, although failing to establish an International Trade Organization (ITO), resulted in a number of GATT Agreements being formulated. Among these was the Agreement on the Implementation of Article VII of GATT, simply known as the Customs Valuation Agreement (CVA). The CVA was signed in Geneva, Switzerland, on 30 October 1947.

In the 1970s, the Customs Cooperation Council (CCC), now known as the World Customs Organization (WCO), had 16 signatories to the CCC's Brussels Definition of Value (BDV). In 1980, the WCO Technical Committee on Customs Valuation was established by the Tokyo Round Agreement on Customs Valuation. GATT Article VII on valuation for customs purposes prescribes that the value for customs purposes should be based on the '*actual value*' of the imported merchandise. It further defines '*actual value*' as the price at which, at a time and place determined by the legislation or the country of importation, such or like merchandise is sold or offered for sale in the ordinary course of trade under fully competitive conditions. The customs valuation mentioned in the Arthashastra is consistent with the spirit of GATT Article VII, denoting nothing other than the '*actual value*' at the time of importation under fully competitive conditions.

§4.02 CUSTOMS VALUATION AGREEMENT

The WTO Customs Valuation Agreement came into effect on 1 January 1995. The WTO Agreement is administered by the WCO, which has devised a number of publications to assist in interpreting the Agreement. The WCO Compendium of Customs Valuation publications contains advisory opinions, commentaries, explanatory notes, and case studies adopted by the WCO Technical Committee on Customs Valuation. They also provide very useful guidelines for addressing various technical questions on customs valuation.

Customs valuation is the only WTO system that is considered '*fun*', as the WTO in its Agreement on Article VII – better known as the Customs Valuation Agreement (CVA) – recognises the need for a fair (f), uniform (u), and neutral (n) system for the valuation of goods for customs purposes (customs valuation) that precludes the use of arbitrary or fictitious customs values.

The CVA stipulates six methods that need to be applied in hierarchical order, starting with Method 1 before moving on to Method 2. The only exception is made where Method 4 and Method 5 could, on request to the Customs Authority, be used interchangeably.

The customs valuation of goods is governed by the WTO CVA, while the WCO Technical Committee on Valuation plays a regulatory role. The intention of customs valuation is to achieve two principal objectives:

- *A fiscal objective* – To ensure the precise levying of customs duties, and other taxes.
- *An Economic objective* – To promote international trade.

In alignment with the objectives, it is an imperative for any business that is engaged in international trade to establish the value of their goods – the '*price actually paid or payable*'. This is the real price paid (positive notion) and not the normal price. To aid businesses in their calculation, the WTO specifies six methods – the primary method, and five secondary methods which need to be employed, in hierarchical order, to establish the value on which customs duties, levies, and taxes, including import VAT, needs to be paid.

On 9 May 2025, the WTO marked the 30th anniversary of the CVA by noting the achievements of the Agreement as well as the future challenges arising from digital trade. One of the prevailing challenges of the CVA is to ensure the uniformity in interpretation and the application of the Agreement in a volatile trading environment and constantly evolving business models:

Methods of Customs Valuation		
	Primary Method	
Method 1	Transaction Value	Transaction
	Secondary Method / Alternative Methods / Replacement Valuation Methods	
Method 2	Transaction Value of Identical Goods	Comparison
Method 3	Transaction Value of Similar Goods	
Method 4	Deductive Method	Calculation
Method 5	Compute Method / Calculation Method	
Method 6	Fallback Method / Residual Method / Reasonable Means Method	Revision

Source: Author's own compilation.

§4.03 PRIMARY METHOD

The transaction value method focuses on the value a buyer and a seller attach to goods in an open market. In most instances, this would imply the selling price in the export transaction or the invoice price.

§4.04 METHOD 1 – TRANSACTION VALUE

The Transaction Value (TV) method is used in over 90% of the instances; however, in the instance of there not being a transaction value or a sale, such as for Research and Development (R&D) goods, the Secondary Methods need to be then considered.

Customs valuation is concerned with the '*actual price, paid or payable*', which implies, as the Union Customs Code (UCC) so succinctly defines as, the '*total payment made or to be made by the buyer to the seller or by the buyer to a third party for the benefit of the seller for the imported goods and include(s) all payments made or to be made as a condition of sale of the imported goods*'.

§4.05 DUTIABLE CHARGES/NON-DUTIABLE CHARGES

Sufficient information is available to enable the specific adjustments to be made under Article 8 to the price paid or payable, such as the following:

- Commissions and brokerage, including selling commission but excluding buying commissions
- Packing and container costs and charges
- Assists (or assistances)
- Royalties and licence fees
- Subsequent proceeds
- The cost of transport, insurance, and related costs is dependent on the basis of customs valuation - FOB or CIF.

The customs value of the imported goods shall be the transaction value:

(1) Price actually paid or payable
(2) For the goods
(3) When sold for export
(4) Adjusted (Article 8) - Only those in Article 8 are allowed.

§4.06 SECONDARY METHODS/ALTERNATIVE METHODS/REPLACEMENT VALUATION METHODS

This is used when the price of the goods is influenced by the restrictions or conditions and in instances where there is no sale.

§4.07 METHOD 2 – TRANSACTION VALUE OF IDENTICAL GOODS

The TV of identical goods method is used where Method 1 cannot be used, such as transactions within companies. The customs valuation of the good to be valued is then based on the TV of identical goods exported at or about the same time, in the same quantities, and at the same level of trade - retail or wholesale.

Goods are considered identical if:

- they are the same in all respects, including physical characteristics, quality, and reputation;
- produced in the same country as the goods being valued; and

- produced by the producer of the goods being valued.

The goods must also be exported at or about the same time as the goods being valued.

The definition excludes imported goods that incorporate engineering, artwork, etc., provided by the buyer to the producer of goods free of charge or at a reduced cost, undertaken in the country of importation for which no adjustment has been made under Article 8.

§4.08 METHOD 3 – TRANSACTION VALUE OF SIMILAR GOODS

The TV of similar goods is based on similar goods produced by the same producer, with corresponding quality, level of trade, etc., as in the instance of Method 2.

The transaction value is calculated in the same manner on similar goods if:

- goods closely resemble the goods being valued in terms of component materials and characteristics;
- goods are capable of performing the same functions and are commercially interchangeable with the goods being valued;
- goods are produced in the same country as and by the producer of the goods being valued. For this method to be used, the goods must be sold to the same country of importation as the goods being valued. The goods must be exported at or about the same time as the goods being valued.

In the instances of Method 4 and Method 5, the importer could request the Customs Authority to change the order.

§4.09 METHOD 4 – DEDUCTIVE METHOD

The Deductive Method determines the customs valuation of the goods based on the sale price in the country of importation from which certain costs, such as expenses and profits, are deducted.

It will be determined on the basis of the unit price at which the imported goods or identical or similar goods are sold to an unrelated buyer in the greatest aggregate quantity in the country of importation. The buyer and the seller in the importing country must not be related, and the sale must take place at or about the time of importation of the goods being valued. If no sale took place at or about the time of importation, it is permitted to use sales up to 90 days after the importation of the goods being valued.

§4.10 METHOD 5 – COMPUTED METHOD/CALCULATION METHOD

The Computed Method determines the customs valuation of the goods based on the costs of material and production in the country of export plus other costs, such as packing, engineering, and development work. Additional amounts for profit, general expenses, and insurance are also included.

To '*compute*' essentially means that a calculation is required by building up the cost to derive a customs valuation. The method is, in the words of the WTO, '*the most difficult and rarely used method*' as the basis used is the cost of production of the goods being valued, adding an amount for profit and general expenses.

§4.11 METHOD 6 – FALL BACK METHOD/RESIDUAL METHOD/REASONABLE MEANS METHOD

As a final resort, if none of the previous Methods can be used to determine a customs valuation, then it requires reverting to Method 1. In doing so, the Methods should now be considered and applied in a reasonably flexible manner, accounting for special circumstances.

§4.12 TARIFF ENGINEERING – REDUCING DUTY OBLIGATIONS

It is possible for importers to consider ways of reducing their value for customs duty purposes and, as a consequence, reduce their duty liability. In the United States of America, the '*first sale*' principle allows importers to use the price of the first sale in a series of transactions (muli-tiered sales) as the basis for customs valuation, thus reducing the customs duty liability.

§4.13 BINDING VALUATION RULING/BINDING VALUATION DETERMINATION/BINDING VALUE INFORMATION

These types of rulings are not nearly as common as those for tariff classifications and origin, with Customs Authorities deliberating on the introduction. For an importer and/or its intermediary to not only mitigate its customs duty liability risk but also provide legal certainty, an application could be made to a Customs Authority to provide a written tariff ruling. In some instances, Customs Authorities also provide a verbal tariff ruling, which indicates the customs duty liability rather than a definitive ruling.

§4.14 ADVANCE VALUATION RULING

In accordance with the Revised Kyoto Convention (RKC) and the WCO Recommendation, importers and related parties can, in advance, request customs valuation rulings from their Customs Authorities. From the WTO's Bali Ministerial decision on the Agreement on Trade Facilitation (TFA), the WCO developed a single document covering procedures for issuing advance rulings on classification, RoO and customs valuation of the goods.

§4.15 DECREED CUSTOMS VALUATION

It is a practice to determine the value of goods by a decree for the purpose of imposition of customs duties and other charges. It is applied as a means to avoid fraud or to protect the domestic industry. The decreed value *de facto* transforms an *ad valorem duty* into a specific duty, called '*valeur mercuriale*', in the Francophone countries. It is possible to apply decreed customs valuation in accordance with the WTO Rules.

§4.16 RELATIONSHIP WITH THE OTHER TAXES – TRANSFER PRICING (TP) AND VALUE ADDED TAX (VAT)

The WCO, WTO, and the Organisation for Economic Co-operation and Development (OECD) acknowledge and continue to pursue initiatives for the possible harmonisation of the rules, objectives and constraints of customs valuation, Transfer Pricing (TP), and Value Added Tax (VAT). The OECD defines TP as *the determination of the price and other conditions for the transfer of goods, services and assets between affiliated companies situated in different tax jurisdictions*'.

The WCO, WTO, and OECD propose a 'whole of government approach' between the Customs Authorities and the Tax Authorities, which they believe could be of mutual benefit.

§4.17 CUSTOMS VALUATION METHODOLOGY VERSUS TP METHODOLOGY

Transfer Pricing (TP) is essentially considered to be the value which is attached to the goods or services transferred between related parties, from one unit of a business to its other units situated in different countries.

To complicate matters, Customs Valuation and TP generally have opposing or competing objectives:

- Customs Valuation:
  - Business objective: A lower customs valuation is desirable as it reduces the duty liability.
  - Customs Authority objective: Wants to ensure that all appropriate costs are included in the customs value and that a related party relationship does not influence the customs value.
- TP:
  - Business objective: A higher TP is desirable as it reduces the taxable profits.
  - Direct Tax Authority objective: Wants to ensure that the TP does not include any inappropriate costs and that the related party relationship does not influence the TP.

The challenge for a business is that it is a '*double obligation*' as its customs valuation practice and its TP practice need to satisfy both the Customs Authority (indirect tax) and the Direct Tax Authority (direct tax):

Customs Valuation *Price Paid or Payable*	*Transfer Pricing* *Arm's-Length Principle*
Transaction Value (TV)	No equivalent
TV of Identical Goods	Compatible Uncontrolled Price (CUP) Method
TV of Similar Goods	CUP Method
Deductive Method	Resale Price Method
Computed Method	Cost Plus Method
Fallback Method	Transactional Net Margin Method (TNMM) Transactional Profit Split Method

Source: Author's own compilation.

Key Differences Between Customs Valuation and TP		
	Customs Valuation	*Transfer Pricing*
Goods, Services, Property	Goods only	Goods, Services, and Property
	Transaction based	Based on aggregates/annual
How do they do that	Import by import	Annual tax return
Confirmation Point	At the point of Customs clearance	Retrospectively (some years after the event)
Method Application	Mandatory hierarchical order alternative methods	Allows choice of the most appropriate method
Test to be applied	Hierarchy to be followed	Most appropriate
Organization	WTO	OECD
Legal basis	OECD Model, Guidelines, and National Legislation	WTO CVA, Regulations, and National Legislation
Authorities' motivation	Application of the WTO CVA is mandatory	Supported by international guidelines, it is not mandatory
What is taxed	Increase the value of the goods	Decrease the value of the goods
Tax/Dutiable Event	Generally – clear goods for home use/free circulation	Generally – change of ownership

Key Differences Between Customs Valuation and TP		
	Customs Valuation	*Transfer Pricing*
Scope	Narrow - value of imported goods	Wide - The profits of the entity
Arm's-length price	Each import must have cost plus profit - no netting	Assessed over the year - can net off profits and losses
How is it tested	Product-by-product test values	Entity comparable
Intercompany concern	Low prices reduce customs duty	High prices reduce income tax

Source: Author's own compilation.

As the table bears out, it makes comparison of Customs Valuation and TP extremely challenging.

§4.18 THE RELATIONSHIP BETWEEN CUSTOMS VALUATION, TP, VAT, AND INCOTERMS®

Although it might not appear apparent, there is an interplay between customs valuation, TP, VAT, and Incoterms®. Since an Incoterms®, which are essentially '*delivery terms*', appears on an invoice, it serves as a reference for a Customs Authority to make a quick assessment of the costs that should be included in the customs valuation. Should, as a consequence, there be costs that are not included in the customs value, then it would impact the VAT payment which would be incorrect as a result. The invoice would further indicate who the buyer and the seller is, and in the instance where a business uses a TP for a customs value, the Customs Authority would have an interest in how the relationship of the two parties influenced the price.

CHAPTER 5

Trade Remedies – Dumping, Countervailing, and Safeguards

Due to a country's commitment to the World Trade Organization (WTO) binding rates, also known as '*binding tariff*' or '*bound rate*' commitments, a country cannot increase the rate of customs duty (tariff) on goods above their '*binding rate*' (also known as a '*ceiling rate*'), without a compensation being negotiated, as the WTO upholds this principle. As a consequence, countries cannot use tariffs as an instrument to protect their domestic manufacturers, but as in the instance of the Most-Favoured Nation (MFN)[66] principle, the WTO does allow exceptions for action to be taken against:

- *dumping* (which implies that the imported good is entering a country at an unfairly low price);
- *countervailing* (or anti-subsidy to offset subsidies);
- safeguards (an emergency measure to temporarily limit the importation of a certain good).

The WTO has three Agreements for this purpose:

- The Anti-Dumping Agreement, or its formal name, Agreement on Implementation of Article VI of the General Agreement on Tariffs and Trade 1994 (GATT 1994).
- Agreement on Subsidies and Countervailing Measures (SCM).
- Agreement on Safeguards.

66. The Most-Favoured-Nation, or MFN treatment, which is the founding principle of the World Trade Organization (WTO), requires Members to not extend better preference to another Member or Members. It is a principle of non-discrimination. But, as with everything in life there are exceptions, and so too is there an exception to the MFN treatment, well two in fact. The exception relates to Customs Unions and Free Trade Areas (FTAs) and to the Generalised System of Preferences (GSP). You can read more in Chapter 13 '*Trade Blocs – Economic Integration*'.

As a collective, trade remedies are known as *'trade defence'*, and then unfortunately as *'trade protection'*, the latter possibly due to its inclusion in the definition of *'contingent protection'*. The definition is that it relates to all measures put in place to serve as a barrier to trade and are then only imposed if certain harmful circumstances on domestic market appear. The *'harmful circumstances'* relate to both fair trade practices and unfair trade practices.

Trade remedies are not one of the three cornerstones, even though it does rely on the imported good's tariff classification, its origin (both the country of origin and country of origin), and its customs valuation in order to determine whether a trade remedy measure would apply to the imported good, and if so, the nature and extent of its imposition. The trade remedy duty level would depend on an investigation by a Government Authority, normally independent from the Customs Authority, of the Trade, Industry, and Finance Departments.

To clarify its naming convention – *'trade remedy'* – its intention is to remedy a trade practice; it does not refer to the remedy itself. Trade remedies intend to normalise the trade practices employed by an overseas exporter and domestic importer. It intends to remedy the unfair trade practices and the unforeseen surges in imports.

Trade remedies' main objective is essentially to level the playing field, as it were, but it should not be concerned with or attempt to remedy *'undervaluation'* in terms of the value for customs duty purposes (customs valuation) values.[67]

There are two categories of trade remedies[68] which can be applied to account for the distorted conditions of competition:

- *Unfair Trade Remedy*
- *Fair Trade Remedy.*

The obvious question to consider here is: Why would the WTO allow a country to take action against another country's exporter or exporters that are not trading unfairly? In this instance, the safeguards, or *'safety value'* as it is best known, allow an importing country to protect or to shield its domestic industry again fairly trade goods. This measure tends to be more often imposed to protect *'infant industries'*;[69] however, this definition is quite nebulous.

The two *'Unfair Trade Remedies'*, which are both company specific and country specific in their application, are:

- dumping, also known as anti-dumping; and
- countervailing, also known as anti-subsidy.

67. *See* Chapter 8 *'Processing – Inward Processing and Outward Processing'* for more on the principles of the value for customs duty purposes.
68. The intention of a trade remedy is to redress the distortion that it is causing rather than to classify the nature of the remedy. Thus, dumping is an unfair trade remedy as its intention is to redress an unfair trade practice, or practices.
69. The *'infant-industry theory'* contends that a new or recently established industry would require protection against competitive overseas industries that export their goods to the country in which the infant industry is based, until the industry had reached a level of maturity.

The single *'Fair Trade Remedy'*, which is imposed against all countries, with the exception of Least-Developed Countries (LDCs), is:

- safeguards.

Interestingly, when the General Agreement on Tariffs and Trade (GATT), the WTO's predecessor, was established, it did not distinguish between developed countries, developing countries, or even LDCs.

Similarly, the Unfair Trade Remedies investigations follow a two-stage investigation process, resulting, following an investigation, in the imposition of provisional anti-dumping duties and provisional countervailing duties before final or definitive anti-dumping duties and final countervailing duties are imposed. The final trade remedy duties are said to be imposed with a *'retrospective effect'*, which tends to confuse. These trade remedy duties are, in fact, imposed from the date that the provisional trade remedy duties were imposed. As for safeguard measures (also known as safeguards), final safeguards are imposed following an investigation. The trade remedy duties are only applicable to goods that are imported from the date on which the trade remedy duties were imposed. If goods were within a Customs Warehousing (CW)[70] or Temporary Admission (TA),[71] Special Customs Procedures/Regimes,[72] the trade remedy duties would not be payable unless the goods are released from the procedure before the trade remedy duties are imposed.

Anti-dumping duties, countervailing duties, and safeguards are imposed and applicable in addition to the duty, tax, and levy. In the instance where the final anti-dumping duty and the final countervailing duty are higher than their provisional equivalent, then a refund of the trade remedy duty could be applied from the Customs Authority.

§5.01 DUMPING AND COUNTERVAILING

The practice is similar, with the only difference being that in the instance of dumping, the decision is the business' (company), and in countervailing, the dumping decision is a consequence of the incentive the exporting business' (company's) government provides. Contrary to popular belief, dumping is not concerned with the comparison of the price of imported goods to that of domestically manufactured equivalents, which are called *'like products'*[73] in the WTO Agreements. So, dumping should not be considered to refer to goods sold at low prices. Dumping is not synonymous with low prices. Dumping is considered to be a form of international price discrimination.

Domestic manufacturers, also called producers, have two options to monitor dumping taking place. In the first instance, the reactive manner would require them to only monitor their own domestic market and to experience price challenges and losses

70. *See* Chapter 9 *'Storage – Customs Warehousing and Free Zones'*.
71. *See* Chapter 10 *'Specific Use – Temporary Admission and End Use'*.
72. *See* section II *'Special Customs Procedures – Regimes'*.
73. A *'like product'* implies that it is a directly competitive good or substitutable good.

due to increased competition from imported goods. Alternatively, they could proactively monitor the import statistics of the *'like products'* (or like goods or equivalent goods) from overseas exporters.

A good is considered to be dumped, and a dumping duty can be imposed against it if the import of the good is at an export price below its *'normal value'*, which is usually the price of the good in its domestic market – the exporting country, and then only if such dumped imports cause material injury to a domestic industry in the importing country. In the instance of countervailing the dumping margin, the difference between the normal value and the export price is due to the government incentives that it receives.

There are essentially four main types of dumping:

- *Persistent dumping*, or *incessant dumping*, occurs when a constant demand for the exported goods continues to be sold at a lower price.
- *Predatory dumping*, also known as *predatory pricing*, attempts to eliminate competition in the exporting market and, ultimately, to create a monopoly.
- *Reverse dumping* sounds like a contradiction in terms but simply implies that where the foreign demand for a good is low, the business (company) will charge a higher price for it in the foreign market than its domestic market. In a similar vein, a business might dump primary goods in a foreign market, only for the process goods (intermediate goods or final goods) being returned to the exporter's market, causing severe material injury to the downstream domestic manufacturers.
- *Sporadic dumping* occurs when exporters sell excess, end-of-the-line goods or unsold inventories, where essentially they have written off the cost of the goods in the accounting systems.

In the instance of countervailing or anti-subsidy, countervailing means to offset an effect by countering it with something of equal impact. Unlike dumping, which is the business' (company's) decision, countervailing dumping is essentially *'incentivised dumping'* as it is a result of government incentives. However, it is not possible for the importing country's government to simply act against another country's companies that receive subsidies. It has to do so with the consideration of the categorisation of the subsidy, which has been done in accordance with the colours of a traffic light:[74]

- *Red Prohibited Subsidy (Forbidden):*
  - It is not permitted under the WTO principles of domestic goods and foreign goods treatment.
  - It simply means that a country can impose trade remedies against another country by imposing countermeasures in the form of countervailing duties, normally without investigation.
- *Amber Actionable Subsidy (Reduced):*

74. Although you might not find a reference to a *'traffic light'* in Customs literature, I found it a helpful and memorable reference when lecturing on the subject matter.

- Normally, these subsidies tend to be specific to an industry.
- A country can impose countervailing duties, but it needs to follow the conclusion of a countervailing investigation (Reduced).

- *Green Non-Actionable Subsidy (Permitted):*
  - A WTO member country would notify other WTO member countries of the nature and the extent of the proposed subsidy.
  - If agreed to by fellow WTO member countries, these subsidies are non-actionable, meaning that countries cannot impose countervailing duties against their use.

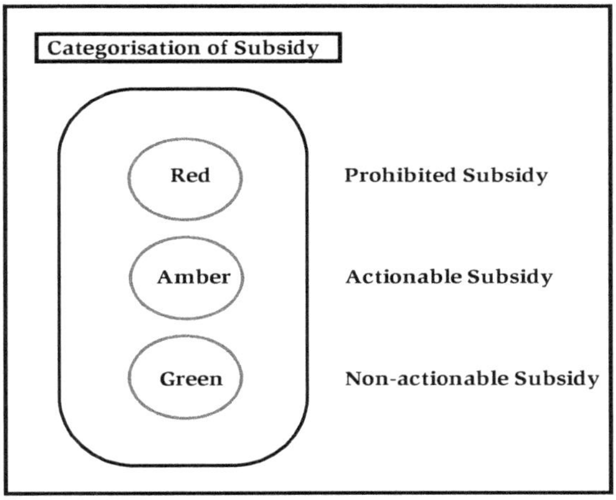

Source: Author's own compilation.

Although the focus of the book is not on agricultural goods, in part due to its complication, suffice to say that the WTO Agriculture Agreement has different boxes. There is no '*Red Box*', domestic support exceeding the reduction commitment levels in the '*Amber Box*' is prohibited, and there is a '*Blue Box*' for subsidies that are tied to programmes that limit production. There are also exemptions for developing countries, called an '*S&D Box*'.

To determine whether a good is dumped requires a series of complex analytical steps in order to determine the appropriate price in the domestic market of the export country - the normal value - and the appropriate price in the market of the importing country - the export price - in order to conduct an appropriate comparison.

The consideration of the imposition of an anti-dumping duty or a countervailing duty is fair and simplistic and subject to the following three considerations - DIC[75] for short:

75. As with so many aspects in Customs, here too you will find a trilogy.

- *Dumping:*
  - First and foremost, consider whether dumping is occurring by comparing the exported good's normal value to the export price.
- *Injury (or Material Injury):*
  - Consider whether the domestic manufacturing industry is experiencing injury, which could be in the form of material injury itself, the threat of material injury, or the material retardation of the establishment of a domestic manufacturing industry.
- *Causality (or Causal Link):*
  - Establishing the existence of a causal link between the dumped imports and the material injury that it is causing. The material injury must be a direct result of the dumping occurring

In the instance where dumping and material injury are demonstrated (two of the three considerations), but the causal link cannot be definitively established or proven, then an anti-dumping duty or a countervailing duty cannot be imposed.

In the instance where exporters have not taken part in a trade remedy investigation, the dumping margin is calculated based on the information supplied by a domestic manufacturer (who initiated the application), normally with the support of a domestic manufacturing industry. The trade remedy duty is called a '*residual duty*'.

In an effort to avoid an anti-dumping duty or a countervailing duty being imposed on its goods, the exporter could commit to a '*price undertaking*'. This commitment could entail the exporter either raising prices or reducing sales in the export market, which the exporter was found to be dumping.

The imposition of anti-dumping duties and countervailing duties remains in place for a period of five years, upon which it becomes due to a mandatory review, known as a '*Sunset Review*'. It is possible for a review of the trade remedy duties to be considered earlier than five years, called an '*Administrative Review*' if:

- the exporter's circumstances have changed; or
- a company (business) that has not previously exported to the country imposing the trade remedy duty, as a consequence its request is only to calculate the dumping margin.

Should the exporter pursue a means to evade the payment of the anti-dumping duty or the countervailing duty, then the domestic manufacturer and domestic industry could request the initiation of a '*Circumvention Investigation*'.

§5.02 TYPES OF REVIEWS

- *Absorption Review:*
  - To determine whether the domestic industry requires an increase in or extension of the scope of applying a trade remedy duty in cases where the exporters and/or the manufacturer or the importer absorbs the trade

remedy duty. The absorption is indicative of no or insufficient price movement following the imposition of a trade remedy duty.

- *Administrative Review (also known as an Interim Review):*
  - A definitive trade remedy duty (anti-dumping or countervailing duty) remains in place for a period of five years. A request to a Trade Remedy Authority to review within a period of one year of its introduction is termed an *'Interim Review'*, or an *'Administrative Review'*.

- *Circumvention Review:*
  - It investigates whether companies are avoiding anti-dumping or countervailing measures by altering their practices, such as modifying products, rerouting goods, or shifting production, to evade duties.
  - It normally considers a change in the pattern of trade, whether the remedial effect of the anti-dumping duty is being undermined, or whether dumping can be found in relation to the normal values previously established for the like products, or similar products.

- *Early Review:*
  - An assessment is made whether the application or suspension of an anti-dumping or countervailing measure should be varied or revoked.

- *Expiry Review:*
  - *See 'Sunset Review'.*

- *Interim Review (also known as an Administrative Review):*
  - *See 'Administrative Review'.*

- *Judicial Review:*
  - An *'interested party'* may challenge the preliminary anti-dumping or countervailing determination, normally when a preliminary anti-dumping duty or countervailing duty is published prior to the final determination of the investigation.

- *Mandatory Review:*
  - *See 'Sunset Review'.*

- *New Exporters Review:*
  - *See 'New Shipper Review'.*

- *New Shipper Review [New Exporters Review]:*
  - If an exporter did not transact with a country during the course of an anti-dumping investigation, and/or countervailing investigation and is in their own view prejudiced by an anti-dumping duty, the exporter may petition for a New Shipper Review. The intention is to have the exporter's goods excluded from the liability of a stipulated anti-dumping duty or countervailing duty.

- *Scope Review:*
  - It investigates whether the goods or the description of the goods subject to an anti-dumping or countervailing measure should be varied. This is to ensure that the right goods are covered.
- *Sunset Review [Expiry Review, Mandatory Review]:*
  - The '*sunset*' requirement establishes that anti-dumping duties and countervailing duties shall normally terminate no later than five years after first being applied unless a review investigation prior to that date establishes that the expiry of the trade remedy duty would be likely to lead to continuation or recurrence of dumping and injury.

§5.03 SAFEGUARDS

Safeguards are considered to act as the '*safety value*' – an emergency measure (also called '*emergency protection*'), which allows a country to act against a surge of imports if the domestic manufacturing industry is experiencing a material injury or the threat of material injury. It is provided for as due to WTO countries' tariff commitments not to exceed their binding rates it is not possible for a country to counteract by increasing its rates of customs duty of an affected good.

A '*surge of imports*' is regarded as a real increase in imports, or in other words, an absolute increase, or it can be an increase in the imports' share of a shrinking market, or even if the import quantity has not increased, in other words, a relative increase.

Unlike dumping and countervailing duties, a safeguard measure, simply known as a '*safeguard*', is not imposed to address unfair trade but rather fair trade.[76] As a consequence, this type of potential action is considered to be a very politically sensitive matter. As a first step, the country whose domestic manufacturing industry is experiencing '*serious injury*' normally tends to engage in diplomacy by attempting to persuade the exporting country's exporter to consider Voluntary Export Restraint (VER). '*Serious injury*' is defined as '*the significant overall impairment in the position of a domestic industry*'.

In essence, a VER is an arrangement between an exporting country of a good and an importing country of the good in which the exporting country agrees to limit the quantity of specific exports of the good below a certain level in order to avoid the imposition of mandatory restrictions by the importing country.

In the instance of an '*unforeseeable surge*' in the imported good, the WTO allows for a safeguard measure, regarded as a short-term measure that allows for the regulation of imports. The safeguard measure, considered a '*temporary relief*',[77] is

76. A '*fair trade remedy*' appears to be a misnomer. It tends to be a highly politically sensitive measure as it deprives the consumers in the import country of the good, of a good which is more price competitive than the domestically manufactured good.
77. Although the meaning and duration of '*temporary relief*' is not defined by the WTO, the imposition of a safeguard for a maximum of 8 years to 10 years, dependent on the classification of the country, does not feel temporary.

imposed against all countries on the clear understanding that during the time of its imposition, the domestic manufacturing industry will adapt. The domestic government will consider policy measures and means to stimulate domestic manufacturing.

According to the WTO Agreement on Safeguards, a WTO member country that imposes or applies a safeguard measure is expected to offer adequate trade compensation to WTO member countries whose trade interests would be adversely affected by the safeguard.

Unlike anti-dumping and countervailing duties, which are imposed for 5 years, safeguard measures are imposed for a maximum initial period of 4 years. Still, they may be extended for up to a maximum of 8 years and 10 years for developing countries.

CHAPTER 6
Excise Duties and Excises

Turning to the national duties, which governments traditionally impose on domestic manufacture, that is collected by its Customs and Excise Authority. Here, too, its application is no longer in line with its origin, as presently, it tends also to be imposed on imported goods. Excise duty originates from the Latin word *'accensare'*, which means *'to tax'*. This is another unhelpful reference perpetuating the interchangeable use of *'duty'* and *'tax'*.

The origin of the term *'Excises'* is also steeped in legend and history. Depending on your source of reference, it is as early as the Han dynasty, from 207 BC to AD 220, where Excises were levied[78] on tea, liquor, fish, and reeds used for fuel and thatching.[79] As for the origin of *'excise duty'*, it is either derived from the Dutch *'accijns'*, for which there is the argument that it originates from the Latin *'accensare'*, which means *'to tax'*, or from the Latin *'excisere'*, which means to *'to carve, to cut out'*. The latter reference is said to refer to the carvings on a stick intended for measuring quantities of beer or liquor. Within this context, it is argued that an 'excise tax' was first imposed by Caesar Augustus, the first Roman Emperor, who reigned from 27 BC to AD 14, before Caesar Caligula abolished it in AD 38. Also not helpful is the conversation about whether excise is a duty, a tax, or a levy. It was only in the mid-17th century that excise duty returned, being reintroduced by the Dutch (The Netherlands). Excise duties tend to be excluded from international trade agreements, including trade blocs, as it is considered a *'national competence'*.

In recent literature, the term *'Excises'* has been conceived, which is defined as *'broadly speaking, the distinguishing features of excise taxation are selectivity in coverage, discrimination in intent, and some form of quantitative measurement in determining the tax liability'*.[80]

78. The reference to *'levied'*, not very helpful.
79. IMF document *'Excises'* Ben JM Terra.
80. The definition is attributable to Sijbren Cnossen.

§6.01 EXCISE DUTY'S EVOLUTION AND APPLICATION

In its truest form, excise duty is concerned with one of the four market failures depicted in international trade known as '*externalities*'.[81] It refers to a situation in which the allocation of goods in a free market is not Pareto efficient. In other words, the resources and, ultimately, the goods are not allocated to their maximum level of efficiency. An '*externality*', in economic terms, is considered a societal cost due to the side effect of an activity that is not reflected in the price of a good and consequently not primarily borne by those involved in the activity, both the producer and the consumer. Consider the classic case of cigarettes, where the consumer is imposing a social cost on those in close proximity without providing compensation for the imposed cost. This cost is not included in the price of the cigarettes (in its both manufacture and use). Although there is a tendency to associate an externality with a negative cost, which it generally is, there are also positive externalities.[82]

Excise duty is considered a '*consumption tax*', which is not helpful, and by definition is also classified as a '*Pigouvian tax*' or '*Pigou tax*'. It is imposed to discourage consumption. This tax is imposed on a market transaction that creates a negative externality or an additional cost to the society. Excise duty is further categorised as a '*sin tax*',[83] another unhelpful reference, as its imposition is not to generate revenue but rather to discourage the consumption of goods such as cigarettes, tobacco, liquor, and fuel. The major argument against a '*sin tax*' is that it is a regressive tax[84] in that it does not account for the ability to pay, with poorer people having to pay a greater share of their income on excise duties than rich people would. A '*sin tax*' is, in essence, adhering to the '*polluter pays principle*', which ultimately attempts to '*internalise an external cost*'. In other words, the polluter is imposing a cost on a third party – the society – a cost which is not included in the cost of the good, and as a consequence, such a cost has to be included in the price of the good.

In essence, an internal cost is the cost of an activity paid for by the consumer of the good. '*External cost*' is the activity being paid for by the non-consumer of the good. The '*social cost*' is the sum or aggregate of the internal and external costs.[85]

The preference for the imposition of excise duties on these types of goods is that their elasticity of demand is either inelastic or, at best, perfectly inelastic. This simply

81. Externalities – the '*social cost*' is the aggregate (sum) of the '*internal costs*' and the '*external costs*'. The internal costs is that of an activity paid by the consumer engaging in the activity, while the external costs is the cost which is not paid by the consumer engaging in the activity.
82. Normally when you consume a good you derive a personal benefit, but it is also possible for there to be a benefit for society. When you are enjoying a barbeque, I know it as a '*braai*', you enjoy the consumption of what you are barbecuing but your neighbours, in close proximity, might enjoy the aroma of what emanates from the barbeque. In other words, for a positive externality, the social benefit exceeds the private benefit.
83. *See* Chapter 7 '*Types of Duties, Taxes, and Levies*'.
84. A '*Regressive Tax*' means that the same rate (percentage) is applied on the goods, regardless of the consumer's income, as a consequence it has a disproportionate effect on poorer consumers. Also *see* Chapter 7 '*Types of Duties, Taxes, and Levies*' for '*Proportional Tax*' and '*Progressive Tax*', which constitute yet another trilogy – tax systems.
85. An external cost, also known as an externalities, refers to the economic principle of uncompensated social or environmental effects.

means that as the price of the good increases (in the case of the excise duty being imposed on it), the quantity demanded by the consumer remains unchanged. It is an ideal good to be subjected to the imposition of a duty as it ensures a consistent duty revenue. In addition to its classification as a '*sin tax*', excise duty is also imposed on luxury goods, more aptly known as non-essential goods that are classified as '*luxury tax*'.[86] Luxury goods tend to individually have varied elasticities of demand, which makes their duty revenue less consistent. An argument for its imposition is that non-essential goods deplete resources, attributing to its '*scarcity*', one of the three cornerstones of Economics (the other two being '*choice*' and '*opportunity cost*').[87] Both the excise duty of '*sin tax*' and '*luxury tax*' are categorised as '*indirect tax*' (another unhelpful reference) as the duty is not paid directly by the seller; it is merely passed on to the consumer by the importer (merchant) or by the manufacturer (producer) of the goods as a part of the price of the goods:[88]

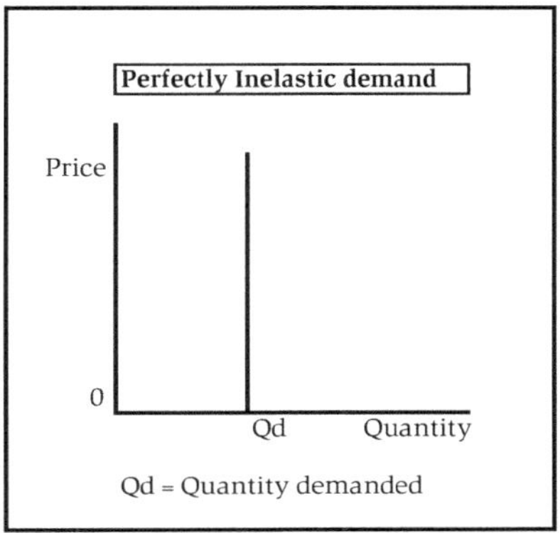

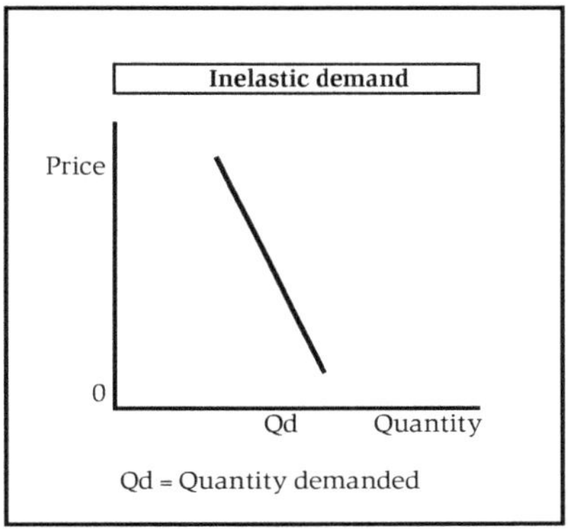

§6.02 EXCISE DUTY VERSUS CUSTOMS DUTY

Traditionally, the distinction lies in a '*customs duty*' being imposed on the goods imported into a country or territory, while an '*excise duty*' is imposed on the manufacture of the goods in a country. Excise duty is thus considered a national duty as it is imposed on domestically manufactured goods, while a customs duty is an international duty as it is imposed on imported goods. Consequently, the World Customs Organization (WCO) and the World Trade Organization (WTO) are concerned

86. *See* Chapter 7 '*Types of Duties, Taxes, and Levies*'.
87. At the heart of Economics are the concepts of scarcity [limited resources and unlimited wants], choice [different incentives in use], and opportunity cost. Resources are scarce, which implies that a choice need to be made as how to utilise the resources, for which there is a cost. The cost being that by choosing one over the other there is a loss of an opportunity, for the alternative being chosen. [Economics define four types of economic resources: land, labour, capital, and technology, with technology also being referred to as entrepreneurship.]
88. The United States of America has a '*Superfund Excise Tax*' that applies to manufacturers, producers or importers who sell or use 'taxable chemicals' or 'taxable substitutes' such as acetic acid, benzoic acid, butanol, chlorine, ethyl chloride glycerine, polypropylene (in many forms).

with customs duties and consider excise duties to be for a country's internal consideration. Excise duty could be considered the autonomous function of a country.

Unfortunately, the distinction is now being confused as excise duty is also unhelpfully imposed on imported goods. The only requirement that the WTO has in the instance of the duty treatment is in the imposition of an excise duty; it should be at the same level as its corresponding additional customs duty. This is an unfortunate state of affairs, and would be better served by keeping to the naming convention and only applying excise duty on domestically manufactured goods.

The *'imported'* component of the excise duty is, in essence, a *'contra duty'*,[89] which simply means that rather than only imposing an excise duty on the domestically manufactured good, the government also imposes a customs duty on the imported good at the same rate of duty. Although this might sound equitable, the basis on which the contra duties are imposed differ, as the basis for the domestically manufactured good basis is on an Ex-Works (EXW) basis, compared to the imported good, which is dutiable on a Free on Board (FOB) or Cost, Insurance, and Freight (CIF) basis:

Differences Between Customs Duty and Excise Duty

	Customs Duty	*Excise Duty*
Imposed	On imports and exports [Goods crossing international borders]	On local manufacture
Scope	All products	Limited (traditional sin goods)
Application through	International Agreement	Domestic Policy
Characteristics	International	National [Internal]
Place of collection	At the country's border [Customs border – Point of Entry]	At the manufacturer's premises [Duty at Source]
Who pays	The importer [Consumer ultimately pays]	The producer [Consumer ultimately pays]
Type of Duty	Predominant *ad valorem* duties [On the value of the goods]	Predominantly specific duties [Also mixed duties]
Rate Amendment	No higher than the WTO binding rate [Higher requires international negotiation]	At any level, as long as the excise duty is at the same level as the customs duty

89. A 'contra duty' simply means that a duty, of the same rate, is applied both on an import good and on a domestically manufactured good, respectively.

	Customs Duty	*Excise Duty*
Objective *[Type of Measure]*	Protective Measure Regulate Trade	Fiscal Measure Discourage consumption
Motivation	Protect local manufacturers	To address negative externalities [Market failure]
Imposed On	Imports All imported goods Broad focus	Production [On specific goods] Narrow focus [*'Sin Taxes'*]
Paid on	Importation	Monthly or Quarterly returns[90]
Applied on	The CIF or FOB value	EXW value
Warehouse	Customs Warehousing procedure can apply	Excise manufacturing warehouse
Market Impact	Influences trade patterns and availability of foreign goods	Affects the price of local goods and, ultimately, their consumption

Source: Author's own compilation.

§6.03 CONTRA DUTIES

Where an excise duty is imposed on both the domestically manufactured good and he imported good, the rate of duty should be the same. At face value, it seems to be equitable and to uphold the principle between a domestically produced good and an imported good. Although the nominal rate of duty is the same, the effective rate of duty differs as the duty is imposed on a different basis.

The duty liability for a domestically produced good is imported on the Ex-Factory price, while for the imported good it is on either the FOB value or the CIF value, depending on the basis for customs valuation of the import country.

This basis of duty liability should not be confused with the International Commercial Terms (Incoterms®),[91] the International Chamber of Commerce (ICC) delivery terms. Consequently, the *'contra customs duty'*, as it rightly should be called, provides additional tariff protection. In accordance with the WTO principles and agreements, imported goods should be treated similarly to a domestically manufactured good, but in this instance, the duty treatment differs.

90. A number of countries have imposed 'Duty at Source' legislation that requires that the excise duty is collected at the premises of the manufacturer.
91. *See* Chapter 18 *'International Commercial Terms (Incoterms®)'*.

The challenge with the imposition of excise duties is that its tax base tends to be very small, as it is imposed on domestic manufacture, which implies the existence of a manufacturing sector. Yes, another seemingly contradictory use of terminology. It is essential that a country's tax base be broad to achieve the greatest level of neutrality and be most efficient in raising revenue – at the lowest possible rates.

An added distinction between excise duty and customs duty is that in the instance of a trade bloc,[92] the excise duty tends to be imposed and collected by individual member countries, while customs duty is uniformly imposed and collected by member countries. In these instances, the revenue collected is distributed or shared between member countries.

It is important to remember that excise duty, similar to customs duty, is only imposed on goods that are domestically consumed. Should the goods be destined for exportation to another country or territory, then the excise duty is not imposed on the good; it is, in effect, exempt.[93] It also applies to instances where goods are re-exported or goods are returned.[94] The latter refers to Returned Goods Relief (RGR), a customs procedure that allows goods to be imported back into the country (return) without incurring duties or taxes, provided certain conditions are met.

§6.04 EXCISE DUTY TYPES

Excise duties comprise the following four main tax categories:[95]

Traditional '*bads*' Sin Taxes
- Tobacco products
- Alcoholic beverages.

New '*bads*' Sin Taxes
- Sugar-sweetened beverages (SSBs).

Nature and Climate
- Carbon–Carbon Border Adjustment Mechanism (CBAM)
- Climate Change Levy
- Deforestation
- Fossil fuels
- Green Taxes
- Plastics.

92. *See* Chapter 13 '*Trade Blocs – Economic Integration*'.
93. To be exempt, or to '*be exempted from*', means that no excise duty is imposed on the good.
94. *See* Returned Goods Relief, or RGR, which is customs procedure.
95. *See* Chapter 7 '*Types of Duties, Taxes, and Levies*'.

Income-elastic goods
- Luxury goods, also known as non-essential goods.

§6.05 EXCISES

Although not adopted as a universal term, there is the odd reference to '*Excises*' for which a definition is lacking, other than to consider it as the plural form of excise duty. As the application of excise duty, which is and should purely be imposed on domestic consumption, is becoming even more blurred, '*excises*' is considered to be the collective for all forms of excise, be it duty, tax, or levy.

CHAPTER 7

Types of Duties, Taxes, and Levies

The interchangeable and indiscriminate use of terminology is no more evident than when considering duty, tax, levy, and tariff. An added challenge is also to consider the context in which the terminology is used, be it as a verb or a noun. The interest (financial interest) is in the movement of the goods, entering and leaving a Customs Authority's territory (country or territory). It is said that a Customs Authority can levy a tax (a tax could also be a duty) or impose a levy or a duty. One might despair that '*a duty is a tax that you levy*'.

Then, not only can a tax, a duty, or a levy be imposed but so too can a surcharge and a toll. To complicate matters further, customs and excise duties are classified as '*indirect taxes*'. Add to this that a '*tariff*' is often confused with duty, which could mean the duty liability or the rate of duty, depending on the context of use. A '*tariff*' has a trilogy of meanings. It could first be a list or a schedule that depicts the rates of duty payable on the importation or the exportation of the good. Second, it could refer to the actual duty being levied on the importation or the exportation of the good. Third, it could be the law that provides for the schedules of the tariff and customs provisions to mitigate the rate of customs duty. So it could, depending on the context, be the list or the schedule, or the duty, or the law.

As for the rate of duty, a rate of 0% is not '*free*'; it simply implies a rate of duty at zero percent. Contrary to popular belief, this distinction does matter. Just as there is nothing that is '*free*' in free trade, there is nothing '*free*' about a rate of duty.

As to the definition of a '*duty*', the Revised Kyoto Convention, or RKC,[96] contains a single definition for '*duty*', that of '*customs duties*', which it defines as meaning '*the duties laid down in the Customs tariff to which goods are liable on entering or leaving the Customs territory*'. This should result in another terminological challenge, as an

96. According to the WCO, the Revised Kyoto Convention, or RKC, promotes trade facilitation and effective controls through its legal provisions that detail the application of simple yet efficient procedures. The RKC also contains new and obligatory rules for its application which all Contracting Parties must accept without reservation.

'*export duty*' is imposed on exported goods. A '*customs duty*' is imposed on imported goods and forms part of the collective of duties, taxes, and levies called '*import duty*'.

§7.01 DUTIES, TAXES, LEVIES, AND TARIFFS

The context in which tariffs are used could result in '*duties*' and '*tariffs*' being used interchangeably, while duties are a measure imposed on goods, either imported or domestically manufactured, and tariffs are the rate of duty. Tariffs[97] could either be a protective measure,[98] in that they protect the domestic industry by restricting the imported good or as a fiscal measure,[99] in that it generates revenue for a government. There are those who are of the belief that a tariff can also serve a punitive function by redressing trade remedy distortions.

As for the rate of the tariff, in the context of the WTO, there is a binding tariff, which means the highest tariff that can be imposed per commodity code, and the applied tariff, which is the prevailing tariff. In the instance of agriculture, the process of converting quotas and import restrictions to tariffs is known as '*tariffication*'. As for pharmaceutical goods, the WTO's Agreement on Trade in Pharmaceutical Products, known as the Pharma Agreement, eliminates tariffs and other duties and charges on a large number of pharmaceutical goods and the substances used to produce them, permanently binding them at duty-free levels.

In essence, a '*duty*' is imposed on an activity which would not have been imposed in its absence. A '*tax*' is imposed on a range of activities that generate revenue, while a '*levy*' tends to be an obligatory payment to the government.

§7.02 THE HISTORY – CUSTOMS DUTY AND EXCISE DUTY

Customs duty,[100] or '*customary due*',[101] was first applied in 609 BC in Egypt. There is the contrary view that the Mesopotamians collected customs duty more than 3,500 years ago. This was, in fact, a '*toll*',[102] meaning the toll was imposed on the movement of the goods itself rather than on the goods being moved to be traded. The Egyptians, in contrast, imposed a customs duty on the goods being traded.

97. Free trade economists tend to argue that tariffs encourage the misallocation of scarce resources.
98. A protective measure or protectionism, also known as trade protectionism, is an economic policy with the intention of restricting the import of goods through the imposition of a number of policy instruments such as tariffs and import quotas.
99. The '*fiscal*' originates from the '*Fiscus*', which translated from Latin means '*basket*' or '*purse*'. It was used to describe all the revenue, which was collected, from taxes, for the Roman Emperor's purse. The collected revenue was literary kept in baskets.
100. Quite surprisingly you will not find many a person/practitioner, involved in Customs, who would be able to explain the origin of '*customs duty*' to you.
101. In times immemorial, an importer, on the importation of a good into a territory, had to pay a due or present the ruler of the territory with something of value, which was customary for the importation of that specific good, essentially making a payment for the right to import the good.
102. A toll is also considered '*passage-money, rent*'. The word originates from the late Latin '*tolonium*' which translates to '*toll house*' or '*custom house*'.

Customs duty (not to be confused with import duty) and excise duty are imposed on imported goods and domestically manufactured goods, while an *'export duty'* is imposed on goods that are exported. The word *'import'* originates from the Latin word *'importare'*, which means to *'carry in'* or to *'bring in'*, while *'export'* originates from the Latin word *'exportare'*, which means to *'to carry out'* or to *'send away'*, and *'manufacture'* from the words *'manu'* meaning *'hand'* and *'factura'* meaning *'a working'*.

§7.03 EXCISE – SIN TAX VERSUS LUXURY TAX

Customs duty and Excise duty, called *'indirect taxes'*, are imposed on the consumers, the persons who ultimately pay the duty, also expressed as *'the person who ultimately meets the levy'*. These are *'consumption taxes'*.

Customs and excise duties are distinctly different, though both are collectively categorised as *'import duty'*. A customs duty tends to serve two purposes: as a fiscal[103] measure, meaning that its intention is to collect revenue. It also serves as a protective measure to make imported goods more expensive in favour of domestically manufactured goods. An *'excise duty'* is a *'consumption tax'*, of which there are two types, namely *'sin tax'* and *'luxury tax'*.

A *'sin tax'* is imposed on the consumption of goods that imposes a cost on society, which is not included in the price of the good. As an example, the consumption of tobacco goods imposes a cost on society for which the producer and the consumer of the goods do not make the full pay, which requires the government to impose a duty so as to *'internalise an external cost'*. The duties imposed are specific, as they are quantitative in nature. A *'luxury tax'* is imposed on the production and consumption of non-essential goods (also known as *'luxury goods'*). The economic argument is that scarce resources are being utilised to produce goods for which there is no real economic need or justification, goods that are considered to be *'vanity goods'* by their mere nature.

§7.04 EXCISE – GREY TAX VERSUS GREEN TAX

Excise(s) can be grouped into two categories, *'grey taxes'* or *'gloomy taxes'*, and *'green taxes'*.

'Grey Taxes', also called *'Gloomy Taxes'*, is the collective categorisation of duties, taxes, and levies imposed on smoking, drinking, petroleum (energy), and health (sugar).

'Green Taxes' is the collective categorisation of duties, taxes, and levies on goods that impact CO_2, plastic, climate change, and the environment.

103. It originates from the word *'fiscus'*, which was the name of the personal chest of the emperors of Rome, which held all the money that were collected from the citizens (normally collected through the imposition of taxes).

§7.05 IMPORT DUTY

An *'import duty'* is the collective term for a range of duties, taxes, surcharges, charges, and levies, which are laid down in a country's Customs Tariff, or tariff that must not be confused with the *'rate of duty'*, which lays down the duty liability on the entering (importation) or leaving (exportation) from the country:

- *Customs duty:*
  - It is imposed by a country on goods imported into a country and is considered an *'international duty'*.[104]
  - There are two types of customs duty, *'fiscal duties'*, also known as revenue-generating duties, and *'protective duties'*.
  - In the instance of a protective customs duty, it tends to be imposed on infant industries, which begs the question as to the qualifying criteria of an *'infant industry'*.
- *Excise duty:*
  - It is a *'consumption duty'* imposed on goods for which the demand is either perfectly inelastic or inelastic, such as petroleum goods, alcohol goods, and tobacco goods, as well as on certain luxury goods, also known as non-essential goods, such as electronics and cosmetics.
  - This is considered a *'national duty'*, as countries can impose these duties on domestically manufactured goods. Excise duties are not regulated by the WTO, which only requires that when an excise duty is imposed, an equivalent needs to be imposed on imported goods, which is called a *'contra customs duty'*. Unfortunately, these duties tend to be called *'excise duty'*, which tends to cause confusion.
  - At issue is the basis on which the duty is imposed. In the instance of *'customs duty'*, it is imposed on a Cost, Insurance, and Freight (CIF) basis or on a Free on Board (FOB) basis, while an *'excise duty'* is imposed on an Ex-Works (EXW) basis.
- *Excises* does not have an official definition; instead, it is considered the collective term for all forms of excise duties, excise taxes, and excise levies. It is broadly defined as *'the distinguishing features of excise taxation are selectivity in coverage, discrimination in intent, and some form of quantitative measurement in determining the tax liability'*.[105] It distinguishes three systems: a limited excise system of between 10 to 15 commodity groups, an intermediate excise system of between 15 to 30 commodity groups, and an extended excise system comprising more than 30 commodity groups spanning almost the whole range of production activities in a particular country.

104. The RKC Chapter 2 *'Definition'* defines *'customs duties'* as the duties laid down in the Customs tariff to which goods are liable on entering or leaving the Customs territory.
105. The definition for *'excises'* is offered by Sijbren Cnossen, in Chapter 8 *'Excises'* in the International Monetary Fund (IMF) *'Tax Law Design and Drafting'*, Volume 1, 1996.

- *Anti-dumping duty* is an '*unfair trade remedy*' imposed on the imported good, for a specified country, and sometimes even identifying the company of manufacture, in order to offset dumping, that is, to bring the price of the imported good in line with the '*normal value*' of that good in its domestic market. The anti-dumping duty cannot exceed the full dumping margin of the good. There is also a '*provisional anti-dumping duty*', which is imposed once a preliminary determination of dumping has been made. These types of duties are imposed on both the exporter and the country.
- *Countervailing (anti-subsidy) duty* is an '*unfair trade remedy*' imposed on an imported good, for a specified country, and sometimes even identifying the company of manufacture, to prevent the dumping of a good due to the export subsidies or incentives it had received in its country. The rate of the countervailing duty cannot exceed the full dumping margin of the good. There is also a '*provisional countervailing duty*', which is imposed once a preliminary determination of dumping due to the utilisation of a subsidy has been made. These types of duties are imposed on both the exporter and the country.
- *Safeguards (safeguard measures)* is a '*fair trade remedy*', also called an '*emergency measure*' or '*safety valve*', imposed on increased imports of particular goods, where such imports have caused or threaten to cause serious injury. It differs from anti-dumping and countervailing in that it is not country and company specific. There is no provisional duty or '*provisional safeguard measure*', as it is imposed once and against all countries, with possible exclusion to Least-Developed Countries (LDCs).
- *Charge* is simply an additional cost that is imposed on a good.
- *Levy*, in its purest application, serves to ringfence the revenue that it collects to remedy an externality or an external cost. There has been a recent rise in the application of levies such as the '*Environmental Levy*', also known as the '*Climate Change Levy*', or '*Carbon Emissions Levy*', and the '*Plastics Bag Levy*' that aims to reduce the use of single-use carrier bags.
- *Surcharge*, as the prefix '*sur*' indicates, means an '*over and above*' charge. Consequently, it takes on various forms and is imposed under various conditions.
- *Import Value Added Tax (VAT)* is a tax paid on goods imported into a country or territory. As VAT is an *ad valorem* duty, it is imposed on the customs valuation of imported goods. [A number of countries have transitioned to VAT from General Sales Tax (GST), although GST is still favoured in other countries.]

In essence, duties, taxes, levies, and charges on the importation of goods, or imports, constitute import duties. To complicate matters further, depending on the context, import duty might also be known as a tariff – import tariff.

§7.06 EXPORT DUTY

An '*export duty*' is not part of a collective; it is a singular duty that is paid on goods being exported from a country or territory. This duty is not as prevalent in use as a customs duty, which tends to be used by LDCs and developing countries, being imposed on primary commodities, especially unprocessed goods. In instances where the price in overseas countries might be higher than in the domestic country, ensure that it does not impact the domestic supply. '*Export duty*' is applied by governments as an industrial policy[106] instrument.

§7.07 TYPES OF DUTIES/TARIFFS

- *Additional duty:*
  - An ad hoc duty that is imposed as either a fiscal measure, to raise revenue, or to protect the domestic industry. It is also called a '*surcharge*' or a '*surtax*'. The prefix '*sur*' indicates, means, an '*over and above*' charge.
- *Ad valorem duty:*
  - It is applied as a percentage, for example, 10%, on the value of the good for customs duty purposes (customs valuation). In the instance of imported goods, the duty is imposed on either the CIF value or the FOB value.[107]
  - The duty is imposed on an ex-factory value for a locally (domestic) manufactured good.
- *Anti-dumping duty:*
  - It is imposed by a country on goods imported into a country and is considered an '*international duty*'.
  - There are two types of customs duty, '*fiscal duties*', also known as revenue-generating duties, and '*protective duties*'.
  - In the instance of a protective customs duty, it tends to be imposed on infant industries, which begs the question as to the qualifying criteria of an '*infant industry*'.
- *Cess*
  - Shortened from '*assess*' is imposed for a specific purpose. The revenue collected from its imposition must be ringfenced; it must be used solely for the intended cause, which could be argued to be the purpose of an excise duty, in its purest form.

106. Trade Policy is traditionally included as an element of Industrial Policy.
107. Do not confuse '*CIF value*' and '*FOB value*' with the CIF Incoterms® and the FOB Incoterms®.

- *Compound duty/Combination duty:*
  - It is based on a combination of both an *ad valorem* duty and a specific rate duty, for example, 10% *ad valorem* plus GBP 5 per kilogram.

- *Contra duty:*
  - It is a customs duty and an excise duty that is imposed at the exact same level or rate of duty.

- *Countervailing duty (Countervailing measure):*
  - Countervailing (anti-subsidy) duty is an '*unfair trade remedy*' imposed on an imported good, for a specified country, and sometimes even identifying the company of manufacture, to prevent the dumping of a good due to the export subsidies or incentives it had received in its country. The rate of the countervailing duty cannot exceed the full dumping margin of the good. There is also a '*provisional countervailing duty*', which is imposed once a preliminary determination of dumping due to the utilisation of a subsidy has been made. These types of duties are imposed on both the exporter and the country.

- *Excise duty:*
  - It is a '*consumption duty*' imposed on goods for which the demand is either perfectly inelastic or inelastic, such as petroleum goods, alcohol goods, and tobacco goods, as well as on certain luxury goods, also known as non-essential goods, such as electronics and cosmetics.
  - This is considered a '*national duty*', as countries can impose these duties on domestically manufactured goods. Excise duties are not regulated by the WTO, which only requires that when an excise duty is imposed, an equivalent needs to be imposed on imported goods, which is called a '*contra customs duty*'. Unfortunately, these duties tend to be called '*excise duty*', which tends to cause confusion.
  - At issue is the basis on which the duty is imposed. In the instance of '*customs duty*', it is imposed on a Cost, Insurance, and Freight (CIF) basis or on a Free on Board (FOB) basis, while an '*excise duty*' is imposed on an Ex-Works (EXW) basis.

- *Excises* does not have an official definition; instead, it is considered the collective term for all forms of excise duties, excise taxes, and excise levies. It is broadly defined as '*the distinguishing features of excise taxation are selectivity in coverage, discrimination in intent, and some form of quantitative measurement in determining the tax liability*'.[108] It distinguishes three systems: a limited excise system of between 10 to 15 commodity groups, an intermediate excise system of between 15 to 30 commodity groups, and an

108. The definition for '*excises*' is offered by Sijbren Cnossen, in Chapter 8 '*Excises*' in the International Monetary Fund (IMF) '*Tax Law Design and Drafting*', Volume 1, 1996.

extended excise system comprising more than 30 commodity groups spanning almost the whole range of production activities in a particular country.

- *Formula duty:*
  - The formula consists of a reference price, above which an *ad valorem* duty would apply to high-cost developed countries and below which, in addition to the *ad valorem* duty, a progressive specific duty (unit of measure) would apply against low-cost developing countries.

- *General tariff:*
  - Imposed on a good imported from a country that is neither granted the Most-Favoured Nation (MFN) status nor is subjected to a preferential arrangement. The reason for the MFN tariff not applying is that the country of export is not a member of the WTO.

- *Levy:*
  - Imposed for a designated purpose. In its purest application, it serves to ringfence the revenue that it collects to remedy an externality or an external cost. There has been a recent rise in the application of levies such as the '*Environmental Levy*', also known as the '*Climate Change Levy*', or '*Carbon Emissions Levy*', and the '*Plastics Bag Levy*' that aims to reduce the use of single-use carrier bags.

- *Luxury tax:*
  - A tax on a luxury good, also known as a non-essential good. This good may be a Veblen good, a good for which the demand increases as the price increases. The argument for its imposition is that an increase in the price of the good will not deter the consumer as the demand for the good is price inelastic.

- *Maximum (minimum) price system:*
  - This is decreed by the importing country, requiring that the price of the imported goods, above or below the stipulated prices, will trigger a protective action, e.g., the imposition of additional duties or quantitative restrictions.
  - The terminology for this system differs between countries and could also be called '*basic import price*', '*minimum import price*', '*reference price*', and '*trigger price*'.

- *Mixed rate duty/Mixed tariff:*
  - It is similar to a '*compound duty*' or a '*combination duty*'. While both duties are listed, when calculating the duties, the one that generates the most, or highest revenue, is the duty imposed.

- *Para-tariff measure:*
  - A measure that intends to increase the cost of an imported good in a similar manner to a tariff. These measures include customs surcharges,

additional taxes and charges, service charges, internal taxes, and decreed customs valuation.

- *Safeguard duty:*
  - Safeguards (safeguard measures) is a '*fair trade remedy*', also called an 'emergency measure' or '*safety valve*', imposed on increased imports of particular goods, where such imports have caused or threaten to cause serious injury. It differs from anti-dumping and countervailing in that it is not country and company specific. There is no provisional duty or 'provisional safeguard measure', as it is imposed once and against all countries, with possible exclusion to Least-Developed Countries (LDCs).

- *Seasonal duty:*
  - The duty is applicable at certain times of the year, usually in connection with agricultural products.

- *Sin taxes:*
  - Also known as a '*Sumptuary Tax*', or a '*Vice Tax*', it is an excise duty levied on goods that are considered harmful to society, such as alcohol, tobacco, drugs, candy, soft drinks, fast foods, coffee, sugar, and vaping. In contrast to a Pigovian tax,[109] whose aim is for the consumer of the good to pay for the damage to society caused by the consumption of the goods. Sin taxes' purpose is to increase the price of a good in an effort to decrease the use of the good.

- *Specific duty:*
  - It is a fixed monetary value per unit imposed on the quantity, weight, or volume of the good, for example, GBP 5 per kilogram.
  - It is effective if protection is required against low-priced imports, such as agricultural goods, as the customs valuation is immaterial.
  - These non-*ad valorem* tariffs are less transparent and more distorting in their application. To analyse their impact, Economists calculate what they call the '*Ad valorem equivalent*'[110] or AVE.

- *Sumptuary tax:*
  - *See* '*Sin Tax*', or '*Vice Tax*'.

- *Surcharge:*
  - The prefix '*sur*' indicates, means, an '*over and above*' charge. Consequently, it takes on various forms and is imposed under various conditions. An ad hoc duty that is imposed as either a fiscal measure, to raise

109. A Pigovian tax, also spelled Pigouvian tax, serves to redress market failures caused by negative externalities, where the consumer of a good's actions impose costs on others without those costs being reflected in the good's market price.
110. It refers to a tariff, also known as a rate of duty, that is not a percentage (quantity, weight, or volume) but which can be estimated as a percentage of the price – AVE.

revenue, or to protect the domestic industry. It is also called an '*additional duty*', or a '*surtax*'.

- *Surtax:*
  - The prefix '*sur*' indicates, means, an '*over and above*' charge. Consequently, it takes on various forms and is imposed under various conditions. An ad hoc duty that is imposed as either a fiscal measure, to raise revenue, or to protect the domestic industry. It is also called an '*additional duty*', or a '*surcharge*'.

- *Tariff:*
  - Is a customs duty on an imported good.

- *Technical tariff:*
  - The tariff rate depends on specific technical factors of the product, its input content, for example, the fat, sugar, or alcohol content of a good.

- *Variable import levy:*
  - A level on imports with the intention to equalise the import price to the domestic price level. In other words, to price of the imported good to at least a level as high as the domestic price.
  - *See* 'Variable levy', and '*Variable tariff formula*'.

- *Variable levy:*
  - A customs duty rate which varies in response to domestic price criterion.
  - *See 'Variable import levy'*, and '*Variable tariff formula*'.

- *Variable tariff formula:*
  - The formula operates on the principle that a country's domestic price should be equal to the domestic prices in developing countries, including the subsidies available to the domestic producers, which constitute the world reference price.
  - The rate of duty will increase or decrease depending on the prevailing international price of the good that will be imported.
  - The duty will be a specific duty.
  - The duty is adjusted or triggered periodically in response to the domestic price criterion without prior publication.
  - *See 'Variable Import Levy'*, and '*Variable levy*'.

- *Sin taxes:*
  - *See 'Sumptuary Tax'*, or '*Vice Tax*'.

§7.08 QUOTAS

It is the explicit limit of the quantity of a good that can be imported or exported during a specified period of time. These limits could either be expressed and measured by physical quantity, or even by value. The quota could be applied on a selective basis, in order to achieve an economic objective, thus imposing limits on the nature of the good and the country of origin. A quota tends to be administered through a system of licensing, though it could be managed on a 'first-come-first-served' basis, which would require:

- *Autonomous tariff quota (ATQ):*
  - Allow limited quantities, up to a given quantity, to be imported at a reduced customs duty rate (lower than the MFN rate of duty), or at a duty-free (0%) rate, for a specified period. Once the limit has been achieved then the MFN rate of duty will apply. This quota is also known as a Tariff Rate Quota (TRQ).

- *Bilateral quota:*
  - A quota that is reserved for a specific exporting country.

- *Global quota:*
  - Is the limit of quantities allowed to enter a country as imports. It is applicable to all import sources combined regardless of the country of origin.

- *Inside quota tariff rate (IQTR):*
  - The rate of customs duty applicable to a good imported within the limits of a tariff quota volume. The quota is the lower rate of customs duty applied to a specific quantity of imports within a TRQ. Once the quota is filled, a higher Outside Quota Tariff Rate (OQTR) applies to any additional imports.
  - *See 'Outside quota tariff rate'.*

- *Outside quota tariff rate (OQTR):*
  - The lower rate of customs duty tariff rate applicable to a specific quantity of imports within a tariff rate quota (TRQ). Once the quota is filled, within a TRQ, the OQTR applies to any additional imports, which is essentially the MFN rate.
  - *See 'Inside quota tariff rate'.*

- *Quota linked with the purchase of local goods:*
  - It limits the amount of goods that can be imported into to country, by linking it to the purchase of domestic (local) good.
  - The quota, allowing for the importation of a good, is normally defined as a percentage of the value of the goods which the importer has purchased domestically, in its country.

- *Seasonal quota:*
  - It is imposed during a given period of the year, usually aligned to the domestic harvest of agricultural goods when the good is available in abundance.

- *Tariff rate quota (TRQ):*
  - Is a combination of an import tariff and an import quota in which imports below a specified quantity enter at a low (or zero) tariff and imports above that quantity enter at a higher tariff. A tariff quota has thus two parts, the IQTR and the OQTR.
  - Also known as an autonomous tariff quota (ATQ).

§7.09 LEVELS OF DUTY (TARIFF)

This is not to be confused with the '*rates of duty*', which is the actual numerical rate that is attributable to the good, i.e., 10% *ad valorem*, or GBP 5 per kilogram, etc. The '*level of duty*' refers to the nature of the tariff.

- *Applied tariff/Applied rate/Prevailing tariff:*
  - Also known as the '*prevailing tariff*', published by Customs Authorities, it can be lower than the bound tariff rate. WTO members have the flexibility to increase or decrease their tariffs, provided that they do not exceed the bound tariff rate.

- *Binding overhang:*
  - It is often used to describe a situation where there is a large difference between the tariff that is actually applied (MFN Applied) and the level at which the tariff is bound in GATT (the ceiling).

- *Bound tariff/Bound rate/Ceiling rate/Ceiling binding/Maximum tariff:*[111]
  - The maximum MFN tariff that an individual WTO Member country commits to impose through the negotiation with the WTO Members.
  - It is referred to by many names: '*bound tariff*', '*bound rate*', '*ceiling rate*', '*ceiling bing*', and '*maximum tariff*'.
  - The bound tariff rate may not be exceeded unless the WTO Members enter into negotiations with all WTO Members and obtain their agreement.
  - The so-called *Schedule of Tariff Concessions* of each WTO member is annexed to its Protocol of Accession.

- *General tariff:*
  - The general tariff is imposed on a good imported from a country that is neither granted the MFN status nor is subjected to a preferential arrangement. In the instance of countries that are not members of the WTO, the general tariff tends to be imposed although the importing country can impose any tariff rate.

111. These terms should not be confused with the '*optimal tariff*', which is a term used to describe a tariff that will raise a country's welfare.

- *Most-Favoured-Nation (MFN) tariff:*
  - The uniform tariff that a World Trade Organization (WTO) Member would impose on the imports from all other WTO members unless the member is part of a trade bloc.[112] The MFN is also called the *'General Tariff'*.
- *Water in the tariff/Tariff overhang/Tariff cliff/Binding overhang principle/Tariff water.*

The difference, or gap, between the *'bound tariff'* and the *'applied tariff'* of MFN is called the *'water in the tariff'* or the *'tariff overhang'*. Economists call it the *'policy space'*, as the government could easily increase the tariff rate from the applied rate to the bound rate. Economists contend that the *'tariff overhang'* makes a country's trade policies less predictable:

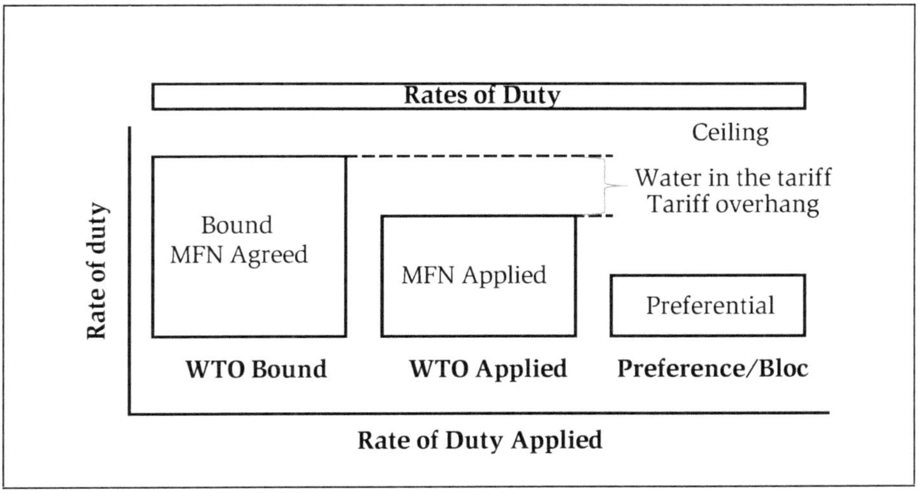

Source: Author's own compilation.

§7.10 TARIFF ESCALATION

As a rule of thumb, the rate of duty tends to be dependent on the nature or stage of manufacture (production) of the good. They are normally applied at an increasing rate of duty as the good is in the process from its primary form to its final or end good. The rate of duty on finished goods is higher on semi-finished goods, and even higher on final goods. This is referred to as *'tariff escalation'*. This practice protects domestic

112. *See* Chapter 13 *'Trade Blocs – Economic Integration'*. As a member of a trade bloc a preferential tariff will apply, which is not within the confines of the WTO.

manufacturing industries and encourages the increase in manufacturing capacity (further processing/manufacture) while discouraging the importation of semi-manufactured goods, as well as final goods.

In instances where developed countries impose duties on primary goods, their government could consider stimulating domestic manufacturing further by extending the Generalised System of Preferences (GSP) to developing countries to provide them with preferential access to their markets:[113]

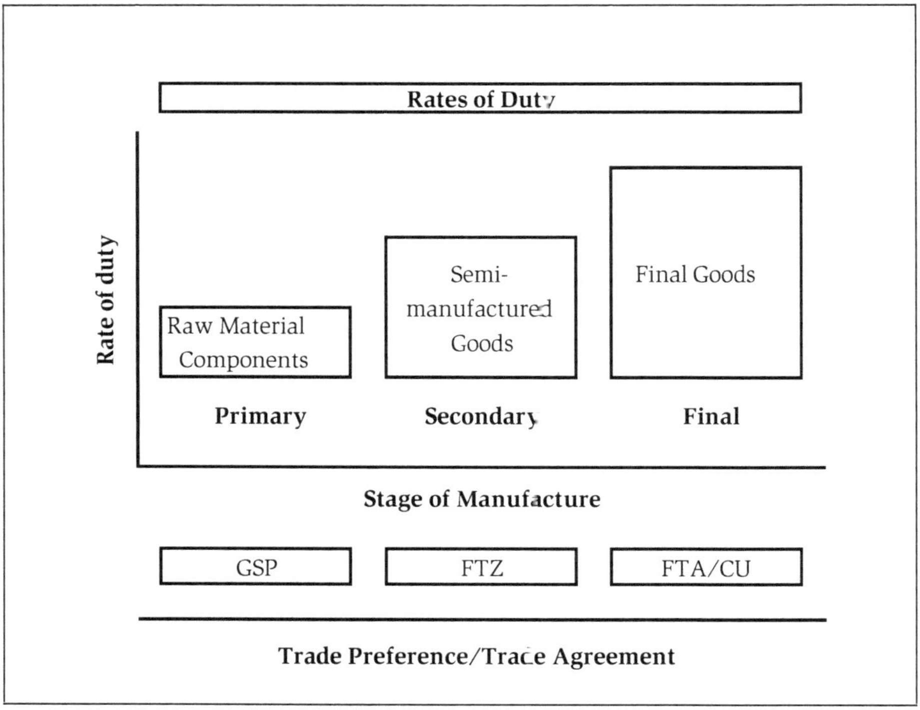

Source: Author's own compilation.

The figure above denotes Free Trade Zone (FTZ), Free Trade Area (FTA), and Customs Union (CU).

In addition to extending GSP preference, a country could also consider extending the following:

- *Tariff suspension:*
  - It suspends the duties on certain goods, normally those used in domestic production. This is also known as a '*rebate*' or a '*manufacturing rebate provision*'.

113. *See* Chapter 13 '*Trade Blocs – Economic Integration*'.

- *Tariff concession:*
  - It removes the duty on certain goods to assist a business (company) in reducing the costs for imported goods, i.e., where suitable alternative goods are not domestically produced or manufactured.

§7.11 TAX SYSTEMS – REGRESSIVE TAX, PROPORTIONAL TAX, AND PROGRESSIVE TAX

When considering the impact that a tax has on an imported good or a domestically manufactured good, it is important to consider the three main tax categories:

- *Regressive tax:*
  - The same rate (percentage) is applied to the goods, regardless of the consumer's income; as a consequence, it has a disproportionate effect on poorer consumers.
- *Proportional tax:*
  - The same rate (percentage) is applied to all goods, regardless of the consumer's income, but as consumption increases, so too does the rate.
- *Progressive tax:*
  - A higher rate (percentage) is applied to more affluent, wealthy consumers than to poorer consumers.

§7.12 OTHER TARIFF DEFINITIONS

- *Bilateral tariff:*
  - A duty, levy, or tax applied on the imports between two countries that have entered into a bilateral trade agreement.
- *Binding coverage:*
  - Statistical measure is defined as the number of bound lines divided by the total number of tariff lines.
- *Border Tax Adjustment (BTA)/Border-Adjusted Tax/Border Tax Assessments:*
  - It is a mechanism that the WTO administers to ensure that a country's internal duties, levies, and taxes on international trade are neutralised, in other words, to prevent trade from being distorted by differing national duties, levies, and taxes policies.
  - Essentially, it aims to level the playing field between domestic producers and foreign producers by ensuring that the duties, levies, and taxes imposed on imported goods are comparable to those imposed on domestically produced goods.

- *Carbon tax:*
  - It is imposed by a government on the greenhouse gas emissions of a producer of a good. The duty, tax, and levy imposed on the domestic producer are also imposed on imported goods which were manufactured in non-carbon taxing countries. The 'tax' is an example of the BTA.
  - '*Not paying the cost of damage to the environment is a subsidy, just as not paying the full costs of workers would be.*'[114] It is a valid economic analogy that holds that failing to pay for the full costs of environmental damage, or for the full costs of labour, is akin to a subsidy as it reduces the overall cost to the company and is willing to, in all likelihood, distort the market.

- *Margin of preference:*
  - The percentage of tariff by which tariffs are reduced on products imported from one Contracting State to another as a result of preferential treatment.

- *Non-reciprocal tariff:*
  - Also known as an '*unilateral tariff*', where a country imposes a duty, tax, or levy on the goods of another country, without the country against which is tariff is imposed, imposing a similar tariff on the goods of the country that imposed the tariff.
  - *See 'Unilateral Tariff'.*

- *Nuisance tariff:*
  - There is no accepted definition for such a tariff. A tariff that is so low that it costs the government more to collect than the revenue it generates. The tariff does not have any protective effect; it is superfluous.

- *Para-tariff:*
  - Is a charge imposed on imports that acts as a tariff in that it increases the cost of the imports. Still, the tariff is not included in the country's tariff schedule. Such charges could include stamp fees, a foreign exchange transactions tax, and a statistical tax.

- *Preferential Tariffs:*
  - A rate of duty, tax, and levy which is lower than the MFN tariff that is levied on an imported good due to a tariff preference which is attributable to a preferential trade arrangement, or a preferential trading arrangement.

- *Punitive Tariff:*
  - A very high rate of duty, levy, and tax imposed on an imported good to protect the domestic manufacturers/producers. Although the WTO has

114. As written by Columbia University Economics Professor and Nobel Laureate Joseph Stiglitz almost a decade ago.

largely curtailed the use of such a tariff, with its imposition, the exporting country could well retaliate by imposing a tariff of equal measure.

- *See 'Retaliatory Tariff'.*

- *Quasi-Tariff:*
  - As the first word 'quasi' suggests, it has some of the features of the tariff, but not all. It is not a traditional tariff in the sense of the word, but it is rather a barrier to trade, an NTB to be specific, that has a similar effect on trade as a tariff has.
  - *See* section IV *'Non-tariff, Tariff and Trade Barriers'.*

- *Retaliatory Tariff:*
  - Not to be confused with a *'safeguard duty'*, which is a fair trade remedy.
  - It is a duty, levy, or tax that a government imposes on another country to effectively punish it for having imposed a duty, levy, or tax on its exports.
  - *See 'Punitive Tariff'.*

- *Tariff celling:*
  - Not to be confused with ceiling rate, bound rate, bound tariff, ceiling binding, ceiling rate, or maximum tariff.
  - It is an authorised quantity for the importation or exportation of a given good during a specified period of time, normally associated with the rate of duty lower than the MFN rate, after which the tariff is suspended.

- *Tariff peaks:*
  - Are considered relatively high rates of duty (tariffs) usually imposed on *'sensitive'* goods. For industrialised countries, tariffs in excess of 15% are generally recognised as *'tariff peaks'*.

- *Unilateral tariff:*
  - Also known as an *'non-reciprocal tariff'*, where a country imposes a duty, tax, or levy on the goods of another country, without this country retaliating itself imposing a tariff on the other country.
  - *See 'Non-Reciprocal Tariff'.*

§7.13 NATURE OF TARIFFS

- *Fiscal measure:*
  - A duty, levy, or tax imposed on an imported good (customs) or a domestically produced good (excises) to generate revenue for the fiscus – the government's national treasury.

- *Protective measure:*
  - A duty, levy, or tax imposed on an imported good (customs) to protect the domestic industry's produced goods.

- Its use tends to be justified and motivated by the infant industry protection argument. The infant industry argument posits that an emerging domestic industry requires temporary protection from international competition in order to be afforded the opportunity to become a competitive industry. The lack of a definition of an *'infant industry'* poses the real challenge.

- *Negotiation measure (tool):*
  - The argument for imposition of tariffs is that it can create economic pressure on the country to which it is targeted, thus encouraging the country to enter into negotiations with the country imposing the tariffs. The tariff could be considered a *'Punitive Tariff'*.
  - Should the two countries be of similar economic strength, it could result in the imposition of a *'Retaliatory Tariff'*.
  - *See 'Punitive Tariff'* and *'Retaliatory Tariff'*.

§7.14 CREATION OF A GOOD

- *Assemble:*
  - Refers to creating a good by putting together pre-made parts. This normally refers to goods that are in a knocked-down format – completely knocked down, and semi-knocked down.

- *Produce:*
  - It tends to be used interchangeably with *'manufacture'*, with its distinguishing application leaning towards the agricultural sector, particularly the farming of fruit, vegetables, and animals.

- *Manufacture:*
  - Its distinguishing feature is that a good is created out of raw materials, that are not in a part assembly format but that are produced by the company or the industry.

§7.15 KNOCKED DOWN GOOD

- *Complete Knocked Down (CKD):*
  - Also known by the acronym CKD, referring to a good that is in a disassembled format and requires full assembly.
  - A good tends to be shipped in a CKD format so as to avoid high import duties, levies, and taxes, to meet the importing country's local content requirements, such as a certain percentage of the value that needs to be added, or to take advantage of the importing country's lower or more competitive labour costs.

  - *See* Semi-Knocked Down.

- *Semi-Knocked Down (SKD):*
  - Also known by the acronym SKD, referring to a good that is partially assembled, or disassembled, depending on your consideration, which requires additional assembly.
  - A good that has been partly or partially assembled, with the final assembly to be completed in the importing country. As with CKD, the good is shipped in this format to avoid high import duties, levies, and taxes, to meet the importing country's local content requirements.
  - *See* Completely Knocked Down.

The Section's Points of Interest

The intention of the points of interest is to provide you with schematics and, in certain instances, a brief explanation that might be useful or of interest. Certain of the schematics might well not have been covered in any of the Section's Chapters, and therefore require explanation.

Collectively, the points of interest of the sections, with a few exceptions, will constitute '*The Lesson's Roadmap*':

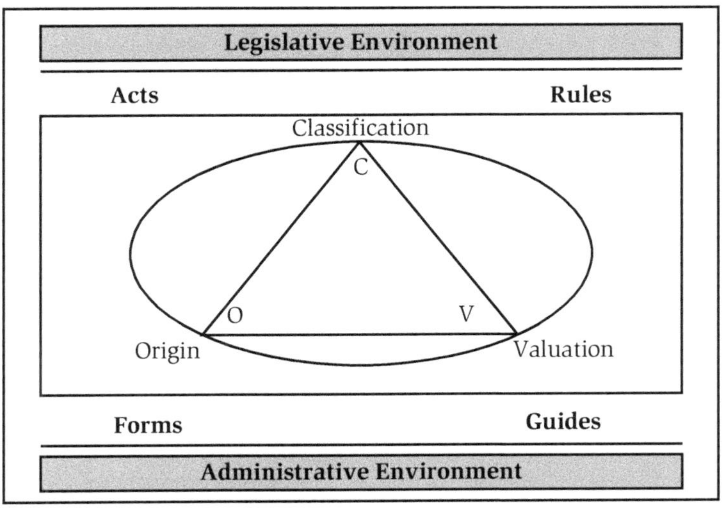

Source: Author's own compilation.

Cornerstones/Types of Duty, Tax & Levy

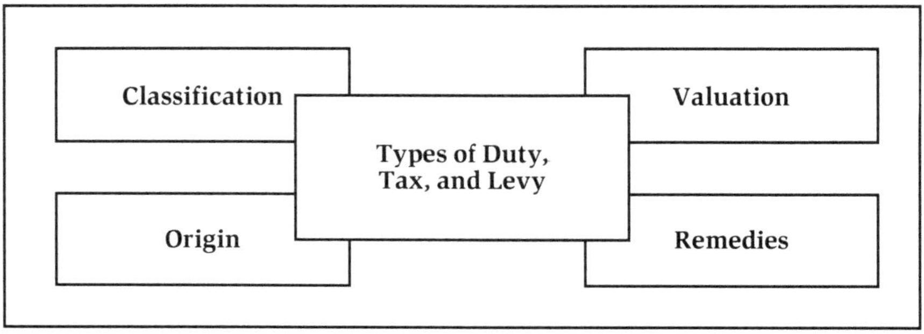

Source: Author's own compilation.

Sections/Chapters/Chapter Description

I LIVE ANIMALS; ANIMAL PRODUCTS
- 1 Live Animals
- 2 Meat and edible meat offal
- 3 Fish and crustaceans, molluscs and other aquatic invertebrates
- 4 Dairy produce; birds' eggs; natural honey; edible products of animal origin, not elsewhere specified or included
- 5 Products of animal origin, not elsewhere specified or included

II VEGETABLE PRODUCTS
- 6 Live trees and other plants; bulbs, roots and the like; cut flowers and ornamental foliage
- 7 Edible vegetables and certain roots and tubers
- 8 Edible fruit and nuts; peel of citrus fruit or melons
- 9 Coffee, tea, maté and spices
- 10 Cereals
- 11 Products of the milling industry; malt; starches; inulin; wheat gluten
- 12 Oil seeds and oleaginous fruit; miscellaneous grains, seeds and fruit; industrial or medicinal plants; straw and fodder
- 13 Lac; gums, resins and other vegetable saps and extracts
- 14 Vegetable plaiting materials; vegetable products not elsewhere specified or included

III ANIMAL, VEGETABLE OR MICROBIAL FATS AND OILS AND THEIR CLEAVAGE PRODUCTS; PREPARED EDIBLE FATS; ANIMAL OR VEGETABLE WAXES
- 15 Animal, vegetable or microbial fats and oils and their cleavage products; prepared edible fats; animal or vegetable waxes

IV PREPARED FOODSTUFFS; BEVERAGES, SPIRITS AND VINEGAR; TOBACCO AND MANUFACTURED TOBACCO SUBSTITUTES; PRODUCTS, WHETHER OR NOT CONTAINING NICOTINE, INTENDED FOR INHALATION WITHOUT COMBUSTION; OTHER NICOTINE-CONTAINING PRODUCTS INTENDED FOR THE INTAKE OF NICOTINE INTO THE HUMAN BODY
- 16 Preparations of meat, fish, crustaceans, molluscs or other aquatic invertebrates, or insects.
- 17 Sugars and sugar confectionery
- 18 Cocoa and cocoa preparations
- 19 Preparations of cereals, flour, starch or milk; pastrycooks' products
- 20 Preparations of vegetables, fruit, nuts or other parts of plants
- 21 Miscellaneous edible preparations
- 22 Beverages, spirits and vinegar
- 23 Residues and waste from the food industries; prepared animal fodder
- 24 Tobacco and manufactured tobacco substitutes; products, whether or not containing nicotine, intended for inhalation without combustion; other nicotine-containing products intended for the intake of nicotine into the human body

V MINERAL PRODUCTS
- 25 Salt; sulphur; earths and stone; plastering materials, lime and cement
- 26 Ores, slag and ash
- 27 Mineral fuels, mineral oils and products of their distillation; bituminous substances; mineral waxes

VI PRODUCTS OF THE CHEMICAL AND ALLIED INDUSTRIES
- 28 Inorganic chemicals; organic or inorganic compounds of precious metals, of rare-earth metals, of radioactive elements or of isotopes
- 29 Organic chemicals
- 30 Pharmaceutical products
- 31 Fertilisers
- 32 Tanning or dyeing extracts; tannins and their derivatives; dyes, pigments and other colouring matter; paints and varnishes; putty and other mastics; inks
- 33 Essential oils and resinoids; perfumery, cosmetic or toilet preparations
- 34 Soap, organic surface-active agents, washing preparations, lubricating preparations, artificial waxes, prepared waxes, polishing or scouring preparations, candles and similar articles, modelling pastes, 'dental waxes' and dental preparations with a basis of plaster
- 35 Albuminoidal substances; modified starches; glues; enzymes

36 Explosives; pyrotechnic products; matches; pyrophoric alloys; certain combustible preparations
37 Photographic or cinematographic goods
38 Miscellaneous chemical products
VII PLASTICS AND ARTICLES THEREOF; RUBBER AND ARTICLES THEREOF
39 Plastics and articles thereof
40 Rubber and articles thereof
VIII RAW HIDES AND SKINS, LEATHER, FURSKINS AND ARTICLES THEREOF; SADDLERY AND HARNESS; TRAVEL GOODS, HANDBAGS AND SIMILAR CONTAINERS; ARTICLES OF ANIMAL GUT (OTHER THAN SILK-WORM GUT)
41 Raw hides and skins (other than furskins) and leather
42 Articles of leather; saddlery and harness; travel goods, handbags and similar containers; articles of animal gut (other than silk-worm gut)
43 Furskins and artificial fur; manufactures thereof
IX WOOD AND ARTICLES OF WOOD; WOOD CHARCOAL; CORK AND ARTICLES OF CORK; MANUFACTURES OF STRAW, OF ESPARTO OR OF OTHER PLAITING MATERIALS; BASKETWARE AND WICKERWORK
44 Wood and articles of wood; wood charcoal
45 Cork and articles of cork
46 Manufactures of straw, of esparto or of other plaiting materials; basketware and wickerwork
X PULP OF WOOD OR OF OTHER FIBROUS CELLULOSIC MATERIAL; RECOVERED (WASTE AND SCRAP) PAPER OR PAPERBOARD; PAPER AND PAPERBOARD AND ARTICLES THEREOF
47 Pulp of wood or of other fibrous cellulosic material; recovered (waste and scrap) paper or paperboard
48 Paper and paperboard; articles of paper pulp, of paper or of paperboard
49 Printed books, newspapers, pictures and other products of the printing industry; manuscripts, typescripts and plans
XI TEXTILES AND TEXTILE ARTICLES
50 Silk
51 Wool, fine or coarse animal hair; horsehair yarn and woven fabric
52 Cotton
53 Other vegetable textile fibres; paper yarn and woven fabrics of paper yarn
54 Man-made filaments; strips and the like of man-made textile materials
55 Man-made staple fibres
56 Wadding, felt and nonwovens; special yarns; twine, cordage, ropes and cables and articles thereof

57 Carpets and other textile floor coverings
58 Special woven fabrics; tufted textile fabrics; lace; tapestries; trimmings; embroidery
59 Impregnated, coated, covered or laminated textile fabrics; textile articles of a kind suitable for industrial use
60 Knitted or crocheted fabrics
61 Articles of apparel and clothing accessories, knitted or crocheted
62 Articles of apparel and clothing accessories, not knitted or crocheted
63 Other made-up textile articles; sets; worn clothing and worn textile articles; rags

XII FOOTWEAR, HEADGEAR, UMBRELLAS, SUN UMBRELLAS, WALKING-STICKS, SEAT-STICKS, WHIPS, RIDING-CROPS AND PARTS THEREOF; PREPARED FEATHERS AND ARTICLES MADE THEREWITH; ARTIFICIAL FLOWERS; ARTICLES OF HUMAN HAIR
64 Footwear, gaiters and the like; parts of such articles
65 Headgear and parts thereof
66 Umbrellas, sun umbrellas, walking-sticks, seat-sticks, whips, riding-crops and parts thereof
67 Prepared feathers and down and articles made of feathers or of down; artificial flowers; articles of human hair

XIII ARTICLES OF STONE, PLASTER, CEMENT, ASBESTOS, MICA OR SIMILAR MATERIALS; CERAMIC PRODUCTS; GLASS AND GLASSWARE
68 Articles of stone, plaster, cement, asbestos, mica or similar materials
69 Ceramic products
70 Glass and glassware

XIV NATURAL OR CULTURED PEARLS, PRECIOUS OR SEMI-PRECIOUS STONES, PRECIOUS METALS, METALS CLAD WITH PRECIOUS METAL, AND ARTICLES THEREOF; IMITATION JEWELLERY; COIN
71 Natural or cultured pearls, precious or semi-precious stones, precious metals, metals clad with precious metal, and articles thereof; imitation jewellery; coin

XV BASE METALS AND ARTICLES OF BASE METAL
72 Iron and steel
73 Articles of iron and steel
74 Copper and articles thereof
75 Nickel and articles thereof
76 Aluminium and articles thereof
77 Reserved for possible future use
78 Lead and articles thereof
79 Zinc and articles thereof
80 Tin and articles thereof
81 Other base metals; cermets; articles thereof
82 Tools, implements, cutlery, spoons and forks, of base metal; parts thereof of base metal

	83	Miscellaneous articles of base metal
XVI		MACHINERY AND MECHANICAL APPLIANCES; ELECTRICAL EQUIPMENT; PARTS THEREOF; SOUND RECORDERS AND REPRODUCERS, TELEVISION IMAGE AND SOUND RECORDERS AND REPRODUCERS, AND PARTS AND ACCESSORIES OF SUCH ARTICLES
	84	Nuclear reactors, boilers, machinery and mechanical appliances; parts thereof
	85	Electrical machinery and equipment and parts thereof; sound recorders and reproducers, television image and sound recorders and reproducers, and parts and accessories of such articles
XVII		VEHICLES, AIRCRAFT, VESSELS AND ASSOCIATED TRANSPORT EQUIPMENT
	86	Railway or tramway locomotives, rolling stock and parts thereof; railway or tramway track fixtures and fittings and parts thereof; mechanical (including electro-mechanical) traffic signalling equipment of all kinds
	87	Vehicles other than railway or tramway rolling stock, and parts and accessories thereof
	88	Aircraft, spacecraft, and parts thereof
	89	Ships, boats and floating structures
XVIII		OPTICAL, PHOTOGRAPHIC, CINEMATOGRAPHIC, MEASURING, CHECKING, PRECISION, MEDICAL OR SURGICAL INSTRUMENTS AND APPARATUS; CLOCKS AND WATCHES; MUSICAL INSTRUMENTS; PARTS AND ACCESSORIES THEREOF
	90	Optical, photographic, cinematographic, measuring, checking, precision, medical or surgical instruments and apparatus; parts and accessories thereof
	91	Clocks and watches and parts thereof
	92	Musical instruments; parts and accessories of such articles
XIX		ARMS AND AMMUNITION; PARTS AND ACCESSORIES THEREOF
	93	Arms and ammunition; parts and accessories thereof
XX		MISCELLANEOUS MANUFACTURED ARTICLES
	94	Furniture; bedding, mattresses, mattress supports, cushions and similar stuffed furnishings; luminaires and lighting fittings, not elsewhere specified or included; illuminated signs, illuminated name-plates and the like; prefabricated buildings
	95	Toys, games and sports requisites; parts and accessories thereof
	96	Miscellaneous manufactured articles
XXI		WORKS OF ART, COLLECTORS' PIECES AND ANTIQUES
	97	Works of art, collectors' pieces and antiques.

Source: World Customs Organization.

		International	National / Country Specific	
SECTION	**I**	**LIVE ANIMALS; ANIMAL PRODUCTS**		
Chapter	01	LIVE ANIMALS		
Section	**II**	**VEGETABLE PRODUCTS**		
Chapter	7	EDIBLE VEGETABLES AND CERTAIN ROOTS AND TUBERS		
Tariff Heading	07.09	Other vegetables, fresh or chilled:		
Tariff Subheading	0709.5	Mushrooms and truffles:		
Tariff Subheading	0709.59	Other		
Tariff Subheading			*0709.59.10*	*Truffle:*
Tariff Subheading			*0709.59.10.10*	*National / Country Specific*
Tariff Subheading			*0709.59.10.10.10*	*National / Country Specific*
Tariff Heading	07.10	Vegetables (uncooked or cooked by steaming or boiling in water), frozen:		
Tariff Subheading	0710.80	Other vegetables:		
Tariff Subheading			*0710.80.10*	*Truffle:*
Tariff Subheading			*0710.80.10.10*	*National / Country Specific*
Tariff Subheading			*0710.80.10.10.10*	*National / Country Specific*
SECTION	**XXI**	**WORKS OF ART, COLLECTORS' PIECES AND ANTIQUES**		
Chapter	97	WORKS OF ART, COLLECTORS' PIECES AND ANTIQUES		
SECTION	***XXII***	***NATIONAL / COUNTRY SPECIFIC***		
Chapter	*98*	*NATIONAL / COUNTRY SPECIFIC*		
Tariff Heading	*9801*	*National / Country Specific*		
Tariff Subheading	*9801.+*	*National / Country Specific*		
Tariff Subheading	*9801.++*	*National / Country Specific*		
Tariff Subheading	*9801.++.++*	*National / Country Specific*		
Tariff Subheading	*9801.++.++.++*	*National / Country Specific*		

(Row groups labelled: International — Sections I to XXI; *National* — Section XXII.)

Source: Author's own compilation.

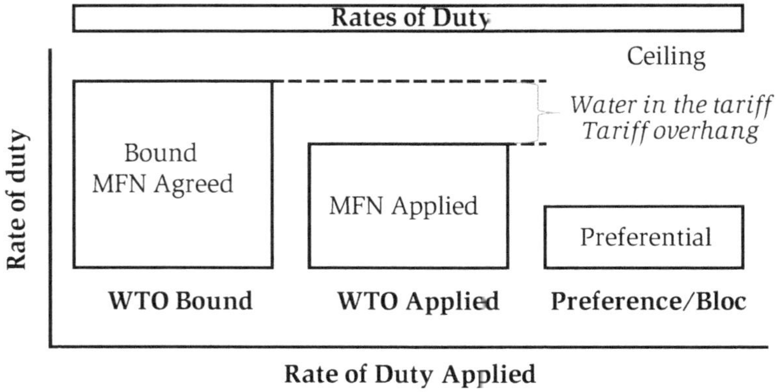

Source: Author's own compilation.

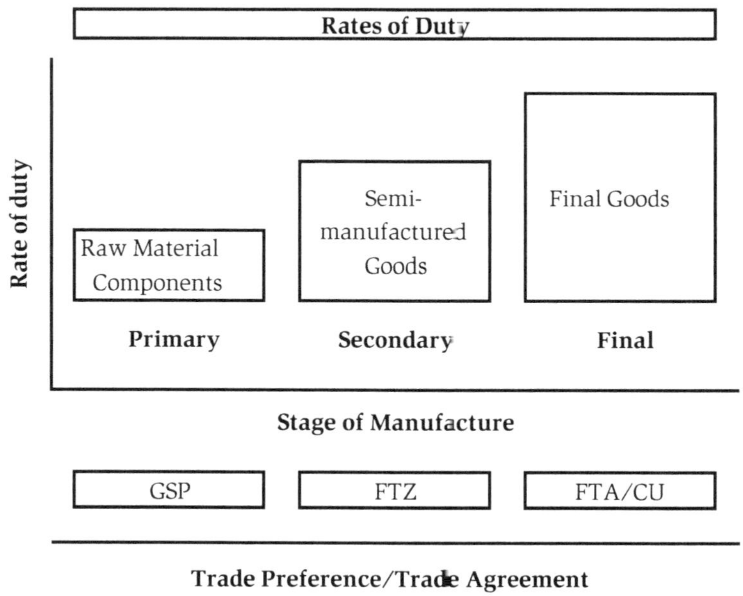

Source: Author's own compilation.

The figure above denotes Free Trade Zone (FTZ), Free Trade Area (FTA), and Customs Union (CU):

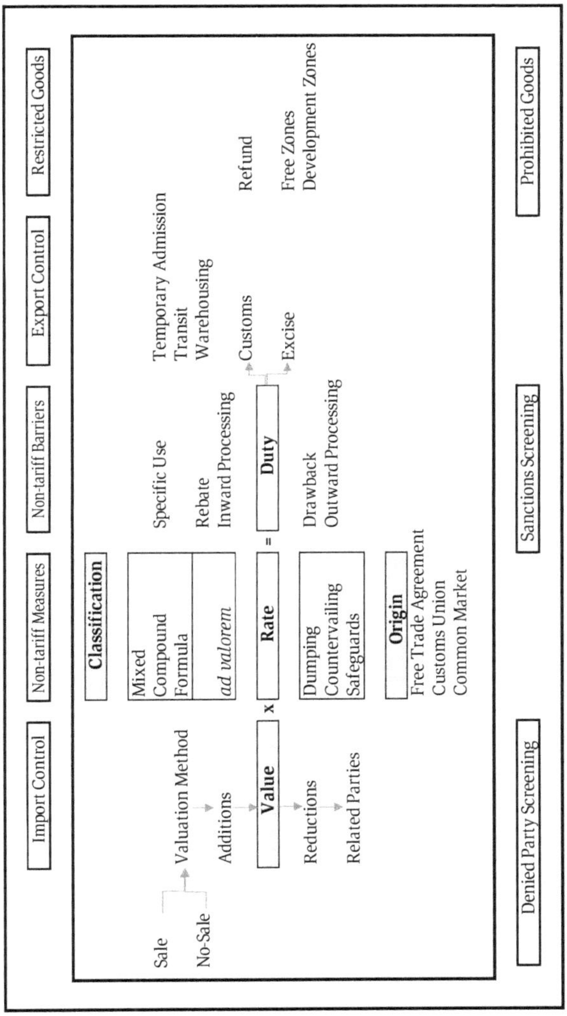

Source: Author's own compilation.

SECTION II

Special Customs Procedures - Regimes

While section I dealt with the nature of the good, the focus being on its tariff classification, origin, and customs valuation, section II is concerned with the treatment of the good. In this instance, Special Customs Procedures or SCP, also known as Special Customs Regimes, aim to stimulate and promote economic activity.

With the potential duty liabilities, barriers, and restrictions known, there are a number of mitigations that could be considered based on the nature and the proposed customs treatment of the goods. You could do so surreptitiously by interjecting - PSST.

Although **P**rocessing, **S**pecific Use, **S**torage, and **T**ransit might not specifically be called by these category names in all Customs jurisdictions, these are the types of SCP that are broadly applied. SCP potentially provides for partial relief, full relief, or, in certain instances, the temporary suspension or the full suspension of the import duty[115] in order to allow for a number of economic activities to be undertaken, such as temporary use, processing or repair of goods. It also allows for the non-economic activity of storage.

Since the Customs Authority has an interest in the imported goods, the use of the SCP is subject to the authorisation by a Customs Authority, with the importer having to have the customs debt that it incurs through its use being underwritten by guarantees (financial) or a surety offered. Once the goods have been discharged under the SCP, the customs debt can be extinguished.

There are, in essence, three types of customs procedures under which goods may normally be placed:

- *Import* - The duty, tax, or levy paid, and the goods released for free circulation [home use]
- *SCP* - Special Customs Procedures/Regimes
- *Export* - The duty, tax, or levy paid on exportation.

115. Remember that '*import duty*' is a collective term, inclusive of among other customs duty.

There are typically four core categories of SCP

- *Processing:*
  - Inward Processing (also known as IP)
  - Outward Processing (also known as OP)
- *Specific Use:*
  - Temporary Admission (also known as TA)
  - End Use (also known as '*Authorised Use*')
- *Storage:*
  - Customs Warehousing (also known as CW)
  - Free Zones (also known as FZ)
- *Transit:*
  - Customs Transit
  - Transhipment.

Three of these tend to be considered as Customs Procedures with Economic Impact or CPEI:

- *Processing*
- *Specific Use*
- *Storage.*

Since the SCP infers a Customs Debt, the use of a procedure is normally subject to, or underwritten by, a guarantee to cover the customs debt, while the release of the good is managed through an authorisation.

The SCP, documented in *The International Convention on the Simplification and Harmonization of Customs Procedures* (as amended), simply known as the Revised Kyoto Convention or RKC, which is the blueprint for modern and efficient Customs procedures in the 21st century, does not contain a provision on Customs Debt. The next RKC review *of Customs Debt* should have a central focus that warrants its inclusion into the RKC, as customs debt constitutes a central aspect of all national Customs Legislation:

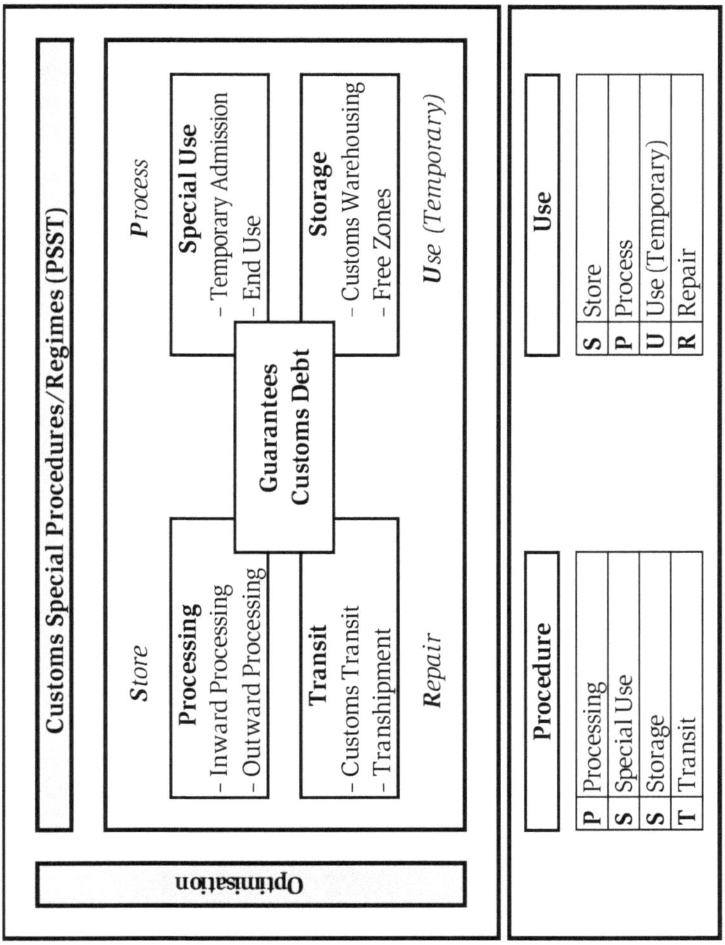

Customs Special Procedures/Regimes (PSST)
Store
Process
Processing
- Inward Processing
- Outward Processing
Special Use
- Temporary Admission
- End Use
Guarantees
Customs Debt
Transit
- Customs Transit
- Transhipment
Storage
- Customs Warehousing
- Free Zones
Repair
Use (Temporary)
Optimisation
Procedure
P Processing
S Special Use
S Storage
T Transit
Use
S Store
P Process
U Use (Temporary)
R Repair

The figure does not deal with:

- *Temporary Storage (TS):*
  - Also known as TS, it is a customs procedure that refers to the period of holding of goods under Customs control in a designated area before the presentation of goods to the Customs Authority and their placement under a customs procedure.
- *Returned Goods Relief (RGR):*
  - Also known as RGR, it is a customs procedure that provides for goods that were previously exported from a country (or territory) to be re-imported into that same country (or territory) without incurring additional customs duties, taxes, or levies.
- *Duty Suspension:*
  - Relief from payment of a part of the total amount of import duties and taxes which would otherwise be payable had the goods been cleared for home use on the date on which they were placed under the temporary admission procedure.[116]

Other Customs Procedures:

- *Refund:*
  - The repayment of the duty, tax, and levy that were paid for which the importer was not liable.
- *Drawback:*
  - The repayment of the duty, tax, and levy that were paid on imported components that were used in the manufacture of goods that were then exported. Similar to IP.
- *Rebate:*
  - The payment of the duty, tax, and levy is suspended (delay), provided that the imported components are used in the manufacture of specified goods, which can then be sold on the domestic market.

116. This term is defined in Annex E to the Istanbul Convention.

CHAPTER 8

Processing – Inward Processing and Outward Processing

Processing is considered a conditional relief of import duties, taxes, and levies of goods, which could be subject to anything from repacking, sorting, repair, destruction, or more complicated manufacturing. There are two types of Processing, which are detailed in the General Annex of the RKC:[117]

- *Inward Processing (IP):*
  - Also known as Rebate provisions or Manufacturing Rebate provisions.
- *Outward Processing (OP):*
  - Also known as Drawback provisions.

IP and OP are mirror images of each other.

Both processing procedures are a suspensive SCP[118] with a CPEI, which simply means that they exist to benefit a country's domestic businesses by stimulating economic activity with the aim of increasing the business' competitiveness.

§8.01 INWARD PROCESSING (IP)

The Customs procedure's basic premise is to provide for goods, normally components or primary inputs, to be imported into a country, conditionally relieved from payment of import duties and taxes. The relief is provided on the basis that the inputs would be manufactured or processed into a final good or end good, or used in the repair and subsequent exportation. The duties, taxes, and levies are suspended. In essence, imported materials undergo processing operations without the imposition of import

117. RKC Special Annexes F1 and F2.
118. CSP generally allows for the storage, temporary use, processing or repair of goods, providing partial or full relief from import duty, or in certain instances suspension.

duties and taxes. IP is the mirror image of Outward Processing or OP. There are two variants: one that allows for the suspension of the duty, tax, or levy and the other under which it is paid and later repaid.

The basic premise of the IP Procedure is to provide for goods, normally components or primary inputs, to be imported into a country where they would be processed into a final good or end good, with the suspension of duties and taxes, as the goods will be exported. In essence, imported materials undergo processing operations without the imposition of import duties and taxes IP is the mirror image of Outward Processing or OP. There are two variants: one that allows for the suspension of the duty, tax, or levy and the other under which it is paid and later repaid.

The processing could require the goods to undergo specified manufacturing, processing, or repair, and the suspension of duties and taxes would typically relate to VAT or import duties.[119]

But IP is not the only SCP or practice that provides for the suspension of duties and taxes, and the processing of goods before their re-exportation. In FZ, another SCP under Storage provides for a similar application and the use of the drawback procedure.

A '*drawback procedure*' is an SCP that provides for the import duties and taxes to be reclaimed – also called a '*clawback*' – either in full (in total) or partially, on the material inputs contained in the manufactured good or consumed in their manufacture.

The manufactured good could be dealt with in alternative ways:

- The import duties and taxes could be brought into account, meaning they could be paid on either:
  - the originally imported raw material/primary material; or
  - on the processed goods.
- The processed goods could be re-exported.

Since a Customs Authority has a financial interest in the imported goods as the duty, tax, and levy need to be paid on them, should they be released for domestic consumption, the imported goods are subject to a Guarantee. The purpose of the Guarantee is to secure that the duty, tax, and levy are suspended on goods imported under an IP authorisation. *See* Chapter 12, '*Customs Debt and Customs Guarantee/Security*'.

A Customs Authority will not issue an authorisation until an appropriate guarantee is in place. The purpose of the guarantee is to secure the duty, tax, and levy that are suspended on the goods imported under the IP authorisation.

As part of the Authorisation, if the intention of the processor is to use identical goods of domestic origin in the processing application, it needs to be made of what is called '*equivalence*'. There could be specific requirements and stipulations which could exclude certain goods and require that the replacement goods be of the same tariff classification and possess the same technical characteristics as the imported goods. In

119. Remember that import duties is a collective term that includes customs duty. *See* Chapter 7 '*Types of Duties, Taxes, and Levies*'.

addition, equivalence can be granted for either all or certain goods. In the instance of repair, the equivalence good would be of a better condition than the original imported good.

The general types of IP authorisations are as follows:

- Authorisation by declaration
- Full authorisation
- Retrospective authorisation.

The discharge of the liability is when all the conditions for the use of the IP have been met or complied with, and the goods have, to name a few examples:

- been re-exported;
- transferred to another SCP, such as CW, which is a Storage procedure;
- customs duties and taxes have been brought into account;
- been abandoned to the Customs Authority;
- been destroyed under Customs supervision.

In the instance of Prohibited Goods and Restricted Goods,[120] goods entered under IP are not exempt from import and/or export prohibitions and restrictions. However, goods subject to Quantitative Restrictions (QRs), tariff quotas or other quantitative import restrictions may be entered under IP suspension. IP also tends to include a provision to sell goods in the domestic market. In this instance, the goods can be cleared and then released to the domestic market, which is known as free circulation. This is considered to be the discharge of the goods which simply means that all conditions for the use of the IP have been complied with.

§8.02 OUTWARD PROCESSING (OP)

The Customs procedure's basic premise is to provide for goods (primary and/or secondary) which are in free circulation in a country (territory) to be temporarily exported for manufacturing, processing or repair overseas (abroad) and then re-imported with total or partial exemption from import duties and taxes. On the return of the final good to the country, the Customs Authority would consider the value added abroad and accordingly only impose duty, tax, and levy on the value-added component. The procedures simply eliminate the need for duty, tax, and levy to be paid on the domestically process goods, as well as on the value added abroad. OP is the mirror image of IP.

OP provides for businesses to take advantage of the benefits that provide it a competitive advantage, such as lower labour costs or specific technical expertise which is not available domestically.

This SCP is subject to an authorisation from the Customs Authorities, which will specify the period within which the OP is to be discharged. Such an authorisation must

120. *See* Chapter 17 '*Prohibited Goods and Restricted Good*'.

also provide for the possibility of the return for export of an inclusion of '*equivalent goods*', the raw materials used in its manufacture. In such instances, a guarantee must be provided. '*Equivalent goods*' should share the same tariff subheading (Commodity Code), be of the same commercial quality, and have the same technical characteristics as the goods they replaced.

For the discharge of the goods from the OP, it would be considered complete when all conditions for the use of the procedure have been complied with and the processed goods have been re-imported.

§8.03 DRAWBACK

The Customs procedure, when goods are exported, provides for a repayment, either partial or total, to be made in respect of the import duties, levies, and taxes charged on the goods, or on materials contained in them or consumed in their production.

CHAPTER 9

Storage - Customs Warehousing and Free Zones

There are two types of Storage detailed in the General Annex of the RKC[121] that are provided for under a system of SCP:[122]

- *Customs Warehousing* (CW), also known as Bonded Warehouse.[123]
- *Free Zone* (FZ).

Both of the Storage procedures are suspensive CPEI.

§9.01 CUSTOMS WAREHOUSING

It is an SCP under which imported goods that arrive in a country are stored under Customs control in a designated warehouse for a period, which could be subject to limitation. During this time, the goods remain under the surveillance of a Customs Authority. These goods are not subject to import duties (the collective term that includes customs duty, excise duty, tax, and levy) or VAT, in which payment is delayed. If the warehouse is not designated as a customs and excise warehouse, then excise duty will become payable when the goods are received in the warehouse.

There are also *tax warehouses* where excise goods are received, processed, produced, held, or stored. The import duties and taxes will become payable after the goods are removed from the warehouse for domestic use, but not if the goods are re-exported or entered under another SCP. Goods can typically be stored in a Bonded

121. RKC Specific Annexes D1 and D2.
122. SCP generally allow for the storage, temporary use, processing or repair of goods, providing partial or full relief from import duty, or in certain instances suspension.
123. A '*Bonded Warehouse*' is considered to be a secured area in which goods which are subject to duties or taxes (dutiable goods) are stored, or undergo processing, or continued manufacturing without payment of duties or taxes.

Warehouse for a period of up to five years, while for goods stored in a Customs Warehouse,[124] there tends not to be a time limit.

The word '*warehouse*' is said to have originated from either the old English '*waru*' or the German '*ware*', meaning '*an article of merchandise*', and its transformation in old English to '*warian*', meaning '*to be wary, guard, protect*'. The latter is, in essence, what a Customs Warehouse, also referred to as a Bonded Warehouse, rather than a Bonded Customs Warehouse, is. It is a licensed facility where imported goods are stored, manipulated, or under processing (manufacturing) operations for either domestic sale or export. It is an authorised place, under the supervision of a Customs Authority, where goods may be stored subject to conditions, such as pending payment of customs and excise duties. The Customs Warehouse allows for the payment of duty, tax, and levy to be deferred until the goods are removed.

There are typically two types of Customs Warehouses, namely the following:

- A *Public Warehouse*[125] is a place that is reserved to store, under the supervision of the Customs Authority on behalf of any trader, all kind of imported goods liable to import duties and taxes or to prohibitions or restrictions, other than those imposed on grounds of: public morality or order, public security, public hygiene or health, or for veterinary or phytosanitary considerations; or the protection of patents, trademarks and copyrights, irrespective of quantity, country of origin, country from which arrived or country of destination. Goods which constitute a hazard, which are likely to affect other goods or which require special installations should be accepted only by Customs warehouses specially designed to receive them.

- A *Private Warehouse*[126] for the use of an authorised trader who is also a depositor of the goods. A depositor is a trader who places goods into a Customs Warehouse. The Customs Authority shall specify the kinds of goods which may be admitted to private Customs warehouses.

The storing of the goods is subject to a guarantee, provided that the user is able to substantiate the economic need for the customs warehousing, and that the goods would primarily be used for the storage of goods.

It is possible for equivalent goods, which are domestic goods that are used instead of imported goods in the processing of goods, to be stored in a Customs Warehouse.

A Customs Warehouse can be used:

- when the final destination of the goods is uncertain;
- when the goods will, in all likelihood, be exported (re-exported);
- to defer or suspend the payment of duty, tax, and levy on the goods;

124. In the instance of a '*Customs Warehouse*', there tends to be two types of customs warehouses in which goods can be stored, namely a public warehouse which is commercially operated by specialist business or a private warehouse which owner of the goods can operate themselves.
125. Also known as '*Public Storage Warehouse*'.
126. Also known as '*Private Storage Warehouse*'.

- while import documentation is awaited;
- to discharge the goods into another SCP, such as IP and TA.

Not to be confused with a customs warehouse is a Transit Shed,[127] which is often operated by railroads to facilitate the loading and discharge of goods. The sheds are typically located on or near a pier (pier shed) or wharf (Wharf Shed). A transit shed is meant for short-term storage only, with charges generally accruing on a daily or weekly basis, making it a very expensive option if used over an extended period of time.

It is not only customs duties and taxes that are deferred for goods being placed in customs warehouses, also no excise duties will be imposed on the transfer between authorised warehouses and upon exportation.

§9.02 TEMPORARY STORAGE (TS)

Although not part of Customs Warehousing, TS[128] is a Customs procedure under which imported goods are temporarily stored under Customs control before they are either placed under an SCP, such as a Transit, or released to free circulation or exported. By placing the goods under this Customs procedure, the full customs declaration, the payment of duties, and VAT can be delayed, generally for only a specified time.

§9.03 FREE ZONES

Although the first *'modern zone'* was established in Shannon Airport, in Ireland, in 1959, the world's oldest document, Free Trade Zones (FTZs), was established on the Greek Island of Delos in 166 BC, before pirates in 69 BC overran it. In a similar vein, the Romans had what they called *'civitas libera'* or *'free cities'*, which were self-governing. After the Irish established zones, there was a proliferation in its use in the late 20th century under various names such as FTZ, free port, industrial zone,[129] and the infamous Export Processing Zones (EPZ). The World Free Zones Organization (WFTO)[130] estimates that there are around 2,260 free zones internationally.

An FZ is a customs enclave in a country, an enclosed area within a country's customs territory where imported goods can be entered into or stored, moved, used, or processed for export outside of the country's customs territory or released under another SCP such as IP, TA, or End Use. Should the goods be exported to the adjacent Customs territory, then the prevailing import duty and taxes need to be accounted for.

127. A *'Transit Shed'* considered a building located on or near a pier or wharf which is used for the short-term storage of cargo which is in transit.
128. Covered in Specific Annex A, Chapter 2 of the RKC.
129. An industrial zone is a zone which focusses on the production of industrial goods which are destined for export out of the zone. The zone is based in a country but is geographically excluded from the administration of the country's Customs Authority.
130. The World Free Zones Organization (World FZO) is a global not-for-profit organisation that provides one authoritative, collective voice representing the interests of free zones around the world [www.worldfzo.org].

An FTZ could also be used as a bonded warehouse for the storage of goods for the local market.

It is possible for goods to enter an FZ from:

- Another SCP.
- Customs Transit.[131]
- Outside the adjacent customs territory.

An FZ tends to be located around international airports, ports, and national frontiers, which offer many geographic advantages for trade and remove the hindrances caused by high tariffs or complex customs regulations, examinations, and formalities.

The International Bank for Reconstruction and Development (IBRD), commonly known as the World Bank (WB),[132] identifies four major free zones:

- A *Free Port* is considered to be the broader term of an FZ as it includes a relatively large area and can cover a wide range of activities and incentives to promote economic development and trade.

- An *FTZ* is considered to be an enclosed duty-free area for the purpose of providing warehousing and distribution facilities supporting trade, particularly re-exports. They are commonly near a point of entry, such as a port, an airport or a land border. The focus is on commerce, such as finished and semi-finished goods.

- An *EPZ* offers incentives for manufacturing and related activities with a particular focus on exports, although several such zones allow non-exporting activities.

- A *Special Economic Zone* (SEZ) is a free port paradigm that has been mainly applied to the Chinese context as a tool to promote foreign direct investments in well-defined areas. The primary purpose is to import parts and raw materials and process them into goods to be exported to international markets.

EPZs used to have a very bad name in years gone by, having been referred to as '*sweatshops*', a stigma which modern-day governments have tried very hard to dispel in favour of focusing on it as a driver of development.

131. In the instance of the European Union (EU), '*customs transit*' is a customs procedure used to move goods between two points of a customs territory, via another customs territory, or between two or more different customs territories.
132. The World Bank established on 27 December 1945 is one of the trilogy of Bretton Woods System institutions, the other two being the IMF and the WTO.

CHAPTER 10

Specific Use – Temporary Admission and End Use

There are two types of Specific Use Procedures provided for under a system of (SCP):[133]

- *Temporary Admission* (TA)
- *End Use.*

There is a Specific Annex in the revised Kyoto Convention (RKC) for TA,[134] but there is not one for End Use.

§10.01 TEMPORARY ADMISSION (TA)

The Customs procedure under which certain goods can be brought into a Customs territory and are conditionally relieved totally or partially from payment of import duties and taxes. Such goods must be imported for a specific purpose and must be intended for re-exportation within a specified period and without having undergone any change except normal depreciation due to the use made of them.

Only certain goods can be brought into a Customs territory for specific use and, consequently, conditionally relieved, either totally or partially, from the payment of import duties or taxes. The goods are not intended to undergo any change and must be re-exported within the specified period.

TA is typically used for goods that are imported to be exhibited at a trade fair or as part of a music or stage show, and typically set the following conditions:

- No alterations may be made to the goods other than normal depreciation that occurs through its use, known as wear-and-tear.

133. SCP generally allow for the storage, temporarily use, processing or repair of goods, providing partial or full relief from import duty, or in certain instances suspension.
134. The RKC Special Annex G1.

- The goods must be clearly identifiable to prevent any abuse.
- All customs requirements and formalities are met.
- A guarantee is provided.

The creation of an international temporary admission scheme is said to date back to 1900 and 1913, depending on your reference. Then, in 1923, Customs specialists convened under the auspices of the LN, but no successful outcome resulted. In 1949, the contracting parties to GATT considered the ICC's report on '*Invisible Barriers to Trade and Travel*', and in 1952, adopted the '*International Convention to Facilitate the Importation of Commercial Samples and Advertising Material*', which entered into force on 20 November 1955. Then, the CCC, with the cooperation of the International League of Commercial Travellers and Agents and of the ICC's International Information Bureau of Chambers of Commerce, prepared the Customs Convention Regarding the E.C.S. Carnets for Commercial Samples, which entered into force on 3 October 1957. Due to the E.C.S. Carnet's success, in 1961, the CCC adopted the '*Customs Convention on the ATA Carnet for the Temporary Admission of Goods*', commonly known as the ATA Convention, which entered into force on 30 July 1963. At the '*CCC's 47th/48th Sessions in June 1976, the Council recommended Contracting Parties to the Customs Convention Regarding the E.C.S. Carnets for Commercial Samples*' denounced as duplicating the ATA Convention.

For its part, the Carnet de Passages en Douane (CPD) was created in 1911 and first entered into use in 1913 as a document serving to simplify customs formalities for motoring tourists and travellers.

As for the Transports Internationaux Routiers or International Road Transports (TIR) Carnet, the TIR Agreement was concluded in 1949. Its success led to the establishment in 1959 of the first TIR Convention. The current Customs Convention on the International Transport of Goods Under Cover of TIR Carnets in 1975 replaced the 1959 Convention.

Even in the instance of SCP, they cannot be neatly classified without some overlap. The TA and Transit procedures can be applied to the movement of goods.[135]

§10.02 CARNETS

The mention of TA cannot but include the consideration of international Carnets (pronounced kar-nays), originating in the 1920s from the French '*notebook*', the more prominent of which are as follows:

- *ATA Carnet*
- *CPD Carnet*
- *TIR Carnet.*

Carnets can be used for three main categories of goods:

135. *See* Chapter 11 '*Transit – Customs Transit and Transhipment*'.

- Commercial samples
- Good for presentation or use at exhibitions, shows, trade fairs, or similar events
- Professional equipment, which is solely used by, or under the personal supervision of the holder or their nominated representative.

§10.03 ATA CARNET[136]

The ATA Carnet, a combination of the French and English terms '*Admission Temporaire/Temporary Admission*', is often referred to as the '*Passport for goods*' and is an international Customs document consisting of unified customs declaration forms which permit duty-free and tax-free (and also levy-free) temporary importation, or temporary admission of non-perishable goods for up to one year.

According to the International Chamber of Commerce (ICC), which administers the ATA Carnet with the WCO through its World Chambers Federation, it is the most widely used document by the business community for international operations involving TA of goods.

The ATA Carnet incorporates an internationally valid guarantee to serve as a security of duty, tax, and levy to cover the TA for specific purposes such as displays, exhibitions and fairs, as professional equipment and commercial samples and, where appropriate, the transit of the goods. The ATA Carnet is a unified customs declaration form, a globally accepted guarantee for duty, tax, and levy (and levy), which can replace the security deposit required by each Customs authority. The Carnet cannot last for more than 12 months.

The ATA Carnet can also be used as a transit document to move goods through a territory where the goods will not actually be used.

§10.04 CPD CARNET

The CPD Carnet is issued on the TA of private road vehicles, commercial road vehicles, and aircraft and pleasure boats for personal use. The maximum period during which goods may remain under the Carnet cannot last for more than 24 months. However, the time limit might be shorter. The CPD Carnet incorporates a guarantee, which serves as a security for the duty, tax, and levy.

§10.05 eATA CARNET AND eCPD CARNET

The eATA Working Group is concerned with the digitalising of the ATA Carnet and the CPD Carnet, which will facilitate the free movement of goods and vehicles across borders and their TA into a Customs territory with relief from duties and taxes.

136. There is an A.T.A. Convention '*Customs Convention on the A.T.A. Carnet for the Temporary Admission of Goods*'.

The WCO and the ICC are in a critical phase during which the members must decide when to transition to digital Carnets and notify the WCO and the ICC of their single point of contact for further collaboration and a smooth transition to the digital ATA Carnets by the end of 2027.[137]

§10.06 TIR CARNET

The TIR Carnet serves to simplify the administrative formalities of transiting commercial goods carried by international road transport. It can be argued that it is both an SCP for Specific Use and Transit. The TIR Carnet not only covers customs transit by road but also a combination is possible with other modes of transport, as long as at least one part of the total transport is made by road.

The TIR Convention establishes an international customs transit system with maximum facilities to move goods:

- Sealed vehicles or containers are also said to be under a Customs seal.
- From a customs office of departure in one country to a customs office of destination in another country.
- Without requiring extensive and time-consuming border checks at intermediate borders.

As with the other Carnets, an international guarantee is required to serve as security for the duty, tax, and levy. The Carnet cannot last for more than 75 days.

§10.07 TEMPORARY STORAGE (TS)

Although not part of TA, TS[138] is a Customs procedure under which imported goods are temporarily stored under Customs control before they are either placed under an SCP, such as a Transit, or released to free circulation or exported. By placing the goods under this Customs procedure, the full customs declaration, the payment of duties, and VAT can be delayed, generally for only a specified time.

§10.08 END USE

Since there is no Specific Annex in the RKC for End Use, it is generally considered the ultimate specific use to which a manufactured good is put or restricted. Also known as '*authorised used*', it is a procedure that provides specified industries with a reduced or zero rate of customs duty on certain goods imported into a country, provided that it meets the defined criteria and is put to prescribed (specific) use, the final item that a

137. The working group's discussion will continue at the next ATA/Istanbul Administrative Committee meeting, scheduled for November 2025.
138. Covered in Specific Annex A, Chapter 2 of the RKC.

product is integrated into, within a set time period. The provision does not apply to VAT, excise duty or anti-dumping duty.

Goods that are normally identified in a country's Tariff, Customs Tariff Schedule to be put to End Use tend to include the following:

- Shipwork goods
- Helicopters, aeroplanes and other aircraft for civil use
- Hydrocarbon oil
- Marine propulsion engines
- Military equipment.

For the authorisation of End Use, the Customs Authority will require that a guarantee be provided and assurances for the proper conduct of the operations.

Imported goods eligible for UK and EU End Use relief include the following:

- Shipwork goods
- Aircraft and parts
- Hydrocarbon oil
- Marine propulsion engines
- Military equipment
- Fish
- Cheese.

CHAPTER 11

Transit - Customs Transit and Transhipment

Transit is considered to be the movement of goods from one place to another under Customs control, while *transhipment*[139] is when goods or a container is moved from one means of transport to another while in transit to its final destination. The word '*transit*' originates from the Latin word '*transire*', which means to '*go across*', and the Latin word '*transitus*', which means '*going over, passing over*'. The concept of '*transhipment*' is also steeped in history, first referenced in the 17th century as an '*entrepôt*', which is derived from the Latin roots '*inter*', meaning '*between*', and '*positum*', meaning '*position*', that literally means '*that which is placed between*'.

Historically, an '*entrepôt*', also called a '*transhipment port*', is a trading post, port, city, or warehouse where merchandise may be imported, stored, or traded before re-export, with no additional processing taking place and with no customs duties imposed. In modern French, '*entrepôt*' also means '*warehouse*'. Due to the efficiency of transportation options, the use of trade entrepôts has mainly become obsolete.

Even in the instance of SCP,[140] they cannot be neatly classified without some overlap. The Customs Transit and TA procedures can apply to the movement of goods. Under both Customs Transit and TA, Carnets[141] can apply, such as the ATA Carnet[142] and the TIR Carnet.[143]

139. The RKC defines '*Transhipment*' as '*the Customs procedure under which goods are transferred under Customs control from the importing means of transport to the exporting means of transport within the area of one Customs office which is the office of both importation and exportation*'.
140. SCP generally allow for the storage, temporary use, processing or repair of goods, providing partial or full relief from import duty, or in certain instances suspension.
141. The word '*Carnet*' is the French word for 'notebook', originating from Middle French '*quernet*', which means '*group of four sheets*'.
142. ATA Carnet, which is often referred to as the '*Passport for goods*', is an international customs document that permits the tax- and duty-free temporary export and import of non-perishable goods for up to one year. It also functions as a transit document.
143. *See* Chapter 10 '*Specific Use – Temporary Admission and End Use*'.

§11.01 CUSTOMS TRANSIT

The Specific Index in the RKC defines the *Customs Transit*[144] as the Customs procedure where goods are transported (moved) under Customs control from one Customs office to another with the temporary suspension of the duty, tax, and levy. Unlike the other SCP – Processing, Storage, and Specific Use, Transit is not considered a CPEI.

The RKC distinguishes two types of Customs Transit:

- *'National Transit'* operations, which should be National Customs Transit, are the transport of goods between departure Customs offices and destination Customs offices within the same country or territory.
- *'International Customs Transit'* is the transport of goods across one or more borders, also known as frontier, in accordance with a bilateral or multilateral agreement.

Consequently, Customs clearance can take place at the point of destination rather than at the point of entry into the Customs territory or country.

The two types of Customs Transit should not be confused with *'Internal Transit'* and *'External Transit'*, which are designations which apply in the European Union (EU). In this instance, it does not refer to the Customs territory or country in which the goods are moved but rather to the status of the goods, whether it is from EU origin or not. *'Internal Transit'* is concerned with the movement of EU goods, and *'External Transit'* is concerned with the movement of non-EU goods.

Since the goods being moved are not Customs cleared, a guarantee is required to secure all the duty, tax, and levy liabilities that were temporarily suspended on the goods and any other obligations arising from the operations under the procedure that would need to be fulfilled.

There is a link between *'Customs Transit'* and the *'ATA Carnet'* in that an ATA Carnet can be used as a transit document. As a transit document, the ATA Carnet can be used to move goods through a country where the goods will not actually be used.

§11.02 TEMPORARY STORAGE (TS)

Although not part of TA, TS[145] is a Customs procedure under which imported goods are temporarily stored under Customs control before they are either placed under an SCP, such as a Transit, or released to free circulation or exported. By placing the goods under this Customs procedure, the full customs declaration, the payment of duties, and VAT can be delayed, generally for only a specified time.

144. The EC defines *'Customs transit'* as a customs procedure which is used to move goods: (i) between two points of a customs territory, via another customs territory; (ii) or between two or more different customs territories.
145. Covered in Specific Annex A, Chapter 2 of the RKC.

§11.03 TRANSHIPMENT

The Specific Index in the RKC defines '*transhipment*', also known as '*transshipment*' or '*trans-shipment*', as the Customs procedure under which goods are transferred under Customs control from the importing means of transport to the exporting means of transport within the area of one Customs office which is the office of both importation and exportation. In other words, it is the unloading of the goods from one mode of transport and being loaded onto another mode of transport to complete the journey to a further destination. In the instance of cargo arriving by ship, the cargo may have had to remain ashore for some time before its onward journey. Transhipment can also be applied to other transport modes, such as freight transport by road, rail, air, or any combination of them. It applies to all modes of transport, also known as multimodal transport.[146]

The goods admitted to '*transhipment*' shall not be subject to the payment of the duty, tax, and levy, provided the conditions laid down by the Customs Authority are complied with. The RKC further stipulates that transhipment should not be refused solely on the grounds of the Country of Origin of the goods, the country from which they arrived or their country of destination.

Since the goods being moved are not Customs cleared, a guarantee is required to secure all the duties, taxes, and levies that were temporarily suspended on the goods. Any other obligations arising from the operations under the procedure will be fulfilled.

Under certain tariff and trade preference agreements, the RoO provisions could have a requirement known as a *direct consignment rule*, also known as the *direct shipment rule*, which effectively prohibits or disqualifies goods that are more under the Transhipment procedure. Certain agreements replace the direct shipment rule with a non-manipulation rule for which Transhipment goods could qualify. The requirement is simply that the goods may not be further processed during transportation, for which documentary evidence of non-manipulation could be required on importation.

§11.04 CARRIAGE OF GOODS COASTWISE

The carriage of goods coastwise procedure[147] means the Customs procedure under which: (1) goods in free circulation and (2) imported goods that have not been declared under the condition that they must be transported in a vessel other than the importing vessel in which they arrived in the Customs territory are loaded on board a vessel at a place in the Customs territory and are transported to another place in the same Customs territory where they are then unloaded.

The Specific Index E3 in the RKC includes an SCP for the carriage of goods coastwise, which consists of two parts. The first relates to goods which are already customs cleared. The second is of interest in the context of Transit as, in this instance,

146. Multimodal transport, also known as combined transport, refers to the transportation of goods under a single contract, but performed with at least two different modes of transport.
147. The Specific Index E3 in the RKC i

the goods have not been declared under the condition that they must be transported in a vessel other than the importing vessel in which they arrived in the Customs territory and are loaded on board a vessel at a place in the Customs territory and are transported to another place in the same Customs territory where they are then unloaded.

Since the goods being moved are not Customs cleared, a guarantee is required to secure all the duties, taxes, and levies that were temporarily suspended on the goods. Any other obligations arising from the operations under the carriage of goods coastwise procedure will be fulfilled.

When considering this procedure, you might come across the term '*cabotage*', which is the French word for '*transport along a coast*'. It was originally applied to the coastwise shipping of goods between two places in the same country by a shipping line from another country. Its application has been extended to include aviation, railway and road transport.

CHAPTER 12

Customs Debt and Customs Guarantee/Security

'*Customs debt*' is presently not part of the RKC, although a substantive case could be made for it to contain comprehensive rules, as customs debt law constitutes a central aspect of all national customs legislation. This could imply the next consequential step in harmonising customs processes and improving the transparency of customs rules with predictable enforcement, which is the essence of the RKC.

Although the RKC does not define a '*customs debt*', nor for that matter a '*customs guarantee*', it does define '*security*', which means that '*which ensures to the satisfaction of the Customs that an obligation to the Customs will be fulfilled*'. *Security is described as 'general'* when it ensures that the obligations arising from several operations will be fulfilled.

§12.01 CUSTOMS DEBT

Customs debt means the obligation of a customs representative to pay the amount of import duty or export duty, which applies to specific goods under the country's Customs legislation. It refers to '*import duty*' and not '*customs duty*', and it does so as customs duty is one of the various duties, taxes, and levies that constitute an import duty.[148]

A '*customs debt*' on import is incurred when goods are placed under a SCP – Processing, Storage, Specific Use, and Transit. The extent of the customs debt would be dependent on the coverage of the procedure as to whether the import duty relief would be partial or full. Should the goods be released for free circulation, or in other words, cleared for domestic consumption, then the import duty liability will arise, and the import duty needs to be paid. The customs debt will also be incurred when the goods

148. Refer to Chapter 7 '*Types of Duties, Taxes, and Levies*' for insight into the elements of import duty.

are removed from a procedure or consumed without the conditions of the procedure being met. In another instance, a customs debt could also arise if the goods were unlawfully introduced into the country or removed from Customs supervision. This is also called Customs non-compliance. If the goods should leave the country through export or completing their transit, then the customs debt would no longer apply or be liquidated.

A '*customs debt*' could also result should there be an underpayment of import duty and export duty, which will bring into question who is liable for the payment of the duty. In the instance where the importer becomes aware of the underpayment, the importer should make a voluntary disclosure.

A consideration in the instance of customs debt, and ultimately the duty liability, is to consider the type of Customs presentation of which there tends to be two:

- *Direct representation* is the instance where a Customs representative acts in the principal's name.
- *Indirect representation* is the instance where a Customs representative acts in their own name but on behalf of the principal.

It is imperative that a business (company) is aware of what type of Customs representation they have.

As for the treatment of customs debt, a Customs Authority has two options; it can either:

- *repay*, also referred to as a refund, not to be confused with a customs refund, which is an amount of import duty or export duty that has been paid; or
- *remit*, also known as waiving, which is the payment of import duty or export duty that has not yet been paid.

§12.02 CUSTOMS GUARANTEE

A '*customs guarantee*', also known as a '*security*', is an agreement to cover import duty, import VAT, and excise duty, which have not been paid at the time of importation or at the time of exportation. Although used interchangeably, a '*guarantee*' is a legal term that is more comprehensive than a '*security*'.

The customs debt that the guarantee needs to cover can arise in two ways:

- *actual debt*, meaning that it has arisen; or
- *potential debt* means that it will arise from certain special customs procedures, as the debts are not chargeable straight away.

There are essentially two types of guarantees:

- An '*individual guarantee*' is a guarantee that covers the customs debt for a single operation, which is considered to be the default case.

- A '*comprehensive guarantee*', also known as a *customs comprehensive guarantee*, covers the *customs debt* and other charges of multiple operations and can be used for a longer time period.

As there could be a cost of capital associated with a guarantee, a business (company) might consider a '*customs guarantee waiver*', which tends to be associated with a Duty Deferment Account.[149] This account allows for a singular payment at the end of a month rather than making payments for individual shipments (consignment).

§12.03 CUSTOMS BOND

Although a Customs bond might be used interchangeably with a customs guarantee, a customs bond constitutes a contract between three parties - the Customs, the principal, normally an importer, and a surety, which serves to ensure that all the duties, taxes, and levies are paid to Customs by the principal. The bond should not be read as singular, as there is an array of customs bonds.

§12.04 DUTY DEFERMENT[150] (ACCOUNT)

Customs deferment is also not presently part of the RKC, although the facility is available in most, if not all, countries. In instances where a comprehensive guarantee is applied for a facility, a '*Duty Deferment Account*' usually is part of the same process. This allows for the payment of duties, taxes, and levies to be delayed until a later prescribed payment day.

§12.05 SECURITY

The RKC does not refer to a '*Guarantee*' but rather a '*Security*', which is covered in Chapter 5. In essence, the RKC requires that:

- national legislation shall enumerate the cases in which security is required. It shall specify the forms in which security is to be provided;
- the Customs shall determine the amount of security;
- any person required to provide security shall be allowed to choose any form of security provided that it is acceptable to the Customs;
- where national legislation provides, the Customs shall not require security when they are satisfied that an obligation to the Customs will be fulfilled;

149. Duty Deferment Account (DDA) allows for the delay of paying most customs or tax charges (normally customs duties, excise duties, and import VAT) when goods are imported into a country or of the release of goods from an excise warehouse. Normally under certain conditions, a DDA can be applied for without using a guarantee by applying for a guarantee waiver approval as part of the DDA application.
150. The RKC Chapter 4 '*Duty and Taxes*', Part B '*Deferred Payment of Duties and Taxes*'.

- when security is required to ensure that the obligations arising from a Customs procedure will be fulfilled, the Customs shall accept general security, in particular from declarants who regularly declare goods at different offices in the Customs territory;
- where security is required, the amount of security to be provided shall be as low as possible and, with respect to the payment of duties and taxes, shall not exceed the amount potentially chargeable;
- where security has been furnished, it shall be discharged as soon as possible after the Customs are satisfied that the obligations under which the security was required have been duly fulfilled.

The Section's Points of Interest

The intention of the points of interest is to provide you with schematics and, in certain instances, a brief explanation that might be useful or of interest. Certain of the schematics might well not have been covered in any of the Section's Chapters, and therefore require explanation.

Collectively, the points of interest of the sections, with a few exceptions, will constitute '*The Lesson's Roadmap*'.

The CSP allows the authorised user to store, temporarily use, process or repair their goods and get partial or full relief from import duty or, in some cases, suspension. Consider it for a moment in the context of processing, special use, storage, or transit – PSST.

The use of the CSP could be summarised:

- *S tore*
- *P rocess*
- *U se* (Temporarily)
- *R epair:*

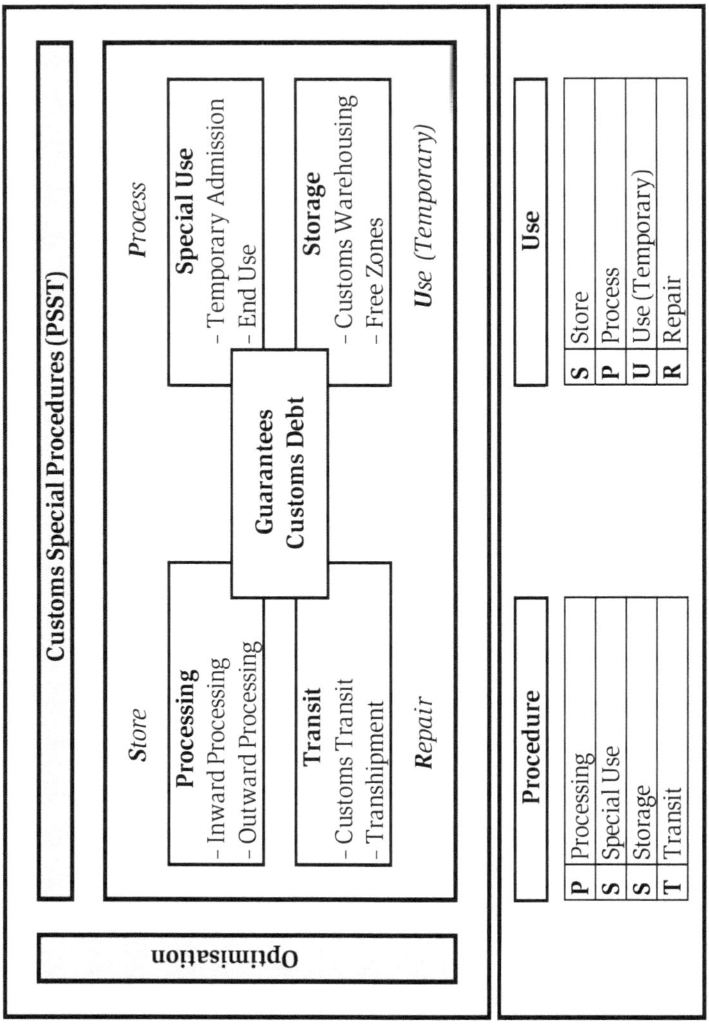
Customs Special Procedures (PSST)
Store
Process
Processing
- Inward Processing
- Outward Processing
Special Use
- Temporary Admission
- End Use
Guarantees
Customs Debt
Transit
- Customs Transit
- Transhipment
Storage
- Customs Warehousing
- Free Zones
Repair
Use (Temporary)
Optimisation
Procedure
P Processing
S Special Use
S Storage
T Transit
Use
S Store
P Process
U Use (Temporary)
R Repair

Customs and Excises		Acronym	Convention	RKC①	Agreement	Methods	WTO TFA④	CPEI	Relief	Guarantee
Cornerstones										
	Codification – Tariff Classification	HS	WCO	-	-	6	3.9 ⑤⑥	-	-	-
	Origination – Origin	-	-	K	WTO	-	3.9 ⑤	-	-	-
	Valorisation – Customs Valuation	CV	-	-	WTO	6	3.9 ⑤⑥	-	-	-
Imports – Importation										
	Clearance for Home Use	-	-	B1	-	-	-	-	-	-
	Re-importation in the Same State	-	-	B2	-	-	-	-	D/VAT	-
	Relief from Import Duties and Taxes	-	-	B3	-	-	3.9	-	D/VAT	-
Customs Special Procedures										
Processing③	Inward Processing	IP	-	F1	-	-	9.2	CPEI	D / VAT	G
	Outward Processing	OP	-	F2	-	-	9.2	CPEI	D* / VAT	G
Storage	Customs Warehousing	CW	-	D1	-	-	-	CPEI	D/VAT	G
	Free Zones	FZ	-	D2	-	-	-	CPEI	D/VAT	G
Special Use	Temporary Admission	TA	WCO	G1	-	-	9.1	CPEI	D/VAT	G
	End Use	-	-	-	-	-	-	CPEI	D/VAT	-
Transit②	Customs Transit	-	-	E1	-	-	11	-	D/VAT	G⑦
	Transhipment	-	-	E2	-	-	-	-	D/VAT	G
Miscellaneous Customs Procedures / Provisions										
	Carriage of Goods Coastwise	-	-	E3	-	-	-	-	D/VAT	G
	Drawback	-	-	F3	-	-	-	CPEI	D/VAT	G
	Processing of Goods for Home Use	-	-	F4	-	-	-	CPEI	-	G
	Relief Consignments	-	-	J5	-	-	-	-	D/VAT	-
	Returned Goods Relief/Rejected Goods	RGR	-	B2, B3	-	-	-	-	-	-
	Temporary Admission	TA	-	G1	-	-	-	-	-	G
	Temporary Storage	TS	-	A2	-	-	-	-	-	G
Exports – Exportation										
	Outright Exportation	-	-	C1	-	-	1.10	-	-	-

①	Specific Annex
②	E3 – Carriage of Goods Coastwise
③	F3 – Drawback
	F4 – Processing of Goods for Home Use
④	Article
⑤	Advance Ruling
⑥	Not Require Preshipment Inspection (PSI)
⑦	RKC Article 11

HS	Harmonised System
CV	Customs Valuation
TA	Istanbul TA Convention / A.T.A. Convention
CPEI	Customs Procedures with Economic Impact
D	Duty
D*	Duty only payable on the value added to the good
VAT	Value Added Tax
D/VAT	No Duty and No VAT

SECTION III

Trade Blocs – Economic Integration

Customs and Excises have their quirks, as the English language does too, which is so eloquently illustrated by David Burge's assessment, '*Yes, English can be weird. It can be understood through tough thorough thought, though*'. In Customs and Excises, there are '*trade blocs*', also called '*trading blocs*', but they are not trade blocks to which they are often erroneously referred.

The reason for its spelling is that a '*bloc*' is, by definition, a group of countries that have an alliance, are united by a common or aligned interest, striving to achieve a specific purpose. A '*trade bloc*' is a type of intergovernmental agreement whose core preoccupation is the elimination of tariffs and trade-restrictive measures between contracting parties or member countries. In international economics, trade blocs are viewed as forms of economic integration, with a progression towards ultimate full economic and commercial integration.

'*Trade blocs*' are also considered to be '*building blocks*', but an argument could also be made that they could be '*stumbling blocks*'.

CHAPTER 13

Trade Blocs – Economic Integration

§13.01 HISTORY – REGIONAL TRADE AGREEMENTS (RTAs)

The origin of '*trade blocs*' is not as recent as might be expected when compared to many customs provisions. The oldest trade bloc dates to the Hanseatic League, which existed between the 12th and 17th centuries which resulted in what would ultimately become Germany. Quite ironically, the establishment of the WTO on 1 January 1995 has led to regionalisation rather than multilateral trade liberalisation. This is evident from the marked increase in Regional Trade Agreements, or RTAs. This seems contradictory to the central principle on which the WTO is built, the principle of non-discrimination or the MFN provision. The MFN principle is fundamental to the whole edifice of the GATT, the WTO's predecessor.

So, by its very nature, RTAs are an exclusive measure of trade liberalisation rather than an inclusive measure. RTAs are essentially formed between countries which are in geographic proximity. An added challenge with RTAs is that countries tend to conclude numerous such agreements, which are referred to as 'spaghetti-bowl' RTAs due to their overlapping nature. Consequently, a country that concludes multiple RTAs needs to maintain and administer different RoO[151] provisions. Observations have been made that RTAs, operating alongside the WTO with its multilateral agreements, cover more than half of international trade and are growing in preference. This could indicate that regional trade liberalisation is preferred to multilateral trade liberalisation.

The RTAs' exception to the MFN clause, which is covered in Article XXIV of GATT, is permitted as long as they meet certain conditions, that Agreement:

- must lower trade barriers within the regional trading partners;
- must not raise trade barriers against non-members;

151. RoO are concerned where imported goods originate, where they were produced or manufactured, and not from where they have been shipped from. As a consequence, the '*origin*' is the '*economic nationality*' of the goods.

- is supposed to cover substantially all trade among RTA partners.

However, these conditions are seldom met, partially due to '*sensitive*' sectors being excluded from the '*trade liberalisation*' under the RTA,[152] generally referred to as '*market access*'. As for MFN treatment, some argue that the spirit of the WTO is maintained as all the members treat each other equally as '*most-favoured trading partners*'.

Although the MFN provision sounds contradictory, it suggests non-discrimination, both outside of and within its exception.

§13.02 MOST-FAVOURED NATION (MFN)

At its heart is that no WTO member country (member country) can extend '*more favourable treatment*' to another WTO member country. All member countries are expected to receive equal favourable treatment; in other words, they are entitled not to be discriminated against. The MFN obligation applies duties, taxes, and levies (charges), associated with importing and exporting. However, MFN status did not always mean equal treatment.

Yet, worthy of the quote from George Orwell's Animal Farm, '*All animals are created equal, but some are more equal than others.*' There is an exception, or rather two, to the MFN principle. There is, for example, in MFN that is often referred to as a '*major exception*'. In the first instance, a WTO Member country could extend a non-reciprocal market access to another WTO Member country, which is usually in the form of the GSP.[153] The idea for GSP emanated from the United Nations Conference on Trade and Development (UNCTAD)[154] in the 1960s as a tariff preference that developed countries granted to developing countries.

The basic premise of the GSP is that developed countries provide developing countries with non-reciprocal preferential duty rate access to their markets. In other words, a developed country would unilaterally reduce the tariffs on imports from developing countries, also called '*beneficiary countries*'. There is another trade preference programme that offers preferential tariff treatment to eligible sub-Saharan African (SSA) countries, which is called the African Growth and Opportunity Act (AGOA). GSP and AGOA differ in that a GSP is a broader programme applicable to various developing countries, while AGOA is specifically designed to benefit eligible SSA countries.

152. The WTO uses the term '*RTAs*' as a generic name for all reciprocal agreements such as customs unions, and FTAs, which can be explained by the fact that, initially, such treaties were within the jurisdiction of the WTO's Committee on Regional Trade Agreements.
153. Generalised System of Preference or GSP is a scheme which provides non-reciprocal preferential market access for goods, normally originating in developing countries to developed countries' markets. The preferential treatment could be provided in the form of reduced or duty-free rates of customs duty. The emphasis is on customs duty and not on other duties, taxes, and levies.
154. *See* Chapter 23 '*International Customs and Trade Organisations, Committees, Agreements, and Conventions*'.

In the second instance, the MFN exception allows members of Free Trade Areas, FTAs,[155] and Customs Unions to extend more favourable treatment to each other's imports. The reference to two trade blocs - FTAs and Customs Unions - might reasonably create the impression that there are only two types of trade blocs. As you will see later, this is not the case.

§13.03 TRADE BLOCS – FORMS AND STATES OF ECONOMIC INTEGRATION

The added challenge in dealing with trade blocs is that the terminology is used interchangeably. Free Trade Agreements and Free Trade Areas, both abbreviated as FTAs, have already been sighted. Then, there are Preferential Trade Areas, PTA, and FTA, with the aforementioned also referenced as Preferential Trade Agreements or PTAs. PTA relates to the GSP MFN exception, which might not technically qualify as a trade bloc. Still, an argument could be made that non-reciprocal trade preferences could evolve into reciprocal trade preferences.

The premise of trade blocs remains integration, but the extent and nature of it differs. Accordingly, it is crucial to consider the various trade blocs. The best way of doing this is ironically through the use of blocks.

It is quite possible for a country to belong to more than one trade bloc which the economist Jagdish Bhagwati termed the *'spaghetti bowl'* to describe the complex and often confusing tangle of trade agreements that countries can get caught up in.

The table below illustrates the trade blocs, also known as the stages of economic integration, by denoting the characteristics with an 'X'. The trade blocs are grouped in Shallow Integration Stages, or Shallow Integration Agreements, and in Deep Integration Stages, or Deep Integration Stages:

155. FTAs should be not be confused with Free Trade Agreements, which share the same acronym. In this context, FTAs refer to set of rules and provisions agreed to by the FTAs' members.

Forms and Stages of Economic Integration	*Free Trade Zone*	*Preferential Trade Area*	*Free Trade Area*	*Customs Union*	*Common Market or Single Market*	*Economic Union*	*Political Union*
Free movement of goods	–	–	**X**	**X**	**X**	**X**	**X**
Common external tariff	–	–	–	**X**	**X**	**X**	**X**
Free movement of factor endowments	–	–	–	–	**X**	**X**	**X**
Common economic policies	–	–	–	–	–	**X**	**X**
Common political environment	–	–	–	–	–	–	**X**
	Shallow Integration Stages[156]			*Deep Integration Stages*[157]			

156. '*Shallow Integration*' is considered to be integration that is only of an economic or trade policy nature, with a focus on the trade in goods. Its concern is with tariffs, either its reduction or its elimination, and the elimination of quantitative restrictions (QR).
157. '*Deep Integration*', which moves beyond the removal of border barriers, is considered to be integration that is of both an economic and a political nature and impacts a country's autonomy. Its primary focus is on NTMs and NTBs. *See* Chapter 15 '*Non-tariff Measures*', and Chapter 16 '*Non-tariff Barriers*'.

§13.04 STAGES OF ECONOMIC INTEGRATION: FROM AUTARKY TO A POLITICAL UNION

As a starting point, a country has economic independence, it has autarky, but as it embarks on an economic policy of economic integration, it explores various forms of economic integration and as a consequence it migrates through the stages of economic integration.

It is quite possible for a country to be a member of different types of trade blocs, which increases the challenge of, among others, the origin determination of goods, giving rise to its own '*spagetti bowl*'. It is not that rare to see a country which a member of a Customs Union is also a member of FTAs.

§13.05 FREE TRADE ZONE (FTZ)

The first FTZ was established on the Greek island of Delos in 166 BC, and the first '*modern*' day FTZ the Shannon Free Zone, which was established in Shannon, Ireland in 1959. A FTZ, also known as an Export Processing Zone (EPZ),[158] Industrial Development Zone, and Special Economic Zone (SEZ),[159] is not universally accepted as the first stage of economic integration. Still, it is included as it signals a country's intention for enhanced trade preferences and to stimulate economic activity and growth through the application of tariff preferences. A FTZ denotes a geographical area or a Customs enclave, meaning that it is outside of the jurisdiction of a country's Customs and Excises laws, and generally located near or adjacent to a seaport or an airport. The general intention of the FTZ is to allow for the manufacture, production of goods with the intention of exporting the goods.

§13.06 PREFERENTIAL TRADE AREA (PTA)

A Preferential Trade Area (PTA), also known as Preferential Trading Agreement and Preferential Trade Arrangements, extends partial preference to trading partners. The WTO-preferred Preferential Trade Arrangement offers a trading partner a non-reciprocal tariff preference, such as the GSP. It could also include non-reciprocal preferential schemes granted through a waiver, providing for the exemption from applying the MFN principle.

158. An EPZ tends to be a fenced-in zone that allows a business import inputs customs duty, levy, and tax free as long as the inputs will be used in the production of exported goods. Should the goods be exported to the adjacent Customs territory then the customs duty, levy and taxes need to be brought into account and be paid.
159. SEZs are designated areas within a country that offer favourable business and trade conditions, such as tax breaks, simplified regulations, and other incentives, to encourage investment and economic activity. The zones often have different business and trade laws than the rest of the country.

§13.07 FREE TRADE AREA (FTA)

The first FTA, the Cobden-Chevalier Treaty, was put in place on 23 January 1860 between Great Britain and France which led to successive agreements between other countries in Europe, leading to what was considered a '*free trade epidemic*' in Europe.

This should not be confused with a Free Trade Agreement, abbreviated as FTA, but refers to the Agreement itself. It allows for eliminating tariffs, quantitative restrictions (QRs) and NTBs between member countries while each contracting member retains their own external tariff.

§13.08 CUSTOMS UNION

The first Customs Union, the South African Customs Union, was established by the Orange River Colony and the Transvaal Colony in 1889. On 1 July 1893, it became known as the Southern African Customs Union (SACU) with neighbouring British territories joining.

In addition to the customs duty-free movement of goods between the member countries, which defines an FTA, a single common external tariff (CET) is adopted. It implies that each member country has to impose the same level of customs duty.

§13.09 COMMON MARKET OR SINGLE MARKET

The first reference to such a Common Market or Single Market is made in 1818, at the close of the Napoleonic Wars. At the time Germany was made up of 39 states, among them four city-states. As it had abolished its own internal tariff, Prussia began inviting individual states to eliminate tariffs. Through agreement it set the foundation for Zollverein, which served to align the Prussian and Hohenzollern territories.

In addition to the free movement of goods, and a CET, this is an agreement on the part of a set of member countries to eliminate trade restrictions among themselves, adopt a CET, and allow the free movement of factors of production among member countries. The factors of production refer to labour and physical capital.

§13.10 ECONOMIC UNION

The European Economic Community (EEC), also known as the European Common Market, was established on 1 January 1993.

An Economic Union's primary concern, in addition to the free movement of goods, the CET, and the free movement of factors of production, is common economic policies – macroeconomic policy coordination. It involves the integration of national economic policies and a common currency.

§13.11 POLITICAL UNION

The Union of Soviet Socialist Republics, known as the USSR, is an example of a Political Union whose ultimate aim is for a common political environment.

It spans all the stages of economic integration, in that includes the free movement of goods, a CET, the free movement of factor endowments, common economic policies (macroeconomic policy coordination), and a common political environment.

§13.12 MONETARY UNION

The Monetary Union, which is not included in the table, refers to a trade bloc adopting a single currency for all member countries.

Since its establishment, SACU has had a single currency, most recently the South African Rand (ZAR); although Botswana uses the Pula, which it introduced in 1976, trading on parity with the ZAR, it still accepts ZAR. The most recent Monetary Union of sorts is the 20 of the 27 EU Member States which use the Euro as their official currency.

§13.13 THE CATEGORIES OF THE INTEGRATION STAGES

Now that the forms and stages of economic integration have been elucidated, their classification in the two categories of integration stages should be considered.

The first is referred to as the '*shallow integration stages*'; its only concern is dismantling the classical barriers to trade at the border, such as tariffs and other measures. These are essentially considered border measures.

The second, the '*deep integration stages*', is concerned with the '*behind-the-border measures*', in other words, once the goods are in the country. These stages are concerned with the protection of intellectual, industrial, and commercial property rights. Their intent is to reduce trade costs, and if efficiently designed, they can increase international trade, investment, economic growth, and social welfare.

A benefit can be derived from '*Shallow Integration Stages*', which stimulate the deliberation between lobbyists for export promotion and import-competing lobbyists. The '*Deep Integration Stages*' tend to have a negative impact on a country's economy if they deal with consumption-side policies and a positive impact when focused on production-side policies, but only when there are strong lobbyists.

In the instance of Common Market (Single Market), and Economic Unions, these agreements are now called '*Deep Trade Agreements*' or DTAs, which are in addition to multilateral trade rules, bilateral investment agreements, labour regulations, protection of intellectual property rights and the environment. DTAs' goals tend to extend beyond trade or deep integration.

[A] Three Shallow Integration Stages

- *PTA*
- *FTA*
- *Customs Union.*

[B] Four Deep Integration Stages

- *Common Market or Single Market*
- *Economic Union*
- *Political Union*
- *Monetary Union.*

§13.14 TRADE BLOC'S ECONOMIC EFFECTS – '*TRADITIONAL*' EFFECTS

The creation of trade blocs does have an impact or an economic effect, which can be broadly classed into two categories.

'*Trade creation*', also known as '*trade expansion*' and '*trade integration*', refers to the increase in internal trade within the trade bloc as tariffs and NTBs are reduced between member countries. This positive effect leads to a more efficient allocation of factors of production within the agreement area, in line with the different members' comparative advantages.

'*Trade diversion*', also known as '*trade deflection*', on the other hand, has an adverse effect on the trade bloc's member countries as trade is diverted from a previously more efficient supplier outside of the trade bloc to a less efficient one within the trade bloc. Consequently, a higher price might now be paid both financially and ultimately economically due to the inefficient use of resources within the trade bloc.

§13.15 THE THREE TYPES OF TRADE AGREEMENTS

There are essentially three types of trade agreements:

- *Unilateral Trade Agreements*
- *Bilateral Trade Agreements*
- *Multilateral Trade Agreements.*

[A] Unilateral Trade Agreements

'*Uni*' means one. A unilateral trade agreement is a one-sided arrangement that a country makes to lower trade barriers for other countries. A prime example is the GSP; under such agreement, a developed country or countries extends non-reciprocal preferences to a developing country with the intention of providing the developing country or countries with the opportunity to grow its economy by removing tariff and trade barriers to its exports.

[B] Bilateral Trade Agreements

'*Bi*' means two. A bilateral trade agreement is an agreement between two countries to lower, or partially remove tariff and trade barriers with each other. These agreements tend to be concluded between countries which are either in geographic proximity or that could derive comparative advantages from trading with each other.

[C] Multilateral Trade Agreements

'*Multi*' means many. A multilateral trade agreement is an agreement between multiple countries to lower tariff and trade barriers between one another. These agreements tend to be exclusively between countries which are in regional geographic proximity and have aligned aims to foster regional economic growth and development.

§13.16 OTHER CONSIDERATIONS

The tariff and trade preferences within trade blocs are administered by means of the RoO provisions of that trade bloc. However, the borders of the trade blocs could be quite porous as countries could be members of multiple trade blocs which are in different stages of economic integration. Consequently, other member countries to a given trade bloc need to rely on the other countries to ensure that the RoO provisions are effectively applied for if they are not. Non-member countries could use these trade blocs to gain preferential access to other markets. This practice might well occur in an FTA where the external rates of customs duty could be significantly higher. Consequently, a country that imposes a low tariff could be used as a thoroughfare for a non-member country to gain access to a member country that imposes a high tariff.

Although much is made of free trade, when it comes to trade blocs, these blocs, at best, promote '*fair*' trade. It remains of great concern that regional trade blocs are not only permitted but also allowed to continue to expand within a world of supposed multilateral trade liberalisation.

§13.17 MEGA FREE TRADE AGREEMENTS

These are '*deep integration*' partnerships between countries and/or regions that aim to improve regulatory compatibility and provide a '*rules-based framework*'[160] to align investment and business climates. It is contended that these agreements differ from

160. The reference to '*rules-based framework*' is interesting, as the WTO refers to a '*rule-based system*'. It begs the question of whether trade blocs are in competition with the WTO, and are complementary to the WTO?

other agreements in their economic significance (due to their sizeable geographic scale) and the width of trade-related issues.

§13.18 GEOPOLITICS

Politics and Economics tend to be more interrelated than might always be appreciated, and the same holds true for trade blocs. Are trade blocs pursued due to their economic returns or due to their political returns? In your journey, you might be confronted by Geopolitics, which is considered the study of how geography, economics, and demography have an influence on politics and the relations between nations, especially a government's foreign policy, including international trade policy.

§13.19 NOT STAGES OF FORMS AND STAGES OF ECONOMIC INTEGRATION

[A] Tax-Free Shops

Several WCO members have authorised the creation of '*tax-free shops*' and similar establishments in their countries. These shops and establishments allow travellers who are leaving for abroad to acquire goods free of the countries' customs duties, internal consumption taxes or monopoly taxes.[161]

The WCO expressed concern that the existence or installation of '*tax-free shops*', on land frontiers (road or rail traffic), gives rise to a grave risk of fraudulent importation. As a consequence, the WCO recommended that:

- '*tax-free shops*' and similar establishments should not be installed at places other than seaports or Customs airports; and that
- sales in '*tax-free shops*' should be limited to travellers leaving for abroad by sea or air.

161. Recommendation of the Customs Co-Operation Council Concerning Tax-Free Shops, 16 June 1960.

The Section's Points of Interest

The intention of the points of interest is to provide you with schematics and, in certain instances, a brief explanation that might be useful or of interest. Certain of the schematics might well not have been covered in any of the Section's Chapters, and therefore require explanation.

Collectively, the points of interest of the sections, with a few exceptions, will constitute '*The Lesson's Roadmap*'.

The table below illustrates the trade blocs, also known as the stages of economic integration, by denoting the characteristics with an 'X':

Forms and Stages of Economic Integration	*Free Trade Zone*	*Preferential Trade Area*	*Free Trade Area*	*Customs Union*	*Common Market or Single Market*	*Economic Union*	*Political Union*
Free movement of goods	–	–	X	X	X	X	X
Common external tariff	–	–	–	X	X	X	X
Free movement of factor endowments	–	–	–	–	X	X	X
Common economic policies	–	–	–	–	–	X	X
Common political environment	–	–	–	–	–	–	X
	Shallow Integration Stages[162]			*Deep Integration Stages*[163]			

162. '*Shallow Integration*' is considered to be an integration that is only of economic in nature. The primary focus tends to be on tariffs, either its reduction, or its elimination, and the elimination of QR.
163. '*Deep Integration*' is considered to be an integration that is of both an economic and a political nature and impacts a country's autonomy. Its primary focus is on NTMs and NTBs. *See* Chapter 15 '*Non-Tariff Measures*', and Chapter 16 '*Non-Tariff Barriers*'.

Section IV

Non-Tariff, Tariff and Trade Barriers

Traditionally, tariffs are considered the *'visible' barriers*, or *'explicit barriers'* to international trade, as these are published as schedules, regulations or policies and, by their very nature, easily assessable for scrutiny. NTBs or NTMs are considered the *'invisible barriers'* or *'implicit barriers'* to international trade. Although NTBs[164] and NTMs[165] are technically different, they tend to be used interchangeably.

NTBs are actually a subset of NTMs and are considered measures that have potentially trade-inhibiting effects. To add to the complication, some NTMs are not actually barriers. They can increase the volume of trade. While this might introduce an administrative burden and a cost on imported goods, it might also give consumers more confidence to buy if they can see that foreign products conform to local standards.

To add to the complication, there are quasi-tariff measures which result in increased tariff protection without actually amending the rate of duty, rather than amending the reference price, the minimum value, the minimum duty imposed, or the administrative value.

The severity of the tariff and trade barriers would depend on the elasticity of demand for the imported goods. If the demand is elastic or perfectly elastic, then the demand for the imported good would significantly reduce in favour of a similar good, which is not subject to NTBs.

This Section will not deal with the WTO's Import Licensing Agreement,[166] which requires governments to publish sufficient information on how and why licences are granted and inform how countries should notify the WTO.

164. *See* Chapter 15 '*Non-Tariff Measures*'. To date, there has been no clear definition of NTB.
165. *See* Chapter 16 '*Non-Tariff Barriers*'.
166. More information is available on the WTO's Import Licensing Gateway.

CHAPTER 14

Import Control and Export Control

There is nothing mysterious or nuanced about Import Control and Export Control. Every country has it as part of the measures to protect and safeguard its citizens.

The crucial role of Import Control and Export Control is essentially to enforce health, environmental, security and safety, and technical standards that arise from the country's domestic laws and its obligation under International Agreements. International Agreements, in this context, generally refer to the Montreal Protocol on Substances that Deplete the Ozone Layer, the Basel Convention on the Control of Transboundary Movements of Hazardous Wastes and Their Disposal, and the 1988 UN Convention Against the Illicit Traffic in Narcotic Drugs and Psychotropic Substances.

The Import and Export Control measures or restrictions are limited to those allowed under the relevant WTO Agreements.

There are essentially three types of Import Control and Export Control:

- *Bans* refer to instances where no imported goods and exported goods are permitted.
- *Quotas*, where the volume of imported goods and exported goods are restricted.
- *Surveillance* is where the importation and exportation of goods are monitored and subject to licences or other specifications.

It is imperative that the cornerstones of Customs and Excises - codification, origination, and valorisation - be correctly applied to ensure that the imported good or the exported good that complies with the Import Control or Export Control provisions should as such be specified.

CHAPTER 15

Non-Tariff Measures

NTMs are considered '*implicit barriers*'; although these tend to be used interchangeably with NTBs, there is a difference. NTBs are subsets of NTMs and are considered measures that have potentially trade-inhibiting effects. NTMs are considered '*implicit barriers*' to trade, which can potentially have an economic effect on international trade in goods. Even though the primary aim of many NTMs is to protect public health or the environment, it negatively impacts compliance costs and procedural costs. Increased transparency of NTMs and, subsequently, a better understanding of NTMs can assist policymakers, trade negotiators, and researchers to zone in on, and to deliberate on, the reduction of international trade costs.

In defining and categorising the NTMs, the United Nations Conference on Trade and Development (UNCTAD)[167] categorises NTMs into three groups:

- *Import-Related Measures*:
  - Technical Measures
  - NTMs
- *Export-Related Measures*
- *Non-Technical Measures*.

The three groups are itself classified into 16 chapters, or types – A to P – as per the table:

167. *See* Chapter 23 '*International Customs and Trade Organisations, Committees, Agreements, and Conventions*'.

International Classification of NTMs by Chapter				
Import-Related Measures	*Technical Measures*	**A**	Sanitary and Phytosanitary measures	SPS
		B	Technical Barriers to Trade	TBT
		C	Pre-shipment Inspection and other formalities	PSI
	Non-technical Measures	**D**	Contingent trade-protective measures	
		E	Non-automatic licensing, quotas, prohibitions and quantity control, measures other than for SPS or TBT reasons	
		F	Price-control measures, including additional taxes and charges	
		G	Finance measures	
		H	Measures affecting competition	
		I	Trade-Related Investment Measures	TRIMS
		J	Distribution restrictions	
		K	Restrictions on post-sale services	
		L	Subsidies	
		M	Government procurement restrictions	
		N	Intellectual Property	IP
		O	Rules of Origin[168]	RoO
Export-Related Measures		**P**		

Source: Adapted from UNCTAD, 2021.

As per UNCTAD's explanation, the first 15 Chapters (Chapters A to O) cover import-related NTMs, which encompass the requirements imposed by a country on imported products. The final Chapter (P) covers export-related measures that encompass the requirements imposed by a country on exported products.

A distinction is made between technical measures (Chapters A to C) and non-technical measures (Chapters D to O). Technical measures comprise SPS measures and TBT, as well as pre-shipment inspections and other formalities. They are primarily aimed at fulfilling public policy objectives, such as concerning the protection of human, plant, and animal life and health, as well as national security or environmental well-being.

Although their primary focus is not related to trade, and they may apply equally to domestic producers, such measures nevertheless regulate and affect international trade and are therefore considered NTMs. Non-technical measures cover a range of policies, including traditional trade policies such as contingent trade-protective

168. *See* Chapter 3 '*Origination – Origin*'.

measures, including anti-dumping and countervailing duties (Chapter D), quotas and non-automatic import licensing (Chapter E) and price controls and para-tariff measures (Chapter F).

As a further explanation and enhancement of the UNCTAD table, the following table serves as a '*Brief Explanation*':

Non-tariff Measure (NTM)	*Acronym*	*Explanation (Brief)*
Sanitary and Phytosanitary measures	SPS	Plant and animal health regulations.
Technical Barriers to Trade	TBT	Regulations on the contents of goods, the process by which they were manufactured, their labelling, etc.
Pre-shipment Inspection and other formalities	PSI	Requirements that goods be checked or licences secured before they can be imported.
Contingent trade-protective measures		Policies that protect the economy from the impact of certain imports, such as trade remedies (anti-dumping duties, countervailing duties, and safeguards) for agriculture, etc.
Non-automatic licensing, quotas, prohibitions and quantity control, measures other than for SPS or TBT reasons		Policies that limit the total number of imports of a certain good, such as quotas, rules stating that the imported goods can only be used in certain industries or temporary bans on certain goods
Price-control measures, including additional taxes and charges		Charges or taxes (other than tariffs) that change the price of those imports, for example, by ensuring that imports do not undercut the price of domestically produced goods.
Finance measures		Policies that regulate access to foreign exchange for imports, for example, by requiring deposits to be paid in advance, or that customs duties must be paid ahead of time.

Non-tariff Measure (NTM)	*Acronym*	*Explanation (Brief)*
Measures affecting competition		For example, compulsory requirements to use national services or the use of a single state-owned importer for some goods.
Trade-Related Investment Measures	TRIMS	Policies stating that post-sale services (customer services, repair services, etc.) must be provided by a local company.
Distribution restrictions		Measures which make it harder to sell imported goods in all parts of a market, for example, by stating that goods can only be sold in areas that meet certain conditions.
Restrictions on post-sale services		Policies stating that post-sales services (customer services, repair services etc.) must be provided by a domestic company.
Subsidies		Money from the government for domestic producers makes it harder for importers to compete.
Government procurement restrictions		Ensuring that the government departments buy goods from domestic producers.
Intellectual Property	IP	Ensuring that imports comply with patents, trademarks, industrial designs copyright, and GI
Rules of Origin	RoO	Requiring that goods be able to demonstrate in which countries they were produced, often so that it can be determined whether the good can benefit from preferential access under a bilateral FTA.
Export-related measures		Policies undertaken by the exporter's government, for example, limit exports to a certain country through trade embargos or reduce exports to keep domestic prices low.

Source: Institute of Government.

CHAPTER 16
Non-Tariff Barriers

Unfortunately, there is no clear definition of NTBs, which is frequently used interchangeably with NTMs, which is a subcomponent. To add complication, governments might well legitimately employ measures other than tariffs as policy instruments, which might then be deemed as NTBs. Its identification could be subjective, as viewing it from another perspective could be considered to meet a public policy objective. It is reminiscent of Darrell Trent's quote, *'One man's terrorist is another man's freedom fighter.'* NTBs are considered *'implicit barriers'* to trade.

Even the WTO does not explicitly deal with NTBs, but under the headline *'NTBs: red tape, etc. – A number of agreements deal with various bureaucratic or legal issues that could involve hindrances to trade'*, the WTO offers the following:

- Import Licensing.
- Rules for the valuation of goods at customs (customs valuation).
- Pre-shipment inspection (PSI):[169] further checks on imports.
- RoO: made in ... where?
- Investment measures.

Undoubtedly, a number of arguments could be offered to the contrary.

The only comprehensive reference to NTBs, which itself could be contested as to whether it is indeed NTBs or rather NTMs, is a website[170] which defines NTBs *as referring 'to restrictions that result from prohibitions, conditions, or specific market requirements that make importation or exportation of products difficult and/or costly. NTBs also include unjustified and/or improper application of NTMs such as SPS measures and other BT'*. It continues that *'NTB arise from different measures taken by governments and authorities in the form of government laws, regulations, policies, conditions, restrictions or specific requirements, and private sector business practices, or prohibitions that protect the domestic industries from foreign competition.'*

169. There is a WTO Preshipment Inspection Gateway.
170. *See* the website – www.tradebarriers.org.

It offers the following categories of classification:

- Category 1 Government participation in trade and restrictive practices tolerated by governments
- Category 2 Customs and administrative entry procedures
- Category 3 TBT
- Category 4 SPS measures
- Category 5 Specific limitations
- Category 6 Charges on imports
- Category 7 Other procedural problems
- Category 8 Transport, Clearing and Forwarding.

  Category 1: Government Participation in Trade and Restrictive Practices Tolerated by Governments:
  - Export subsidies
  - Government monopoly in export/import
  - State subsidies, procurement, trading, state ownership
  - Preference is given to domestic bidders/suppliers
  - Requirement for counter-trade
  - Domestic assistance programmes for companies
  - Discriminatory or flawed government procurement policies
  - Import bans
  - Determination of eligibility of an exporting country by the importing country
  - Determination of eligibility of an exporting establishment (firm, company) by the importing country
  - Occupational safety and health regulation
  - Multiplicity and Controls of the Foreign Exchange Market
  - *'Buy National'* policy
  - Lack of coordination between government institutions.

  Category 2: Customs and Administrative Entry Procedures:
  - Government imposing anti-dumping duties
  - Arbitrary customs tariff classification
  - Issues related to the RoO
  - Import licensing
  - Decreed customs surcharges
  - Additional taxes and other charges
  - International taxes and charges levied on imports and other tariff measures
  - Lengthy and costly customs clearance procedures
  - Issues related to transit fees
  - Inadequate or unreasonable customs procedures and charges
  - Lack of control in Customs infrastructure
  - Lack of capacity of Customs officers
  - Issues related to Pre-Shipment Inspections (PSI).

Temporary Trade Barriers
Temporary trade barriers in the form of anti-dumping, countervailing, and safeguard measures
Hindsight
Insight
Foresight

Category 3: TBT
Category 4: SPS Measures
Category 5: Specific Limitations:
- QR[171]
- Exchange controls
- Export taxes
- Quotas
- Import licensing requirements[172]
- Proportion restrictions of foreign to domestic goods (local content requirement)
- Minimum import price limits
- Embargoes
- Non-automatic licensing
- Prohibitions[173]
- Quantitative safeguards (safeguard measures)[174]
- Export restraint arrangements
- Other quantity control measures
- Restrictive licences.

Category 6: Charges on Imports:
- Prior import deposits and subsidies
- Administrative fees
- Special supplementary duties
- Import credit discriminations
- Variable levies
- Border taxes.

Category 7: Other procedural problems:
- Arbitrariness
- Discrimination
- Corruption
- Costly procedures
- Lengthy procedures
- Lack of information on procedures (or changes thereof)

171. The WTO has a Quantitative Restrictions Gateway.
172. The WTO has an Import Licensing Gateway.
173. *See* Chapter 17 *'Prohibited Goods and Restricted Goods'*.
174. *See* Chapter 5 *'Trade Remedies – Dumping, Countervailing and Safeguards'*.

- A complex variety of documentation is required
- Consular and Immigration Issues
- Inadequate trade-related infrastructure.

Category 8: Transport, Clearing and Forwarding:

- Government Policy and Regulations
- Administrative (Border Operating Hours, delays at border posts, etc.)
- Immigration requirements (Visa, travel permit)
- Transport-related corruption
- Infrastructure (Air, Port, Rail, Road, Border Posts)
- Vehicle standards
- Costly Road user charges/fees
- Issues related to Transit.[175]

175. *See* Chapter 11 '*Transit – Customs Transit and Transhipment*'.

CHAPTER 17

Prohibited Goods and Restricted Goods

All countries tend to have a '*Prohibited Goods and Restricted Goods List*' of some kind of description, which is either published as a singular document or across its Customs Authorities' administration. The two terms '*prohibited*' and '*restricted*' are distinctly different and cannot be used interchangeably. In another instance, the WTO classifies subsidies as red, or prohibited subsidies, and amber which are actionable subsidies.[176] As a consequence, countries could impose countervailing, anti-subsidy (duties on subsidies).

§17.01 PROHIBITED GOODS

'*Prohibited goods*' are goods where importation or exportation is forbidden or completely banned by law or authority due to a possible health threat, environmental danger, protection of endangered species of flora and fauna - Convention on International Trade in Endangered Species (CITES), security, dangerous chemicals - Authorisation and Restriction of Chemicals (REACH), the Basel Convention on hazardous waste,[177] counterfeit or pirated goods, to name but a few. The reason for the imposition of prohibitions or restrictions is broadly categorised as agricultural, economic, health, political, security, and social protection.

In essence, prohibited goods are never, under any circumstances, allowed to enter or exit a country.

176. *See* Chapter 5 '*Trade Remedies – Dumping, Countervailing and Safeguards*', and specifically the two colours of a traffic light.
177. Basel Convention on the Control of Transboundary Movements of Hazardous Wastes and Their Disposals.

§17.02 RESTRICTED GOODS

'Restricted goods', also known as controlled goods are goods where importation or exportation is limited or restrained, and is only possible should specific conditions be met or complied with. The control of these goods could, in its interpretation and administration, be regarded as NTBs, which implies that restriction diverts from its original intent to a protectionist measure.

'Restricted goods' are allowed to enter or exit a country only in certain circumstances or under certain conditions, for example, on production of a permit, certificate or letter of authority from the relevant government department, institution or body.

A Customs Authority normally administers certain prohibitions or restrictions on behalf of a number of government departments, institutions, or bodies. In essence, restricted goods tend to require permits, certificates or authorisations before a Customs declaration can be processed, as it is regulated under a national legislation.

§17.03 PROHIBITIONS AND RESTRICTIONS

'Prohibitions and restrictions' are not limited to goods carried by travellers but are applicable to all modalities of transport (road, rail, air, sea, post or other). This means that products subject to any prohibitions or restrictions will be subject to those no matter in what form of package or packaging they are imported or exported.

The *'prohibitions and restrictions'* from all different government departments, institutions or bodies are normally incorporated in a *'Consolidated List of Prohibited and Restricted Imports and Exports'*. The list tends to be categorised according to the tariff structure of the Harmonised Commodity Coding and Description System – commonly known as the HS Tariff or Tariff Book

International Instruments:

- Kyoto Convention Specific: General Annex Chapter 3 – Clearance and other Customs formalities
- Chapter 6 – Customs Control
- Chapter 8 – Relationship between the Customs and third parties
- WCO SAFE Framework of Standards: Annex 1 Standard 1.2, 1.3, 2.1, 2.2, and 2.3.

In the instance of the imposition of a quantitative restriction or QR, the severity of its implementation would depend on the form that it takes. The severity of the restrictive measure is dependent on the elasticity of demand for the imported good. Elasticity, in Economics, is used to measure the change in the quantity demanded for a good should the price change.

Article XI of the GATT 1994 regulates QRs. The Article provides for the general elimination of all *'prohibitions or restrictions other than duties, taxes or other charges' on imports and exports of goods, which can be 'made effective through quotas, import or export licences or other measures'*. The WTO has created a *'Quantitative Restrictions*

Database', which provides a platform to search and retrieve information concerning trade prohibitions and other restrictions that its Members have notified.

What possibly best illustrates the challenge experienced by Customs Authorities relates to '*grey goods*' and '*counterfeit goods*'. '*Grey goods*', also known as '*parallel imports*', are genuine or non-counterfeit goods of a trademark owner. It means that the trademark's owner or their assigned agent in a certain country did not import the goods, and as a consequence, technical and repair support would be provided for the goods. Counterfeit goods are those imitating recognised brands, also known as fakes or pirated goods. The goods are not generally only of poor quality, but also could be potentially harmful to use and expose buyers to harm and injury, particularly in the instance of electronic goods.

In addition to restricted and prohibited goods, government authorities distinguish between '*controlled goods*' and '*non-controlled goods*'. The latter two normally refer to people who are travelling with commercial goods which are accompanying them, in their baggage or luggage, or on their person.

In essence, the word '*restricted*' tends to indicate a country-specific or national competence, while '*prohibited*' has an international connotation.

The Section's Points of Interest

The intention of the points of interest is to provide you with schematics and, in certain instances, a brief explanation that might be useful or of interest. Certain of the schematics might well not have been covered in any of the Section's Chapters, and therefore require explanation.

Collectively, the points of interest of the sections, with a few exceptions, will constitute '*The Lesson's Roadmap*':

International Classification of NTMs by Chapter				
Import-Related Measures	*Technical Measures*	**A**	Sanitary and Phytosanitary measures	SPS
		B	Technical Barriers to Trade	TBT
		C	Pre-shipment Inspection and other formalities	PSI
	Non-technical Measures	**D**	Contingent trade-protective measures	
		E	Non-automatic licensing, quotas, prohibitions and quantity control, measures other than for SPS or TBT reasons	
		F	Price-control measures, including additional taxes and charges	
		G	Finance measures	
		H	Measures affecting competition	
		I	Trade-Related Investment Measures	TRIMS
		J	Distribution restrictions	
		K	Restrictions on post-sale services	
		L	Subsidies	
		M	Government procurement restrictions	
		N	Intellectual Property	IP
		O	Rules of Origin	RoO
Export-Related Measures		**P**		

Source: Adapted from UNCTAD, 2021.

Non-tariff Measure (NTM)	Acronym	Explanation (Brief)
Sanitary and Phytosanitary measures.	SPS	Plant and animal health regulations.
Technical Barriers to Trade.	TBT	Regulations on the contents of goods, the process by which they were manufactured, their labelling, etc.
Pre-shipment Inspection and other formalities.	PSI	Requirements that goods be checked, or licences secured before they can be imported.
Contingent trade-protective measures.		Policies that protect the economy from the impact of certain imports, such as trade remedies (anti-dumping duties, countervailing duties, and safeguards) for agriculture, etc.
Non-automatic licensing, quotas, prohibitions and quantity control, measures other than for SPS or TBT reasons.		Policies that limit the total number of imports of a certain good, such as quotas, rules stating that the imported goods can only be used in certain industries or temporary bans on certain goods.
Price-control measures, including additional taxes and charges.		Charges or taxes (other than tariffs) that change the price of the imports, for example, by ensuring that imports do not undercut the price of domestically produced goods.
Finance measures.		Policies that regulate access to foreign exchange for imports, for example, by requiring deposits to be paid in advance, or that customs duties must be paid ahead of time.
Measures affecting competition.		For example, compulsory requirements to use national services, or use of a single state-owned importer for some goods.
Trade-related Investment Measures.	TRIMS	Policies stating that post-sale services (customer services, repair service, etc.) must be provided by a local company.
Distribution restrictions.		Measures which make it harder to sell imported goods in all parts of a market, for example, by stating that goods can only be sold in areas that meet certain conditions.
Restrictions on post-sale services.		Policies stating that post-sales services (customer services, repair services, etc.) must be provided by a domestic company.
Subsidies.		Money from government for domestic producers, making it harder for importers to compete.
Government procurement restrictions.		Ensuring that government departments buy goods from domestic producers.
Intellectual Property	IP	Ensuring that imports comply with patents, trademarks, industrial designs, copyright, and GI.
Rules of Origin	ROO	Requiring that goods be able to demonstrate in which countries they were produced, often so that it can be determined whether the good can benefit from preferential access under a bilateral FTA.
Export-related measures.		Policies undertaken by the exporter's government, for example, to limit exports to a certain country through trade embargos or reduce exports to keep domestic prices low.

SECTION V

International Commercial Terms (Incoterms®)[178]

International **Co**mmercial **Terms**, abbreviated as Incoterms®, is a generic term unless it is Incoterms®, a set of 11 internationally recognised three-letter trade terms that is under a registered trademark of its creator, the ICC – '*The merchants of peace*'. Incoterms® are not mandatory rules. It simply defines the risks, obligations, and costs of sellers and buyers in the sale of goods for both international and national transactions.[179] It does not constitute a complete contract for Incoterms® to have legal effect when incorporated by the seller and the buyer into their contract. Incoterms® are '*delivery terms*' and are not concerned with the transfer of the title of the goods. Its introduction is in line with the ICC's founders' conviction that the private sector is best qualified to set global standards for business.

It is puzzling why it is called '*International Commercial Terms*' and not simply '*Commercial Terms*', as it is used for both international or cross-border trade and national or domestic trade.

If the Incoterms is not denoted by the '®' in the contract or on purchase order (PO), it would imply that it is not an ICC Incoterms®, and thus a generic Incoterms.

The '*Chambre de Commerce*' of Marseille, the oldest in the world, was founded in 1599 with the appointment of four deputies in charge of defending the interests of trade and, consequently, the port. After years of civil and religious war, in August 1599, King Henry IV established the Chamber to 'raise *the kingdom's economy*'. The members met in a room, a '*chambre*', hence chamber, to discuss their shared business concerns. After operating for 65 years, it expanded in the Spanish Netherlands in 1664 before spreading around the world. After being suppressed by the French Revolution due to its links to the aristocracy, Napoleon revived it. Today, it forms a worldwide network of over 10,000 CCIs that share the same universal mission and philosophy.

178. Incoterms® is a trademark used to brand the Rules devised by ICC and is copyright protected.
179. Incoterms® only relates to goods, and not services.

CHAPTER 18

International Commercial Terms (Incoterms®)

The Incoterms® are a series of pre-defined commercial terms published by the ICC relating to international commercial law. Incoterms® is a registered trademark of the ICC.

§18.01 THE HISTORY

The first ICC Incoterms® consisted of six trade terms – Free Alongside Ship (FAS), Free on Board (FOB), Cost and Freight (C&F), Cost Insurance and Freight (CIF), Ex Ship and Ex Quay. Their rules of interpretation were published in 1936, following the ICC's 1923 study into the most commonly used trade terms and their disparities. This was the first effort for the introduction of international standard trade terms.

The first Incoterms, FOB (which had been used in British Courts since 1812), is widely considered the antecedent of the transport clauses, predating the Incoterms by 111 years. The second Incoterms, CIF (Cost, Insurance, and Freight), was introduced in 1895 and became the international standard with the introduction of Incoterms® 1936.

Following the Second World War (WWII), the first periodical review accounting for the changing trade practices was released in 1953, with three new non-maritime transport Incoterms® being introduced – Free on Rail (FOR), Free on Truck (FOT), and Delivered Costs Paid (DCP). It also saw the introduction of the Ex-Works (EXW).

In 1967, misinterpretations were corrected, and two terms were added – Delivery at Frontier (DAF) and Delivery at Destination (DDP). The latter must not be confused with the present-day Delivered Duty Paid (DDP).

Then, in 1976, the FOB Airport (FOBA) was replaced by Free Carrier (FCA), which was introduced for air freight to distinguish it from FOB.

In 1980, the first of the now customary decade review of Incoterms®, which accounted for the advent of containerisation, was released with the addition of two new Incoterms® – Free Carrier, then called FRC, now FCA, and Freight Cost and

Insurance (FCI), now Carriage and Insurance Paid To (CIP). At the time, there were 14 Incoterms®.

The year 1990 saw the complete revamp of Incoterms®, which led to the simplification of FCA to include by deletion of FOR, FOT and FOBA Airport and consideration for the increased use of Electronic Data Interchange (EDI). In 2000, the Incoterms® formats were simplified, and clarity was provided on the customs clearance responsibility. At this stage, there were 13 Incoterms®.

The year 2010 saw the elimination of four terms – Delivered at Frontier (DAF), Delivered Ex Ship (DES), Delivered Ex Quay (DEQ) and Delivered Duty Unpaid (DDU), and the addition of two Incoterms® – adding Delivered at Terminal (DAT) and Delivered at Place (DAP). This reduced it to the present-day 11 Incoterms®. The modifications ensured obligatory cooperation between the buyer and the seller in the exchange of information as a security measure.

The 2020 and ninth iteration, consisting of 11 Incoterms®, saw the removal of DAT and being replaced by Delivered at Place Unloaded (DPU), and the insurance to be provided under the CIF and CIP was also changed.

It is important to bear in mind that the latest Incoterms® iteration does not replace the previous ones. It is possible to continue to use the previous iterations, provided that the chosen version is clearly specified in the contract of sale or on the Purchase Order (PO) – Incoterms®1990. An additional safeguard would be to specify '[The chosen Incoterm® rule] [Named port, place or point] Incoterms® 2020', for example, '*DAP 10 Downing Street, London, Great Britain Incoterms® 2020*'.

§18.02 WHAT INCOTERMS® RULES DO COVER

Incoterms® is concerned with dealing with three aspects between the buyer and the seller:

- obligations,
- risks, and
- costs.

§18.03 WHAT INCOTERMS® RULES DO NOT COVER

Incoterms® is not concerned with the following issues, to name but a few, between the buyer and seller:

- A substitute for a contract of sale does not address all the conditions of a sale.
- Concerned with the goods sold, nor their contract price.
- Indicative of when title or ownership of the goods passes.
- Specifying the documentary requirements.
- The method of payment or when the payment is due.
- Liability for the failure to provide the goods in conformity with the contract of sale.

- Sanctions and prohibitions.
- Tariff and customs duties.

§18.04 THE GROUPS OF INCOTERMS®

There are seven Incoterms® that can be used for any mode of transport and four for sea, land or inland waterway transport.

The seven Incoterms® rules for any mode(s) of transport, in previous iterations known as '*multimodal transport*', are:

- EXW Ex-Works (Place of Delivery)
- FCA Free Carrier (Place of Delivery)
- CPT Carriage Paid To(Place of Destination)
- CIP Carriage and Insurance Paid To(Place of Destination)
- DAP Delivered at Place (Place of Destination)
- DPU Delivered at Place Unloaded (Place of Destination)
- DDP Delivered Duty Paid (Place of Destination).

The four Incoterms® rules for Sea and Inland Waterway Transport are:

- FAS Free Alongside Ship (Port of Loading)
- FOB Free on Board (Port of Loading)
- CFR Cost and Freight (Port of Destination)
- CIF Cost Insurance and Freight (Port of Destination).

§18.05 THE CATEGORIES OF INCOTERMS®

The types of Incoterms® are divided into four principal categories – E, F, C and D, which are classified according to the delivery location, the fees, responsibilities for formalities, and responsibility for covering the cost of each part of the journey. These categories are further classified into subcategories.

Category E (Departure Term)

- EXW Ex-Works (Place of Delivery).

Category F (Shipment Terms – Main Carriage Unpaid)

- FCA Free Carrier (Place of Delivery)
- FAS Free Alongside Ship (Port of Loading)
- FOB Free on Board (Port of Loading)

Categories E and F are '*Freight Collect Terms*'.

Category C (Shipment Terms – Main Carriage Paid Terms)

- CFR Cost and Freight (Port of Destination).
- CIF Cost Insurance and Freight (Port of Destination).
- CPT Carriage Paid To (Place of Destination).
- CIP Carriage and Insurance Paid To(Place of Destination).

Category D (Arrival Terms)

- DAP Delivered at Place (Place of Destination).
- DPU Delivered at Place Unloaded (Place of Destination).
- DDP Delivered Duty Paid (Place of Destination).

Categories C and D are '*Freight Prepaid Terms*'.

§18.06 THE ICC'S INCOTERMS® 2020 – A BRIEF DESCRIPTION

[A] EXW – Ex-Works (Place of Delivery) Incoterms® 2020

The seller delivers the goods to the buyer when it places the goods at the disposal of the buyer at a named place, and that named place may or may not be the seller's premises. The seller does not need to load the goods on any collecting vehicle, nor does it need to clear the goods for export.

[B] FCA – Free Carrier (Place of Delivery) Incoterms® 2020

The seller delivers the goods to the buyer in one of two ways. First, when the named place is the seller's premises, the goods are delivered when they are loaded on the means of transport arranged by the buyer. Second, when the named place is another place, the goods are delivered when having been loaded on the seller's means of transport, they reach the named other place and are ready for uploading from that seller's means of transport and at the disposal of the carrier or of another person nominated by the buyer.

[C] FAS – Free Alongside Ship (Port of Shipment) Incoterms® 2020

The seller delivers the goods to the buyer when the goods are placed alongside the ship nominated by the buyer at the named port of shipment or when the seller procures goods already so delivered. The risk of loss of or damage to the goods transfers when the goods are alongside the ship, and the buyer bears all costs from that moment onwards.

[D] FOB – Free On Board (Port of Shipment) Incoterms® 2020

The seller delivers the goods to the buyer on board the vessel nominated by the buyer at the named port of shipment or procures the goods already so delivered. The risk of loss of or damage to the goods transfers when the goods are on board the vessel, and the buyer bears all costs from that moment onwards.

[E] CFR – Cost and Freight (Port of Destination) Incoterms® 2020

The seller delivers the goods to the buyer on board the vessel or procures the goods already so delivered. The risk of loss of or damage to the goods transfers when the goods are on board the vessel, such that the seller is taken to have performed its obligation to deliver the goods whether or not the goods actually arrive at their destination in sound condition, in the stated quantity or, indeed, at all. In CFR, the seller owes no obligation to the buyer to purchase insurance cover: the buyer would be well-advised therefore to purchase some cover for himself.

[F] CIF – Cost, Insurance and Freight (Port of Destination) Incoterms® 2020

The seller delivers the goods to the buyer on board the vessel or procures the goods already so delivered. The risk of loss of or damage to the goods transfers when the goods are on board the vessel, such as the seller is taken to have performed its obligation to deliver the goods whether or not the goods actually arrive at their destination in sound condition, in the stated quantity or, indeed, at all.

[G] CPT – Carriage Paid To (Place of Destination) Incoterms® 2020

The seller delivers the goods – and transfers the risk – to the buyer by handing them over to the carrier contracted by the seller or by procuring the goods so delivered. The seller may do so by giving the carrier physical possession of the goods in the manner at the place appropriate to the means of transport used. Once the goods have been delivered to the buyer in this way, the seller does not guarantee that the goods will reach the place of destination in sound condition, in the stated quantity or indeed at all. This is because the risk transfers from the seller to the buyer when the goods are delivered to the buyer by handing them over to the carrier; the seller must nonetheless contract for the carriage of the goods from delivery to the agreed destination.

[H] CIP – Carriage Insurance Paid To (Place of Destination) Incoterms® 2020

The seller delivers the goods – and transfers the risk – to the buyer by handing them over to the carrier contracted by the seller or by procuring the goods so delivered. The seller may do so by giving the carrier physical possession of the goods in the manner and at the place appropriate to the means of transport used. Once the goods have been delivered to the buyer in this way, the seller does not guarantee that the goods will reach the place of destination in sound condition, in the stated quantity or indeed at all. This is because the risk transfers from the seller to the buyer when the goods are delivered to the buyer by handing them over to the carrier; the seller must nonetheless contract for the carriage of the goods from delivery to the agreed destination.

[I] DAP – Delivered At Place (Place of Destination) Incoterms® 2020

The seller delivers the goods – and transfers risk – to the buyer when the goods are placed at the disposal of the buyer on the arriving means of transport ready for unloading at the named place of destination or at the agreed point within that place if any such point is agreed. The seller bears all risks involved in bringing the goods to the named place of destination or to the agreed point within that place. In this Incoterms® rule, therefore, delivery and arrival at the destination are the same.

[J] DPU – Delivered at Place Unloaded (Place of Destination) Incoterms® 2020

The seller delivers the goods – and transfers risk – to the buyer when the goods, once unloaded from the arriving means of transport, are placed at the disposable of the buyer at a named place of destination or at the agreed point within that place, if any such point is agreed. The seller bears all risks involved in bringing the goods to and unloading them at the named place of destination. In this Incoterms® rule, therefore, the delivery and arrival at the destination are the same. DPU is the only Incoterms® rule that requires the seller to unload the goods at the destination. The seller should, therefore, ensure that it is in a position to organise unloading at the named place. Should the parties intend the seller not to bear the risk and cost of unloading, the DPU rule should be avoided, and the DAP rule should be used instead.

[K] DDP – Delivered Duty Paid (Place of Destination) Incoterms® 2020

The seller delivers the goods to the buyer when the goods are placed at the disposal of the buyer, cleared for import, on the arriving means of transport, ready for unloading, at the named place of destination or at the agreed point within that place, if any such point is agreed. The seller bears all risks involved in bringing the goods to the named place of destination or to the agreed point within that place. In this Incoterms® rule, therefore, delivery and arrival at destination are the same.

§18.07 THE PARTIES' OBLIGATIONS UNDER THE ICC'S INCOTERMS®

Seller's Obligations Buyer's Obligations

A1. General Obligations B1. General Obligations
A2. Delivery B2. Taking Delivery
A3. Transfer of Risks B3. Transfer of Risks
A4. Carriage B4. Carriage
A5. Insurance B5. Insurance
A6. Delivery/Transport Document B6. Proof of Delivery
A7. Export/Import Clearance B7. Export/Import Clearance
A8. Checking/Packaging/Marking B8. Checking/Packaging/Marking
A9. Allocation of Costs B9. Allocation of Costs
A10. Notices B10. Notices

§18.08 THE USE OF OLDER INCOTERMS® ITERATIONS (VERSIONS)

A contract is governed by the version of Incoterms® rules that are referred to in the contract, which implies that earlier versions of Incoterms® rules can still be used if agreed by the contracting parties – buyer and seller. Should the contract only refer to Incoterms® rules but not to a specific version, then the Incoterms® rules version that was in force at the time of the conclusion of the contract will, in all likelihood, be applied should a dispute arise:

	1990	2000	2010	2020	Incoterms®	Delivery	Mode	Category
1	EXW	EXW	EXW	EXW	Ex Works	(named place of delivery)	Any	Departure
2	FCA	FCA	FCA	FCA	Free Carrier	(named place of delivery)	Any	Main Carriage Unpaid
3	FAS	FAS	FAS	FAS	Free Alongside Ship	(named port of shipment)	Water	Main Carriage Unpaid
4	FOB	FOB	FOB	FOB	Free on Board	(named port of shipment)	Water	Main Carriage Unpaid
5	CFR	CFR	CFR	CFR	Cost and Freight	(named port of destination)	Water	Main Carriage Paid
6	CIF	CIF	CIF	CIF	Cost Insurance and Freight	(named port of destination)	Water	Main Carriage Paid
7	CPT	CPT	CPT	CPT	Carriage Paid To	(named place of destination)	Any	Main Carriage Paid
8	CIP	CIP	CIP	CIP	Carriage and Insurance Paid To	(named place of destination)	Any	Main Carriage Paid
9	DAF	DAF			Delivered at Frontier	(named place)	Any	Arrival
10			DAT		Delivered at Terminal	(named terminal at port or place of destination)	Any	Arrival
11			DAP	DAP	Delivered at Place	(named place of destination)	Any	Arrival
12	DES	DES			Delivered Ex Ship	(named port of destination)	Water	Arrival
13	DEQ	DEQ			Delivered Ex Quay	(named port of destination)	Water	Arrival
14	DDU	DDU			Delivered Duty Unpaid	(named place of destination)	Any	Arrival
15				DPU	Delivered at Place Unloaded	(named place of destination)	Any	Arrival
16	DDP	DDP	DDP	DDP	Delivered Duty Paid	(named place of destination)	Any	Arrival

§18.09 INCOTERMS® RELATIONSHIP WITH SANCTIONS

The EU' Sanctions Law *'Incoterms "Ex Works" rule (EXW)'* notice directed that contracts between buyers and sellers cannot derogate from EU sanctions. Consequently, using Incoterms® rules such as the EXW Incoterms® does not modify sanctions-related obligations in any way. The notice indicated that this includes the obligation to ensure that certain goods do not end up in a prohibited destination. It is important that exporters and/or sellers take all necessary measures to that end.

The Section's Points of Interest

The intention of the points of interest is to provide you with schematics and, in certain instances, a brief explanation that might be useful or of interest. Certain of the schematics might well not have been covered in any of the Section's Chapters, and therefore require explanation.

Collectively, the points of interest of the sections, with a few exceptions, will constitute '*The Lesson's Roadmap*':

Incoterms® 2020

Category E	**(Departure)**		*'Freight Collect Term'*
EXW	Ex Works	Place of Delivery	Any mode
Category F	**(Main Carriage Unpaid)**		*'Freight Collect Term'*
FCA	Free Carrier	Place of Delivery	Any mode
FAS	Free Alongside Ship	Port of Loading	Sea/Waterway
FOB	Free on Board	Port of Loading	Sea/Waterway
Category C	**(Main Carriage Paid)**		*'Freight Prepaid Term'*
CFR	Cost and Freight	Port of Destination	Sea/Waterway
CIF	Cost Insurance and Freight	Port of Destination	Sea/Waterway
CPT	Carriage Paid To	Place of Destination	Any mode
CIP	Carriage and Insurance Paid To	Place of Destination	Any mode
Category D	**(Arrival)**		*'Freight Prepaid Term'*
DAP	Delivered at Place	Place of Destination	Any mode
DPU	Delivered at Place Unloaded	Place of Destination	Any mode
DDP	Delivered Duty Paid	Place of Destination	Any mode

Incoterms® Relationship with Customs Valuation

Incoterms® are '*delivery terms*' that determine the responsibilities and obligations of the buyer and the seller, and by definition it deals with the costs and the risk. In the instance of risk, this could be mitigated through insurance, which may or may not be included in the price that would be declared for customs duty purposes. The insurance cost and other costs associated with the goods are included in the calculation of the value for customs duty purposes (customs valuation), and there is a direct link between Incoterms® and customs valuation. As a consequence, Incoterms® can assist in identifying the costs that have been included in the '*price actually paid or payable*' for the invoiced goods. This is arguably the route that a Customs Authority can explore to challenge a customs valuation.

SECTION VI

Denied Party Screening and Sanctions Screening

Although not traditionally associated with Customs and Excise, '*Denied Party Screening*' and '*Sanctions Screening*' have been included as part of this specialisation due to their general inclusion in the Trade Compliance function.

The screening focus tends to be on the individuals and the entities involved in the cross-border transaction. Due to its classification, parties may be prohibited or restricted in their transactions by government agencies. Companies and individuals are expected to undertake screening activities of all the business partners in their transactions, with such screening not being a once-off, but a continuous process, which tends to be added with electronic solutions.

It is important that companies have documented processes and procedures to identify and prevent business interaction with individuals and companies, and to ensure compliance with national and international rules, regulations, and laws.

CHAPTER 19

Denied Party Screening and Sanctions Screening

As with Customs and Excises, sanctions are steeped in history, their first recorded use dating to 432 BC, when the Athenian-led Delian League[180] banned traders from Megara from its marketplaces. In modern times, it was not until the 20th century that sanctions increased in prominence and use.

The League of Nations (LN), the predecessor to the United Nations (UN), played a crucial role in forging country-based sanctions, which are a restrictive measure imposed by one country on another with the aim of limiting or impeding its trade and business relations. Its use was adopted following the enactment of the LN Covenant on 28 June 1919, authorising the use of economic sanctions against countries which had committed military aggression against other states. The application of sanctions has become one of the most favoured tools for governments to respond to foreign policy challenges.

Similar to Customs and Excises, its terminology offers similar challenges. Economic sanctions could, for instance, include export restrictions, trade embargoes, and asset seizures and typically regulate individuals' activities. While regulating individuals, export controls are typically designed to promote national interests such as national security, foreign policy, and multilateral non-proliferation. Adding to the challenge of terminology and focus, there is the overlapping nature of sanctions which could be imposed by the UN, or country specific. The adherence to the compliance of the sanction becomes more challenging where goods move across international borders in an international supply chain which could include manufacturing and processing.

In the application of Sanctions, unlike Customs and Excises, which have international agreements, conventions, and international organisations that strive for

180. The Delian League was a confederacy of Greek city-states, founded in 478 BC under the hegemony of Athens whose primary purpose was to continue fighting the Persian Empire, also known as the Achaemenid Empire.

uniformity, this simply does not exist in Sanctions and Screening. Even as far as guidance is concerned, it is left at the discretion of the business, which then tends to be managed by the direction of its risk appetite. The challenge that companies experience are what processes and procedures it needs to introduce to ensure that it effectively accounts for an ever changing environment, to evaluate and interpret the nature and the extent of the sanctions, and the appropriate screening technology that is required to avoid penalties, fines, or even severe sanction for non-compliance.

§19.01 DENIED PARTY SCREENING

Denied Party Screening, also known as '*Denied Trade Screening*' or '*Sanctions Party Screening*', is often used interchangeably with '*Restricted Party Screening*'. The differing terminology is not very helpful and causes confusion to the layperson, who could be under the impression that each term is of different significance while it is, in effect, one and the same. The only constant is that screening purports to detect, prevent and manage risk as part of export, trade and financial compliance.

Even as per definition, the terms '*denied party*', '*sanctioned party*', and '*restricted party*' are essentially the same. A '*denied party*' means a business (company) or an individual restricted or prohibited from engaging in transactions. A '*sanctioned party*' or a '*blocked party*' means a business (company) or an individual which is subjected to trade control or sanctions restrictions. A '*restricted party*' means a business (company) or individual with whom business is restricted, either partially or totally.

There is a difference between '*Denied Party Screening*' (or '*Sanctions Party Screening*') and '*Restricted Party Screening*' in that '*Denied Party Screening*' relates to export privileges being revoked or denied. Businesses are still able to engage with a denied party by selling goods to them. However, in the event of the denied party exporting or re-exporting the goods, it would constitute an export compliance violation. In such an instance, the business that sold the goods to the denied party would be complicit in the violation.

In essence, '*Denied Party Screening*' entails the process of checking or comparing, normally through automated means, a potential business partner or customer against denied party lists and sanctioned party lists to ensure that they are not violating any export control regulations. '*Denied Party Screening*' is a crucial element of a business' export compliance processes. The '*Denied Party Lists and Sanctioned Party Lists*', or '*Restricted Lists*', are maintained by government and international bodies.

The denied party lists and sanctioned party lists are normally published and maintained by government agencies and international organisations. In the instance where a business (company), entity or an individual (person) appears to be a potential match, additional due diligence is required.

§19.02 TYPICAL TYPES OF SCREENING

There are essentially three types of screening.

– Client Screening or Party-Based Screening

The screening of all business partners, clients, businesses (companies), and entities against the denied party lists and sanctioned party lists, and in the matching accounting for any false positives that might arise.

– Transaction Screening or Transaction-Based Screening

The screening of only the relevant business partners and clients for suspicious activity, and only doing so prior to each business transaction and/or business opportunity. It allows for decisions on the risk level associated between the payment beneficiaries and originators.

– Hybrid Screening

The periodic screening of all business partners and clients. This is in addition to screening the relevant business partners and clients prior to each business transaction and/or opportunity.

§19.03 SANCTIONS SCREENING

A '*sanction*' is considered to be a preventative measure that tends to be implemented by governments and international bodies in an effort to change behaviour, prohibit illicit activity and curb undesirable actions by certain high-risk persons or groups.

It is imperative to understand the extent of the sanction which may be comprehensive, prohibiting any and all commercial activities, or may be more targeted with the intent to restrict or block the transactions of particular businesses, group companies, or individuals.

'*Sanctions screening*'[181] is broadly defined as a control employed by financial institutions to detect, prevent, and manage the disruption of financial crime and, in particular, sanctions risk. The screening should be undertaken by a business as part of its Financial Crime Compliance programme. In essence, the screening involves comparing Financial Institutions' data against the lists of names of sanctioned parties or locations. The obvious challenge is to determine or establish a '*true match*' and to guard against '*fuzzy matching*', which could arise from not using an updated automated system. Adding to the challenging is the generation of '*false positives*', which is time-consuming due to its manual review.

181. The Wolfberg Group.

§19.04 SANCTIONS LIST

It is broadly considered to be a compilation of sanctions, usually collated by governments or international bodies, that can be applied to individuals, countries, groups or companies. Another reason for staying current is that Sanctions Lists are constantly evolving with additions being made to account for political foreign policy, and with new companies and individuals being added to and removed from lists, all the time.

An added challenge is the increasing complexity of sanctions which no longer target specific companies and individuals; now, narrative sanctions and sectoral sanctions are introduced which simply target specific sector and prohibit specific activities, both of which are subjective and open to interpretation.

§19.05 SCREENING FUNCTIONALITY REQUIREMENTS

The general functional support that would be required to ensure screening compliance is as follows:

- Global Sanctions
- Political Exposed Persons
- Adverse Media
- Business Information Monitoring.

SECTION VII

The Lesson's Roadmap, Timeline, Milestones, Elucidations of Trade Terms, Organisations, Agreements, Conventions, Resources, and In a Minute (I'm ^{TM})

Customs and Excises can be reduced to a single lesson and itself into a single sentence:

> The art of Customs and Excises consists in not merely accepting the terminology for its linguistic meaning; it consists of ensuring that the terminology, its context, its meaning, and its effective, efficient, and compliant application is fully understood, and appreciated, in both its reference and application.

CHAPTER 20

The Lesson's Roadmap

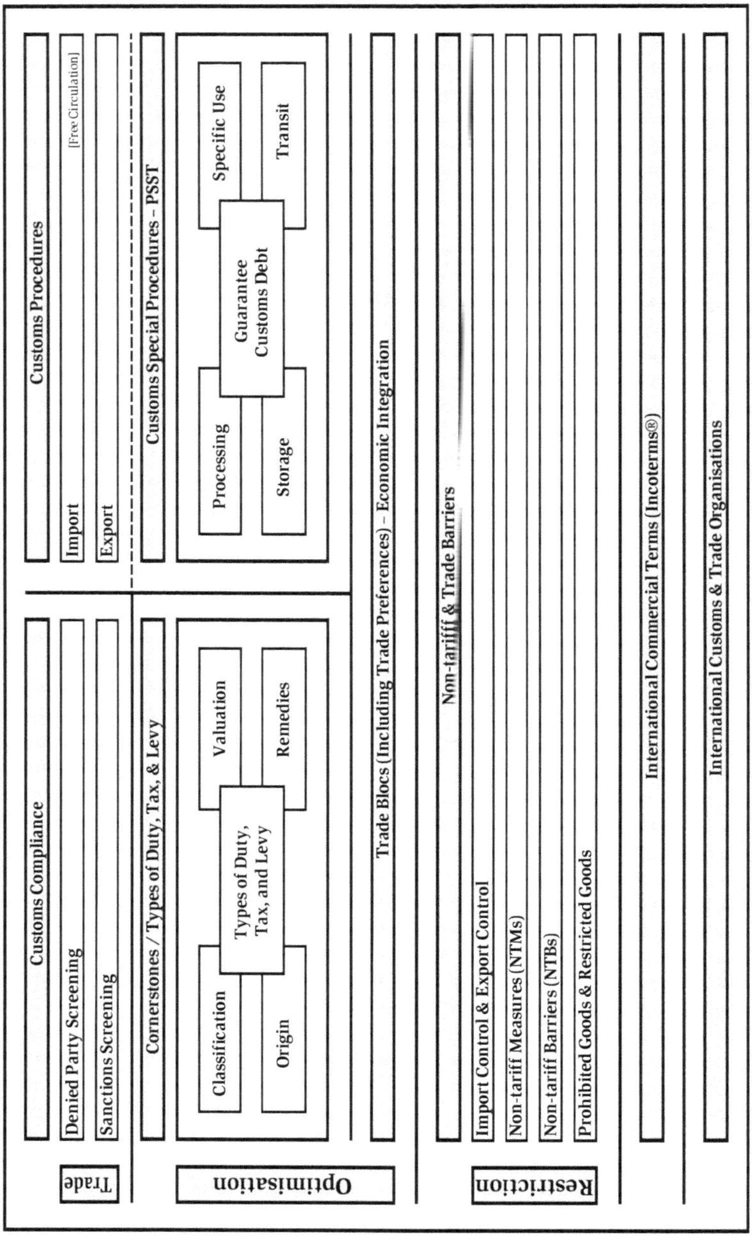
Trade
Optimisation
Restriction
Customs Compliance
Denied Party Screening
Sanctions Screening
Customs Procedures
Import
[Free Circulation]
Export
Cornerstones / Types of Duty, Tax, & Levy
Classification
Valuation
Types of Duty, Tax, and Levy
Origin
Remedies
Customs Special Procedures - PSST
Processing
Specific Use
Guarantee Customs Debt
Storage
Transit
Trade Blocs (Including Trade Preferences) - Economic Integration
Non-tariff & Trade Barriers
Import Control & Export Control
Non-tariff Measures (NTMs)
Non-tariff Barriers (NTBs)
Prohibited Goods & Restricted Goods
International Commercial Terms (Incoterms®)
International Customs & Trade Organisations

§20.01 *'THE LESSON'S ROADMAP'* EXPLAINED

A *'roadmap'* represents a plan or strategy with the sole intention of achieving a particular goal. The goal of this book is contained in its title, which is to provide you with the shortest and surest way to understand basic Customs and Excises.

If you have worked your way through the book in the traditional way or turned to this chapter, you can now access *'The Lesson's Roadmap'*. Although the table has been designed to be self-explanatory, it might be beneficial to provide you with a brief insight into its interpretation.

There are three category rows on the far left:

- *Trade*
- *Optimisation*
- *Restriction.*

There are two columns for *'Trade'*, which are headed:

- Customs Compliance/Cornerstones/Types of Duty, Tax, & Levy
- Customs Procedures/Customs Special Procedures - PSST.

There are two columns for *'Optimisation'*:

- Cornerstones/Types of Duty, Tax, & Levy
- Customs Special Procedures - PSST.

There is one category row for *'Optimisation'*:

- Trade Blocs (Including Trade Preferences) - Economic Integration.

There is a dotted line between:

- Customs Compliance; and
- Customs Special Procedures.

The reasoning being that:

- Import [Free Circulation];
- Export; and
- Customs Special Procedures

are all three Customs Procedures.

The book considers that Customs Special Procedures/Regimes are procedures/regimes that could be employed to optimise the duty, tax, and levy liability of the goods.

There is one category row for *'Restriction'*:

- Non-tariff & Trade Barriers.

of which there are four categories.

Then, there are two rows:

- International Commercial Terms (Incoterms®)
- International Customs & Trade Organisations.

§20.02 EMPLOYING *'THE LESSON'S ROADMAP'*

How you employ the roadmap would be dependent on your focus or approach. If you are looking at the import of the goods, then you will turn to the column rows for *'Optimisation'*.

If you are looking at the parties who are involved in the transacting and the movement of the goods, then you will turn to the column *'Customs Compliance'* and the category row *'Trade'*, where the consideration would be *'Denied Party Screening'*, and *'Sanctions Screening'*.

Although International Commercial Terms (Incoterms®) is in a category row of its own, it does not diminish its importance in trade due to its interaction with, particularly, valorisation (customs valuation), VAT, and sanctions.

The concluding category row, *'International Customs & Trade Organisations'*, serves as a reminder that trade is conducted in a rule-based system. There is not a single organisation that has the responsibility for or administers trade; it is multidirectional – a collective endeavour.

I trust that *'The Lesson's Roadmap'* will serve you well as you embark on your Customs and Excises journey or continue on the road.

§20.03 THE CUSTOMS OPTIMISATION PROCESS [A PRACTICAL APPROACH DERIVED FROM THE LESSON]

The Customs Optimisation Process [A Practical Approach Derived from the Lesson]

Company Information – Data – Statistics

- Customs Statistics [Imports (Arrivals), Exports (Dispatches), and Import VAT]:
  - Reconciliation and analysis from:
  - Company information:
  - Monthly Customs Duty Deferment Schedules
  - Customs Authority Data/Broker Data [Imports, Export, etc.].

Desk Review – Analysis

- Codification – Tariff Classification:
  - Rulings – Advanced and Binding
- Origination – Origin:
  - Rulings – Advanced and Binding

- Valorisation – Customs Valuation:
  - Rulings – Advanced and Binding
  - TP
  - VAT
  - Incoterms®.

Business Insight

- Engaging business stakeholders to gain management insight:
  - Customs processes, procedures and treatments
  - Engaging with suppliers/contractors
- Duty Deferment Account – Use
- Guarantees – Nature and Extent.

Desk Review – Analysis [PSST]

- Customs Reliefs (Applicability, Use, and Potential Financial Benefit):
  - Processing: IP and OP
  - Specific Use: TA and End Use (Prescribed Use)
  - Storage: CW and FZ
  - Transit: Customs Transit and Transhipment.

Other Customs Procedures

- TS, RGR, and Duty Suspension.

Business Process Redesign

- Recommendations:
  - Resulting from analysis:
  - Mitigate risk
  - Exploit opportunity
  - Structural/Procedural change.
- Implementation – Embedding Compliance:
  - Implement the recommendations
  - Risk/Opportunity:
  - Customs Authorities
  - Taking Corrective Action and Preventive Action (CAPA)
  - System/Structural change.

Continual Improvement

- Government Engagement – Advocacy:
  - Engaging the Government in defining the duty/tariff environment
  - Consider the possible/Future duty/tariff environment

- Self-Defined Customs Landscape.

§20.04 THE CUSTOMS & EXCISES: REFRACTION AND SPECTRUM

Another summary that provides a different insight into the essential elements of Customs and Excises equates the movement of the goods to the travel of light through a prism, its refraction, and its dispersion into a spectrum of colours.

The '*Cornerstone: Refraction*' considers the three elements of codification, origination, and valorisation, which, once established, provide the '*Customs: Spectrum*' which could be employed to mitigate the goods' duty liability (customs and excise), namely trade remedies, processing, storage, specific use, transit, trade blocs and trade preferences, non-tariff barriers, non-tariff measures, and trade barriers, with RGR.

Customs Valuation's interaction with Incoterms®, TP, and VAT, which is increasing in importance, is called out.

Customs and Excises operate within a '*Rule-Based System*' based on International Organisations, International Agreements, and International Conventions:

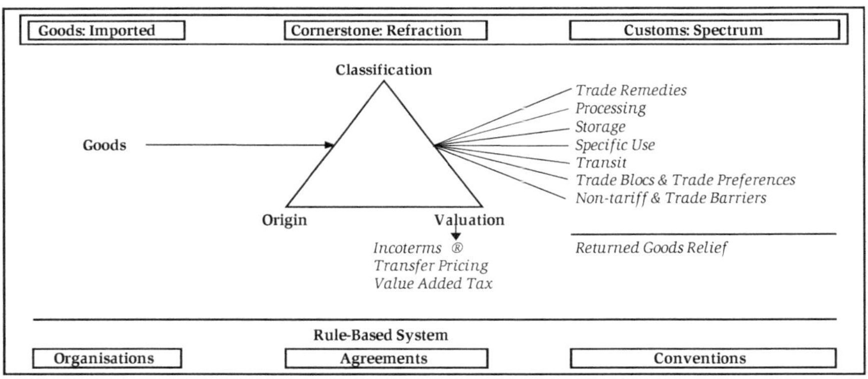

CHAPTER 21

Customs & Excises Timeline and Milestones

The Customs & Excises' Guardians – 'The gods and an Adam.'

Gud

The Sumerian god, Gud, later known as Hermes (Greek mythology), and Mercury (Roman mythology), favoured rains, agricultural fertility and harvest abundance. To the Egyptians, he was simply known as '*the messenger*', while the Babylonians called him Nebo or Nebu.

Hermes

In Greek mythology, Hermes was the god of commerce, or trade, who crossed the boundary between life and death. Hermes was widely considered the protector of travellers, merchants, and orators, and he served as the emissary and messenger of the gods, who delivered messages and instructions between the gods and mortals.

Mercury

In Roman mythology, Hermes was known as Mercury, originating from the Latin word '*merx*', which means '*merchandise*', and the origin of the word '*merchant*'. Mercury was the messenger of the gods, guide of the dead, protector of travellers, and the inventor of letters, figures, mathematics, and astronomy. The planet Mercury is named after him.

Adam Smith

The father of Economics, Adam Smith (1723 to 1790), wrote *An Inquiry into the Nature and Causes of the Wealth of Nations* (published on 9 March 1776), with numerous references to customs and trade provisions. Ironically, as a free-trade proponent, he served as the Commissioner of Customs (1778) in Edinburgh, Scotland, in his final years.

The End of the World, the Start of the Tariff – Where Two Continents and Two Oceans Meet

In Greek mythology, Hermes and Heracles (Hercules) are both sons of Zeus, the king of the gods. The myth of the Pillars of Hercules, which marked the end of the world, is the marker of how far Hercules had travelled; it originated with the ancient Greeks and was adopted by the Romans. Depending on the reference, the Pillars of Hercules, signifying the end of the world with the inscription '*Non plus ultra*', meaning '*nothing further beyond*', which were two promontories at the Northern and Southern ends of the Strait of Gibraltar, are said to have been in Tarifa and disputed to be in Gibraltar and Ceuta. Gibraltar is a British Overseas Territory and headland on Spain's south coast, while Ceuta is an autonomous city of Spain on the North African coast, bordered by Morocco, an enclave on the Moroccan coast. Tarifa is the southernmost city in Europe at the end of the Iberian Peninsula. The Pillars appear in the Coat of Arms of Spain.

The Pillar in Tarifa, where two seas – the Mediterranean Sea (calm and warm) and the Atlantic Ocean (wild and rough) – and two continents – Africa and Europe – meet has a link to international trade as it is the city that gave international trade the trade term '*tariff*'. The term originated due to the fact that the port of Tarifa charged and collected revenue (also called '*dues*') for goods passing through the Mediterranean, now the '*Strait of Gibraltar*'. Although the word 'tariff' is used universally, ironically, Spain calls it '*arancel*'.

Tarifa has the distinction of being the town that both introduced tariffs to the world and also marked the end of the ancient world, not that tariffs today are the end of the world.

Before Christ (BC)

2001 BC	In the early Bronze Age, one of the Sumerian (southern Mesopotamia people) gods was called Gud. Gud was later known as Hermes, the Roman god, and Mercury. Gud is the god favouring rains, agricultural fertility and harvest abundance. Later, in Babylonian times, Gud appeared in the Code of Hammurabi as Nebo or Nebu, the scribe of the gods who wrote down the laws and communicated them to ordinary men. To the Egyptians, he was simply known as '*the messenger*'. [*See* 1476 BC and 1754 BC.]

1600 BC	Hermes, the Greek god, has a long history in Greek mythology that dates back to the Mycenaean period, around 1600 BC to 1100 BC.
1476 BC	The Mesopotamians collected '*tolls*' imposed on the movement of the goods rather than on the goods themselves[*Mesopotamia in the West Asia area*] [*see* 2001 BC].
1754 BC	The Babylonians were the first to apply a Financial Penal Code. The Code of Hammurabi, a collection of 282 laws written by the Babylonian king Hammurabi, includes economic provisions (commerce, prices, tariffs, trade) and debt. Penalties imposed vary according to the offenders' status and the offences' circumstances. [*Babylonia in present-day Iraq and parts of Syria and Iran*.] [2001 BC].
609 BC	The first customs duty is applied in Egypt.
495 BC	The worship of the Roman god, Mercury, was introduced in Rome when a temple was dedicated to him near the Circus Maximus. Mercury's annual festival was celebrated on 15 May.
478 BC	The Delian League was founded under the hegemony of Athens with the primary purpose to continue fighting the Persian Empire, also known as the Achaemenid Empire. [*See* 432 BC.]
432 BC	The Athenian-led Delian League imposed sanctions by banning traders from Megara from its marketplaces. [*See* 478 BC.]
400 BC	The customs valuation practice is established in the Arthashastra, an Ancient Indian Sanskrit treatise dealing with, among others, economic policy. [*See* 1 January 1948, 15 December 1950, 1 January 1953, 28 July 1953, 5 September 1969, 1 November 1971, 12 September 1973, 12 April 1979, and 1 January 1995.]
215 BC	Mercury is a major god in the Roman mythology as one of the 12 Dii Consentes ('the council of the divine') within the ancient Roman pantheon.
207 BC	The term '*excises*' originates from the Han dynasty (207 BC to AD 220) and is levied on fish, liquor, fish, tea, and reeds used for fuel and thatching.
199 BC	The Roman Customs Administration was the first to establish tariff classification.

196 BC	The Rosetta Stone, a fragment of a larger slab, was erected at an Egyptian temple during the reign of Ptolemy V, a Ptolemaic king of Macedonian Greek ancestry. Although it serves as the key to unlocking the meaning of hieroglyphics, it is primarily a tax document explaining new tax laws decreed. [*See* 1799 and 1822.]
167 BC	The Palmyra Tariff is a bilingual inscription on limestone that records the trade tariffs and civic authority of the city of Palmyra. The Customs tariff of Palmyra, the centre of modern Syria, is alphabetical. [*See* AD 137.]
166 BC	The world's first Free Trade Zones (FTZs) were established on the Greek Island of Delos, a small island near Mykonos. [*See* 69 BC, 1947, and 1959.]
75 BC	The Lex Portorii Asiae (Customs Law of Asia) deals with the customs dues of the Roman province of Asia and Bithynia (western Türkiye). It was enforced from 75 BC to AD 62 and contained a provision for: - the exemption from customs due (import duty) for conveyances in the course of transit [*see* August 1976]; and - import duty exemptions in Pergamene harbour (enforcing Augustus Caesar decision) and also conceded the ambassadors (diplomats).[*See* 14 and 18 April 1961.]
69 BC	The FTZ on the Greek Island of Delos, a small island near Mykonos, is overrun by pirates. [*See* 166 BC, 1947, and 1959.]
49 BC	Ancient Rome was the first to administer a sales tax. Julius Caesar, a Roman general and statesman, imposed a 1% flat rate sales tax (*centesima rerum venalium*) across the entire Roman Empire. *Centesima rerum venalium*, meaning '*a hundredth of the value of everything sold*', is a tax on goods sold at auction in the Roman Empire. [*See* 1954.]

Anno Domini (AD) – '*In the Year of the Lord*'.

14	Excise duty was imposed by Caesar Augustus, the first Roman Emperor (14 to 27).
38	Excise duty was abolished by Caesar Caligula, the third Roman Emperor (37 to 41), only for it to return in the mid-17th Century in The Netherlands.

62	The Lex Portorii Asiae (Customs Law of Asia) deals with the customs due (customs duty) of the Roman province of Asia and Bithynia (western Türkiye), from 75 BC to AD 62. [*See* 75 BC.]
137	The Palmyra Tariff: The council of the city of Palmyra in Syria agrees to revise and publish the tariff and regulations according to which dues (duties) were levied on goods brought into and exported from the city and services provided within it. [*See* 167 BC.]
476	The collapse of the Western Roman Empire, the half of the Empire that used Latin as its official language. [*See* 1453.]
710	The word '*tarif*' originates from a place, before it became an international trade term, the city of Tarifa, which is located across the Strait of Gibraltar on the southernmost tip of the Iberian Peninsula (Spain). The city in turn derived its name from '*Tarif Ibn Malik*', a Berber general who in AD 710 led the first invasion of Visigothic Hispania under the orders of Commander Tariq ibn Ziyad from the Umayyad Caliphate, an empire based in Damascus, Syria. The port of Tarifa was charged for its use, thus the association of its name to a tax on trade - a tariff. Ironically, Spain calls a tariff an arancel.
907	The Byzantine Empire, the eastern half of the Roman Empire (907 to 911), was the first to introduce the origin of the goods, by applying preferential duty for goods originating in Russia.
1001	The Muziris Papyrus (Papyrus Vindobonensis G 40822), presently housed in the Vienna Museum, is a document that evidences Indo-Roman trade (India-Subcontinent and the Roman Empire) covering a transnational origin-to-destination supply chain secured by seals and validated by customs payment. [*See* 2001 and 2007.]
	This is argued to be evidence of the first Authorised Economic Operator (AEO) and the Customs Trade Partnership Against Terrorism (CTPAT), the two primary globally recognised standards that indicate a business' role in the international supply chain is secure.
1275	England is the first country to impose an export duty on goods that are exported.
1356	The Hanseatic League, in Central and Northern Europe (12th to 17th Century), created the first trade bloc. [*See* 1669.]

1453	The collapse of the Eastern Roman Empire, known as the Byzantine Empire. [*See* 907.]
1542	The Habsburg Council of State in The Netherlands proposed excise taxes on beer, wine, and wool. [*See* 1665 and 17th Century.]
August 1599	The '*Chambre de Commerce*' of Marseille, France, the first chamber of commerce and industry, or the acronym CCI, was established to defend the interests of trade and, consequently, the port. It was established by King Henry IV, after years of civil and religious war, to '*raise the kingdom's economy*'. [*See* 1919 and 19 June 1996.]
17th Century	Excise duty returns in the mid-17th Century in The Netherlands. [*See* 1542 and 1665.]
17th Century	The earliest modern-day reference to a transshipment port or an entrepôt, also known as a warehouse, is found in Amsterdam, The Netherlands. An entrepôt is a place where goods are imported, stored, to be exported again. The word '*entrepôt*' is derived from the Latin roots 'inter' meaning '*between*' and 'positum' meaning '*position*', which means '*that which is placed between*'. The term 'entrepôt' is also used to refer to duty-free ports.
1660	The practice of '*Old Subsidy*', essentially a preferential rate of duty, gives certain imported Colonial products a virtual monopoly in England, effectively starting a form of 'Colonial preference' for sugar.
1664	The '*Chambre de Commerce*' of Marseille (CCI), Marseille, France, after operating for 65 years, expanded in the Spanish Netherlands before spreading around the world.
1664	Customs duty, as a protective measure, was first employed by the French Finance Minister, Jean-Baptise Colbert (1619 to 1683).
1665	The Council of Policy in The Netherlands institutes an excise tax on retailed alcohol. [*See* 1542 and 17th Century.]
1669	The Hanseatic League, a medieval commercial alliance, was formally dissolved. [*See* 1356.]
18th Century	The Customs Tariff of Palmyra, as well as almost all the Nomenclatures in the West that were drawn up before the 18th Century, with the goods listed alphabetically.
5 June 1723	Adam Smith, '*the father of Economics*', was born in Kirkcaldy, Scotland. [*See* 9 March 1776 and 17 July 1790.]

1733	The British Prime Minister Robert Walpole (1676 to 1745) proposed a system to store tobacco and wine in warehouses to reduce fraud and make commerce easier. It was intended to obviate these difficulties and to put a check upon fraud on the revenue. The proposal was unpopular, and it was not until 1803 that the system was adopted. [*See* 1803.]
9 March 1776	The publication of Adam Smith's (1723 to 1790) book *An Inquiry into the Nature and Causes of the Wealth of Nations*, known as *The Wealth of Nations*. [*See* 5 June 1723 and 17 July 1790.]
17 July 1790	Adam Smith, '*the father of Economics*', dies in Edinburgh, Scotland. [*See* 5 June 1723 and 9 March 1776.]
1796	The word '*transhipment*' was first used in the late 1700s, and the earliest known example is from 1796 in the writing of W. Vaughan. The word is derived from the prefix trans and the noun shipment. In this context, an '*entrepôt*' is called a transshipment port.
15 July 1799	The Rosetta Stone was found by a French officer, Pierre-François Bouchard, during the Napoleonic campaign in Egypt. The stone is built into an old wall near the town of Rashid (Rosetta) in the Nile Delta. [*See* 196 BC and 1822.]
1803	The first customs warehouse system, conceptualised in 1733, was established in Great Britain, allowing for imported goods to be stored in customs-approved warehouses. Importers gave bonds to pay duties when the goods are removed from the customs warehouse. [*See* 1733.]
1812	The first Incoterm Free on Board (FOB) was used in British courts. [*See* 1895, 1923, 1936, 1953, 1967, 1976, 1 January 1980, 1 January 1990, 1 January 2000, 1 January 2010, and 1 January 2020.]
1818	At the close of the Napoleonic Wars, Germany was made up of 39 states, among them four city-states. As it had abolished its own internal tariff, Prussia began inviting individual states to eliminate tariffs. Through agreement, it set the foundation for Zollverein, which served to align the Prussian and Hohenzollern territories.

1822	The French Customs tariff grouped goods mainly according to their nature, such as live animals, flour, stone, earth and other minerals. This would later become the basis of the international Customs tariff nomenclature.
14 September 1822	Jean-François Champollion, who dedicated his life to studying historical languages, discovered how, using the Rosetta Stone, to read Egyptian hieroglyphs and unlock the secrets of the ancient civilisation. In the process, he solves one of history's greatest mysteries. [*See* 196 BC and 1799.]
1853	The modern-day tariff classification (Tariff Nomenclature) discussion commenced at the first International Statistical Congress and concluded with the 9th Conference in 1876. [*See* 1876.]
23 January 1860	The first Free Trade Agreement (FTA), the Cobden-Chevalier Treaty, was agreed between Great Britain and France, leading to successive agreements between other European countries. The treaty is considered to have sparked a '*free trade epidemic*' in Europe.
June 1863	The Paris Postal Conference, the first multilateral conference on international postal services, was arranged in Paris, France, by Montgomery Blair, then Postmaster General of the USA. This led to the Berne Conference of 1874, at which the Universal Postal Union (UPU) was founded. [*See* 9 October 1874, 1 July 1875, and 1948.]
9 October 1874	The Universal Postal Union (UPU) was established, through the signing of the Treaty of Berne. It is headquartered in Berne, Switzerland. It operated independently before being incorporated into the UN in 1948 [*See* June 1863 and 1 July 1875.]
1 July 1875	The Treaty of Berne officially came into effect. [*See* June 1863 and 9 October 1874.]
1876	The modern-day tariff classification (Tariff Nomenclature) discussion at the 9th International Statistical Congress concluded, the 1st having commenced in 1853. [*See* 1853.]

1883	The origins of WIPO go back to 1883 when the Paris Convention for the Protection of Industrial Property and to 1886 when the Berne Convention for the Protection of Literary and Artistic Works established an 'International Bureau'. The two bureaus were united in 1893 and, in 1970, were replaced by the WIPO by virtue of the WIPO Convention. [*See* 1893, 14 July 1967, 1970, and 26 April 1970.]
1889	The first Certificate of Origin (CoO) was issued by the Vienna Chamber of Commerce. Chambers of Commerce and Industry (CCI) have been the trusted issuers of CoO ever since. [*See* August 1599 and 1919.]
1889	The first Customs Union, the South African Customs Union, was established between the Orange River Colony and the Transvaal Colony. It later became known as the Southern African Customs Union (SACU). [*See* 1891.]
23 September 1889	The International Commercial Congress in Paris, France, commences with the question challenge on a Customs Nomenclature: '*Would it not be in the interest of all nations to adopt in their Customs tariffs and their official statistics' comparable classifications and uniform vocabularies?*' [*See* 28 September 1889.]
28 September 1889	The International Commercial Congress on a Customs Nomenclature in Paris, France, concluded. [*See* 23 September 1889.]
1890	The United States Congress passed the first anti-subsidy law, from what it views as '*unfair trade*', to offset the payments some European countries granted to sugar exporters. '*Anti-subsidy*' is also known as '*countervailing*'.
1891	Basutoland (*present-day Lesotho*) is admitted as a non-official South African Customs Union member.
25 May 1892	The Austria-Hungary tariff, which is similar to Brussels Nomenclature, is introduced.
1893	The origins of WIPO go back to 1883 when the Paris Convention for the Protection of Industrial Property and to 1886 when the Berne Convention for the Protection of Literary and Artistic Works established an '*International Bureau*'. The two bureaus were united in 1893 and, in 1970, were replaced by the WIPO by virtue of the WIPO Convention. [*See* 1883, 14 July 1967, 1970, and 26 April 1970.]

1893	The Central Office for International Carriage by Rail (OCTI), the predecessor of the Intergovernmental Organization for International Carriage by Rail (OTIF), was established. [*See* 1 May 1985.]
1 July 1893	Bechuanaland (*present-day Botswana*) was admitted as a non-official member of the Southern African Customs Union (SACU).
1894	The first anti-dumping legislation was designed to prevent foreign monopolies from restraining the United States of America (USA) domestic commerce.
1894	The Boer Republic of the South African Republic and Swaziland form a separate Customs Union – the Southern African Customs Union (SACU).
1895	The first Incoterm Free on Board (FOB) predates the International Chamber of Commerce (ICC) International Commercial Terms (Incoterms®) by 111 years, and so the second Cost, Insurance, and Freight (CIF) was introduced. [*See* 1812, 1923, 1928, 1936, 1953, 1967, 1976, 1980, 1990, 2000, 2010, and 2020.]
4 August 1898	The Alliance Internationale de Tourisme (AIT) was established. Its name was later changed to the Ligue Internationale des Associations Touristes (LIAT). [*See* 30 May 1919.]
1900	The creation of an international Temporary Admission (TA) scheme dates back to 1900 or 1913, depending on your reference. [*See* 1913.]
1902	The International Rail Transport Committee (CIT) was established. It is headquartered in Bern, Switzerland.
10 March 1903	Discussion of establishing the SACU commenced. It consisted of Cape Colony, Basutoland, Bechuanaland Protectorate, Natal, Orange River Colony, Transvaal Colony (*the former South African Republic*), and Southern Rhodesia.
May/June 1903	The SACU was signed on 6, 12 and 25 May, and on 3 June 1903 (Governments of the Cape Colony, the Colony of Natal, the Orange River Colony, the Transvaal Colony and Southern Rhodesia (present-day Zimbabwe), the Governor of the Cape Colony also signed on behalf of Basutoland (present-day Lesotho) and the Bechuanaland protectorate (present-day Botswana)).
20 June 1904	The Federation Internationale de l'Automobile was established. It is headquartered in Paris, France.

1904	Swaziland (*present-day Eswatini*) signed supplementary protocol to the SACU Agreement.
8 June 1904	Dumping legislation was first introduced in Canada, with New Zealand following similar legislation in 1905 and Australia in 1906.
1905	North-Western Rhodesia signed supplementary protocol to the SACU Agreement. [Northern Rhodesia is present-day Zambia.]
24 September 1905	The International Conference on World Economic Expansion convened in Mons, Belgium. The conferees indicated that they favoured an '*international entente*' (a type of informal agreement or understanding between nations) for the establishment of customs statistics in all lands according to a uniform classification of products.
29 September 1905	The International Conference on World Economic Expansion concluded in Mons, Belgium. The conferees indicated that they favoured an '*international entente*' (a type of informal agreement or understanding between nations) for the establishment of customs statistics in all lands according to a uniform classification of products.
26 February 1909	The '*International Convention on Prohibited Goods*': The First International Conference took place in Shanghai, the People's Republic of China.
29 June 1910	The SACU Agreement 1910 was signed, excluding the initial member Southern Rhodesia (present-day Zimbabwe).
1911	The Carnet de Passages en Douane (CPD) was created and entered into force in 1913. [*See* 5 July 1913.]
1913	The creation of an international Temporary Admission (TA) scheme dates back to 1913 or 1900, depending on your reference. [*See* 1900.]
5 July 1913	The CPD entered into use, having been created in 1911. The Fédération Internationale de l'Automobile FIA scanned the very first CPD. [*See* 1911.]
31 December 1913	Antecedents of the Brussels Nomenclature of 1913 are the earliest uniform statistical Nomenclature approved by the International Convention. It was signed in Brussels, Belgium.
28 July 1914	World War I (WW I) started. [*See* 11 November 1914.]

11 November 1918	WW I ended. The League of Nations (LN) was conceptualised at the Paris Peace Conference in France and was established on 10 January 1920. [*See* 28 July 1914.]
1919	The International Chamber of Commerce (ICC), known as the '*Merchants of Peace*', was established. It is headquartered in Paris, France. It presently represents over 45 million businesses in over 170 countries, with interests spanning every private enterprise sector. [*See* 1599, and 19 June 1996.]
30 May 1919	LIAT changed its name to the Alliance Internationale de Tourisme (AIT). It is headquartered in Geneva, Switzerland. [*See* 4 August 1898.]
28 June 1919	The enactment of the LN Covenant.
10 January 1920	The LN was established by the Paris Peace Conference. It is headquartered in Geneva, Switzerland. [*See* 11 November 1918, and 18 April 1946.]
15 November 1920	The LN 41 Member States gathered in Geneva, Switzerland, for the opening of its Assembly.
17 October 1922	The International Union of Railways (UIC) was established. It is headquartered in Paris, France.
30 December 1922	The Union of Soviet Socialist Republics, known as the USSR, was established, comprising a confederation of Russia, Belorussia, Ukraine and the Transcaucasian Federation, the latter of which, in 1936, was divided into the Georgian, Azerbaijan and Armenian republics. [*See* 30 December 1922, and 1936.]
1923	The International Convention relating to the Simplification of Customs Formalities, under the auspices of the LN, established the first rules on transactions between countries, storage of goods, and rules of origin (RoO). [*See* 28 July 1914, 11 November 1918, and 10 January 1920.]
1923	The ICC's first Incoterms® study, '*ICC's first sounding of commercial trade terms*', into the most commonly used trade terms (Incoterms®) and their disparities. [*See* 1812, 1895, 1928, 1936, 1953, 1967, 1976, 1980, 1990, 2000, 2010, and 2020.]
1923	The ICC International Court of Arbitration was established in Paris, France, as one of the most experienced and reputable institutions for international commercial arbitration. [*See* 1919.]

7 September 1923	The International Criminal Police Organization (INTERPOL) was established. It is headquartered in Lyon, France. [*See* 1998.]
3 November 1923	The LN '*International Convention relating to the Simplification of Customs Formalities*' was registered with the LN Secretariat.
27 November 1924	The LN '*International Convention relating to the Simplification of Customs Formalities*' entered into force.
31 May 1926	The International Federation of Freight Forwarders Associations (FIATA) was established. It is headquartered in Geneva, Switzerland.
4 May 1927	The LN organised the first World Economic Conference in response to the rise of protectionist trade barriers.
1928	The ICC's second Incoterms® study, '*Clarity improved*', examined the discrepancies with an expanded range of trade terms used in more than 30 countries. [*See* 1812, 1895, 1923, 1936, 1953, 1967, 1976, 1980, 1990, 2000, 2010, and 2020.]
1931	The LN's Sub-Committee of Experts for the Unification of Customs Tariff Nomenclature completed its '*Draft Customs Nomenclature*', commonly called the '*Geneva Nomenclature*'. [*See* 1 July 1937.]
1932	The British Imperial Preference was established. The trade policy involved the British Empire granting preferential treatment to its goods in its colonies. The policy was based on the idea that '*home producers first, empire producers second, and foreign producers last*' [*first established by the Byzantine Empire*].
1936	The first version of the Incoterms® rules, '*Global guidelines for traders*', was published. The rules of the interpretation for the first ICC Incoterms® consisted of six trade terms – Free Alongside Ship (FAS), Free on Board (FOB), Cost and Freight (C&F), Cost Insurance and Freight (CIF), Ex Ship and Ex Quay were published. [*See* 1812, 1895, 1923, 1928, 1953, 1967, 1976, 1 January 1980, 1 January 1990, 1 January 2000, 1 January 2010, and 1 January 2020.]
1936	The Transcaucasian Socialist Federative Soviet Republic, which existed under the USSR from 1922, comprising the Armenian, Azerbaijan, and Georgian Republics was dissolved. The individual Republics became separate constituent Republics of the USSR. [*See* 30 December 1922 and 26 December 1991.]

1 July 1937	The League of Nations (LN) revised version of the *'Draft Customs Nomenclature'* (Tariff Nomenclature), commonly called the Geneva Nomenclature, was issued but halted by WW II. [*See* 1931, 1938, 1 September 1939, and 2 September 1945.]
1938	The League of Nations (LN) published the report of its Committee of Statistical Experts, *'Minimum Lists of Commodities for International Trade Statistics'*. The Minimum List was based on the 1937 revision of the *'Draft Customs Nomenclature'* [*See* 1 July 1937, 1950.]
1 September 1939	WW II started. [*See* 2 September 1945.]
1 to 22 July 1944	The Bretton Woods Conference took place in Bretton Woods, New Hampshire, United States of America (USA).
22 July 1944	The World Bank Group (WBG) was established. It is headquartered in Washington, D.C., USA.
22 July 1944	The International Bank for Reconstruction and Development Bank (IBRD), known as the World Bank, was established. It is headquartered in Washington, D.C., USA.
22 July 1944	The International Monetary Fund (IMF) was established. It is headquartered in Washington, D.C., USA. [*See* 1 March 1947.]
7 December 1944	The Convention on International Civil Aviation (ICA) was signed as the Chicago Convention. [*See* 4 April 1947, 6 June 1945, and October 1947.]
19 April 1945	The International Air Transport Association (IATA) was established. It is headquartered in Quebec, Canada. [*See* 23 June 1986 and 20 June 1988.]
6 June 1945	The Provisional International Civil Aviation Organisation was established. It is headquartered in Montreal, Quebec, Canada. [*See* 7 December 1944, 4 April 1947, and October 1947.]
26 June 1945	The UN Economic and Social Council (ECOSOC) was established. It is headquartered in New York, USA. [*See* 28 March 1947.]
2 September 1945	WW II ends. [*See* 1 September 1939.]
24 October 1945	The UN was established. It is headquartered in New York, NY, USA. [*See* 10 January 1920 and 18 April 1946.]
16 November 1945	The UN Educational, Scientific and Cultural Organization (UNESCO) was established. It is headquartered in Paris, France.

1946	The ICC gained top-level consultative status with the UN and a close working relationship with its specialised agencies. [*See* August 1599, 1919, and 2016.]
1946	The inaugural session of the Preparatory Committee, meeting in Church House, London, UK was charged with creating an International Trade Organization (ITO). [*See* 21 November 1947, December 1947, and 24 March 1948.]
18 April 1946	The LN ceased its operations and was succeeded by the UN. [*See* 10 January 1920 and 24 October 1945.]
1947	Shannon Airport became the world's first duty-free airport. [*See* 1951 and 1959.]
23 February 1947	The International Organization for Standardization (ISO) was established. It is headquartered in Geneva, Switzerland.
1 March 1947	International Monetary Fund (IMF) commenced financial operations. [*See* 22 July 1944.]
28 March 1947	The UN Economic Commission for Europe (UNECE) was set up by the ECOSOC. It is headquartered in Geneva, Switzerland. [*See* 26 June 1945.]
April 1947	The General Agreement on Tariffs and Trade (GATT) first (Trade Round (Tariffs) commenced in Geneva, Switzerland (23 countries). [*See* October 1947.]
4 April 1947	The International Civil Aviation Organization (ICAO) was established. It is headquartered in Montreal, Quebec, Canada. [*See* 7 December 1944, 6 June 1945, 4 April 1947, and October 1947.]
23 August 1947	13 governments represented in the Committee for European Economic Cooperation set up a Study Group to examine the possibility of establishing one or more Customs Unions between the various European countries in accordance with the GATT principles.
October 1947	The GATT first Trade Round (Tariffs) concluded in Geneva, Switzerland, 1947 (23 countries). [*See* April 1947.]
October 1947	The ICAO became an Agency of the UN under its ECOSOL. It is headquartered in Montreal, Quebec, Canada. [*See* 4 December 1944, 7 December 1944, 6 June 1945, 4 April 1947, and October 1947.]
30 October 1947	The General Agreement on Tariffs and Trade (GATT) was signed by 23 countries in Geneva, France. It was never institutionalised. It is headquartered in Paris, France. [*See* 400 BC, 1 January 1948, and 1 January 1995.]

30 October 1947	Article VII of the GATT (Principles for Customs Valuation), known as the Customs Valuation Agreement (CVA), was signed and entered into force on 1 January 1948. The customs value is based on the actual value of the imported merchandise and where it is not ascertainable, such as no sale, use the nearest ascertainable equivalent. [*See* 1 January 1948, 15 December 1950, 1 January 1953, 28 July 1953, 5 September 1969, 1 November 1971, 12 September 1973, 12 April 1979, and 1 January 1995.]
10 November 1947	The Committee for European Economic Cooperation's Customs Union Study Group commenced its first meeting in Brussels, Belgium. The Group decided to examine the possibility of arriving at a common tariff. [*See* 14 November 1947.]
14 November 1947	The Committee for European Economic Cooperation's Customs Union Study Group concluded its first meeting in Brussels, Belgium. The Group decided to examine the possibility of arriving at a common tariff. [*See* 10 November 1947.]
21 November 1947	The UN Conference on Trade and Employment in Havana, Cuba, commenced. The purpose of the Conference was to establish the International Trade Organization (ITO). [*See* 1946 and 24 March 1948.]
1948	The Universal Postal Union (UPU) was incorporated into the UN. [*See* June 1863, 9 October 1874, and 1 July 1875.]
1948	The Committee for European Economic Cooperation's Study Group decided to establish two Committees: an Economic Committee, which later evolved into the Organisation for Economic Cooperation and Development (OECD), and a Customs Committee, which later became the Customs Cooperation Council (CCC). [*See* 30 September 1961 and 15 December 1950.]

1948	The European Customs Union Group continued to work on the Geneva Nomenclature (Tariff Nomenclature), with the result of a preliminary draft containing headings and subheadings being released in 1949. On 15 December 1950, the 1949 draft became the Brussels Convention on Nomenclature for the Classification of Goods in Customs Tariffs (CCCN), which was released and came into force on 11 September 1959, following the adoption on 1 July 1955 of a Protocol of Amendment establishing a revised version of the Nomenclature. [*See* 1882, 1 July 1937, 1 September 1939, 2 September 1945, 1949, 15 December 1950, 1 July 1955, and 11 September 1959.]
1 January 1948	GATT entered into force. It eventually led to the creation of the WTO. [*See* 30 October 1947, 1 January 1948, and 1 January 1995.]
1 January 1948	Article VII of GATT (Principles for Customs Valuation) entered into force. [*See* 400 BC, 30 October 1947, 15 December 1950, 1 January 1953, 28 July 1953, 5 September 1969, 1 November 1971, 12 September 1972, 12 April 1979, and 1 January 1995.]
12 March 1948	The International Road Transport Union (IRU) was established. It is headquartered in Geneva, Switzerland. [*See* 21 September 1987.]
24 March 1948	The UN Conference on Trade and Employment in Havana, Cuba, commenced. The purpose of the Conference is to establish the International Trade Organization (ITO). [*See* 1946 and 21 November 1947.]
7 April 1948	The World Health Organization (WHO) was established. It is headquartered in Geneva, Switzerland. [*See* July 2022.]
September 1948	The Study Group to establish a Customs Union in Europe met for the first time in Brussels, Belgium.
1949	The European Customs Union Group released its preliminary draft Geneva Nomenclature (Tariff Nomenclature) containing headings and subheadings. [*See* 1882, 1 July 1937, 1 September 1939, 2 September 1945, 15 December 1950, 1 July 1955, and 11 September 1959.]
April 1949	The GATT second Trade Round (Tariffs) commenced in Annecy, France (34 countries). [*See* August 1949.]
August 1949	The GATT second Trade Round (Tariffs) concluded in Annecy, France (34 countries). [*See* April 1949.]

1949	The Transports Internationaux Routiers or International Road Transports (TIR) Carnet and the TIR Agreement was concluded. [*See* 1959 and 1975.]
1950	The United Nations (UN) Secretariat drew up the 1950 SITC. [*See* 1 July 1937, 12 July 1950, and 1969.]
12 July 1950	The United Nations (UN) urged Governments to use the 1950 SITC. [*See* 1 July 1937, 1950, and 1969.]
September 1950	The GATT third Trade Round (Tariffs) commenced in Torquay, England (34 countries). [*See* April 1951.]
December 1950	The International Chamber of Commerce (ICC) established the World Chambers Federation (WCF). [*See* 1960 and 2001.]
15 December 1950	The Convention establishing the Customs Cooperation Council (CCC) (the official name of the WCO) was opened for ratification. [*See* 1948.]
15 December 1950	The Brussels Convention on Nomenclature for the Classification of Goods in Customs Tariffs, which was the 1949 draft, was released. The Tariff Nomenclature was initially known as the 'Brussels (Tariff) Nomenclature' (BTN), but in 1974, it was renamed as the 'Customs Co-operation Council Nomenclature' (CCCN). The BTN was set to come into force on 11 September 1959, following the adoption on 1 July 1955 of a Protocol of Amendment establishing a revised version of the Nomenclature. [*See* 1882 1948, 1949, 15 December 1950, 1 July 1955, 11 September 1959, and 1974.]
15 December 1950	The Convention on the Valuation of Goods for Customs Purposes was adopted in Brussels, Belgium in 1950 and opened for national signatures on 15 December 1950. It established a definition of value for customs purposes, known as the Brussels Definition of Value (BDV). [*See* 400 BC, 30 October 1947, 1 January 1948, 15 December 1950, 1 January 1953, 28 July 1953, 5 September 1969, 1 November 1971, 12 September 1973, 12 April 1979, and 1 January 1995.]
1951	Brendan O'Regan opened the world's first duty-free store at Shannon Airport. Initially, the store sold local produce, with everything from meat, eggs and butter to whiskeys and other spirits on offer. Though duty-free farm products did not catch on, alcohol sales proved to be an instant success with passengers. [*See* 1947 and 1959.]
April 1951	The GATT third Trade Round (Tariffs) concluded in Torquay, England (34 countries). [*See* September 1950.]

4 November 1952	The Convention establishing a Customs Cooperation Council (CCC) entered into force. Now known as the WCO. [*See* 22 June 1994.]
7 November 1952	THE '*International Convention to Facilitate the Importation of Commercial Samples and Advertising Material*' was adopted and entered into force on 20 November 1955.
1953	The second version and the first periodical review of the Incoterms® rules, '*Rise of transportation by rail*', was published following WWII. It debuts three new trade terms for non-maritime transport: DCP (Delivered Costs Paid), FOT (Free on Truck), and FOR (Free on Rail). It also sees the introduction of Ex-Works (EXW). [*See* 1812, 1895, 1923, 1928, 1953, 1967, 1976, 1 January 1980, 1 January 1990, 1 January 2000, 1 January 2010, 19 September 2019, and 1 January 2020.]
1 January 1953	The inaugural (first) CCC Council Session was held, with its 17 founding Members. [*See* 22 June 1994.]
1 January 1953	The first meeting of the CCC Permanent Technical Committee was held.
1 January 1953	The Convention on the Valuation of Goods for Customs Purposes, known as the BDV, which was signed on 15 December 1950, entered into force. It established a definition of value for customs purposes, known as the Brussels Definition of Value (BDV). [*See* 400 BC, 30 October 1947, 1 January 1948, 15 December 1950, 28 July 1953, 5 September 1969, 1 November 1971, 12 September 1973, 12 April 1979, and 1 January 1995.] [Note there is a dispute in the date, *see* 28 July 1953.]
26 January 1953	The CCC, now known as the WCO, was established. It is headquartered in Brussels, Belgium. The inaugural session of the CCC Council, attended by 17 European countries, was held in Brussels, Belgium. This date is now celebrated annually as International Customs Day. [*See* 22 June 1994 and 26 January.]
28 July 1953	The Convention on the Valuation of Goods for Customs Purposes, known as the BDV, which was signed on 15 December 1950, enters into force. It established a definition of value for customs purposes, known as the Brussels Definition of Value (BDV). [*See* 400 BC, 30 October 1947, 1 January 1948, 15 December 1950, 28 July 1953, 5 September 1969, 1 November 1971, 12 September 1973, 12 April 1979, and 1 January 1995.] [Note there is a dispute in the date, *see* 1 January 1953.]

10 April 1954	France is the first country to introduce a Value Added Tax (VAT), a consumption tax. VAT has largely replaced General Sales Tax, or Goods and Services Tax internationally, which shares the same acronym '*GST*'. One of the main differences between GST and VAT is that GST is a destination-based tax, while VAT is an origin-based tax. This means that GST is levied at the point of consumption, while VAT is levied at the point of origin. [*See 49 BC.*]
4 June 1954	The Customs Convention on the Temporary Importation of Private Road Vehicles was concluded in New York City, USA. The CPD Carnet de Passages en Douane is used within the legal framework of the UN Customs Convention of 1954 and 1956 on the temporary importation of private and commercial road vehicles and the '*Convention on Temporary Admission*', known as the Istanbul Convention (1990). [*See* 18 May 1956 and 26 June 1990.]
1 July 1955	The Convention on Nomenclature for the Classification of Goods in Customs Tariffs known as the Brussels Tariff Nomenclature or BTN, was adopted and came into force on 11 September 1955. [*See* 1882, 1948, 1949, 15 December 1950, 11 September 1959.]
November 1955	The International Association of Ports and Harbors (IAPH) was established. It is headquartered in Tokyo, Japan. [*See* 1987.]
20 November 1955	The '*International Convention to Facilitate the Importation of Commercial Samples and Advertising Material*' was introduced.
January 1956	The GATT fourth Trade Round (Tariffs) commenced in Geneva, Switzerland (22 countries). Japan participated for the first time. [*See* May 1956.]
May 1956	The GATT fourth Trade Round (Tariffs) concluded in Geneva, Switzerland (22 countries). Japan participated for the first time. [*See* January 1956.]
18 May 1956	The Customs Convention on the Temporary Importation of Commercial Road Vehicles entered into force. [*See* 4 June 1954.]
25 March 1957	The European Economic Community (EEC), also known as the European Common Market, was established with Belgium. France, Italy, Luxembourg, The Netherlands, and West Germany signed a Treaty in Rome, Italy. [*See* 1 January 1993.]

3 October 1957	The Customs Convention Regarding the E.C.S. Carnets for Commercial Samples entered into force.
17 March 1958	The International Maritime Organization (IMO) was established. It is headquartered in London, UK. [*See* 23 July 2022.]
1959	The first Customs Convention on the International Transport of Goods Under Cover of TIR Carnet came into effect. [*See* 1949 and 1975.]
1959	The first *'modern zone'*, the Shannon Free Zone (SFZ), was established at Shannon Airport in Ireland. The world's oldest Free Trade Zones (FTZs) were established on the Greek Island of Delos in 166 BC before pirates overran it in 69 BC. [*See* 166 BC, 69 BC, and 1947.]
11 September 1959	The BTN (Tariff Convention) entered into force, following the adoption, on 1 July 1955, of a Protocol of Amendment establishing a revised version of the Nomenclature for the Classification of Goods in Customs Tariffs. [*See* 1882, 1948, 1949, 15 December 1950.]
1960	The World Chambers Federation (WCF) changes its name to the International Bureau of Chambers of Commerce. [*See* 1950 and 2001.]
September 1960	The GATT fifth Trade Round (Tariffs) commenced in Geneva, Switzerland (45 countries). By then, the European Community (EC) had been set up. It is known as the Dillon Round, named after C Douglas Dillon, the USA Undersecretary of State and Treasury Secretary at the time. [*See* July 1961.]
1961	Due to the E.C.S. Carnet's success, the CCC adopted the '*Customs Convention on the ATA Carnet for the Temporary Admission of Goods*'.
1961	The Generalised System of Preferences (GSP) was proposed by India within the GATT.
18 April 1961	'*The Vienna Convention on Diplomatic Relations*' entered into force, requiring that receiving states must exempt diplomatic missions from customs duties, taxes, and related charges for items used for official purposes. [*See* 75 BC.]
July 1961	The GATT fifth Trade Round (Tariffs) concluded in Geneva, Switzerland (26 countries). Japan participates for the first time. By then, the European Community (EC) had been set up. It is known as the Dillon Round, named after C Douglas Dillon, the USA Undersecretary of State and Treasury Secretary at the time. [*See* September 1960.]

30 September 1961	The Organisation for Economic Cooperation and Development (OECD) was established. It is headquartered in Paris, France. [*See* 1948.]
15 March 1962	'*The Customs Convention on the Temporary Importation of Packings*' entered into force.
1 July 1962	'*The Customs Convention on the Temporary Importation of Professional Equipment*' entered into force.
13 July 1962	The '*Customs Convention concerning Facilities for the Importation of Goods for Display or Use at Exhibitions, Fairs, Meetings, or Similar Events*' entered into force.
30 July 1963	The '*Customs Convention on the ATA Carnet for the Temporary Admission of Goods*', commonly known as the '*ATA Convention*', entered into force.
19 March 1964	The International Trade Centre (ITC) was established. It is headquartered in Geneva, Switzerland. The ITC has a joint mandate with the WTO, formerly GATT, and the UN Conference on Trade and Development (UNCTAD).
23 March 1964	The first UNCTAD started to explore ways and means of granting special trade preferences to developing countries. The beginning of the Generalised System of Preferences (GSP).
May 1964	The GATT sixth Trade Round (Tariffs and Anti-Dumping Measures) commenced in Geneva, Switzerland (48 countries). It is known as the Kennedy Round, named after assassinated USA President John F. Kennedy. Trade Round. [*See* May 1967.]
16 June 1964	The first UNCTAD concluded by exploring ways and means of granting special trade preferences to developing countries. The beginning of the GSP.
30 December 1964	The UN Conference on Trade and Development (UNCTAD) was established. It is headquartered in Geneva, Switzerland. [*See* 2013 and 4 October 2022.]
1 January 1965	The CCCN (Tariff Nomenclature) first of three Recommendations was introduced. [*See* 1882, 15 December 1950, 1 July 1955, 11 September 1959, 1 January 1972, and 1 January 1978.]
11 December 1965	The Customs Convention concerning Welfare Material for Seafarers entered into force. It was established under the auspices of the CCC and in consultation with the International Labour Organisation (ILO). It ensures that import duties and taxes are suspended on such material and that import restrictions are refrained from.

20 June 1966	The World Federation of Pipe Line Industry Associations (WFPIA) was established. It is headquartered in Geneva, Switzerland.
17 December 1966	The UN Commission on International Trade Law (UNCITRAL) was established. It is headquartered in Vienna, Austria.
1967	The third iteration of the Incoterms® rules, '*Misinterpretations corrected*' and Delivery at Frontier (DAF) and Delivery at Destination (DDP), was published. The latter must not be confused with the present-day Delivered Duty Paid (DDP). [*See* 1812, 1895, 1923, 1928, 1936, 1953, 1976, 1980, 1990, 2000, 2010, and 2020.]
May 1967	The GATT sixth (6th) Trade Round (Tariffs and Anti-Dumping Measures) concluded in Geneva, Switzerland (48 countries). It is known as the Kennedy Round, named after assassinated US President John F. Kennedy. [*See* May 1967.]
14 July 1967	The World Intellectual Property Organization (WIPO) was established. It is headquartered in Geneva, Switzerland. [*See* 1883, 1893, 14 July 1967, 1970, and 26 April 1970.]
1968	The GSP, as a voluntary '*autonomous*' trade measure, was established through discussions within UNCTAD. It violates the MFN obligation of GATT and had to await a GATT waiver of this obligation, which came in 1971. [*See* 25 June 1971.]
1 July 1968	The EU Customs Union was established.
1969	The SITC revision, pursuant to a recommendation of the UN Statistical Commission, began. [*See* 1 July 1937, 1950, 12 July 1950.]
5 September 1969	The '*Customs Convention on the Temporary Importation of Scientific Equipment*' entered into force.
5 September 1969	The GATT Agreement on Customs Valuation, which established the basic framework for valuing goods for customs purposes, entered into force; it replaced the BDV. [*See* 400 BC, 30 October 1947, 15 December 1950, 1 January 1953, 28 July 1953, 5 September 1969, 12 September 1973, 12 April 1979, and 1 January 1995.]
27 November 1969	The International Association of Professional Customs Agents (ASAPRA) was established. It is headquartered in Montevideo, Uruguay.

1970	The CCC set up a Study Group to examine the possibility of preparing a Harmonized Commodity Description and Coding System (Tariff Nomenclature) capable of meeting the principal requirements of Customs authorities, statisticians, carriers and producers. The Study Group is also tasked to examine the '*Standard International Trade Classification*' (SITC) as a classification tool to be used by governments for their external trade statistics. The final Report was approved by the CCC in May 1973. [*See* May 1973.]
26 April 1970	The origins of WIPO go back to 1883 when the Paris Convention for the Protection of Industrial Property and to 1886 when the Berne Convention for the Protection of Literary and Artistic Works established an '*International Bureau*'. The two bureaus were united in 1893 and, in 1970, were replaced by the WIPO by virtue of the WIPO Convention, which was signed in Stockholm, Sweden. World Intellectual Property Day is celebrated annually on 26 April. The day was chosen as it coincides with the date on which the Convention Establishing the WIPO entered into force in 1970. [*See* 1883, 1893, and 14 July 1967.]
11 October 1970	The GSP was instituted in 1971 under the aegis of UNCTAD. Delegates of UNCTAD's Special Committee of Preference meeting in Geneva, Switzerland, reached a compromise on the GSP for developing countries' exports. In order to implement the system, a waiver was required from Article 1 of the GATT, which prohibits discrimination. This waiver was granted in 1971 by adopting the 'enabling clause' of the GATT to create the legal framework for the 'Generalized System of Tariff Preferences' (GSP). Under this framework, developed countries were authorised to establish individual Generalised Schemes of Tariff Preferences or GSP. The enabling clause was adopted originally for 10 years and renewed on 28 November 1979 for an indefinite period of time thereafter. [*See* 1968 and 25 June 1971.]
25 June 1971	The European Community (EC), present-day EU, was the first to implement its GSP scheme. [*See* 1968 and 11 October 1970.]

1 November 1971	The GATT Valuation Code Protocol came into effect. It is a significant step in international trade, aiming to standardise the valuation of goods for customs purposes. The Protocol established the principle that customs valuation should be based on the actual value of goods, ensuring fair and consistent trade practices. [*See* 400 BC, 30 October 1947, 15 December 1950, 1 January 1953, 28 July 1953, 5 September 1969, 12 September 1973, 12 April 1979, and 1 January 1995.]
10 December 1971	*The 'Customs Convention on the Temporary Importation of Pedagogic Material'* entered into force.
1972	The *'WCO Handbook Customs Convention on Containers, 1972'* was released. [*See* 6 December 1975.]
1 January 1972	The CCCN (Tariff Nomenclature) second of three Recommendations was introduced. [*See* 1882, 15 December 1950, 1 July 1955, 11 September 1959, 1 January 1965, and 1 January 1978.]
3 March 1973	The Convention on International Trade in Endangered Species of Wild Fauna and Flora (CITES) was established. It is headquartered in Geneva, Switzerland. [*See* 1 July 1995.]
January 1973	The International Convention on the Simplification and Harmonization of Customs Procedures, known as the Kyoto Convention, replaced the LN Convention. The Convention was adopted on 19 May 1973 and entered into force on 25 September 1974. [*See* January 1920, 19 May 1973, 25 September 1974, June 1999, and 3 February 2006.]
3 March 1973	The Convention on International Trade in Endangered Species of Wild Fauna and Flora (CITES) was established. It is headquartered in Geneva, Switzerland. [*See* 1 July 1975.]
May 1973	The CCC Study Group (Tariff Nomenclature) Final Report was approved by the CCC, which concluded that the development of an HS Commodity Description and Coding System is not only feasible but also essential in the longer-term interests of facilitating international trade. [*See* 1970.]
May 1973	The CCC establishes a Harmonized Systems Committee to prepare the HS. [*See* 1970, May 1973, and 1981.]
19 May 1973	The Kyoto Convention was adopted and entered into force on 25 September 1974. [*See* 25 September 1974.]

12 September 1973	The GATT seventh Trade Round (Tariffs, Non-tariff Measures, Plurilateral Agreements) commenced in Tokyo, Japan (102 countries). It was known as the Tokyo Round, and it was the first time held outside of Europe. [*See* 12 April 1979.]
12 September 1973	The Tokyo Round Valuation Code established a customs valuation system based on the price actually paid or payable for imported goods, known as the '*transaction value*'. [*See* 400 BC, 30 October 1947, 15 December 1950, 1 January 1953, 28 July 1953, 5 September 1969, 12 April 1979, and 1 January 1995.] [The Tokyo Round took place from 12 September 1973 to 12 April 1979.]
12 September 1973	The WTO Ministerial Meeting hosted in Tokyo, Japan, commenced. [*See* 14 September 1973.]
14 September 1973	The WTO Ministerial Meeting hosted in Tokyo, Japan, concluded. [*See* 12 September 1973.]
1 January 1974	The BTN (Tariff Nomenclature) was renamed Customs Cooperation Council Nomenclature (CCCN). It comprises 1,241 headings, divided among 96 Chapters, arranged into 21 Sections. The CCCN was updated with three Recommendations. [*See* 1882, 15 December 1950, 1 July 1955, 11 September 1959, 1 January 1965, 1 January 1972, and 1 January 1978.]
25 September 1974	The '*International Convention on the Simplification and Harmonisation of Customs Procedures*', known as the '*Kyoto Convention*', entered into force.
1 July 1975	CITES entered into force. [*See* 3 March 1973.]
14 November 1975	The second Customs Convention on the International Transport of Goods Under Cover of TIR Carnet came into effect. [*See* 1949, 1959, and 6 December 1975.]
6 December 1975	The '*Customs Convention on Containers*' entered into force. [*See* 1972 and 14 November 1975.]
1976	The fourth version of the Incoterms® rules, 'Advances in air travel', was published. It is published due to the increased use of air transportation, which includes the new term 'FOB Airport' or 'FOBA' (Free on Board Airport) aimed to address confusion around the term 'FOB' (Free on Board) by signifying the exact 'vessel' used. [*See* 1812, 1895, 1923, 1928, 1936, 1953, 1967, 1 January 1980, 1 January 1990, 1 January 2000, 1 January 2010, 19 September 2019, and 1 January 2020.]

July 1976	The OECD published its first Transfer Pricing Guidelines. These are voluntary guidelines for multilateral enterprises. [*See* 30 September 1961.]
August 1976	The stone on which the text of the Lex Portorii Asiae (Customs Law of Asia) is inscribed was found during work in the Church of Saint John in Selçuk, Türkiye. It was displayed in the courtyard of the Ephesus Archaeological Museum. The Lex Portorii Asiae is concerned with the customs dues of the Roman province of Asia from 75 BC to AD 62 and contains a provision for the exemption from customs due (import dues) for conveyances in the course of transit and customs due exemptions in Pergamene harbour in light of what Caesar Augustus 'decided and conceded or replied to the ambassadors'. [*See* 75 BC and August 1976.]
9 June 1977	The Nairobi Convention on Mutual Administrative Assistance was signed. [*See* 21 May 1980.]
1 January 1978	The CCCN (Tariff Nomenclature) second of three Recommendations was introduced. [*See* 1882, 15 December 1950, 1 July 1955, 11 September 1959, 1 January 1965, and 1 January 1972.]
12 April 1979	The GATT seventh Trade Round (Tariffs, Non-tariff Measures, Plurilateral Agreements) concluded in Tokyo, Japan (102 countries). It was known as the Tokyo Round, and it was the first time held outside of Europe. [*See* 12 September 1973.]
12 April 1979	The Tokyo Round Valuation Code established a customs valuation system based on the price actually paid or payable for imported goods, known as the '*transaction value*'. [*See* 400 BC, 30 October 1947, 15 December 1950, 1 January 1953, 28 July 1953, 5 September 1969, 1973 to 1979, and 1 January 1995.] [The Tokyo Round took place from 12 September 1973 to 12 April 1979.]
28 November 1979	The GSP enabling clause was renewed, and a permanent GATT most-favoured-nation (MFN) waiver was granted. The waiver was to expire after 10 years, but the authority for preferences was extended by the GATT Contracting Parties' Decision of 28 November 1979 on Differential and More Favourable Treatment, Reciprocity and Fuller Participation of Developing Countries, popularly known as the '*Enabling Clause*'. [*See* 1968, 12 September 1973, and 12 September 1979.]

1 January 1980	The fifth version of the Incoterms® rules, *'Proliferation of container traffic'*, the first of the now customary decade review of Incoterms®, was published. The addition of two new Incoterms® – Free Carrier, called FRC, now FCA, and Freight Cost and Insurance (FCI), now Carriage and Insurance Paid To (CIP). There are 14 Incoterms®. [*See* 1812, 1895, 1923, 1928, 1936, 1953, 1967, 1976, 1 January 1990, 1 January 2000, 1 January 2010, and 1 January 2020.]
21 May 1980	The Convention on Mutual Administrative Assistance in the Prevention, Repression and Investigation of Customs Offences (Nairobi Convention) entered into force. [*See* 9 June 1977.]
1980	The WCO Technical Committee on Customs Valuation (TCCV) was established by the Tokyo Round Agreement on Customs Valuation. [*See* 400 BC, 30 October 1947, 15 December 1950, 1 January 1953, 28 July 1953, 5 September 1969, 1 November 1971 and 1973 to 1979.]
1981	The CCC Harmonized Systems Committee (Tariff Nomenclature) completed the preparatory work of the entire HS.
1981	The Automated System for Customs Data (ASYCUDA) programme at the UN Conference on Trade and Development (UNCTAD) was established. It is headquartered in Geneva, Switzerland.
1 January 1981	The GATT Valuation Code entered into force. [*See* 1 January 1995.]
1982	The International Federation of Inspection Agencies (IFIA), presently the TIC Council, was established. It is headquartered in Brussels, Belgium. [*See* 10 March 2019.]
1983	The Global Express Association (GEA) was established. It is headquartered in Geneva, Switzerland.
May 1983	The CCC Harmonized Systems Committee and its Working Party (Tariff Nomenclature) hold their 31st and last Session, resulting in the completion of the 'Harmonized Commodity Description and Coding System' and the establishment of a new international Convention (Harmonized System Convention) for its implementation. [*See* 14 June 1983.]

14 June 1983	The International Convention on the Harmonized Commodity Description and Coding System, also known as the Harmonized System Convention, which replaced the CCCN, previously known as the BTN, was signed in Brussels, Belgium. [*See* 1974, 14 May 1983, 1 January 1965, and 1 January 1988.]
1 May 1985	The Intergovernmental Organization for International Carriage by Rail (OTIF) was established, replacing OCTI. It is headquartered in Berne, Switzerland [*See* 1893.]
23 June 1986	IATA and the WCO signed an MoU. [*See* 19 April 1945 and 20 June 1988.]
20 September 1986	The GATT 8th Trade Round (Tariffs, Non-tariff Measures (NTMs), Rules, Services, Intellectual Property, Dispute Settlement, Textiles, Agriculture, creation of the WTO, etc.) commenced in Geneva, Switzerland (123 countries). It was known as the Uruguay Round. [*See* 15 December 1993.]
1987	The IAPH and the WCO signed an MoU. [*See* November 1955.]
January 1987	The original intention of the CCC was to implement the HS Convention (Tariff Nomenclature), but a new target date was set for 1 January 1988. [*See* 1 January 1988.]
21 September 1987	The IRU and the WCO signed an MoU. [*See* 12 March 1948.]
1 January 1988	The HS Nomenclature 1988 Edition entered into force, replacing the CCCN. [*See* 1 January 1987, 1 January 1992, 1 January 1996, 1 January 2002, 1 January 2007, 1 January 2012, 1 January 2017, 1 January 2022, 1 January 2027, and 1 January 2028.]
1 January 1988	The first meeting of the HS Committee took place.
13 April 1988	The Global System of Trade Preferences (GSTP) among Developing Countries, negotiated with the United Nations Conference on Trade and Development (UNCTAD) framework, was signed.
20 June 1988	IATA and the WCO signed an MoU. [*See* 19 April 1945 and 23 June 1986.]

1 January 1990	The sixth version of the Incoterms®, '*A complete revision*', which led to the simplification of FCA to include by deletion of FOR, FOT and FOBA Airport and consideration for the increased use of Electronic Data Interchange (EDI). The Incoterms® formats of the 13 Incoterms® had been simplified, and clarity was provided on the customs clearance responsibility. [*See* 1812, 1895, 1923, 1928, 1936, 1953, 1967, 1976, 1 January 1980, 1 January 2000, 1 January 2010, and 1 January 2020.]
26 June 1990	The Convention on Temporary Admission (TA) was signed in Istanbul, Türkiye/ [*See* 4 June 1954.]
1990	The International Air Cargo Association (TIACA) was established. It is headquartered in Miami, Florida, USA. [*See* 25 June 2010.]
November 1990	The International Federation of Customs Brokers Associations (IFCBA) was established. It is headquartered in Ottawa, Ontario, Canada. [*See* 25 June 1990.]
26 December 1991	The USSR was formally dissolved as a sovereign state. [*See* 30 December 1922 and 1936.]
1 January 1992	The HS Nomenclature 1992 Edition, the first Revision, entered into force. [*See* 1 January 1987, 1 January 1988, 1 January 1996, 1 January 2002, 1 January 2007, 1 January 2012, 1 January 2017, 1 January 2022, 1 January 2027, and 1 January 2028.]
January 1993	The EU Single Market, formerly known as the European Common Market, was established. It guarantees the free movement of goods, services, people, and capital (the '*four freedoms*') within the EU. [*See* 25 March 1957.]
3 July 1993	The adoption of the Arusha Declaration concerning Integrity in Customs. [*See* 27 June 2003.]
27 November 1993	The Convention on Temporary Admission (Istanbul Convention) entered into force.
15 December 1993	The GATT eighth Trade Round (Tariffs, Non-tariff Measures, Rules, Services, Intellectual Property, Dispute Settlement, Textiles, Agriculture, creation of the WTO, etc.) concluded in Geneva, Switzerland (102 countries). It was known as the Uruguay Round. [*See* 20 September 1986.]
1993	Adoption of the Arusha Declaration concerning Integrity in Customs.

22 June 1994	The CCC adopted the WCO as the working name (informal name) to better reflect the worldwide nature of the Organization. [*See* 26 January 1953 and 4 November 1952.]
15 April 1994	The Uruguay Round concluded, seven years after the Round began, resulting in GATT going out of existence. [*See* 1 January 1995.]
1 January 1995	The WTO was established. It is headquartered in Geneva, Switzerland. [*See* 30 October 1947, 1 January 1948, and 15 April 1994.]
1 January 1995	The WTO Agreement on Origin entered into force.
20 July 1995	The negotiations for Harmonised Non-Preferential RoO at the WTO commenced. [*See* July 2007.]
1 January 1995	The first meeting of the WCO Technical Committee on RoO, following the WTO Agreement on RoO entry into force.
1 January 1995	The WTO Customs Valuation Agreement came into effect. [*See* 400 BC, 30 October 1947, 15 December 1950, 1 January 1953, 28 July 1953, 5 September 1969, 1 November 1971 and 1973 to 1979.]
1 January 1995	The first meeting of the WCO Technical Committee on Customs Valuation, following the entry into force of the WTO Agreement on Customs Valuation. [*See* 400 BC, 30 October 1947, 15 December 1950, 1 January 1953, 28 July 1953, 5 September 1969, 1 November 1971 and 1973 to 1979.]
1 January 1996	The HS Nomenclature 1996 Edition, the second Revision, entered into force. [*See* 1 January 1987, 1 January 1988, 1 January 1992, 1 January 2002, 1 January 2007, 1 January 2012, 1 January 2017, 1 January 2022, 1 January 2027, and 1 January 2028.]
19 June 1996	The ICC and the WCO signed an MoU. [*See* August 1599 and 1919.]
9 December 1996	The WTO's first Ministerial Conference (MC1) commenced in Singapore.
13 December 1996	The WTO MC1 concluded in Singapore.
1998	INTERPOL and the WCO signed an MoU. [*See* 7 September 1923.]
1998	The WCO's establishment of the Tariff and Trade Affairs Directorate, through the merger of the Nomenclature Directorate and the Valuation Directorate.

18 May 1998	The GATT, the Multilateral Trading System, celebrated its 50th anniversary.
18 May 1998	The WTO's second Ministerial Conference (MC2) commenced in Geneva, Switzerland.
20 May 1998	The WTO MC2 concluded in Geneva, Switzerland.
1 January 1999	The EU launched the Euro, which is now the official currency of 20 of the 27 EU Member States.
26 June 1999	The WCO Council adopted the '*revised International Convention on the Simplification and Harmonisation of Customs Procedures*', known as the Revised Kyoto Convention, abbreviated to RKC, which entered into force on 3 February 2003. [*See* 1999 and 3 February 2003.]
30 November 1999	The WTO's third Ministerial Conference (MC3) commenced in Seattle, United States of America.
3 December 1999	The WTO MC3 concluded in Seattle, United States of America.
1 January 2000	The seventh version of the Incoterms® rules, '*Amended customs clearance obligations*', was published. The FAS and DEQ Incoterms® rules were modified to comply with how most customs authorities address the issues of Exporter of Record (EOR) and Importer of Record (IOR). [*See* 1812, 1895, 1923, 1928, 1936, 1953, 1967, 1976, 1 January 1980, 1 January 1990, 1 January 2010, 19 September 2019, and 1 January 2020.]
July 2000	The Customs Enforcement Network (CEN) became operational.
November 2001	The Customs-Trade Partnership Against Terrorism (CTPAT) was launched shortly after the 9/11 attacks - 11 September 2001. The USA Customs and Border Protection (CBP) administered the programme. [*See* 1001 and 2007.]
June 2001	The International Bureau of Chambers of Commerce changed its name to the World Chambers Federation. [*See* 1599 August, 1919, 1950, December, and 1960.]
6 July 2001	The WTO Public Forum '*Symposium on issues confronting the world trading system*' commenced.
7 July 2001	The WTO Public Forum '*Symposium on issues confronting the world trading system*' concluded.

November 2001	The GATT ninth Trade Round (Tariffs, non-tariff measures (NTMs), agriculture, labour standards, environment, competition, investment, transparency, patents) commenced in Doha, Qatar (159 countries). It was known as the Doha Round. The Trade Round was yet to conclude.
9 November 2001	The WTO's fourth Ministerial Conference (MC4) commenced in Doha, Qatar.
13 November 2001	The WTO MC4 concluded in Doha, Qatar.
1 January 2002	The HS Nomenclature 2002 Edition, the third Revision, entered into force. [*See* 1 January 1987, 1 January 1988, 1 January 1992, 1 January 1996, 1 January 2007, 1 January 2012, 1 January 2017, 1 January 2022, 1 January 2027, and 1 January 2028.]
29 April 2002	The WTO Public Symposium (now called Public Forum) '*The Doha Development Agenda and Beyond*' commenced.
1 May 2002	The WTO Public Symposium (now called Public Forum) '*The Doha Development Agenda and Beyond*' concluded.
July 2002	The WHO and the WCO signed an MoU. [*See* 7 April 1948.]
23 July 2002	The IMO and the WCO signed an MoU. [*See* 17 March 1958.]
2003	The WCO Council adopted the Convention on Mutual Administrative Assistance in Customs Matters (Johannesburg Convention).
3 February 2003	The '*revised International Convention on the Simplification and Harmonisation of Customs Procedures*', simply known as the Revised Kyoto Convention, and abbreviated to RKC, entered into force.
16 June 2003	The WTO Public Symposium (now called Public Forum) '*Challenges ahead on the Road to Cancun*' commences.
18 June 2003	The WTO Public Symposium (now called Public Forum) '*Challenges Ahead on the Road to Cancun*' concluded.
27 June 2003	The adoption of the Revised Arusha Declaration. [*See* 3 July 1993.]
10 September 2003	The WTO fifth (5th) Ministerial Conference (MC5) commenced in Cancún, Mexico.
14 September 2003	The WTO MC5 concluded in Cancún, Mexico.
26 January 2004	International Customs Day theme '*Role of Customs in the Protection of Society*'.

25 May 2004	The WTO Public Forum '*Multilateralism at a Crossroads*' commenced.
27 May 2004	The WTO Public Forum '*Multilateralism at a Crossroads*' concluded.
20 April 2005	The WTO Public Symposium (now called Public Forum) '*WTO After 10 Years: Global Problems and Multilateral Solutions*' commenced.
22 April 2005	The WTO Public Symposium (now called Public Forum) '*WTO After 10 Years: Global Problems and Multilateral Solutions*' concluded.
25 June 2005	The adoption of the first version of the SAFE Framework (Standards to **S**ecure **a**nd **F**acilitate Global Trad**e**). The AEO programme was part of the SAFE, which was adopted by the WCO Council.
July 2005	The International Network of Customs Universities (INCU) was established. It is headquartered in Barton, Australian Capital Territory (ACT), Australia. [*See* 30 September 2009.]
13 December 2005	The WTO's sixth Ministerial Conference (MC6) commenced in Hong Kong, China
18 December 2005	The WTO MC6 concluded in Hong Kong, China
2006	The WCO HS '*Customs Compendium*' series was published.
2006	The WCO and the OECD held a joint '*Conference on Transfer Pricing and Customs Valuation*' in Brussels, Belgium. [*See* 2007.]
January 2006	The WCO launched the Columbus Programme, the largest ever Customs capacity-building initiative focused on promoting customs modernisation and supporting the implementation of the Framework Standards to **S**ecure **a**nd **F**acilitate Global Trad**e** (SAFE). [*See* 28 June 2014.]
26 January 2006	International Customs Day theme '*Safer World Trade through Security and Facilitation*'.
3 February 2006	The '*Revised Kyoto Convention on the Simplification and Harmonisation of Customs Procedures*', abbreviated to RKC, entered into force following its adoption on 26 June 1999. [*See* 26 June 1999.]
March 2006	The Standard International Trade Classification (SITC) Revision 4 was accepted by the United Nations (UN) Statistical Commission at its 37th session.

1-3 March 2006	The launch of the Partnerships in Customs Academic Research and Development (PICARD) at its first Conference held at the WCO headquarters in Brussels, Belgium.
30-31 March 2006	First meeting of the Private Sector Consultative Group (PSCG), its establishment having been agreed at the WCO Council's June 2005 annual sessions in Brussels, Belgium.
25 September 2006	The WTO Public Forum '*What WTO for the XXIst Century?*' commenced.
26 September 2006	The WTO Public Forum '*What WTO for the XXIst Century?*' concluded.
2007	The WCO and the OECD held a joint '*Conference on Transfer Pricing and Customs Valuation*' in Brussels, Belgium. [*See* 2006.]
2007	The WCO launched the Authorized Economic Operators (AEO) programme in 2007. The AEO programme is a voluntary accreditation programme that aims to strengthen supply chain security, safety, and compliance. [*See* 1001, 2001, and 25 June 2005.]
1 January 2007	The HS Nomenclature 2007 Edition, the fourth Revision, entered into force. [*See* 1 January 1987, 1 January 1988, 1 January 1992, 1 January 1996, 1 January 2002, 1 January 2012, 1 January 2017, 1 January 2022, 1 January 2027, and 1 January 2028.]
26 January 2007	International Customs Day theme '*No to Counterfeiting and Piracy*'.
27 March 2007	*The World Customs Journal*, a peer-reviewed academic journal published twice a year, was launched at the WCO's second annual PICARD conference, held in Brussels, Belgium.
July 2007	Negotiations for Harmonised Non-Preferential RoO at the WTO were halted. [*See* 20 July 1995.]
4 October 2007	The WTO Public Forum '*How the WTO can help harness globalization?*' commenced.
5 October 2007	The WTO Public Forum '*How the WTO can help harness globalization?*' concluded.
26 January 2008	International Customs Day theme '*Combating Illicit Trafficking in Drugs and Psychotropic Substances*'.
24 September 2008	The WTO Public Forum '*Trading into the Future*' commenced.
25 September 2008	The WTO Public Forum '*Trading into the Future*' concluded.

26 January 2009	International Customs Day theme '*Environment*'.
28 September 2009	The WTO Public Forum '*Global Problems, Global Solutions: Towards Better Global Governance*' commenced.
30 September 2009	The WTO Public Forum '*Global Problems, Global Solutions: Towards Better Global Governance*' concluded.
30 September 2009	INCU and the WCO signed an MoU.
30 November 2009	The WTO's seventh Ministerial Conference (MC7) commenced in Geneva, Switzerland.
2 December 2009	The WTO MC7 concluded in Geneva, Switzerland.
1 January 2010	The eighth iteration of Incoterms® rules, '*Reflections on the contemporary trade landscape*', was published. The iteration eliminated four terms – Delivered at Frontier (DAF), Delivered Ex Ship (DES), Delivered Ex Quay (DEQ) and Delivered Duty Unpaid (DDU) – and added two Incoterms® – adding Delivered at Terminal (DAT) and Delivered at Place (DAP). There are 11 Incoterms®. [*See* 1812, 1895, 1923, 1928, 1936, 1953, 1967, 1976, 1980, 1990, 2000, and 2020.]
26 January 2010	International Customs Day theme '*Customs-Business Partnerships*'.
13 April 2010	The WCO celebrated 30 years of Customs Valuation.
25 June 2010	The IFCBA and the WCO signed an MoU. [*See* November 1990.]
25 June 2010	The TICA and the WCO signed an MoU. [*See* 1990.]
15 September 2010	The WTO Public Forum '*The Forces Shaping World Trade*' commenced.
17 September 2010	The WTO Public Forum '*The Forces Shaping World Trade*' concluded.
26 January 2011	International Customs Day theme '*Knowledge*'.
19 September 2011	The WTO Public Forum '*Seeking answers to global trade challenges*' commenced.
21 September 2011	The WTO Public Forum '*Seeking answers to global trade challenges*' concluded.
16 November 2011	The GATT ninth Trade Round (Tariffs, non-tariff measures, agriculture, labour standards, environment, competition, investment, transparency, patents) failed (159 countries). It was known as the Doha Round.
15 December 2011	The WTO eighth Ministerial Conference (MC8) commenced in Geneva, Switzerland.
17 December 2011	The WTO MC8 concluded in Geneva, Switzerland.

1 January 2012	The HS Nomenclature 2012 Edition, the fifth Revision, entered into force. [*See* 1 January 1987, 1 January 1988, 1 January 1992, 1 January 1996, 1 January 2002, 1 January 2007, 1 January 2017, 1 January 2022, 1 January 2027, and 1 January 2028.]
26 January 2012	International Customs Day theme '*Connectivity*'.
28 September 2012	The International Chamber of Commerce (ICC) World Chambers Federation (WCF) launched the International Certificates of Origin (CoO) Chain.
24 September 2012	The WTO Public Forum '*Is Multilateralism in Crisis?*' commenced.
26 September 2012	The WTO Public Forum '*Is Multilateralism in Crisis?*' concluded.
2013	The WCO and UNCTAD, on 4 October 2022, signed an MoU, updating the MoU between the two organisations dating back to 2013. [*See* 17 December 1966 and 4 October 2022.]
26 January 2013	International Customs Day theme '*Innovation*'.
June 2013	The recommendation concerning Customs formalities in connection with the temporary admission of container security devices (CDSs) was adopted.
1 October 2013	The WTO Public Forum '*Expanding Trade through Innovation and the Digital Economy*' commenced.
3 October 2013	The WTO Public Forum '*Expanding Trade through Innovation and the Digital Economy*' concluded.
3 December 2013	The WTO's ninth Ministerial Conference (MC9) commenced in Bali, Indonesia.
6 December 2013	The WWTO MC9 concluded in Bali, Indonesia.
7 December 2013	The WTO Trade Facilitation Agreement (TFA) was signed as the first multilateral trade agreement since the founding of the WTO. [*See* 1 January 1995 and 11 December 2013.]
11 December 2013	The WCO Dublin Resolution on the conclusion of the WTO TFA was adopted by the WCO. [*See* 1 January 1995 and 7 December 2013.]
26 January 2014	International Customs Day theme '*Communication*'.
19 May 2014	The World Free Zones Organization (WFZO) was established. It is headquartered in Dubai, United Arab Emirates (UAE).
28 June 2014	Launch of the Mercator Programme to support the implementation of the WTO Trade Facilitation Agreement (TFA). [*See* January 2006.]

1 October 2014	The Public Forum *'Why trade matters to everyone'* commenced.
3 October 2014	The WTO Public Forum *'Why trade matters to everyone'* concluded.
26 January 2015	International Customs Day theme *'Coordinated Border Management'*.
30 September 2015	The WTO Public Forum *'Trade Works'* commenced.
2 October 2015	The WTO Public Forum *'Trade Works'* concluded.
10 December 2015	Punta Cana Resolution on the Role of Customs in the Security Context.
15 December 2015	The WTO's 10th Ministerial Conference (MC10) commenced in Nairobi, Kenya.
18 December 2015	The GATT ninth Trade Round (Tariffs, NTMs, agriculture, labour standards, environment, competition, investment, transparency, patents), the Doha Round (159 countries), was declared dead by the WTO.
19 December 2015	The WTO MC10 concluded in Nairobi, Kenya.
21 December 2015	The GATT ninth Trade Round (Tariffs, non-tariff measures, agriculture, labour standards, environment, competition, investment, transparency, patents) failed (159 countries). It was known as the Doha Round.
26 January 2016	International Customs Day theme *'Digital Customs'*.
16 July 2016	The WCO's Council Resolution on the Role of Customs in Preventing Illicit Trafficking of Cultural Objects was adopted.
27 September 2016	The WTO Public Forum 'Inclusive Trade' commenced.
29 September 2016	The WTO Public Forum *'Inclusive Trade'* concluded.
13 December 2016	The ICC was granted Observer Status by 193 members of the UN General Assembly. [*See* 1 January 2017.]
1 January 2017	The ICC took up its position as Observer to the General Assembly. [*See* 13 December 2016.]
1 January 2017	The HS Nomenclature 2017 Edition, the sixth Revision, entered into force. [*See* 1 January 1987, 1 January 1988, 1 January 1992, 1 January 1996, 1 January 2002, 1 January 2007, 1 January 2012, 1 January 2022, 1 January 2027, and 1 January 2028.]
26 January 2017	International Customs Day theme *'Data Analysis'*.
22 February 2017	The WTO Trade Facilitation Agreement (TFA) entered into force.
26 September 2017	The WTO Public Forum *'Trade: Behind the Headlines'* commenced.

28 September 2017	The WTO Public Forum '*Trade: Behind the Headlines*' concluded.
10 December 2017	The WTO 11th Ministerial Conference (MC11) commenced in Buenos Aires, Argentina.
13 December 2017	The WTO MC11 concluded in Buenos Aires, Argentina.
26 January 2018	International Customs Day theme '*A secure business environment*'.
30 June 2018	Adoption of the Framework of Standards on Cross-Border E-Commerce.
2 October 2018	The WTO Public Forum '*Trade 2030*' commenced.
4 October 2018	The WTO Public Forum '*Trade 2030*' concluded.
8 October 2019	The WTO Public Forum '*Trading Forward: Adapting to a Changing World*' commenced.
11 October 2019	The WTO Public Forum '*Trading Forward: Adapting to a Changing World*' concluded.
26 January 2019	International Customs Day theme '*SMART borders*'.
10 March 2019	The TIC Council replaced the International Federation of Inspection Agencies (IFIA). It is headquartered in Brussels, Belgium. [*See* 1982.]
19 September 2019	Incoterms® 2020 was launched but entered into force on 1 January 2020. [*See* 1812, 1895, 1923, 1928, 1936, 1953, 1967, 1976, 1 January 1980, 1 January 1990, 1 January 2000, 1 January 2010, and 1 January 2020.]
1 January 2020	The ninth iteration of Incoterms® rules, '*Looking Ahead/Revision*' was published. The iteration saw the removal of the Delivered at Terminal (DAT) Incoterms® and its replacement by Delivered at Place Unloaded (DPU) Incoterms®. The insurance to be provided under the Cost Insurance and Freight (CIF) Incoterms® and the Cost and Insurance Paid (CIP) Incoterms® was also changed. There are 11 Incoterms®. [*See* 1812, 1895, 1923, 1928, 1936, 1953, 1967, 1976, 1980, 1990, 2000, 2010, and 19 September 2019.]
26 January 2020	International Customs Day theme '*Customs fostering Sustainability*'.
4 March 2020	The 25th anniversary of the WTO Agreement on Rules of Origin (RoO).
29 September 2020	The WTO Public Forum '*Building on 25 Years of the WTO*' commenced.
2 October 2020	The WTO Public Forum '*Building on 25 Years of the WTO*' concluded.

12 October 2020	The WCO 50th Session was marked, as well as the 25 years of existence of the WTO Customs Valuation Agreement (CVA). [*See* 400 BC, 30 October 1947, 15 December 1950, 1 January 1953, 28 July 1953, 5 September 1969, 1 November 1971 and 1973 to 1979.]
11 December 2020	WCO Council Resolution on the Role of Customs in Facilitating the Cross-Border Movement of Situationally Critical Medicines and Vaccines.
26 January 2021	International Customs Day theme '*Customs bolstering Recovery, Renewal and Resilience*'.
24 June 2021	Adoption of the WOC's 'Guidelines on Disaster Management and Supply Chain Continuity'.
28 September 2021	The WTO Public Forum '*Trade Beyond COVID-19: Building Resilience*' commenced.
1 October 2021	The WTO Public Forum '*Trade Beyond COVID-19: Building Resilience*' concluded.
1 January 2022	The HS Nomenclature 2022 Edition, the seventh Revision, entered into force. [*See* 1 January 1987, 1 January 1988, 1 January 1992, 1 January 1996, 1 January 2002, 1 January 2007, 1 January 2012, 1 January 2017, 1 January 2027, and 1 January 2028.]
26 January 2022	International Customs Day theme '*Scaling up Customs Digital Transformation*'.
12 June 2022	The WTO 12th Ministerial Conference (MC12) commenced in Geneva, Switzerland.
17 June 2022	The WTO MC12 concluded in Geneva, Switzerland.
4 October 2022	The WCO and UNCTAD signed an MoU, updating the MoU between the two organisations dating back to 2013. [*See* 30 December 1964 and 2013.]
14 November 2022	The WCO ATA Carnet for the Temporary Admission of Goods (ATA Convention) was held.
27 September 2023	The WTO Public Forum '*Towards a sustainable and inclusive recovery: ambition to action*' commenced.
30 September 2023	The WTO Public Forum '*Towards a sustainable and inclusive recovery: ambition to action*' concluded.
26 January 2023	International Customs Day theme '*Nurturing the next generation*'.
12 September 2023	The WTO Public Forum '*It is time for action*' commenced.
15 September 2023	The WTO Public Forum '*It is time for action*' concluded.

31 October 2023	Adoption of the WCO (WCO)-International Association of Ports and Harbors (IAPH) 'Guidelines on Cooperation between Customs and Port Authorities'.
2 November 2023	The WCO ATA/Istanbul Convention Administrative Committee meeting.
2024	ICC Genesis, a tool to verify an origin statement to facilitate smoother Customs checks, was launched.
26 January 2024	International Customs Day theme '*Customs Engaging Traditional and New Partners with Purpose*'.
26 February 2024	The WTO 13th Ministerial Conference (MC13) commenced in Abu Dhabi, United Arab Emirates (UAE).
2 March 2024	The WTO MC13 concluded in UAE.
10 September 2024	The WTO Public Forum '*Re-globalisation: Better Trade for a Better World*' commenced.
13 September 2024	The WTO Public Forum '*Re-globalisation: Better Trade for a Better World*' concluded.
27 November 2024	The LN '*International Convention relating to the Simplification of Customs Formalities*' celebrated its centenary.
9 December 2024	The WCO ATA/Istanbul Convention Administrative Committee meeting.
18 December 2024	The WCO launched the '*Smart Customs Community Portal*' to bridge the digital divide among WCO Members by leveraging disruptive technologies to enhance global supply chain security and efficiency.
26 January 2025	International Customs Day theme '*Commitment to Efficiency, Security and Prosperity*'.
2 April 2025	In the White House's Rose Garden, USA President Donald J. Trump declared '*Liberation Day*', announcing the introduction of tariffs against all countries.
22 May 2025	The World Customs Organization (WCO) held the 23rd meeting of the digitalising the ATA Carnet (eATA) Working Group. Each year, the Working Group discusses progress on the eATA and the Carnet de Passages en Douane (eCPD).
17 September 2025	The WTO Public Forum 'Enhance, Create and Preserve' will commence.
18 September 2025	The WTO Public Forum 'Enhance, Create and Preserve' will conclude.
November 2025	The WCO ATA/Istanbul Administrative Committee meeting.

26 March 2026	The WTO 14th Ministerial Conference (MC14) will commence in Cameroon, quite possibly in Yaoundé.
29 March 2026	The WTO MC14 will conclude in Cameroon, quite possibly in Yaoundé.
1 January 2027	The HS Nomenclature 2027 Edition, the eighth Revision, will not enter into force as originally envisaged, having been delayed by a year. [*See* 1 January 2028.]
1 January 2028	The HS Nomenclature 2028 Edition, the eighth Revision, will enter into force. [*See* 1 January 1987, 1 January 1988, 1 January 1992, 1 January 1996, 1 January 2002, 1 January 2007, 1 January 2017, 1 January 2022, 1 January 2027, and 1 January 2028.]

CHAPTER 22

Acronyms and Elucidation of Trade Terms

§22.01 ACRONYMS

The challenge, for the uninitiated, with using an acronym is that its meaning is not immediately known, which could lead to an exclusion in discussion or an obstruction when reading. An added challenge is that multiple acronyms could denote different Customs and Excises terms. Additionally, acronyms could be written differently.

What follows is a quick reference to the acronyms used in this book. To further aid in its reference, at the end of each acronym, there is a square bracket '[]', which contains the reference to either the Chapter or the Section that deals with the trade term. When there is a cross-reference, round brackets '()' are used:

ACV	Agreement on Customs Valuation [Trade Remedies]
AD	Anno Domini [In the year of the Lord] [The Lesson]
ADA	Anti-Dumping Agreement [WTO Agreement]
AGOA	African Growth and Opportunity Act [Trade Bloc]
AIT	Alliance Internationale de Tourisme (*see* LIAT) [Temporary Admission]
ARO	Agreement on Rules of Origin [Origination]
ATQ	Autonomous Tariff Quota [Types of Duties]
ASYCUDA	Automated Systems for Customs Data (*see* UNCTAD) [Organisations]
ATA Carnet	Admission Temporaire/Temporary Admission Carnet [Temporary Admission]

ATA Convention	Admission Temporaire/Temporary Admission Convention [Temporary Admission]
ATQs	Autonomous Tariff Quotas [Types of Duties]
AVE	*Ad Valorem* Equivalent [Types of Duties]
BC	Before Christ
BDV	Brussels Definition of Value [Customs Valuation]
BTA	Border Tax Adjustment/Border Tax Assessment [Types of Duties]
BTN	Brussels Tariff Nomenclature [Tariff Classification]
C&F	Cost and Freight (Incoterms®) 1936 [Incoterms®]
CAPA	Corrective Action and Preventive Action [The Lesson]
CCC	Customs Co-operation Council (*see* WCO) [Organisations]
CCI	Chamber of Commerce and Industry (*see* ICC) [Organisations]
CCCN	Customs Co-operation Council Nomenclature [Classification]
CCV	WTO Committee on Customs Valuation [Customs Valuation]
CET	Common External Tariff [Trade Blocs]
CIF	Cost, Insurance and Freight (Incoterms® 1895, 1936, 1990, 2000, 2010, 2020, or the basis of customs valuation) [Incoterms®]
CIP	Carriage and Insurance Paid To (Incoterms® 1990, 2000, 2010, 2020) [Incoterms®]
CITES	Convention on International Trade in Endangered Species [Prohibited/Restricted]
CO_2	Carbon dioxide [The Lesson]
CoO	Certificate of Origin [Origin], not to be confused with '*Country of Origin*'.
CPD Carnet	Carnet de Passage and Douane [Temporary Admission]
CPEI	Customs Procedures with Economic Impact [SCP]
CRO	WTO Committee on Rules of Origin [Origin]
CRTA	WTO Committee on Regional Trade Agreements [Trade Blocs]
CROSS	US Customs Ruling Online Search System [Tariff Classification]
CTS	WTO Consolidated Tariff Schedule [Types of Duties]
CU	Customs Union [Trade Blocs]
CUP	Compatible Uncontrolled Price Methods [Transfer Pricing]

CVA	Countervail Agreement [WTO]
CW	Customs Warehousing [Special Customs Procedure]
DAF	Delivered at Frontier (Incoterms® 1990, 2000) [Incoterms®]
DAP	Delivered at Place (Incoterms® 2010, 2020) [Incoterms®]
DAT	Delivered at Terminal (Incoterms® 2010) [Incoterms®]
DCP	Delivered Cost Paid (Incoterms® 1953) [Incoterms®]
DDP	Delivered at Destination (Incoterms® 1967) [Incoterms®]
DDP	Delivered Duty Paid (Incoterms® 1990, 2000, 2010, 2020) [Incoterms®]
DDU	Delivered Duty Unpaid (Incoterms® 1990, 2000) [Incoterms®]
DES	Delivered Ex Ship (Incoterms® 1990, 2000) [Incoterms®]
DEQ	Delivered Ex Quay (Incoterms® 1990, 2000) [Incoterms®]
DIC	Dumping, Injury (Material Injury), and Causality [Trade Remedies]
DPU	Delivered at Place Unloaded (Incoterms® 2020) [Incoterms®]
eATA	The digitalising of the ATA Carnet [Temporary Admission]
EC	European Commission [Organisation]
ECS Carnet	Carnets for Commercial Samples [Temporary Admission]
EDI	Electronic Data Interchange [Incoterms®]
EN	Explanatory Notes [Classification]
EOR	Exporter of Record
EPZ	Export Processing Zone [Trade Blocs]
EU	European Union [Trade Blocs]
Ex Quay	Ex Quay (Incoterms® 1936) [Incoterms®]
Ex Ship	Ex Ship (Incoterms® 1936) [Incoterms®]
EXW	Ex-Works (Incoterms® 1990, 2000, 2010, 2020) (or basis for domestic manufacture) [Incoterms®]
FAN	Fictitious, Arbitrary, and Nominal customs values [Customs Valuation]
FAS	Free Alongside Ship (Incoterms® 1936, 1990, 2000, 2010, 2020)
FCA	Free Carrier (Incoterms® 1990, 2000, 2010, 2020, previously FRC) [Incoterms®]
FCI	Freight Cost and Insurance (Incoterms® 1980, now CIP) [Incoterms®]
FIA	Federation Internationale de l'Automoblile [Organisations]
FIATA	International Federation of Freight Forwarders Associations [Organisations]

FOB	Free on Board (Incoterms® 1812, 1936, 1990, 2000, 2010, 2020, or basis of customs valuation) [Incoterms®]
FOBA	Free on Board Airport (Incoterms®1976) [Incoterms®]
FOR	Free on Rail (Incoterms® 1953) [Incoterms®]
FOT	Free on Truck (Incoterms® 1953) [Incoterms®]
FRC	Free Carrier (Incoterms® 1980, now FCA) [Incoterms®]
FTA	Free Trade Agreements [Trade Blocs]
FTA	Free Trade Area [Trade Blocs]
FTZ	Free Trade Zone [Trade Blocs]
FZ	Free Zones [Trade Blocs]
G20	Group of 20 [Organisations]
GATS	General Agreement on Trade in Services [Organisations]
GATT	General Agreement on Tariffs and Trade [Agreements]
GATT 1994	General Agreement on Tariffs and Trade 1994 [Agreements]
GIs	Geographical Indications [Origin]
GPTAD	Global Preferential Trade Agreements Database [Trade Blocs]
GRI	General Rules of Classification [Tariff Classification]
GSP	Generalised System of Preferences [Origin]
GST	General Sales Tax [Indirect Tax] [Types of Duties]
HRO	Harmonised Rules of Origin [Origin]
HS	Harmonized Commodity Description and Coding System (Harmonized System) [Classification]
HSC	WCO Harmonized System Committee [Classification]
IAPH	International Association of Ports and Harbors [Organisations]
IATA	International Air Transport Association [Organisations]
IBRD	International Bank for Reconstruction and Development (*see* WB) [Organisations]
ICC	International Chamber of Commerce (*see* ICC) [Organisations]
ICSID	International Centre for Settlement of Investment Disputes [Organisations]
IDA	International Development Association [Organisations]
IDB	WTO Integrated Database [Types of Duties]
IFC	International Finance Corporation [Organisations]
IFCBA	International Federation of Customs Brokers Associations [Organisations]

IFIA	International Federation of Inspection Agencies (*see* TIC Council) [Organisations]
IMF	International Monetary Fund [Organisations]
IMO	International Maritime Organization [Organisations]
IMPACT	International Medical Products Anti-Counterfeiting Taskforce [Organisations]
Incoterms®	International Commercial Terms [Incoterms®]
INCU	International Network of Customs Universities [Organisations]
INTERPOL	International Criminal Police Organization (abbreviated to ICPO–INTERPOL, but simply called INTERPOL) [Organisations]
IOR	Importer of Record
IP	Inward Processing [Special Customs Procedures]
IP	Intellectual Property [NTMs/NTBs]
IPR	Intellectual Property Rights
IQTR	Inside quota tariff rate [Types of Duties]
IRU	International Road Transport Union [Organisations]
ISO	International Standards Association [Organisations]
ITC	International Trade Centre [Organisations]
ITI	Customs Convention on the International Transit of Goods [Special Customs Procedures]
ITO	International Trade Organization (*see* GATT, WTO) [Organisations]
LIAT	Ligue Internationale des Associations Touristes (*see* AIT) [Organisations]
LDCs	Least-Developed Countries [Trade Remedies]
MFN	Most-Favoured Nation [Origin]
MIGA	Multilateral Investment Guarantee Agency [Organisations]
MoU	Memorandum of Understanding [Organisations]
MNC	Multinational Company [Transfer Pricing]
NGO	Non-governmental Organisation [Organisations]
NTBs	Non-tariff Barriers [Trade Barriers]
NTMs	Non-tariff Measures [Trade Barriers]
OECD	Organisation for Economic Co-operation and Development [Organisations]
OP	Outward Processing [Special Customs Procedures]
OQTR	Outside Quota Tariff Rate [Types of Duties]

PICARD	Partnerships in Customs Academic Research and Development
PSCG	Private Sector Consultative Group [Organisations]
PSI	Pre-Shipment Inspection [Non-tariff Barriers]
PSST	Processing, Storage, Specific Use, and Transit [Procedures]
PTA	Preferential Trade Area [Trade Blocs]
QRs	Quantitative Restrictions [Trade Barriers]
R&D	Research & Development [Customs Valuation]
REACH	Authorisation and Restriction of Chemicals [Prohibited/Restricted]
RGR	Returned Goods Relief [Procedures]
RKC	Revised Kyoto Convention [Organisations]
RoO	Rules of Origin [Origin]
RSC	WCO Harmonized System Review Subcommittee [Customs Tariff]
RTA	Regional Trade Agreement [Trade Blocs]
SAFE Framework	Standards to **S**ecure **a**nd **F**acilitate Global Trad**e** [Committees]
SCP	Special Customs Procedures (also known as Regimes) [SCP]
SCM	Subsidies and Countervailing Measures [Trade Remedies]
SEZ	Special Economic Zone [Trade Blocs]
SITC	Standard International Trade Classification [Tariff Classification]
SMEs	Small and Midsize Enterprises [Organisations]
SPS	Sanitary and Phytosanitary (measures) [Agreements]
SPUR	Store, Process, Use (Temporary), and Repair [Procedures]
SSA	Sub-Saharan African countries [Trade Blocs]
SSC	WCO Scientific Subcommittee [Tariff Classification]
TA	Temporary Admission [Procedures]
TBT	Technical Barriers to Trade [NTMs/NTBs]
TCRO	WCO Technical Committee on Rules of Origin [Origin]
TCCV	WCO Technical Committee on Customs Valuation [Customs Valuation]
TFA	Trade Facilitation Agreement [Agreement]
TIACA	International Air Cargo Association [Organisations]
TIC	Testing, Inspection, and Certification industry
TIC Council	TIC Council (IFIA) [Organisations]

TIR Carnet	Transports Internationaux Routiers or International Road Transports Carnet [Customs Procedures]
TNMM	Transactional Net Margin Method (*see* Transfer Pricing) [Customs Valuation]
TRIMS	Trade-Related Investment Measures [NTMs/NTBs]
TRIPS	Trade-Related Aspects of Intellectual Property Rights [Origin]
TRQ	Tariff Rate Quota
TS	Temporary Storage [Customs Procedures]
TV	Transaction Value [Customs Valuation]
UN	United Nations [Organisation]
UCC	Union Customs Code [EU]
UNCITRAL	Union Nations Commission on International Trade Law [Organisation]
UNCTAD	United Nations Conference on Trade and Development [Organisation]
UNSD	United Nations Statistics Division
US	United States of America
VAT	Value Added Tax [Indirect Tax]
VER	Voluntary Export Restraint [The Lesson]
WATAC	World ATA Carnet Council (Within the WCF-ICC) [Organisations]
WB	World Bank (*see* IBRD) [Organisations]
WBG	World Bank Group (*see* IDA, IFC, MIGA, ICSID) [Organisations]
WCF	World Chambers Federation - ICC [Organisations]
WCO	World Customs Organization (*see* CCC) [Organisations]
WHO	World Health Organization [Organisations]
WIPO	World Intellectual Property Organization [Organisations]
WTO	World Trade Organization [Organisations]
WWI	World War I - First World War
WWII	World War II - Second World War

§22.02 ELUCIDATION OF TRADE TERMS

The Customs and Excises terminology might well appear impenetrable to the non-specialist, while practitioners' tendency to use the trade terms interchangeably and then incorrectly adds to the challenge and confusion in their understanding and interpretation. The latter is mainly due to significant parts of the law, rules, regulations, and practices steeped in centuries-old jargon. As a consequence, the terms and the terminology should under no circumstances be accepted for their linguistic appearance and meaning; they should be understood for their meanings in customs and excises.

What follows is a quick reference to the terms, terminology, and expressions that tend to be used more regularly and written in everyday language. To further aid in its reference, at the end of each elucidation, there is a square bracket '[]', which contains the reference to either the Chapter or the Section that deals with the trade term. Where there are interchangeable trade terms, it is cross-referenced:

25% Local Content Rule	National Customs and Excises' legislation tends to specify a minimum local content requirement, typically 25%, of a locally manufactured good's ex-factory selling price, where imported material is used, in order for the good to be considered to be of the country's origin. [Origin]
Absorption Principle	*See Roll-Up Rule.* [Origin]
Absorption Review	To determine whether the domestic industry requires an increase in or extension of the scope of applying a trade remedy duty in cases where the exporters and/or the manufacturer or the importer absorbs the trade remedy duty. The absorption is indicative of no or insufficient price movement following the imposition of a trade remedy duty. [Trade Remedies]
Ad Hoc	A Latin term meaning '*when necessary or needed*'. [Types of Duties]
Ad Valorem	A Latin term meaning '*on value*'. [Types of Duties]
Ad Valorem Duty	The duty is expressed as a percentage of the CIF value or the FOB value of the imported goods and on the ex-factory selling price of the domestically (locally) manufactured goods. [Types of Duties]
Ad Valorem Equivalent	A tariff that is not a percentage can be calculated as a percentage of the price – the *ad valorem* equivalent, abbreviated as AVE. The AVE is the equivalent of the percentage of a specific duty, mixed, compound, or other duty containing a specific element. The AVE is calculated from the actual duty collection or the unit value of imports. *See Specific Duty.* *See Mixed Duty.* *See Compound Duty.* [Types of Duties]

Ad Valorem Rule	*See Value Content Rule.* [Origin]
Additional Duty	Also known as '*Customs Surcharge*', '*Surtax*' and '*Surcharge*'. *See Customs Surcharge.* *See Surcharge.* *See Surtax.* [Types of Duties]
Administrative Review	*See Interim Review.* [Trade Remedies]
Administered Protection	*See Contingent Protection.* *See Contingent Trade-Protective Measures.* [Non-tariff Measures]
Advance Ruling	Also known as a '*Binding Ruling*', it is a written decision issued by a Customs Authority to an importer or exporter, defining the treatment of the good at the time of import or export. The treatment is normally set for a specified period and guarantees the treatment for this period. *See Binding Ruling.* [Tariff Classification, Origin, Customs Valuation]
Advance Binding Ruling	*See Advance Ruling.* [Tariff Classification, Origin, Customs Valuation]
Advance Classification Ruling	*See Advance Ruling.* [Tariff Classification]
Advance Origin Ruling	*See Advance Ruling.* [Origin]
Advance Valuation Ruling	*See Advance Ruling.* [Customs Valuation]
Agent	An intermediary engaged by one party to bring about a contractual relation with another. *See Direct Agent.* *See Indirect Agent.*
Alliance Internationale de Tourisme	One of the two international organisations, along with the FIA, which administers the CPD Carnet system. [Organisations]
Alphabetical Index	An alphabetical list of the articles and products mentioned in the HS and its EN. [Tariff Classification]

Alternative Methods	The second category of customs valuation methods. *See Replacement Valuation Methods.* *See Secondary Methods.* [Customs Valuation]
Anti-Dumping Duty	A duty that is imposed on goods that are deemed to be dumped and causing material injury to domestic producers of a competing good in the importing country. These duties are equal to the difference between the goods' export price and their normal value if dumping causes injury. *See* Anti-dumping Measure. [Trade Remedies]
Anti-dumping Measure	Known as an '*Anti-dumping Duty*'. [Trade Remedies]
Anti-Subsidy Duty	Known as a '*Countervailing Duty*'. *See Countervailing Duty* [Trade Remedies]
Appeal	The act by which a person who is directly affected by a decision or omission of the Customs and who considers himself to be aggrieved thereby seeks redress before a competent authority. Covered in Annex H.1. to the Kyoto Convention of 1974 and the General Annex, Chapter 10 of the RKC.
Applied Rate	Also known as the '*Applied Tariff*' and the 'Prevailing Tariff Rate', it might well be below the '*Bound Rate*', known as the '*Water in the Tariff*'. WTO members have the flexibility to increase or decrease their tariff rate, provided that they do not exceed the '*Bound Rate*' and '*Ceiling Rate*'. *See Applied Rate.* *See Prevailing Tariff Rate.* *See Bound Rate.* *See Water in the Tariff Rate.* *See Ceiling Rate.* [Types of Duties]
Applied Tariff	*See Applied Rate.* *See Prevailing Tariff Rate.* *See Bound Rate.* *See Water in the Tariff Rate.* *See Ceiling Rate.* [Types of Duties]

Assessment of Duties and Taxes	The determination of the amount of duties and taxes that are payable. Covered in The General Annex, Chapter 4 of the RKC. [Types of Duties]
ATA Carnet	Often referred to as the '*Passport for goods*', it is an international customs document issued under the terms of the ATA Convention and the Istanbul Convention that incorporates an internationally valid guarantee and may be used in lieu of national Customs documents and as security for import duties and taxes, to cover the TA of goods, and where appropriate, the transit of goods. The term '*ATA*' is a combination of the initial letters of the French words '*Admission Temporaire*' and the English words '*Temporary Admission*'. *See ATA Convention.* *See Istanbul Convention.* [Temporary Admission]
ATA Convention	An international Customs Convention adopted by the WCO, on the use of ATA carnets for the TA of goods. *See ATA Carnet.* *See Istanbul Convention.* [Temporary Admission]
Audit-Based Control	The measures and means by which a Customs Authority satisfies itself as to the accuracy and authenticity of declarations through the examination of the relevant books, records, business systems and the commercial data held. It is covered in the General Annex, Chapter 6 of the RKC.
Authorisation	The process of obtaining permission and approval from a Customs Authority before the importation of the goods under a Customs facility. The granting of the authorisation is subject to a guarantee, security, or a bond being lodged to cover the importer's Customs debt or potential duty and tax liability. *See Customs Debt.* *See Prior Authorisation.* [Special Customs Procedures]
Authorised Economic Operation	Better known by its acronym AEO, it refers to the approval that a national Customs Authority gave a party involved in the international movement of goods that it is in compliance with the WCO or equivalent supply chain security standards. AEO is dealt with in the WCO SAFE Frameworks of Standards.

	AEOs may include brokers, carriers, consolidators, distributors, exporters, freight forwarders, importers, integrated operators, intermediaries, manufacturers, ports (air and sea), terminal operators, and warehouses. AEOs operate under different names; for instance, in the US, it is known as Customs Trade Partnership Against Terrorism (CTPAT) and Partners in Protection (PIP) in Canada. [Timeline and Milestones]
Autonomous Duty	*See Statutory Duty.* [Types of Duties]
Autonomous Tariff Quota	Known as TRQ or Autonomous Tariff Quotas (ATQs), it is a measure under which a good is subject to an MFN tariff, but only a certain quantity, referred to as the '*quota*', is admitted into a country at a lower rate of duty, sometimes even at a rate of 0%. TRQ tend to be applied mainly to the agricultural trade and then tends to be seasonal. *See Tariff Rate Quota or TRQ.* [Types of Duties]
Bilateral Cumulation	As the name suggests, '*bi*' meaning '*twice each*' allows the materials from the two contracting parties to be considered originating. This cumulation may stipulate that the rules of '*sufficient worked or processed*' or '*substantial transformation*' be adhered to. *See Cumulation.* *See Diagonal Cumulation.* *See Extended Cumulation.* *See Full Cumulation.* *See Multilateral Cumulation.* *See Multilateral Extended Cumulation.* *See Regional Cumulation.* [Origin]
Bilateral Quota	As the name suggests, '*bi*' means '*twice each*'; this is a quota that the two contracting parties reserve for each other. [Types of Duties]
Bilateral Trade Agreement	As the name suggests, '*bi* means '*twice each*' and is a trade agreement between two contracting parties. *See Multilateral Trade Agreement.* *See Unilateral Trade Agreement.* [Trade Blocs]
Binding Origin Determination	*See Binding Origin Information.* *See Binding Origin Ruling.* [Origin]

Binding Origin Information	For an importer and/or its intermediary to mitigate its customs duty liability risk and provide legal certainty, an application could be made to a Customs Authority to provide a written tariff ruling. *See Binding Origin Determination.* *See Binding Origin Ruling.* [Origin]
Binding Origin Ruling	*See Binding Origin Determination.* *See Binding Origin Information.* [Origin]
Binding Overhang Principle	*See Water in the Tariff.* *See Tariff Cliff.* *See Tariff Overhang.* [Types of Duty]
Binding Ruling	*See Advance Ruling.* [Tariff Classification, Origin, Customs Valuation]
Binding Tariff Determination	*See Binding Tariff Ruling* *See Binding Tariff Information* [Tariff Classification]
Binding Tariff Information	For an importer and/or its intermediary to mitigate its customs duty liability risk and provide legal certainty, an application could be made to a Customs Authority to provide a written tariff ruling. *See Binding Tariff Determination.* *See Binding Ruling.* [Tariff Classification]
Binding Tariff Ruling	*See Binding Tariff Determination.* *See Binding Tariff Information.* [Tariff Classification]
Binding Valuation Determination	*See Binding Valuation Information.* *See Binding Valuation Ruling.* [Customs Valuation]
Binding Valuation Information	For an importer and/or its intermediary to mitigate its customs duty liability risk and provide legal certainty, an application could be made to a Customs Authority to provide a written tariff ruling. *See Binding Valuation Determination.* *See Binding Valuation Ruling.* [Customs Valuation]
Binding Valuation Ruling	*See Binding Valuation Ruling.* *See Binding Valuation Information.* [Customs Valuation]

Bond	A financial guarantee given by an importer, exporter, or manufacturer to the Customs and Excise Authority to secure the payment of duties and taxes. *See Customs Comprehensive Guarantee.* *See Guarantee.* *See Individual Guarantee.* [Special Customs Procedures]
Bonded Goods	Goods that are kept in a Customs warehouse and Excise warehouse or a Customs and Excise warehouse.
Bonded Warehouse	Is a facility, a building or a secure area in which dutiable goods (subject to duties and taxes) may be stored, manipulated, or undergo repair or manufacturing operations without the payment of duties or taxes until they are ready to be released. It allows for duties, levies, and taxes to be deferred until the goods are either cleared for free circulation, home use, or export.
Border Tax Adjustment	It is a mechanism that the WTO administers to ensure that a country's internal duties, levies, and taxes on international trade are neutralised, in other words to prevent trade from being distorted by differing national duty, levy, and tax policies. Essentially, it aims to level the playing field between domestic producers and foreign producers by ensuring that the duties, levies, and taxes imposed on imported goods are comparable to those imposed on domestically produced goods. [Types of Duties]
Bound Rate	Also known as the '*bound tariff*', a tariff fixed in GATT, a country cannot increase the rate of customs duty (tariff) on goods above their '*binding rate*' (also known as a '*ceiling rate*') without compensation being negotiated, as the WTO upholds this principle. *See Bound Tariff.* *See Ceiling Rate.* *See Maximum Tariff.* [Types of Duty]
Bound Tariff	*See Bound Rate.* *See Ceiling Rate.* *See Maximum Tariff.* [Types of Duty]
Calculation Method	*See Computed Method.* [Customs Valuation]

CAPA	The purpose of Corrective and Preventive Action is to collect information, analyse the information, identify and investigate product and quality problems, and subsequently take appropriate and effective corrective and preventive action to prevent their recurrence. [The Roadmap]
Carnet	Pronounced '*kar-nay*', it is an international Customs document which allows for the temporary export or import of goods for commercial purposes to and from a country without having to pay duties or VAT on the goods. The word '*carnet*' is the French for '*booklet*' which describes the physical appearance of the document *See ATA Carnet.* *See CPD Carnet.* *See ECS Carnet.* *See TIR Carnet.* [Temporary Admission]
Carnet de passages en Douane carnets	Also known as CPD Carnets, it is an international customs document administered by AIT and FIA for the temporary importation/exportation of motor vehicles. It is regulated by the ATA Convention and by the Istanbul Convention. *See ATA Convention.* *See CPD Carnet.* *See Istanbul Convention.* [SCP: Temporary Admission]
Carriage of Goods Coastwise Procedure	The Customs procedure under which: (a) goods in free circulation and (b) imported goods that have not been declared under the condition that they must be transported in a vessel other than the importing vessel in which they arrived in the Customs territory are loaded on board a vessel at a place in the Customs territory and are transported to another place in the same Customs territory where they are then unloaded. [*See* Customs Transit, Transhipment.]
Carrier	The person who is transporting the goods or in charge of or responsible for the operation of the means of transport. Covered in Annex A.1. to the Kyoto Convention and Specific Annex A, Chapter 1 and Specific Annex J, Chapter 4 of the RKC

Category C	The category for '*Main Carriage Paid*' Incoterms®, of which there are four: Cost and Freight (CFR), Cost Insurance and Freight (CIF), Carriage Paid To (CPT), Carriage and Insurance Paid To (CIP). [Incoterms®]
Category D	The category for '*Arrival*' Incoterms® of which there are three: Delivered at Place (DAP), Delivered at Place Unloaded (DPU), and Delivered Duty Paid (DDP).
Category E	The category for '*Departure*' Incoterms®, of which there is only one Ex-Works (EXW). [Incoterms®]
Category F	Categorised as '*Main Carriage Unpaid*' Incoterms®, of which there are three: Free Carrier (FCA), Free Alongside Ship (FAS), and Free on Board (FOB). [Incoterms®]
Causal Link	No anti-dumping duty may be imposed until the Remedy Authority has determined that dumped imports have caused material injury, threatened material injury to or materially retarded the establishment of the domestic industry. *See Causality.* [Trade Remedies]
Causality	*See Causal Link.* [Trade Remedies]
Ceiling Binding	A binding is '*ceiling*' if the applied duty is lower than the bound duty. *See Binding Overhang* [Types of Duties]
Ceiling Rate	The maximum MFN tariff that individual WTO Members commit to impose through negotiation with the WTO Members is referred to by many names: '*bound tariff*', '*bound rate*', '*ceiling rate*' and '*maximum tariff*'. The bound tariff rate may not be exceeded unless the WTO Members enter into negotiations with all WTO Members and obtain their agreement. A country cannot increase the rate of customs duty (tariff) on goods above their '*binding rate*', also known as a '*ceiling rate*'. *See Bound Rate.* *See Bound Tariff.* *See Maximum Tariff.* [Types of Duties]

Certificate of Origin	The CoO is a prescribed form identifying the good to which the Authority or Body is empowered to issue. It certifies expressly that the good to which the CoO relates originates in a specific country. In addition, the imported goods were grown, produced, or manufactured in the country. The CoO may also include a declaration by the manufacturer, producer, supplier, exporter or other competent person. The specific forms for CoO are covered in Annex D.2 to the Kyoto Convention and the Specific Annex K, Chapters 2 and 3 of the RKC and in the framework of preferential arrangements such as the GSP. [Origin]
Certificate Declaration of Origin	A certification by an Authority or Body empowered to do so. Covered in Annex D.2. to the Kyoto Convention and Specific Annex K, Chapters 2 and 3 of the RKC. [Origin]
CFR	Under Cost and Freight Incoterms® 2020, the seller delivers the goods to the buyer on board the vessel or procures the goods already delivered. The risk of loss of or damage to the goods transfers when the goods are on board the vessel, such that the seller is taken to have performed its obligation to deliver the goods whether or not the goods actually arrive at their destination in sound condition, in the stated quantity or, indeed, at all. In CFR, the seller owes no obligation to the buyer to purchase insurance cover: the buyer would be well advised, therefore, to purchase some cover for himself. [Incoterms®]
Chamber of Commerce and Industry	The postfix '*CCI*' that appears in a Chamber's acronym is a voluntary or mandatory association of businesses with the express purpose of promoting the commercial interests of an area. The first Chamber – '*Chambre de Commerce*' – was founded in 1599 in Marseille, France. [Organisations]
Change of Tariff Classification Rule	*See Tariff Shift Rule.* *See Specified Processed Rule.* [Origin]
Chapter	Tariff Chapter *See Heading.* *See Section.* *See Subheading.* [Tariff Classification]

Charge	*See Surcharge.* [The Lesson]
CIF	Cost, Insurance and Freight serve as the basis of value for customs duty purposes (customs valuation), not to be confused with the CIF Incoterms®. CIF customs valuation involves determining the value of imported goods for customs purposes, considering the cost of the goods, insurance, and freight (CIF). It is a crucial process for calculating import duties and other taxes, as these are often calculated as a percentage of the CIF value. The CIF value is the price of goods delivered at the frontier of the importing country, before any import duties or taxes. [Customs Valuation]
CIF Incoterms®	Under Cost Insurance and Freight Incoterms® 2020, the seller delivers the goods to the buyer on board the vessel or procures the goods already so delivered. The risk of loss of or damage to the goods transfers when the goods are on board the vessel, such as the seller is taken to have performed its obligation to deliver the goods whether or not the goods actually arrive at their destination in sound condition, in the stated quantity or, indeed, at all. *See Incoterms®.* [Incoterms®]
CIP Incoterms®	Carriage Insurance Paid To Incoterms® 2020, the seller delivers the goods – and transfers the risk – to the buyer by handing them over to the carrier contracted by the seller or by procuring the goods so delivered. The seller may do so by giving the carrier physical possession of the goods in the manner and at the place appropriate to the means of transport used. Once the goods have been delivered to the buyer in this way, the seller does not guarantee that the goods will reach the place of destination in sound condition, in the stated quantity or indeed at all. This is because the risk transfers from the seller to the buyer when the goods are delivered to the buyer by handing them over to the carrier; the seller must nonetheless contract for the carriage of the goods from delivery to the agreed destination. *See Incoterms®.* [Incoterms®]

Circumvention Review	Investigates whether companies are avoiding anti-dumping or countervailing measures by altering their practices, such as modifying products, rerouting goods, or shifting production, to evade duties. It normally considers a change in the pattern of trade, whether the remedial effect of the anti-dumping duty is being undermined, or whether dumping can be found in relation to the normal values previously established for the like products, or similar products. [Trade Remedies]
Classification	The process of determining the most appropriate class or code in the Tariff is attributable to a particular good. *See Tariff Classification.* [Tariff Classification]
Clearance	The completion or accomplishment of the Customs formalities necessary to allow the goods to enter for free circulation (home use), to be exported, or to be placed under another Customs procedure, such as an SCP. Covered in General Annex, Chapter 2 of RKC.
Clearance for Home Use	The Customs procedure provides that imported goods enter into free circulation, or home use, in the Customs territory upon the payment of any import duties and taxes chargeable on the completion of all Customs formalities. Covered in Annex B.1. to the Kyoto Convention and Specific Annex B, Chapter 1 of the RKC.
Client Screening	Also known as '*Party-Based Screening*', it refers to the screening of all business partners, clients, businesses (companies), and entities against the denied party lists and sanctioned party lists, and in the matching accounting for any false positives that might arise. It is one of the three types of '*Screening*', the others being Transaction Screening or Transaction-Based Screening, and Hybrid Screening. *See Party-Based Screening.* *See Transaction Screening.* *See Transaction-Based Screening.* *See Hybrid Screening.* [Screening]
Combination Duty	Is a tariff comprising the combination of an *ad valorem* duty and specific duty, which are either added to each other or subtracted from each other. *See Compound Duty* [Types of Duties]

Commercial Samples	Goods owned abroad and imported for the purpose of being shown or demonstrated in the country for the soliciting of orders to be supplied from abroad. [Temporary Admission]
Commodity Code	Also known as an HS code, it is a standardised, internationally recognised system for classifying traded products. It uses a numerical code to identify goods for customs purposes, ensuring consistent and accurate documentation during import and export. [Tariff Classification]
Common Market	Also known as a '*Single Market*'. This is an agreement on the part of a set of countries to eliminate trade restrictions among themselves, adopt a CET, and allow the free movement of factors of production among member countries, also known as the factors of production. The factors of production refer to labour and physical capital. *See Trade Blocs.* *See Single Market.* [Trade Blocs]
Comparable Price	Refers to the comparison of prices at the same levels of trade.
Comparative Advantage	Occurs when one country is able to produce a good at a lower opportunity cost than another.
Compensating Products	Products: (a) obtained within a country resulting from the manufacturing, processing or repair of the goods for which the use of the inward processing procedure is authorised; or (b) obtained abroad and resulting from the manufacturing, processing or repair of goods for which the use of the outward processing procedure is authorised. Covered in Annexes E.6. and E.8. to the Kyoto Convention and Specific Annex B, Chapter 2 and Specific Annex F, Chapters 1 and 2 of the RKC.
Completely Knocked Down	Also known by the acronym CKD, referring to a good that is in a disassembled format and requires full assembly. A good tends to be shipped in a CKD format so as to avoid high import duties, levies, and taxes, to meet the importing country's local content requirements, such as a certain percentage of the value that needs to be added, or to take advantage of the importing country's lower, or more competitive labour costs. *See Semi-Knocked Down.* [Types of Duties]

Compound Duty	It is a tariff comprising the combination of an *ad valorem* duty and a specific duty, which is either added to each other or subtracted from each other. *See Combination Duty.* [Types of Duties]
Comprehensive Guarantee	A guarantee to cover the amount of import or export duty corresponding to the existing and/or potential customs debt and other charges, if applicable, in connection with two or more operations, declarations or customs procedures. [Customs Debt]
Computed Method	Also known as the '*Calculation Method*', or Method 5. The customs valuation of the goods is calculated based on the costs of material and production in the country of export, plus other costs, such as packing, engineering, and development work. Additional amounts for profit, general expenses, and insurance are also included. The computed value is considered the most difficult method as the Customs value is determined on the basis of the costs or value of material and production costs; plus profit and general expenses equal to those usually reflected in the sale of goods of the same class or kind, and, depending on the basis of customs valuation (FOB or CIF), the Cost of transport, loading, handling and insurance up to the point of entry. *See Customs Valuation.* *See Calculation Method.* [Trade Remedies]
Concession	A tariff reduction, tariff binding or other agreement to reduce import restrictions: usually accorded pursuant to negotiation in return for concessions by other parties. *See Tariff Concession.*
Consumption Duty	Imposed on goods for which the demand is either perfectly inelastic or inelastic, such as petroleum goods, alcohol goods, and tobacco goods, as well as on certain luxury goods, also known as non-essential goods, such as electronics and cosmetics. *See Consumption Tax.* *See Indirect Tax.* [Types of Duties]
Consumption Tax	*See Consumption Duty.* *See Indirect Tax* [Types of Duties]

Contingent Protection	All measures put in place to form a certain barrier to trade. These measures are only imposed if certain harmful circumstances on domestic market appear. *See Contingent Trade-Protective Measures.* *See Administered Protection.* [Non-tariff Measures]
Contingent Trade-Protective Measures	Trade barriers, imposed under certain circumstances, arise to protect the economy from the adverse effects of the impact of certain imports, such as trade remedies – anti-dumping or countervailing duties (unfair trade practices). Also called '*Administered Protection*'. *See Non-tariff Measures (NTMs).* *See Contingent Protection.* *See Administered Protection* *Contingent Trade-Protective Measures* [Non-tariff Measures]
Contra Customs Duty	*See* Contra Duty. [Types of Duties]
Contra Duty	Excise duties are not regulated by the WTO, which only requires that when an excise duty is imposed, an equivalent needs to be imposed on imported goods, which is called a 'contra customs duty'. Unfortunately, these duties tend to be called 'excise duty', which tends to cause confusion. It is a tariff imposed at the same rate on imports and manufacturing. Although the rate of duty is the same, the basis differs. For imports, it is on either the FOB value or the CIF basis, while for manufacture, it is on the EXW basis. *See Contra Customs Duty.* [Types of Duties]
Controlled Goods	Also known as '*Restricted Goods*', these are goods where importation or exportation is limited or restrained, and is only possible should specific conditions be met or complied with. The control of these goods could, in its interpretation and administration, be regarded as NTBs, which implies that restriction diverts from its original intent to a protectionist measure. *See Restricted Goods.* [Prohibited Goods and Restricted Goods]
Convention	A practice is consistently followed, although it does not have the force of law. [Convention]
CPEI	Customs Procedures with Economic Impact apply to the SCP of Storage, Specific Use, and Processing. [Special Customs Procedures]

Cost, Insurance and Freight	If it is not specifically denoted as an Incoterms®, it refers to the basis of customs valuation. *See Free on Board.* [Customs Valuation]
Cost, Insurance and Freight Incoterms®	Better known by the acronym CIF. The seller delivers the goods to the buyer on board the vessel or procures the goods already so delivered. The risk of loss of or damage to the goods transfers when the goods are on board the vessel, such as the seller is taken to have performed its obligation to deliver the goods whether or not the goods actually arrive at their destination in sound condition, in the stated quantity or, indeed, at all. [Incoterms®]
Counterfeit	Unauthorised representation of a registered trademark carried on goods identical or similar to goods for which the trademark is registered, with a view to deceiving the purchaser into believing that he/she is buying the original goods.
Countervailing Duty	A duty levied on imports of goods that have benefited from production or export subsidies. The duty is intended to offset, or to counter, the effect of the subsidy. *See Anti-Subsidy Duty.* [Trade Remedies]
Countervailing Measures	Action taken by the importing country, usually in the form of increased duties to offset subsidies given to producers or exporters in the exporting country. [Trade Remedies]
Country-Specific Tariff	National Tariff, HS8, HS10, and HS12. [Tariff Classification]
Country of Origin	*See Country of Origin of Goods.* [Origin]
Country of Origin of Goods	Country in which the goods have been produced or manufactured, according to the criteria laid down for the purposes of application of the Customs tariff, of quantitative restrictions or any other measure related to trade. The word '*country*' may include a group of countries, a region or a part of a country. It is covered in Annex. D.1. to the Kyoto Convention and Specific Annex K, Chapter 1 of the RKC. [Origin]

CPD Carnet	The Carnet de Passages en Douane is a customs document issued under the Istanbul Convention, the Customs Convention on the temporary importation of private road vehicles, the Customs Convention on the temporary importation of commercial road vehicles and the Customs Convention on the temporary importation for private use of aircraft and pleasure boats. *See ATA Convention.* *See Istanbul Convention.* [Specific Use, Customs Special Procedures]
Cumulation	Cumulation is a deviation from the principle that goods must be produced entirely in the country of exportation, or have undergone sufficient working or processing there, in order to qualify as originating goods. It allows producers in one country to source components and inputs from other countries without losing the originating status of that component or input. Under cumulation, foreign components and inputs are not considered imported (non-originating) for purposes of '*substantial transformation*' requirements. *See Bilateral Cumulation.* *See Diagonal Cumulation.* *See Extended Cumulation.* *See Full Cumulation.* *See Multilateral Cumulation.* *See Multilateral Extended Cumulation.* *See Regional Cumulation.* *See Full Cumulation.* [Origin]
CPT Incoterms®	Under Carriage Paid To Incoterms® 2020, the seller delivers the goods – and transfers the risk – to the buyer by handing them over to the carrier contracted by the seller or by procuring the goods so delivered. The seller may do so by giving the carrier physical possession of the goods in the manner at the place appropriate to the means of transport used. Once the goods have been delivered to the buyer in this way, the seller does not guarantee that the goods will reach the place of destination in sound condition, in the stated quantity or indeed at all. This is because the risk transfers from the seller to the buyer when the goods are delivered to the buyer by handing them over to the carrier; the seller must nonetheless contract for the carriage of the goods from delivery to the agreed destination. [Incoterms®]

Cumulation of Imports	In determining whether imports of countries are causing material injury to the domestic industry, the investigating authority should consider each import individually. [Trade Remedies]
Custom	A local rule, which is both reasonable and certain, that is deemed to have existed for a considerable time and has become accepted as part of the law of the land – the country.
Custom House	Without '*s*', it is the traditional term for the public office at which the Customs business of a port is carried out.
Customary Due	*See Customs Duty.* [Types of Duties]
Customs	The Government Authority that is responsible for the administration of the Customs law and the collection of duties and taxes. It has the added responsibility for the application of other laws and regulations relating to the importation, exportation, movement or storage of goods. Covered in General Annex, Chapter 2 of the RKC. *See Customs Authority.*
Customs Agent	The word '*Customs*' tends to mask the word '*Agent*', which is a person who acts on behalf of another person or group. *See Customs Broker* *See Direct Representation,* *See Indirect Representation,*
Customs and Excise Tariff	A volume that contains the duties, drawbacks and allowances of Customs and Excise. [The Lesson]
Customs and Excise Warehouse	A warehouse that is approved by the Customs Authority as both a Customs and an Excise warehouse. [The Lesson]
Customs-Approved Route	Any road, railway, waterway, airway and any other route, such as a pipeline, which is to be used for the importation, exportation, and Customs transit of the goods.
Customs Authority	*See Customs*
Customs Bond	An undertaking in due legal form by which a person binds himself to the Customs to do or not to do some specified act. Although a Customs bond might be used interchangeably with a customs guarantee, a customs bond constitutes a contract between three parties – the Customs, the principal, normally an importer, and a surety, which serves to ensure that all the duties, taxes, and levies are paid to Customs by the principal. [Customs Debt]

Customs Broker	Acts as an intermediary between traders and Customs in the clearance process. The Customs Broker completes the declaration forms for importing and/or exporting the goods; however, the Customs Broker does not primarily deal with the physical movement of goods. The RKC makes the usage of Customs Broker services '*optional*' for both the importer/exporter. Covered in Chapter 8 of the General Annex (GA) to the RKC. *See Customs Clearing Agent.* *See Customs Intermediaries* *See Direct Representation.* *See Indirect Representation.*
Customs Clearing Agent	A person who carries on the business of arranging for the Customs clearance of goods and who deals directly with the Customs for and on behalf of another person. This could include Customs Agents, Customs Brokers and Freight Forwarders. Countries tend to require that these companies be approved or licensed by the Customs Authority. It is covered in Annex G.2. to the RKC. *See Customs Broker.* *See Direct Representation.* *See Indirect Representation.*
Customs Compliance	*See Trade Compliance.*
Customs Cooperation Council	*See WCO.* [Organisations]
Customs Control	Measures are applied by a Customs Authority to ensure compliance with Customs law. The measures may be general, in relation to all goods entering the Customs territory, or may be specifically related to the location of the goods, the nature of the goods, and the Customs procedure applied to the goods. It is covered in General Annex, Chapters 2 and 6 of the RKC.
Customs Declaration	Any statement or action, in any form prescribed or accepted by the Customs, giving information or particulars required by the Customs.
Customs Debt	The obligation on a person to pay the amount of import or export duty which applies to specific goods under the customs legislation in force. It relates to the amount of import duty, levy, and tax and export duty that is due to a Customs Authority. [Customs Debt]

Customs Duty	The duty laid down in the Customs tariff is to which goods are liable for entering or leaving a country of Customs territory. The rates of duty are specified in the national tariff schedule, also known as the Tariff Book. It is covered in General Annex, Chapters 2 and 4 of the RKC.
Customs Facilitation	Refers to measures that streamline and simplify technical and legal procedures for a good at a Customs border.
Customs Formalities	All Customs processes, procedures, and operations must be carried out by the person concerned and by the Customs Authority in order to comply with the Customs law, its rules, and its regulations. It is covered in General Annex, Chapter 2 of the RKC, and in the Specific Annex A, Chapter 1 of the RKC.
Customs Fraud	Any act by which a person deceives, or attempts to deceive, the Customs and thus evades, or attempts to evade, wholly or partly, the payment of duties and taxes or the application of prohibitions or restrictions laid down by Customs law or obtains, or attempts to obtain, any advantage contrary to Customs law, thereby committing a Customs offence.
Customs Frontier	The boundary of a Customs territory. *See Customs Border.*
Customs Guarantee	A customs guarantee, also known as a security, is an agreement to cover import duty, import VAT, and excise duty, which have not been paid at the time of importation or at the time of exportation. Although a '*security*' is used interchangeably, a guarantee is a legal term that is more comprehensive than a security.
Customs Intermediaries	Assist traders in moving goods across borders by ensuring they are meeting their obligations and moving goods efficiently through the customs system. Customs Intermediaries are a crucial component in the operation of the border and the facilitation of trade. Customs Intermediaries tend to complete customs declarations on behalf of traders, sometimes alongside other services, like paying duties, levies, taxes, and tariffs and providing or arranging transportation of goods. A range of businesses acts as Customs Intermediaries, including customs brokers, agents or advisors, fast parcel operators (FPOs), freight forwarders, warehouse operators and hauliers. *See Customs Brokers.* *See Customs Clearing Agent.* *See Customs Intermediaries* *See Direct Representation.* *See Indirect Representation.*

Customs Law	The statutory and regulatory provisions relating to the importation, exportation, movement or storage of goods, the administration and enforcement of which are specifically charged to the Customs, and any regulations made by the Customs under their statutory powers. Customs law generally includes provisions concerning: the functions, powers and responsibilities of the Customs, as well as the rights and obligations of the persons concerned; the various Customs procedures, together with the conditions and formalities relating to their application; the factors relating to the application of import and export duties and taxes; the natural and legal consequences of Customs offences; and the ways and means of appeal. It is covered in General Annex, Chapter 2 of the RKC.
Customs Maritime Zone	The sea area is under the control of a Customs Authority in accordance with their domestic legislation. The sea area may also include a zone continuous with the territorial sea.
Customs Offence	Any breach, or attempted breach, of Customs law. It is covered in the Nairobi Convention and Annex H.2 to the Kyoto Convention of 1974 and Specific Annex H, Chapter 1 of the RKC.
Customs Office	The Customs Authority is empowered to perform the Customs formalities, and the premises or other areas are approved. It is covered in General Annex, Chapter 2 of the RKC.
Customs or Economic Union	In addition to the customs duty-free movement of goods between the member countries, a CET tariff is adopted. It implies that each member country has to impose the same level of customs duty. [Trade Blocs]
Customs Procedure	The treatment the Customs Authority applies to the goods, including the means of transport and the procedure, which are subject to Customs control. The RKC identifies a set of customs procedures and provides standards and recommended practices regarding those activities. *See Customs Regime.* [Special Customs Procedures]
Customs Regime	Means a Customs Procedure. *See Customs Procedures.* [Special Customs Procedures]

Customs Special Procedure	A range of mechanisms that allow for the temporary or partial suspension of import duties, levies, and taxes on imported or exported goods. *See Special Customs Procedure.* [Special Customs Procedure]
Custom Surcharge	*See Surcharge.* [Types of Duties]
Customs Tariff	A customs tariff schedule essentially comprises two elements: a goods nomenclature and a list of tariff rates.
Customs Territory	A geographic territory in which the Customs law and Customs regulations apply.
Customs Transit	The Customs procedure under which goods are transported under Customs control from one Customs office to another. It is covered in Annex E.1. to the Kyoto Convention and Specific Annex E, Chapter 1 of the RKC. [Special Customs Procedures: Transit]
Customs Union	In addition to the customs duty-free movement of goods between the member countries, a single CET tariff is adopted. It implies that each member country has to impose the same level of customs duty. [Trade Bloc]
Customs valuation	It is a customs procedure applied to determine the customs value of imported goods. If the rate of duty is *ad valorem*, the customs value is essential to determine the duty to be paid on an imported good. *See* Valorisation. [Customs Valuation]
Customs value	It is essentially the transaction value of a good (the price paid or payable) providing for Customs permitted adjustments, and deductions.
Customs warehousing	It is a Special Customs Procedure under which imported goods are stored under Customs control in a designated place (a Customs warehouse) without the payment of import duties and taxes. The duties and taxes only become payable on releasing the goods into free circulation (home use). The benefit of using this procedure is that it preserves a business' cash flow. There tend to be two types of Customs warehouses: Public Customs Warehouse for general use and Private Customs Warehouses for specified person's use only. It is covered in Annex E.3. to the Kyoto Convention of 1974 and Specific Annex D, Chapter 1 of the RKC. [Storage, Customs Special Procedure]

Customs warehousing procedure	The Customs procedure under which imported goods are stored under Customs control in a designated place (a Customs warehouse) without payment of import duties, levies, and taxes [Storage, Customs Special Procedure]
DAP Incoterms®	Under Delivered At Place Incoterms® 2020, the seller delivers the goods - and transfers risk - to the buyer when the goods are placed at the disposal of the buyer on the arriving means of transport ready for unloading at the named place of destination or at the agreed point within that place if any such point is agreed. The seller bears all risks involved in bringing the goods to the named place of destination or to the agreed point within that place. In this Incoterms® rule, therefore, delivery and arrival at the destination are the same. [Incoterms®]
DDP Incoterms®	Under Delivered Duty Paid Incoterms® 2020, the seller delivers the goods to the buyer when the goods are placed at the disposal of the buyer, cleared for import, on the arriving means of transport, ready for unloading, at the named place of destination or at the agreed point within that place, if any such point is agreed. The seller bears all risks involved in bringing the goods to the named place of destination or to the agreed point within that place. In this Incoterms® rule, therefore, delivery and arrival at destination are the same. [Incoterms®]
De Minimis	A Latin term that translates to '*of the least significance*' or '*too small to be meaningful*'
De Minimis Rule [Tolerance]	It allows, under certain conditions, that a small amount of non-originating materials to be used in the production of the good without affecting its originating status. The provision acts as the relaxation of the RoO, and the threshold is usually set at around 5% to 15%. [Origin]
Declarant	Any person who makes a Goods declaration or in whose name such a declaration is made. It is covered in General Annex, Chapter 2 of the RKC.
Declaration of Origin	An appropriate statement as to the origin of the goods made in connection with their exportation by the manufacturer, producer, supplier, exporter or other competent person on the commercial invoice or any other document relating to the goods. It is Covered in Annex D.2. to the Kyoto Convention of 1974 and Specific Annex K, Chapters 2 and 3 of the RKC. [Origin]

Decreed Customs Valuation	The practice to determine the value of goods by a decree for the purpose of imposition of customs duties and other charges. It is applied as a means to avoid fraud or to protect the domestic industry. The decreed value *de facto* transforms an *ad valorem* duty into a specific duty, called '*valeur mercuriale*', in the Francophone countries. It is possible to apply decreed customs valuation in accordance with the WTO Rules. [Customs Valuation]
Deductive Method	A Second Method of customs valuation, also called Method 4, where the customs value is calculated on the basis of the unit price at which the imported goods, or identical or similar goods, are sold in the country to an unrelated buyer in the greatest aggregate quantity. As a consequence of the starting point being the sales value in the country of importation, various deductions are necessary to reduce the price to the relevant customs value. [Customs Valuation]
Deep Integration [Stages]	It is concerned with behind-the-border measures, in other words, once the goods are in the country. *See Shallow Integration.* [Trade Blocs]
Deep Trade Agreements	*See Deep Integration [Stages].* [Trade Blocs]
Demurrage	A charge for detaining a freight car, ship, or other vehicle beyond the free time stipulated for loading or unloading. Demurrage may also be levied by a shipper on a consignee for containers held beyond an agreed date or for failure to take delivery of stored goods within a specified time.
Denied Party Screening	Also known as Denied Trade Screening, or Sanctions Party Screening, it tends to be used interchangeably with Restricted Party Screening. It is the process of checking or comparing, normally through automated means, a potential business partner or customer against denied party lists and sanctioned party lists to ensure that they are not violating any export control regulations. [Screening]
Denied Trade Screening	*See Denied Party Screening.* *See Sanction Party Screening.* [Screening]

Deposit	A sum of money provisionally paid, or title deeds, bearer bonds, etc., lodged as security for the payment of such duties, levies, taxes or other sums as may become chargeable. [Customs Debt]
Diagonal Cumulation	It is essentially similar to '*Bilateral Cumulation*', with the only difference being that it applies to more than two contracting parties. *See Cumulation.* *See Bilateral Cumulation.* *See Extended Cumulation.* *See Full Cumulation.* *See Multilateral Cumulation.* *See Multilateral Extended Cumulation.* *See Regional Cumulation.* *See Full Cumulation.* [Origin]
Direct Tax	A tax, such as income tax, is levied on the income or profits of the person who pays it rather than on goods or services. [Types of Duties]
Direct Transport Rule	The GSP rule requires that the good eligible for preferential treatment is transported directly from the exporting country to the importing country without significant manipulation in a third country. The intention of the rule is to maintain the originating status of the goods and prevent the exploitation of the GSP by third non-beneficiary countries [Origin]
Disassembled Goods	Also known as '*Unassembled Goods*', it is covered in GRI 2(a) Part 2, which describes how to classify the good. GRI 2(a) Part 1 describes how to classify '*Incomplete Goods*' and '*Unfinished Goods*'. [Tariff Classification]
Discharge of a Special Procedure	Completing a Customs Special Procedure of CSP. [Special Customs Procedure]
Dispersion (Tariff)	The tariff dispersion is generally analysed by compiling tariff profiles. Tariff profiles show a distribution of tariff lines according to duty ranges as follows.
Documentary Evidence of Origin	A certificate of origin, a certified declaration of origin or a declaration of origin. Covered in Annex D.2. to the Kyoto Convention of 1974 and Specific Annex K, Chapters 2 and 3 of the RKC.
Domestic Industry	It collectively refers to all the producers of a good, in a certain industry, in a country.

DPU	Under Delivered at Place Unloaded Incoterms® 2020, the seller delivers the goods – and transfers risk – to the buyer when the goods, once unloaded from the arriving means of transport, are placed at the disposable of the buyer at a named place of destination or at the agreed point within that place, if any such point is agreed. The seller bears all risks involved in bringing the goods to and unloading them at the named place of destination. In this Incoterms® rule, therefore, the delivery and arrival at the destination are the same. DPU is the only Incoterms® rule that requires the seller to unload the goods at the destination. The seller should, therefore, ensure that it is in a position to organise unloading at the named place. Should the parties intend the seller not to bear the risk and cost of unloading, the DPU rule should be avoided, and the DAP rule should be used instead. [Incoterms®]
Drawback	A drawback is a special customs regime that allows the exemption, suspension or refund of the payment of taxes on the import of inputs (raw material) used in the production of goods for export. It is covered in Annex E.4. to the Kyoto Convention and Specific Annex F, Chapter 3 of the RKC. [Types of Duties]
Drawback Procedure	The Customs procedure which, when goods are exported, provides for a repayment (total or partial) to be made in respect of the import duties and taxes charged on the goods, or on materials contained in them or consumed in their production. [Types of Duties.]
Due	It is an *'obligatory payment'*, and the origin of the word *'duty'* in *'customs duty'*.
Dumping	A good is sold in an overseas market at a price lower than the price at which it is sold in the country of its origin. Or putting it another way, the good is exported at a price less than its normal value, generally meaning they are exported for less than they are sold in the domestic market or third-country markets or at less than production cost. [Trade Remedies]
Dumping Margin	The extent to which the normal value, after adjustments, is higher than the export price after adjustments. *See Margin of Dumping.* [Trade Remedies]
Dutiable Charges	The costs added to the value of an imported good in order to calculate the customs value of the good. [Customs Valuation]

Duties and Taxes	Import duties, taxes, and/or export duties and taxes. It is covered in General Annex, Chapters 2 and 4 of the RKC. [Types of Duties]
Duty	It is traditionally known as a 'due'. [Types of Duties]
Duty Drawback	A customs procedure that allows the manufacturer or producer of a good to recover or claim all or part of the customs duties and taxes paid on imported raw material or components used in the manufacture or production of a good that is subsequently exported. This tends to be incorrectly referred to as a 'refund', which it is not, as a refund allows for the recovery of duties or taxes that have been overpaid or in error. It is also known as a clawback provision as the duties and taxes are being '*clawed back*'. *See Drawback.*
Duty-Drawback Scheme	A duty-drawback scheme (often administratively demanding) is a form of Border Tax Adjustment whereby the duties or taxes levied on imported goods are refunded, in whole or in part, when the goods are re-exported. The idea is to reduce the burden on exporters while maintaining tariffs for revenue or protective purposes.
Duty Deferments	It is not covered in the RKC. In the normal course of trade, an importer needs to pay the duties and taxes for every imported shipment and export shipment, while a manufacturer or producer will need to pay the domestic duties and taxes. Countries tend to have a facility for the deferment of the payment of the duties and taxes when it becomes due through the means of a '*Duty Deferment Account*'. [Types of Duties]
Duty Deferment Account	Duty deferment is not covered in the RKC, although the facility is available in most, if not all, countries. The account allows for the delay in the payment of the duties and taxes to a later prescribed payment date. It will be a single payment for the movement (import or local manufacture) of the goods for a particular period. The use of this facility needs to be applied for, with the approval being subject to a guarantee, bond, or a surety. The advantage of the use of this facility is that payments will tend to be made on the same day each month, allowing for efficient cash flow management and planning. *See Duty Deferment.* [Types of Duties]

Duty-Free Shop	A premise, which is under Customs control, allows goods to be provided for sale without the payment of the import duties, including excise duties and taxes. The sale of the duty-free and tax-free goods tends to be limited to travellers leaving a country or a Customs territory by sea (seaport) or air (airport).
Duty Suspension	It is a temporary reduction or elimination of the import duties, levies, and taxes paid on certain goods imported into a country. *See Tariff Suspensions on GSP.*
Economic Integration	The unification of economic policies between different states through the partial or full abolition of tariff and non-tariff restrictions on trade. [Trade Blocs]
Effective Rate of Protection	Better known by its acronym EROP, it is the measure of the protection afforded by an import restriction calculated as a percentage of the value added to the good concerned. The calculation accounts for the protection of output and the cost-raising effects of protection on inputs. *See Nominal Rate of Protection.* *See Natural Rate of Protection.*
Elasticity	A measure of a variable's sensitivity in accordance with another variable's change. Consequently, it measures the change in aggregate product demand with respect to price change. This is called elasticity of demand.
End Use	Also known as *'Authorised Use'*, it is a procedure that provides specified industries with a reduced or zero rate of customs duty on certain goods imported into a country, provided that it meets the defined criteria and is put to prescribed (specific) use, the final item that a product is integrated into, within a set time period. The provision does not apply to VAT, excise duty or anti-dumping duty. [Specific Use, Special Customs Procedures]
Equivalence	In SPS, a government recognises other countries' measures as acceptable even if they are different from their own, so long as an equivalent level of protection is provided.
Equivalent Compensation	System allowing, under certain Customs procedures, the exportation or importation of goods identical in type, description, quality and technical characteristics to those previously imported or exported. In the context of the ECE Convention on Customs treatment of pool containers used in international transport, this term means the system that

	allows the re-exportation or re-importation of a container of the same type as that of another container previously imported or exported. In certain countries, this system only allows a temporary admission for IP procedure or a temporary exportation for OP procedure is to be discharged upon presentation of a compensating product obtained from goods equivalent to those that have been exported or imported. In certain countries, this system can also be applied to goods that will be imported or exported. It is covered in the Guidelines to Chapters 1 and 2 of Specific Annex F to the RKC.
Equivalent Goods	Goods identical in description, quality and technical characteristics to those imported or exported for inward or outward processing. It is covered in Annexes E.4. (drawback), E. 6 (TA for IP), E.7. (duty-free replacement of goods) and E. 8. (temporary exportation for OP) to the Kyoto Convention, and in Specific Annex F Chapters 1 and 2 of the RKC.
Essential Character	The attribute which strongly marks and serves to distinguish what an article is – that which is indispensable to the structure, core, or condition of the article. [Tariff Classification]
Ex-factory Selling Price	Although still widely used, the term is being replaced by the EXW Incoterms®. It refers to all costs incurred by the seller up to the point where the seller places the goods at the disposal of the buyer on the seller's premises. This price does not include any further costs associated with transportation, insurance, or import duties. It is essentially the manufacturer's list price before any discounts or rebates.
Ex Ship	Incoterms® 1936 [Incoterms®]
Ex Quay	Incoterms® 1936 [Incoterms®]
Ex-Works	Under Ex-Works Incoterms® 2020, the seller delivers the goods to the buyer when it places the goods at the disposal of the buyer at a named place, and that named place may or may not be the seller's premises. The seller does not need to load the goods on any collecting vehicle, nor does it need to clear the goods for export. [Incoterms®]

Examination of Goods	The physical inspection of goods by the Customs is done to satisfy themselves that the nature, origin, condition, quantity, and value of the goods are in accordance with the particulars furnished in the Goods declaration. It is covered in General Annex, Chapter 2 of the RKC.
Excise Duty	A duty on domestic manufacture was never intended to be a duty on importation. [Types of Duties]
Excises	Broadly speaking, the distinguishing features of excise taxation are selectivity in coverage, discrimination in intent, and some form of quantitative measurement in determining the tax liability. [Types of Duties]
Explanatory Notes	Provide a commentary on the scope of each heading, giving a list of the main products included and excluded, together with technical descriptions of the goods concerned (their appearance, properties, method of production and uses) and practical guidance for their identification. Where appropriate, EN also clarify the scope of particular subheadings. It does not form an integral part of the HS Convention. However, as approved by the WCO Council, they constitute the official interpretation of the HS at the international level. They are an indispensable complement to the HS. [Tariff Classification]
Export	The word originates from the Latin word '*exportare*', which means to '*carry out*' or to '*send away*'. [The Lesson]
Export Controls	Essentially enforce health, environmental, security and safety, and technical standards that arise from the country's domestic laws and its obligation under International Agreements. *See Import Control.* [Export Control]
Export Duty	Customs duties and all other duties, taxes or charges which are collected on or in connection with the exportation of goods, but not including any charges which are limited in amount to the approximate cost of services rendered or collected by the Customs on behalf of another national authority. Covered in General Annex, Chapter 2 of the RKC. [Types of Duties]

Export Processing Zone	It denotes a geographical area or a customs enclave located near or adjacent to a seaport or airport. The general intention of the zone is to allow for the manufacture of goods with the intention of exporting the goods. [Trade Blocs]
Export Prohibitions and Restrictions	Export measures that have a limiting effect on the quantity or amount of a product being exported. They can take the form of a tax or a quantitative restriction. The latter is generally prohibited with some exceptions, notably those applied to prevent or relieve critical shortages of foodstuffs.
Export-Related Measures	It is one of the three groups of NTMs. *See Non-tariff Measures.* [Non-tariff Measures]
Export Restrictions	Restrictions on goods exported to a specific country or countries by the government of the exporting country for reasons such as a shortage of goods in the domestic market, regulating domestic prices, avoiding anti-dumping measures or for political reasons.
Export Taxes	Customs duties and all other duties, taxes or charges which are collected on or in connection with the exportation of goods, but not including any charges which are limited in amount to the approximate cost of services rendered or collected by the Customs on behalf of another national authority.
Exportation	The act of taking out or causing to be taken out any goods from the Customs territory. Covered in Specific Annex C Chapter 1 of the RKC.
Exporter of Record	Also known as EOR, it is the legal exporting entity for goods exiting a country. Fundamentally, the EOR is the person who owns and ships the product, which is a stereotypical quality equal to the Importer of Record. However, suppose an EOR is not designated. In that case, the EOR may default to the shipment's foreign recipient (foreign principal party).
Extended Cumulation	Allows materials from countries that do not necessarily have FTAs with each other to be considered as originating in the country of export, for purposes of preferential treatment. It provides more flexibility than traditional cumulation, which may require identical RoOs between all contracting countries. *See Cumulation.* *See Diagonal Cumulation.*

	See Extended Cumulation. *See Full Cumulation.* *See Multilateral Cumulation.* *See Multilateral Extended Cumulation.* *See Regional Cumulation.* *See Full Cumulation.* [Origin]
Externality	In economic terms, it is considered a societal cost due to the side effect of an activity that is not reflected in the price of a good and consequently not primarily borne by those involved in the activity, both the producer and the consumer. It is an external cost that can be either positive or negative, depending on the cost of the benefit that it expends. *See Negative Externality.* *See Positive Externality.* [Excises]
Factors of Production	In Economics, four categories are distinguished that are used in the production of the goods – capital, labour, land, and entrepreneurship. [Trade Blocs]
Fall Back Method	A Secondary Method in customs valuation, also called Method 6, which is used when the previous five methods could not be applied. It implies reverting back to the previous customs valuation methods and then this time around to apply it with a reasonable degree of flexibility, accounting for special circumstances. *See Residual Method.* *See Reasonable Means Method.* [Customs Valuation]
False Positives	Matches that are not actually sanctioned parties. [Screening]
Fair Trade Remedy	The measure is imposed against a good which is traded fairly in compliance with international trade practice. [Safeguards]
FAS	Free Alongside Ship Incoterms® 2020, the seller delivers the goods to the buyer when the goods are placed alongside the ship nominated by the buyer at the named port of shipment or when the seller procedures goods already delivered. The risk of loss or damage to the goods transfers when the goods are alongside the ship, and the buyer bears all costs from that moment onwards. [Incoterms®]
Fast Parcel Operators	Transport items worldwide in a specific time frame, including documents, parcels, and freight.

Federation Internationale de l'Automoblile	Abbreviated as FIA, it is one of the two international organisations, along with the AIT, that administers the CPD Carnet system.
Final Products	*See Finished Products.*
Finished Products	These are processed products which can be sold to consumers without further processing. *See Final Products.*
FCA Incoterms®	Under Free Carrier Incoterms® 2020, the seller delivers the goods to the buyer in one of the two ways. First, when the named place is the seller's premises, the goods are delivered when they are loaded on the means of transport arranged by the buyer. Second, when the named place is another place, the goods are delivered when having been loaded on the seller's means of transport, they reach the named other place and are ready for uploading from that seller's means of transport and at the disposal of the carrier or of another person nominated by the buyer. [Incoterms®]
FOB	FOB customs valuation means the value of imported goods for customs purposes is determined without including the cost of international freight or insurance between the exporter's and importer's customs frontiers. The FOB value essentially represents the value of the goods at the point of loading onto the vessel or other mode of transport at the exporter's frontier. This FOB should not be confused with the FOB Incoterms®. *See Free on Board.* [Customs Valuation]
FOB Incoterms®	In accordance with Incoterms®, the seller delivers the goods to the buyer on board the vessel nominated by the buyer at the named port of shipment or procures the goods already so delivered. The risk of loss of or damage to the goods transfers when the goods are on board the vessel, and the buyer bears all costs from that moment onwards. [Incoterms®]
Force Majeure	A superior or irresistible force, an event or effect that cannot be reasonably anticipated or controlled. This will include natural calamities such as storms, lightning, shipwreck, inundations, fires, hostile incursions, exceptional droughts or frosts. It is the same as *Vis Major.* [*See* Vis Major]

Foreign Trade Zone	*See Free Zone.* *See Free Port.* *See Free Warehouse.* *See Foreign Trade Zone.* [Trade Blocs]
Formula duties	The formula consists of a reference price, above which an *ad valorem* duty would apply to high-cost developed countries and below which, in addition to the *ad valorem* duty, a progressive specific duty (unit of measure) would apply against low-cost developing countries. [Types of Duties]
Forwarder	Also known as a '*Forwarding Agent*', '*Freight Forwarder*' and '*Shipping Agent*', it facilitates the movement of goods between countries. *See Forwarding Agent.* *See Freight Forwarder.* *See Shipping Agent.*
Forwarding Agent	*See Forwarder.* *See Freight Forwarder.* *See Shipping Agent.*
Free Circulation	Also known as '*Home Use*', it is a customs procedure where the goods are cleared; in other words, all Customs formalities are concluded, and the goods are then released to the domestic market.
Free on Board	If it is not specifically denoted as an Incoterms®, it refers to the basis of customs valuation. *See Cost, Insurance and Freight.* [Customs Valuation] Better known by its acronym FOB. [Incoterms®]
Free Ports	*See Free Trade Zone.* [Trade Blocs]
Free Rider	A term that infers that a country that does not make any trade concessions profits, nonetheless, from tariff cuts and concessions made by other countries in negotiations under the MFN principle.
Free Trade Agreement	Not to be confused with a Free Trade Area, it provides for the elimination of tariffs, QRs and NTBs between member countries while each contracting member retains their own external tariff. [Trade Bloc]

Free Trade Area	Known as an FTA, it should not be confused with a Free Trade Agreement, which shares the same abbreviation but refers to the Agreement itself. It provides for the elimination of tariffs, QRs and NTBs between member countries while each contracting member retains their own external tariff. [Trade Bloc]
Free Trade Zone	A customs enclave is an enclosed area within a customs territory where imported goods can be entered into or stored, moved, used, or processed for export outside of the customs territory or released under another SCP such as IP, TA, or End Use. Should the goods be exported to the adjacent Customs territory, then the prevailing import duty and taxes need to be accounted for. Known under various other names, such as '*Free Port*', '*Free Warehouse*', or '*Foreign Trade Zone*'. Covered in Specific Annex D, Chapter 2 of the RKC. *See Free Port.* *See Free Warehouse.* *See Foreign Trade Zone.* [Trade Blocs]
Free Warehouse	*See Free Trade Zone.* *See Free Zone.* *See Free Port.* *See Foreign Trade Zone.* [Trade Blocs]
Free Zone	An FZ is a customs enclave in a country, an enclosed area within a country's customs territory where imported goods can be entered into or stored, moved, used, or processed for export outside of the country's customs territory or released under another SCP such as IP, TA, or End Use. Should the goods be exported to the adjacent Customs territory, then the prevailing import duty and taxes need to be accounted for. An FTZ could also be used as a bonded warehouse for the storage of goods for the local market. *See Storage.* *See Foreign Trade Zone.* *See Free Zone.* *See Free Port.* *See Free Warehouse.* [Trade Blocs, SCP]

Freight Forwarder	Also known as a '*Forwarder*', '*Forwarding Agent*', and '*Shipping Agent*', it facilitates the movement of goods between countries. *See Forwarder.* *See Forwarding Agent* *See Shipping Agent.*
Full Cumulation	This is the most preferential and flexible of the types of cumulation as it allows for components (inputs) that are not sufficiently worked or processed or originating in any of the contracting parties to be considered originating. *See Cumulation.* *See Bilateral Cumulation.* *See Diagonal Cumulation.* *See Extended Cumulation.* *See Multilateral Cumulation.* *See Multilateral Extended Cumulation.* *See Regional Cumulation.* [Origin]
Fuzzy Matching	Rather than flagging records as a '*match*' or a '*non-match*', fuzzy matching identifies the likelihood that two records are true matches based on whether they agree or disagree on the various identifiers. To reduce the number of false positives, organisations can use advanced screening solutions that utilise fuzzy matching algorithms and other techniques to improve accuracy. [Screening]
General Rules of Classification	The GRI are rules that govern the classification of goods under the Harmonized Commodity Description and Coding System. [Tariff Classification]
Generalised System of Preferences	Also called the Generalised System of Trade Preferences, better known by its acronym GSP, it is a system through which industrialised high-income countries grant preferential access to their markets to developing countries, with special preferences to LDCs. [Origin]
Geographical Indications	GIs are indications that identify a good as originating in a place or a region, where a given quality, reputation or other characteristic of the good is essentially attributable to its geographic origin. Examples include '*Rooibos*', '*Tequila*' '*Champagne*' or '*Roquefort*'. Interestingly, the cheese from the town of 'Cheddar' is not considered a GI. [Origin]

Gloomy Taxes	It is the collective categorisation of duties, taxes, and levies imposed on smoking, drinking, petroleum (energy), and health (sugar). *See Gray Taxes* [Types of Duties]
Good	It is the merchandise or the item, also known as a product. *See Incomplete Goods.* *See Unfinished Goods.* *See Unassembled Goods.* *See Disassembled Goods.*
Goods Declaration	A statement made in the form prescribed by a Customs Authority, by which the '*persons interested*' indicate the Customs procedure to be applied to the goods and furnish the particulars which the Customs require to be declared for the application of that procedure. The '*persons interested*' may be the importer, the exporter, the owner, the consignee, or the carrier of the goods or their legal representative, according to the country concerned.
Goods in Free Circulation	Goods for which Customs formalities have been concluded, or which require no formalities, which may be disposed of without Customs restriction. Covered in Specific Annex B, Chapters 1 and 2 of the RKC.
Grey Taxes	Excises can be grouped into two categories, 'grey taxes', or '*gloomy taxes*', and '*green taxes*'. '*Grey taxes*' tend to be imposed on smoking, drinking, petroleum (energy), and health (sugar). *See Gloomy Taxes.* [Types of Taxes]
Green Subsidy	Also known as *Non-Actionable Subsidy.* *See Trade Remedies.* *See Amber Subsidy.* *See Red (Prohibited Subsidy).* [Trade Remedies]
Green Taxes	Excises can be grouped into two categories, '*Grey Taxes*' or '*Gloomy Taxes*' and '*Green Taxes*'. '*Green Taxes*' tend to impose levies on goods that impact CO_2, plastic, climate change, and the environment. *See Grey Taxes.* *See Gloomy Taxes.* [The Lesson]
Grey Imports	*See Parallel Imports.*

Guarantee	A customs guarantee is an agreement (usually from a bank or insurer) to pay the Customs Authority if the importer does not pay debts arising from duties, levies, and taxes. It is a commitment which is provided through financial means to secure the payment of import or export customs duties and, if applicable, other charges. *See Bond* *See Individual Guarantee.* *See Customs Comprehensive Guarantee.* [Customs Debt]
Harmonized System	The HS or '*Harmonized Commodity Description and Coding System*' is a nomenclature developed by the WCO for customs tariffs and international trade statistics to organise products through hierarchical categories. [Tariff Classification]
Harmonized System Convention	It commonly refers to the International Convention of the Harmonized Commodity Description and Coding System, adopted by the CCC in 1988. The HS Convention requires that HS headings, subheadings and numerical codes be used without addition or modification and that the GRI be used for its application. [Conventions]
Harmonising Formula	Used in tariff negotiations for much steeper reductions in higher tariffs than in lower tariffs, the final rates being '*harmonised*', brought closer together.
Haulier	A business or a person that deals mainly with the physical transportation of goods
Heading	Tariff Heading *See Section.* *See Chapter.* *See Subheading.* [Tariff Classification]
Hybrid Screening	This is one of the three types of Screening *See Transaction-Based Screening.* *See Transaction Screening.* [Screening]
Party-Based Screening	Also known as 'Client Screening', 'Party-Based Screening' refers to screening all business partners, clients, businesses (companies), and entities against the denied party lists and sanctioned party lists, and in the matching accounting for any false positives that might arise. It is one of the three types of '*Screening*', the others being Transaction Screening or Transaction-Based Screening, and Hybrid Screening.

	See Client Screening. *See Party-Based Screening.* *See Transaction Screening.* *See Transaction-Based Screening.* *See Hybrid Screening.* [Screening]
Identical Goods	The first Secondary Method of customs valuation, and the first following the Primary Method, also known as Method 2, where the price of goods is the same in all respects, including physical characteristics, quality and reputation. [Customs Valuation]
Incomplete Goods	Also known as '*Unfinished Goods*', it is covered in GRI 2(a) Part 1, which describes how to classify the good. *See Unfinished Goods.* [Tariff Classification]
Incoterms®	*See International Commercial Terms.* [Incoterms®]
International Commercial Terms	Incoterms® rules are a set of standards used in international and domestic contracts for the delivery of goods. UNCITRAL recognises them as the global standard for the interpretation of the most common terms in foreign trade, helping to avoid costly misunderstandings by clarifying the tasks, costs and risks involved in the delivery of goods from sellers to buyers. [Incoterms®]
Indirect Tax	It is imposed on the consumers, the persons who ultimately pay the duty, also expressed as '*the person who ultimately meets the levy*'. These are '*consumption taxes*'. *See Consumption Taxes.* *See Customs Duty.* *See Excise Duty.* *See Value Added Tax.* [Types of Duties]
Import	The act of bringing or causing any goods to be brought into a Customs territory, or a country.
Import Control	Essentially to enforce health, environmental, security and safety, and technical standards that arise from the country's domestic laws and its obligation under International Agreements. *See Export Control.* [Import Control]

Import Duty	The collective term for charges, duties, levies, taxes, and surcharges imposed on the importation of goods. *See Import Duties and Taxes.* [Types of Duties]
Import Duties and Taxes	Customs duties and all other duties, taxes or charges which are collected on or in connection with the importation of goods, but not including any charges which are limited in amount to the approximate cost of services rendered or collected by the Customs on behalf of another national authority. It is covered in General Annex, Chapter 2 of the RKC. *See Import Duty.* [Types of Duties]
Import Licensing	The requirement to obtain a permit for importing a product; administrative procedures for obtaining an import licence.
Import-Related Measures	It is one of the three groups of NTMs. *See Non-tariff Measures.* [NTMs]
Importation	The act of bringing or causing any goods to be brought into a Customs territory.
Import monitoring	It is a measure to monitor the import value and volume of specified products, which may be applied with the purpose of signalling concern over import surges.
Importer of record	Also known as the IOR, it is the fiscal entity taking responsibility for the import of goods into a different customs territory from where they were sent. It is the person responsible for ensuring that imported goods comply with all customs and legal requirements of the country of import whose name appears on the Customs clearance documentation as the importer of the goods.
Indirect agent	An agent who acts in their own name but on behalf of another person.
Individual guarantee	A guarantee covering a single operation for an existing or potential customs debt and, if applicable, for other charges. [Customs Debt]
Injury	*See Material Injury.* *See Dumping.* [Trade Remedies]

Infant Industry Protection	The infant industry argument posits that an emerging domestic industry requires temporary protection from international competition in order to be afforded the opportunity to become a competitive industry. The lack of a definition of an 'infant industry' poses the real challenge. [Types of Duties]
Intellectual Property	Known as IP, it refers to creations of the mind, such as inventions, literary and artistic works, designs, symbols, names and images used in commerce. *See IP Non-tariff Measures.*
Intellectual Property Rights	The term is defined by the World Intellectual Property Organization (WIPO), it is a collective referring to the following rights: (1) Copyright and related rights; (2) Trademarks: any sign, including words, names, letters, numerals, figurative elements and combinations of colours, or combinations of these are used by a manufacturer or merchant to identify its goods and distinguish them from those manufactured or sold by others; (3) geographical indications (GIs), which identify a good as originating in the territory of a State, or a region or locality in that territory, where a given quality, reputation or other characteristics of the good is essentially attributable to its geographical origin; (4) industrial designs; (5) patents which shall be available for any inventions, whether products or processes, in all fields of technology, provided that they are new, involve an inventive step and are capable of industrial application;
	(6) layout design (topographies) of integrated circuits: either a protected layout design or an integrated circuit in which a protected layout design is incorporated; (7) protection of undisclosed information such as trade secrets and other business confidential information.
Interim Review	A definitive trade remedy duty (anti-dumping or countervailing duty) remains in place for a period of five years. A request to a Trade Remedy Authority to review within a period of one year of its introduction is termed an 'Interim Review', or an 'Administrative Review'. *See* Administrative Review. [Trade Remedies]
Intermediate	Goods sold on to a manufacturer for additional processing prior to final sale. *See Secondary Goods.*

Intermediary	Customs intermediaries are businesses that help traders in moving goods across borders. They offer a range of different services, including providing/arranging transportation of goods, completing customs declarations and paying tariffs/import duties.
International Chamber of Commerce	Known as the ICC, it is the institutional representative of 45 million companies in more than 170 countries, making it easier for businesses to trade internationally. It believes in the power of the private sector to change the world for the better. It is uniquely positioned to ensure the voice of businesses, large and small, is heard where it matters most. [Organisations]
International Convention	Or treaty is an agreement between different countries that is legally binding to the contracting States.
International Entente	(a type of informal agreement or understanding between nations)
International Organisations	*See* ICC, WCO, WTO.
Inward Processing	Or IP is the Customs procedure under which certain goods can be brought into a Customs territory conditionally relieved from payment of import duties and taxes, on the basis that such goods are intended for manufacturing, processing or repair and subsequent exportation. *See Rebate Provisions* *See Manufacturing Rebate Provisions*
Issuing Authority	An association approved by the Customs Authorities to issue ATA Carnet, CPD Carnet, or TIR Carnet, which is affiliated directly or indirectly with a guaranteeing chain. The issuing association must be approved by the Customs Authorities of the Contracting Party.
Istanbul Convention	The expression commonly refers to the Convention on TA, adopted by the WCO in Istanbul in 1990.
Johannesburg Convention	It is commonly used to refer to the International Convention on Mutual Administrative Assistance in Customs Matters, adopted by the WCO in Brussels in 2003.
Judicial Review	An 'interested party' may challenge the preliminary determination of the Trade Remedy Authority, prior to the finalisation of an investigation. [Trade Remedies]
Kyoto Convention	The expression commonly used to refer to the International Convention on the simplification and harmonisation of Customs procedures adopted by the WCC in Kyoto in 1973.

League of Nations	Was an international diplomatic group developed after World War I to solve disputes between countries before they erupted into open warfare. A precursor to the UN, the League achieved some victories but had a mixed record of success, sometimes putting self-interest before becoming involved with conflict resolution and contending with governments that did not recognise its authority. The League effectively ceased operations during World War II. [Organisations]
Levels of Duty	*See Types of Duties.*
Levy	It is imposed for a designated purpose.
Lisbon Agreement	Treaty, administered by the WIPO, for the protection of geographical indications and their international registration.
Long-Haul Destination Country	*See Natural Protection.*
Luxury Goods	Non-essential means not absolutely necessary. *See Non-Essential Goods.*
Luxury Taxes	Or '*non-essential taxes*' are taxes imposed on goods which could well be considered vanity goods, which are not really needed and merely contribute to the depletion of the world's natural resources. In the instance of Customs and Excises, they should really be 'luxury duties'. [Types of Duties]
Mandatory Review	*See Sunset Review.* [Trade Remedies]
Manufacturing Rebate Provisions	*See IP/Rebate Provisions.*
Margin of Preference	The difference between the duty paid on an MFN basis and the duty paid under a preferential system.
Market Access	Market access for goods in the WTO means the conditions, tariff measures, and NTMs agreed upon by members for the entry of specific goods into their markets.
Material Injury	*See Injury.* [Trade Remedies]
Maximum Price System	Decreed by the authorities of the importing country and above which price(s) imports may not enter the domestic market. Actual import prices below the decreed minimums trigger a protective action, such as the imposition of

	additional duties or a quantitative restriction. Different terms are used in different countries and different sectors: basic import price, minimum import price, reference price, and trigger price. *See Minimum Price System.* *See Trigger Price.* [Types of Duties]
Maximum Tariff	*See Ceiling Rate.* *See Bound Rate.* *See Bound Tariff.* [Types of Duties]
Mega Free Trade Agreements	Also known as Mega Regionals, they are deep integration partnerships between countries or regions with a major share of world trade and foreign direct investment (FDI). Beyond simply increasing trade links, the deals aim to improve regulatory compatibility and provide a rules-based framework for ironing out differences in investment and business climates. [Trade Blocs]
Mercantilism	A nationalist economic policy whose purpose is to maximise exports, thus increasing the prosperity and power of a country, while minimising imports through restrictive trade practices. [The Lesson]
Minimum Import Price	A tariff regime seeks to ensure that imports do not enter a member's domestic market below a certain minimum price. Should the price of an individual consignment be below the specified minimum import price, an additional charge is imposed corresponding to the difference between the two prices.
Minimum Price System	Decreed by the authorities of the importing country and below which price(s) imports may not enter the domestic market. Actual import prices below the decreed minimums trigger a protective action, such as the imposition of additional duties or a quantitative restriction. Different terms are used in different countries and different sectors: basic import price, minimum import price, reference price, and trigger price. *See Maximum Price System.* *See Trigger Price.* [Types of Duties]

Most-Favoured Nation Tariff	The MFN tariff, Normal non-discriminatory tariff, charged on imports (excludes preferential tariffs under free trade agreements and other schemes or tariffs charged inside quotas).
Most-Favoured Nation Treatment	The MFN principle, for goods, requires that each WTO member must extend to all other Members treatment no less favourable than it accords to imports from any other country. It is covered in GATT Article I, GATS Article II and TRIPS Article 4, the principle of non-discrimination between a country's trading partners.
Multimodal	*See Multimodal Transport.* [Incoterms®]
Multimodal Transport	The transportation of goods under a single contract, normally by one transport provider, using at least two different modes of transport in the movement of the goods by either road, rail, sea, waterway, or air. [Incoterms®]
Multilateral Cumulation	Materials or processing from multiple countries within an FTA are considered when determining the origin of a good. Essentially, it allows for a good to be treated as originating from one country within the FTA even if they were partially produced or sourced in other contracting countries. *See Cumulation.* *See Diagonal Cumulation.*
	See Extended Cumulation. *See Full Cumulation.* *See Multilateral Extended Cumulation.* *See Regional Cumulation.* [Origin]
Multilateral Extended Cumulation	An FTA provision where multiple countries can consider products originating in any of the contracting countries as if they originated in the final country of production, even if the countries do not all have identical RoO. This is a more flexible approach to RoO than other forms of cumulation that require similar RoO between all participating countries. *See Cumulation.* *See Diagonal Cumulation.* *See Extended Cumulation.* *See Full Cumulation.* *See Multilateral Cumulation.* *See Regional Cumulation.* [Origin]

Multilateral Trade Agreement	These are intergovernmental agreements aimed at expanding and liberalising international trade under non-discriminatory, predictable and transparent conditions set out in an array of rights and obligations. *See Bilateral Trade Agreement.* *See Unilateral Trade Agreement.* [Trade Blocs]
Multilateral Trading System	The multilateral trading system is a non-discriminatory arrangement for international trade, which came into existence with the GATT in 1947 and is now represented by the WTO system.
National Treatment	Once foreign goods and services have entered a country and satisfied its formalities, they are required to be treated in exactly the same way as national goods and services. It is imperative that they are subject to the exact same duties, levies, and taxes and are subject to no additional restrictions, or any form of disparity, or discrimination.
Natural Protection	The protection that a country's domestic industry is afforded is simply due to the cost that an importer incurs to land the goods in a country. Long-haul destination countries tend to have a higher level of natural protection, and the basis of their customs valuation tends to be FOB.
Nature of Duties	It refers to the different kinds of duty, be it customs duty or excise duty, which can, among others, be either *ad valorem*, specific, compound, mixed, or variable. [Types of Duties]
Negative Externality	*See Externality.* *See Positive Externality.*
New Shipper Review	If an exporter did not transact with a country during the course of an anti-dumping investigation, and/or countervailing investigation and is in their own view prejudiced by an anti-dumping duty, the exporter may petition for a New Shipper Review. The intention is to have the exporter's goods excluded from the liability of a stipulated anti-dumping duty, or countervailing duty. [Trade Remedies]
Nomenclature	An agreed system for classifying goods according to defined criteria and in given detail and order by associating a number of the specific goods with the nomenclature used by all contracting parties to the nomenclature. *See Tariff Nomenclature.* [Tariff Classification]

Nominal Rate of Protection	The proportion by which an import's (tariff-inclusive) domestic price exceeds the landed price. *See also Effective Rate of Protection.*
Non-actionable Subsidies	Also known as non-actionable subsidies, it means that a WTO Member country cannot initiate a countervailing (anti-subsidy) investigation against another Member for the use of such a subsidy. *See Trade Remedies.* *See Green Light Subsidy.* *See Amber Light Subsidy (Actionable).* *See Red Light Subsidy (Prohibited).*
Non-discrimination	The WTO operates on the principle of non-discrimination, ensuring fair and consistent treatment of trade between members. This principle is embodied in two key concepts: MFN treatment and National Treatment. MFN prohibits countries from discriminating between trading partners, while National Treatment ensures that foreign goods and services are treated no less favourably than domestic counterparts after they have been imported. The MFN treatment excludes GSP and trade blocs.
Non-dutiable Charges	The costs deducted from the value of an imported good in order to calculate the customs value of the good. [Customs Valuation] [Customs Valuation]
Non-essential Goods	Also known as '*Luxury Goods*', these are considered, by Customs Authorities, to be non-essential, meaning that there is a cheaper alternative and that the good is not absolutely necessary. *See Luxury Goods.*
Non-preferential Rules of Origin	Primarily used to determine the country of origin of the good for the application of the MFN. It has further trade policy application through protective measures such as trade remedies (anti-dumping, countervailing, and safeguards), trade embargoes, tariff quotas, and quantitative restrictions. Its use extends to, among others, trade statistics and origin marking. *See Rules of Origin.* [Origin]
Non-qualifying Operation	An operation that does not confer origin. It is considered below the threshold of sufficient production or processing. In order to obtain preferential status, the good would need to undergo further processing. [Origin]

Non-reciprocal agreement	Unilateral trade agreement A non-reciprocal agreement, also called *'one-sided'*, where a country lowers or removes trade restrictions and barriers to trade for the imports of another country or countries. The preferential arrangement is normally extended by a developed country to a developing country, an example of which is the GSP. The objective of such an agreement is to provide the developing country or countries with increased market access to the developing country's market and to increase its exports, aiding its economic growth. *See Bilateral Trade Agreement.* *See Multilateral Trade Agreement.* [Trade Blocs]
Non-tariff Barriers	Known as NTBs, they refer to the restrictions resulting from prohibitions, conditions, or specific market requirements that make the importation or exportation of products difficult and/or costly. It also includes the unjustified and/or improper application of NTMs, such as SPS measures and other TBT. NTBs arise from measures taken by governments and authorities in the form of laws, regulations, policies, conditions, restrictions, specific requirements, or prohibitions that protect its domestic industries from foreign competition. [Non-tariff Measures and Trade Barriers]
Non-tariff Measures	Known as NTMs, these are policy measures other than tariffs that can potentially have an economic effect on international trade in goods. They are increasingly shaping trade, influencing who trades what and how much. There are three groups (categories) of NTMs, namely Import-Related Measures, Export-Related Measures, and Non-technical Measures. [Non-tariff Measures] Groups or Categories
Non-technical Measures	It is one of the three groups of NTMs. *See Non-tariff Measures.* [Non-tariff Measures]
Non-trade Measures	NTMs [Non-tariff Measures]
Notification of Intended Return	Goods exported with notification of *'intended return'* means goods specified by the declarant as intended for re-importation. Consequently, identification measures may be taken by the Customs to facilitate re-importation in the same state. It is covered in Specific Annex B, Chapter 2 of the RKC.

Nuisance Tariff	A tariff that is so low that it costs the government more to collect than the revenue it generates. There is no accepted definition for such a tariff. The tariff does not have any protective effect; it is superfluous. [Types of Duties]
Omission	It is considered the failure by the Customs Authority to act or to make a decision required by the Customs law within a reasonable time on a matter duly submitted to the Authority. It is covered in General Annex, Chapter 2 of the RKC.
One Stop Border Post	A border crossing point where goods and their means of transport stop once only to undertake both exit formalities from one country and entry formalities into the other.
Origin	It is quite simply the place where a good is produced or created. Origin is the '*economic nationality*' of a good, meaning where it was substantially transformed or produced. [Origin]
Origin Engineering	The relocation of part of a good's manufacturing from one country to another country to avoid unfavourable trade restrictions, such as higher duty rates or quotas. *See RoO.* [Origin]
Origination	It refers to the country where a good is produced or manufactured, which is distinct from the country where it is shipped from. This determination is crucial for international trade as it affects how much duty is paid on imports and whether goods can be exported to specific countries.
Outright Exportation	Where goods, which are in free circulation or home use, leave the country or a Customs territory with the express intention to remain permanently outside it. It is covered in Specific Annex C, Chapter 1 of the RKC.
Outside Quota Tariff Rate (OQTR)	Known as OQTR, it is the tariff rate applicable to imported goods that are in excess of a tariff quota volume. The tariff rate is usually much higher than the tariff rate applied to imports within the quota. [Types of Duties]
Outsourcing	It is when a function is tasked or delegated by the principal to an intermediary to complete. In a customs context, it could be the completion of a Customs Declaration.

Outward Processing	Also known as OP, it is the Customs procedure under which goods which are in free circulation in a Customs territory may be temporarily exported for manufacturing, processing or repair abroad and then re-imported with total or partial exemption from import duties and taxes. [*See* Outward Processing, Special Customs Procedure.]
Para-tariff	Is a charge imposed on imports that acts as a tariff in that it increases the cost of the imports. Still, the tariff is not included in the country's tariff schedule. Such charges could include stamp fees, a foreign exchange transactions tax, and a statistical tax. [Types of Duties]
Parallel imports	Also known as *'Grey Imports'*, it means that although the good is legally manufactured abroad, it is imported without the permission of the IP-holder, for instance, the holder(s) of the trademark, copyright, or patent. It is considered an arbitrage activity as the importer imports the goods from a lower-priced market into a higher-priced country.
Party-Based Screening	Also known as *'Client Screening', 'Party-Based Screening'* refers to screening all business partners, clients, businesses (companies), and entities against the denied party lists and sanctioned party lists, and in the matching accounting for any false positives that might arise.
	It is one of the three types of *'Screening'*, the others being Transaction Screening or Transaction-Based Screening, and Hybrid Screening. *See Client Screening.* *See Party-Based Screening.* *See Transaction Screening.* *See Transaction-Based Screening.* *See Hybrid Screening.* [Screening]
Partial Relief	The relief from payment of a part of the total amount of import duties and taxes which would otherwise be payable had the goods been cleared for free circulation or home use on the date on which they were placed under the TA procedure. It is covered in Annex E of the Istanbul Convention. [Special Customs Procedures – TA]

Percentage Rule	Also known as the *'Ad Valorem Rule'*, *'Value-Added Rule'*, *'Value Content Rule'*, and *'Percentage Rule'*. The 25% RoO is based on *'value thresholds'* – *'local content'* or *'regional content'*. When the value added of a good increases up to a specified level expressed by an *ad valorem* percentage. The value-added criterion can be expressed in two ways: a maximum allowance for non-originating materials or a minimum requirement for domestic content. *See Value Content Rule.* [Origin]
Pigouvian Tax	*See Pigovian Tax.* [Types of Duties]
Pigovian tax	Also spelled Pigouvian tax, it serves to redress market failures caused by negative externalities, where the consumer of a good's actions impose costs on others without those costs being reflected in the good's market price. *See Pigouvian Tax.* [Types of Duties]
Policy Space	The difference, or gap, between the 'bound tariff' and the 'applied tariff' of MFN. *See Water in the Tariff.* *See Tariff Overhang.* *See Tariff Cliff.* *See Binding Overhand Principle.* [Types of Duties]
Political Union	The ultimate aim is for a common political environment, which is an additional stage to an Economic Union. [Trade Blocs]
Positive Externality	*See Externality.* *See Negative Externality.*
Post Clearance Audit	A systematic Customs control measure to ensure the accuracy and authenticity of declarations through the examination of the relevant books, records, business systems, and commercial data kept by persons/companies directly or indirectly involved in international trade.
Pre-shipment Inspection	Also known as PSI, it is the physical inspection of a good before it is shipped from the country of export, which establishes the exact nature of the good. It assures that the good conforms with the accompanying documents that specify their tariff classification (commodity or HS code), origin, customs valuation, quality, and quantity, to name the most prominent. [Non-tariff Measures]

Preferential Rules of Origin	Used to determine whether goods qualify as originating from certain countries, for which special arrangements and agreements apply. *See Non-preferential Rules of Origin.* [Origin]
Preferential Trade Area	Also known as a *'Preferential Trading Agreement'* and a Preferential Trade Arrangement, which removes the trade barriers - tariff and NTBs - between members, offering preferential access to markets on a non-reciprocal basis. This is one of the exceptions permitted under the WTO's MFN principle, known as the GSP. *See Preferential Trade Arrangement.* *See Preferential Trading Agreement.* *See Generalised System of Preferences (GSP).* [Trade Blocs]
Preferential Trade Arrangement	*See Preferential Trade Area.* *See Preferential Trading Agreement.* *See Generalised System of Preferences (GSP).* [Trade Blocs]
Preferential Trading Agreement	*See Preferential Trade Area.* *See Preferential Trade Arrangement.* *See Generalised System of Preferences (GSP).* [Trade Blocs]
Preferential Tariffs	Tariffs are lower than the MFN tariffs, which are levied on an imported good from a country that is being given favoured treatment through a preferential trade area, a preferential trade arrangement, or a preferential trading arrangement. These are effectively unilateral tariff preferences. *See Preferential Trade Area.* *See Preferential Trade Arrangement.* *See Preferential Trading Agreement.* *See Generalised System of Preferences (GSP).* [Trade Blocs] [Types of Duties]
Prevailing Tariff	Also known as the *'Applied Tariff'* or *'Applied Rate'*, it might be lower than the country's bound tariff rate. The reason is that WTO members have the flexibility to increase or decrease their tariffs, provided that the prevailing tariff does not exceed the bound tariff rate. *See Applied Tariff.* *See Applied Rate.* *See Bound Rate. WHAT ABOUT BOUND TARIFF* *See Ceiling Tariff.* [Types of Duties]

Price-Control Measures	Price-control measures are measures implemented to control the prices of imported articles in order to support the domestic price of certain products when the import price of these goods is lower, establish the domestic price of certain products because of price fluctuation in domestic markets or price instability in a foreign market and counteract the damage resulting from the occurrence of '*unfair*' foreign trade practices.
Price Undertaking	It is a Commitment by an exporter to either raise prices or reduce sales in a market as a way of settling an anti-dumping suit brought by import-competing domestic firms. It tends to have an effect analogous to a quota. [Trade Remedies]
Prima Facie	The Latin expression means '*at first sight*', '*at first view*', or '*based on first impression*'. At first sight, accepted as such until proved otherwise. [Trade Remedies]-
Primary Method	There is the first and only one method, the transaction value (TV) method, which requires the determination of the '*actual price paid or payable*' for the imported good. The addition of 'payable' for the customs valuation accounts for all payments made in procuring the goods, including future payments. This method applies first; should it fail to determine a customs value of the goods, then the five secondary methods need to be considered. [Customs Valuation]
Primary Products	Also called commodities or primary goods, these are goods sold for production or consumption just as they were found in nature.
Prior Authorisation	The process of obtaining permission from a Customs Authority before the importation of the goods. Such permission is subject to a guarantee or security being lodged that essentially covers the extent of the importer's Customs debt or potential duty and tax liability. *See Customs Debt.* *See Authorisation.* [Special Customs Procedures]
Processing	*See Inward Process (IP)* *See Outward Processing (OP)* [Special Customs Procedures]

Processing of Goods for Home Use	The Customs procedure under which imported goods may be manufactured, processed or worked before clearance for home use and under Customs control, to such an extent that the amount of the import duties and taxes applicable to the products thus obtained is lower than that which would be applicable to the imported goods. *See Processing.*
Production of Goods to Customs	It is one of the Customs formalities, the act of presenting a good to the Customs authority at the place designated or accepted by them for completion of the Customs formalities.
Progressive Tax	A higher rate (percentage) of tax is applied to more wealthier consumers than to poorer consumers. *See Regressive Tax.* *See Proportional Tax.* [Types of Duties]
Prohibited Goods	The importation or exportation of a good is forbidden or completely banned by law or authority. A good is never allowed, under any circumstances, to enter or exit a country. Such treatment is possibly due to a possible health threat, environmental danger, or protection of endangered species of flora and fauna. Conventions such as the Convention in International Trade in Endangered Species (CITES), Authorisation and Restriction of Chemicals (REACH), and the Basel Convention on hazardous waste, counterfeit or pirated goods are examples of the stipulation of prohibited goods.
Prohibited Subsidy	Also known as '*Red Subsidy*', it is a subsidy that is prohibited from being used by a WTO Member country to incentivise its manufacturers to export goods. Require recipients to meet certain export targets or to use domestic goods instead of imported goods. They are prohibited because they are specifically designed to distort international trade and are, therefore, likely to hurt other countries' trade. *See Amber (Actionable Subsidy).* *See Green (Non-actionable Subsidy).* [Trade Remedies]
Proportional Tax	The same rate (percentage) is applied to all goods, regardless of the consumer's income, but as consumption increases, so does the rate. *See Proportional Tax.* *See Progressive Tax.* [Types of Duties]

Punitive Tariff	A very high rate of customs duty (tariff) imposed on an imported good to protect the domestic manufacturers/producers. Prior to the establishment of the WTO, the imposition of such a tariff would have resulted in the exporting country imposing a tariff in kind, called a Retaliatory Tariff. *See Retaliatory Tariff.* [Types of Duties]
Quasi-Tariff	As the first word 'quasi' suggests, it has some of the features of the tariff, but not all. It is not a traditional tariff in the sense of the word, but it is rather a barrier to trade, an NTB to be specific, that has a similar effect on trade as a tariff has. [Types of Duties]
Quantitative Restrictions	Known as QRs, these are specific limits on the quantity or value of goods that can be imported (or exported) during a specific time period. [Non-tariff Barriers]
Quantitative Quotas	Any pre-set quantity authorised for importation or exportation of given goods during a specified period, beyond which no additional quantity of these goods can be imported or exported.
Quantity Control Measures	Aimed at restraining the quantity of goods that can be imported, regardless of whether they come from different sources or one specific supplier. These measures can take the form of restrictive licensing, fixing of a predetermined quota, or through prohibitions. [Non-tariff Barriers]
Raw Materials	The first stage of processing is the measurement of tariff escalation. The material is in its primary form and will be used in the manufacture/production of a good. *See Semi-manufactures.* *See Finished Products.*
Re-exportation	Exportation from a Customs territory of goods previously imported into that territory.
Re-exports	Foreign goods that are re-exported in the same state as previously imported. They are included in the country's exports. It is recommended that customs offices record them separately for analytical purposes; however, this is rarely done in practice.
Re-importation	Importation into a country (Customs territory) of goods previously exported from that country. [Special Customs Procedures]

Re-importation in the Same State	*See Re-imported.* *See Re-imports.*
Re-imported	*See Returned Goods Relief or RGR.* [Special Customs Procedures]
Re-imports	Refer to the import of goods in the same state as it was previously exported. The country of origin of the goods is, in this case, the compiling country itself, which is reflected as a country's trade with itself. The Customs procedure under which goods which were exported may be taken into home use free of import duties and taxes, provided they have not undergone any manufacturing, processing or repairs abroad and provided that any sums chargeable as a result of repayment or remission of or conditional relief from duties and taxes or of any subsidies or other amounts granted in connection with exportation must be paid. The goods that are eligible for re-importation in the same state can be goods that were in free circulation or were compensating products. It is covered in Specific Annex B, Chapter 2 of the RKC. *See Re-importation in the Same State.* *See Re-imported.* [Special Customs Procedures]
Reasonable Means Method	*See Fall Back Method.* *See Residual Method.* [Customs Valuation]
Rebate	Allows for the reduction or waiving of the import duties.
Rebate Provisions	*See Inward Process or IP.* *See Manufacturing Rebate Provisions.* [Special Customs Procedures]
Red Subsidy	*See Prohibited Subsidy.* *See Amber (Actionable Subsidy).* *See Green (Non-Actionable Subsidy).* [Trade Remedies]
Refund	The repayment of the duty, tax, and levy that were paid for which the importer was not liable.
Regional Appellation Certificate	A certificate drawn up in accordance with the rules laid down by an authority or approved body, certifying that the goods described therein qualify for a designation specific to the given region - Champagne, Karoo meat, Port wine, and Parmesan cheese. It is covered in Annex D.2 to the RKC.

Regional Cumulation	Is a form or diagonal cumulation that only applies to the GSP and, in some instances, between members of a regional group of beneficiary countries. GSP, discussed under '*Trade Blocs*', refers to tariff preferences on imported goods being extended by developed countries to developing countries. *See Bilateral Cumulation* *See Cumulation.* *See Diagonal Cumulation.* *See Extended Cumulation.* *See Full Cumulation.* *See Multilateral Cumulation* *See Multilateral Extended Cumulation.* [Origin]
Regional Trade Agreements	Known as RTAs, these are a generic name for all reciprocal agreements such as customs unions, FTAs, and partial scope agreements. This can be explained by the fact that, initially, such treaties were within the jurisdiction of the WTO's Committee on RTAs. In reality, such trade agreements do not have to include members from the same region. [Trade Blocs]
Regressive Tax	The same rate (percentage) is applied to the goods, regardless of the consumer's income; as a consequence, it has a disproportionate effect on poorer consumers. *See Proportional Tax.* *See Progressive Tax.* [Types of Duties]
Regulation	A legal document issued officially by a government, such as an act, law, decree, rule, order, directive, and notice. The regulations collected are those imposing mandatory NTMs that affect imported or exported products. An official regulation could bear several NTMs. Regulations are active from their date of entry into force (implementation date) to their revoke date (repeal date).
Retaliatory Tariff	It is a rate of customs duty (tariff), normally very high, imposed by a country on imported goods from another country as a response to that country's imposition of a similar tariff on its own exports. There was a tendency to use it before establishing the WTO. *See Punitive Tariff.*
Release of Goods	The action by Customs is to permit goods undergoing clearance to be placed at the disposal of the persons concerned. It is covered in General Annex, Chapter 2 of the RKC.

Relief	*See Relief Consignments.* *See Relief from Import Duties and Taxes.*
Relief Consignments	Goods, including vehicles and other means of transport, foodstuffs, medicaments, clothing, blankets, tents, prefabricated houses, water purifying and water storage items, or other goods of prime necessity, forwarded as an aid to those affected by the disaster; and all equipment, vehicles and other means of transport, specially trained animals, provisions, supplies, personal effects and other goods for disaster relief personnel to perform their duties and support them in living and working in the territory of the disaster throughout the duration of their mission. It is covered in Specific Annex J, Chapter 5 of the RKC.
Relief from Import Duties and Taxes	Clearance of goods for home use free of import duties and taxes, irrespective of their normal tariff classification or normal liability, provided that they are imported in specified circumstances and for specified purposes. It is covered in Annex B.2. to the Kyoto Convention and in Specific Annex B, Chapter 3 of the RKC.
Remission of Import Duties and Taxes	The waiver of payment, in whole or in part, of import duties and taxes where payment has not been made. It is covered in Annex F.6. to the RKC. The Annex also covers the refund, in whole or in part, of import duties and taxes paid on goods declared for home use.
Remit	To waive the payment of import duty or export duty that has not yet been paid.
Replacement Methods	*See Alternative Methods.* *See Replacement Methods.* *See Secondary Methods.* [Customs Valuation]
Repayment	The refund, in whole or in part, of duties and taxes paid on goods and the remission, in whole or in part, of duties and taxes where payment has not been made. It is covered in General Annex, Chapter 2 of the RKC.
Residual Method	*See Fall Back Method.* *See Reasonable Means Method.* [Customs Valuation]
Restricted Goods	Also known as '*Controlled Goods*', these are goods where importation or exportation is limited or restrained and is only possible should specific conditions be met or complied with.

	The control of these goods could, in its interpretation and administration, be regarded as NTBs, which implies that restriction diverts from its original intent to a protectionist measure. *See Restricted Goods.*
Retaliatory Tariff	A very high tariff is imposed on an imported good in order to protect domestic manufacturers. Prior to the WTO, the imposition of such a tariff would have resulted in the exporting country imposing a tariff in kind, called a retaliatory tariff. *See Punitive Tariff.*
Returned Goods Relief	Also known as RGR, it is a customs procedure that allows goods to be imported back into the country, normally within a specified period of the original export, without duties or taxes, such as VAT payable, provided certain conditions are met. Typically, proof is required that the goods have not been altered. The procedure serves to facilitate the re-importation of goods that have previously been exported from the country, either temporarily or permanently. Goods under RGR cannot be processed or repaired in any way unless the work carried out on the goods was routine maintenance. [SCP]
Revised Kyoto Convention	Best known by its acronym RKC, it refers to the International Convention on the Simplification and Harmonization of Customs Procedures (amended), adopted by the WCO in 1999. [Conventions]
Roadmap	It is simply a plan or guide to illustrate how something is arranged. [The Lesson]
Roll-Up Rule	Also the known as the '*Absorption Principle*', it allows originating materials to be considered originating even when used as input in a subsequent transformation. This means that non-originating materials that have acquired originating status through a previous process are treated as originating in the final product. The rule aims to encourage regional trade by allowing materials that have been processed to an originating level in one stage of manufacture to be treated as originating in all subsequent stages of production. *See Absorption Principle.*

Rule-Based Framework	A trading system based on rules helps ensure that trade flows as smoothly, predictably and freely as possible. The WTO agreements are described as '*rules-based*'. The WTO deals with the global rules of trade between nations. Its primary function is to ensure that trade flows as smoothly, predictably and freely as possible.
Rules of Origin	Specific origin criteria, provisions, regulations, and administrative procedures devised from national legislation or international agreements to establish a good's economic nationality. The RoO tends to vary from country to country and even between a country's trade agreements that it has concluded with other countries. The imported good must satisfy the RoO provision in order to be considered as the country of origin of the good. There are two types of RoO, namely preferential and non-preferential. It is covered in Annex D.1. to the Kyoto Convention and in Specific Annex K, Chapter 1 of the RKC. [Origin]
SAFE Framework of Standards	The expression commonly refers to the WCO SAFE Framework of **S**tandards to Secure **a**nd **F**acilitate Global Trad**e**, adopted by the WCO in 2005.
Safeguard	It is a fair trade remedy, incorrectly called a '*Protective Measure*'. It is imposed as a '*Corrective Measure*' rather than a '*Protective Measure*', as it is imposed on a good imported at a fair market price, not at a dumped price. *See Fair Trade Remedy.* [Trade Remedies]
Safeguard Duty	Also known as a '*Safeguard Measure*', it is a duty that is applied when a domestic manufacturing industry is impacted by an unforeseen, sharp, and sudden increase in imports. These goods are imported at a fair market price, not a dumped price. *See Safeguard Measure.* [Types of Duties]
Safeguard Measure	A WTO member may take safeguard measures to temporarily restrict the import of a good to protect a specific domestic industry from an increase in imports of any product which is causing or is threatening to cause serious injury to the industry. The WTO Agriculture Agreement and the WTO Textiles and Clothing Agreement have different specific types of safeguards: '*Special Safeguards*' in agriculture and '*Transitional Safeguards*' in textiles and clothing.

	See Special Safeguards. *See Transitional Safeguards.* [Trade Remedies]
Sample	It is considered to be an article that is representative of a particular category of a good already produced or serves as an example of a good for which its production is still under consideration. The TA facilities for samples are covered in Annex B.3. to the Istanbul Convention.
Samples of No Commercial Value	An article regarded by a Customs Authority to be of negligible value and only to be used for soliciting orders for the good of the kind they represent. Such articles are normally allowed relief from import duties and taxes. It is covered in Annex B.2. to the Kyoto Convention, and there is also an International Convention to facilitate the importation of commercial samples and advertising material.
Sanctions Party Screening	*See Denied Party Screening.* *See Denied Trade Screening.* [Screening]
Sanitary and Phytosanitary Measures	Known as measures that deal with food safety and animal and plant health. '*Sanitary*' refers to human and animal health, while '*Phytosanitary*' refers to plants and plant products. These measures are applied to protect humans, animals, plants, and plant goods from risk to health and from diseases. *See SPS Measures.* [Non-tariff Measures]
Screening	In a Customs context, it simply implies the evaluation of information and intelligence relating to a good, the means of transport, the transaction parties and their intermediaries. The screening process would take the form of a manual process, an automated process, or a combination of both. There are various types of screening, such as '*Client Screening/Party-Based Screening*', '*Transaction Screening*', '*Transaction-Based Screening*', and '*Hybrid Screening*'. [Screening]
Seasonal Duty	It is a rate of customs duty (tariff) that is imposed on seasonal produce in order to protect the domestically produced goods. It tends to be used for agricultural goods, particularly when there is an abundant domestic harvest. [Types of Duties]
Seasonal Quota	It is a quota that is established for a given period of the year, usually set for certain agricultural goods when the domestic harvest is in abundance. [Types of Duties]

Second-best argument (for protection)	Any argument for protection that can be countered by pointing to a less costly policy that would achieve the same desired result. It also refers to rationales for protection to partially correct a distortion in the economy when the first-best policy for that purpose is not available. For example, if domestic production generates a positive externality and a production subsidy to internalise it is not available, then a tariff may be the second-best optimal.
Secondary Good	*See Intermediary Good.* *See Semi-manufacturers.*
Secondary Methods	In the instance where there is no transaction value (for instance, there is no sale), or where the transaction value is not acceptable, five alternative methods of customs valuation need to be applied in the prescribed hierarchical order. Method 2: Transaction Value of Identical Goods Method 3: Transactional Value of Similar Goods Method 4: Deductive Method Method 5: Computed Method or Calculation Method Method 6: Fall Back Method, Residual Method, or Reasonable Means Method. *See Alternative Methods.* *See Replacement Valuation Methods.* [Customs Valuation]
Section	*See Tariff Section.* *See Chapter.* *See Heading.* *See Subheading.* [Tariff Classification]
Security	Also called a '*Customs Guarantee*', it ensures that an obligation to Customs will be fulfilled to the satisfaction of the Customs Authority. Security is described as 'general' when it ensures that the obligations arising from several operations will be fulfilled. Security usually takes the form of a deposit or a legal obligation, such as a bond. *See Customs Guarantee.* [Customs Guarantee]
Semi-Knocked Down	Also known by the acronym SKD, referring to a good that is partially assembled, or disassembled, depending on your consideration, which requires additional assembly. A good that has been partly or partially assembled, with the final assembly to be completed in the importing country. As with

	CKD, the good is shipped in this format to avoid high import duties, levies, and taxes, to meet the importing country's local content requirements. *See Completely Knocked Down.* [Types of Duties]
Semi-manufactures	The second stage of processing is the measurement of tariff escalation. The product is not yet in the form where it can be sold to the consumer, as it requires further processing. *See Raw Materials.* *See Finished Products.*
Shallow Integration [Stages]	The only concern in these stages is with the border and, consequently, dismantling the classical barriers to trade, such as tariffs and other border measures. *See Deep Integration.* [Trade Blocs]
Shipping Agent	Also known as a '*Forwarder*', '*Freight Forwarder*', and '*Forwarding Agent*', it facilitates the movement of goods between countries. *See Forwarder.* *See Forwarding Agent.* *See Freight Forwarder.*
Similar Goods	A Secondary Method, the third customs valuation method known as Method 3, where goods which, although not alike in all respects, have like characteristics and like component materials which enable them to perform the same functions and to be commercially interchangeable. The quality of the goods, their reputation and the existence of a trademark are among the factors to be considered in determining whether goods are similar. [Customs Valuation]
Sin Taxes	Levied on goods which, through their manufacture or use, are considered to be harmful or costly to society. In the instance of Customs and Excises, it should really be '*Sin Duties*'. *See Luxury Taxes.* [Types of Duties]
Single Market	This is an agreement on the part of a set of countries to eliminate trade restrictions among themselves, adopt a CET, and allow the free movement of factors of production among member countries, also known as the factors of production. The factors of production refer to labour and physical capital. *See Common Market.* [Trade Bloc]

Special Customs Procedures	Allow an importer to store, temporarily use, process, or repair your goods with payment of import duties, levies, and taxes (in certain instances) suspended. These become payable if you release the goods to the country's home market (free circulation) but are relieved if the goods are re-exported. These procedures support various kinds of economic activity that takes place in the country using imported goods. *See Processing.* *See Inward Processing.* *See Outward Processing.* *See Specific Use.* *See Temporary Admission.* *See End Use.* *See Storage.* *See Customs Warehousing.* *See Free Zones.* *See Transit.* *See Customs Transit.* *See Transhipment.* *See Customs Special Procedure.* [Special Customs Procedures]
Special Safeguard	The WTO Agreement on Agriculture allows for this protectionist measure to be triggered automatically should there be a decline in prices or an increase in imports. *See Safeguard.* *See Safeguard Measure.* [Trade Remedies]
Specific Duty	Also known as a '*Specific Tariff*', it is a customs duty which is not related to the value of the imported good but rather to its quantity, weight, volume, and its alcoholic strength by volume, to name but a few. *See Specific Tariff.* *See Ad Valorem Tariff.* [Types of Duties]
Specific Tariff	*See Ad Valorem Tariff.* *See Specific Duty.* *See Ad Valorem Duty.* [Types of Duties]
Specific Use	Although there is a Specific Annex in the RKC for TA, there is no one for End Use. *See Temporary Admission (TA).* *See End Use.* [Special Customs Procedures]

Specified Process Rule	*See Tariff Shift Rule.* *See Change of the Tariff Classification Rule.* [Origin]
Specified Product or Process Rules	*See Specified Rules.* *See Technical Rules.* [Origin]
Specified Rules	*See Specified Product or Process Rules.* *See Technical Rules.* [Origin]
Split Consignment	*See Staggered Consignment.* *See Staged Consignment.* *See Split Consignment.* [Tariff Classification]
Split Shipment	*See Staggered Consignment.* *See Staged Consignment.* *See Split Consignment.* [Tariff Classification]
Staged Consignment	A Customs Authority will consider the classification of the good in the manner in which it is presented for clearance. In instances where a consignment consists of more than one shipment, it will arrive separately but needs to be considered a single consignment. An application needs to be made for the Customs Authority to consider the multiple shipments as a single consignment. These types of consignments tend to apply to goods which are too large to be transported as a single shipment. The various shipments contain goods that are in an unassembled or disassembled state. *See Staggered Consignment.* *See Split Consignment.* *See Split Shipment.* [Tariff Classification]
Stages of Processing	For the analysis of the tariff escalation, products are classified according to their stage of processing. Products can be classified, in general, according to three stages of processing, namely, raw materials, semi-manufactures and finished products.
Staggered Consignment	*See Staged Consignment.* *See Split Consignment.* *See Split Shipment.* [Tariff Classification]
Standard Industrial Classification	The SIC provides an established framework to classify businesses by the type of economic activity in which they are engaged.

Standard International Trade Classification	The SITC classification was developed by the UN for the statistical analysis of trade data. Articles are grouped by classes of goods such as food, raw materials, chemicals, machinery and transport equipment, stage of fabrication, and industrial origin. The SITC was first revised in 1960 to match the CCCN. The second revision served to the CCCN in 1972, while the third revision of 1985 was to establish a match to the HS.
Statutory Duty	It is also called the '*Autonomous* Duty' or the '*Legal Duty*'. It appears in the Customs Tariff of a country. WTO Members cannot impose a '*Statutory Duty*' that is higher than their GATT-bound duty. *See Autonomous Duty.* *See Legal Duty.*
Storage	The SCP provides for two types of storage, namely CW, also known as Bonded Warehouse, and FZ. Both of the storage procedures are suspensive CPEI. It is covered in the General Annex of the RKC. *See Customs Warehousing (CW).* *See Free Zones (FZ).* [Special Customs Procedures: Storage]
Strategic Trade and Export Control	It is defined as the control of the export, import, international transit, and transhipment of certain commodities to certain recipients or for certain end uses/end users and in certain circumstances. [Export Control]
Subheading	A six-digit numerical designation (when international), an eight-digit numerical designation (when national), used to classify goods for import and export purposes. *See Section.* *See Chapter.* *See Heading.* [Tariff Classification]
Subsidies	Subsidies are grants given to enterprises/firms by their governments. There are two main types of subsidies – export and domestic. An export subsidy is a grant given to enterprises engaging in international trade through exportations. A domestic subsidy is a grant not directly linked to exports. *See Red (Prohibited Subsidy).* *See Amber (Actionable Subsidy).* *See Green (Non-Actionable Subsidy).* [Trade Remedies]

Subsidy	*See Subsidies.* [Trade Remedies]
Substantial Transformation	*See Sufficiently Worked.* *See Sufficiently Processed.* [Origin]
Sufficiently Processed	*See Sufficiently Worked.* *See Substantial Transformation.* [Origin]
Sufficiently Worked	*See Sufficiently Processed.* *See Substantial Transformation.* [Origin]
Sunset Review	The 'sunset' requirement establishes that anti-dumping duties and countervailing duties shall normally terminate no later than five years after first being applied unless a review investigation prior to that date establishes that the expiry of the trade remedy duty would be likely to lead to continuation or recurrence of dumping and injury. *See Mandatory Review.* [Trade Remedies]
Surcharge	The prefix '*sur*' means '*an over and above*' charge; consequently, it takes on various forms. It is imposed under various conditions dependent on the economic reasoning for the additional charge. An ad hoc charge is imposed in addition to customs duties and taxes to raise fiscal revenues or to protect domestic industries. Also called '*Surtax*' and '*Additional Duty*'. *See Customs Surcharge.* *See Surtax.* *See Additional Duty.* [Types of Duties]
Surety	A natural or legal person (generally a bank or insurance company) who accepts responsibility in due legal form for the financial consequences of non-fulfilment of another's obligations to the Customs. [Customs Debt]
Surtax	Also known as '*Additional Duty*' and '*Customs Surcharge*'. *See Surtax.* *See Additional Duty.* *See Customs Surcharge.*

Suspensions	Provide for either the complete or partial reduction in the standard rate of duty. Alternatively, it allows for only a limited quantity of the good to be imported for a specific period of time at a reduced or zero rate of duty, after which the rate of duty reverts to the standard or 'General' rate of duty.
Tariffication	Tariffication in customs refers to the process of classifying imported goods and assigning applicable customs duties (tariffs) according to a specific system. This system, often referred to as a tariff schedule or a customs tariff, outlines the classification of goods and the corresponding duty rates. The purpose of tariffication is to determine the amount of duty payable on imported goods. [*See* tariffication.]
Tariff	A customs duty, levy, or tax which is imposed on an imported good to provide it with a price advantage over the domestically produced/manufactured good. The majority of tariffs have an *ad valorem* rate of duty/tax, but there are still specific rates of duty/tax and, in some instances, a mixture of the two rates. A tariff can serve two purposes: a protective measure (to protect the domestic industry) or a fiscal measure (to collect revenue). There is a third use of a tariff as a negotiation instrument. *See Protective Measure.* *See Fiscal Measure.* [Types of Duties]
Tariff Binding	Maximum duty level on a product listed in a member's schedule of commitments; it represents the commitment not to exceed the duty applied to the concerned product beyond the level bound in the schedule. Once a rate of duty is bound, it may not be raised without compensating the affected parties. [Types of Duties]
Tariff Celling	Any pre-set value or quantity authorised for importation or exportation of given goods during a specified period, with a reduction of the normal Customs duties, and beyond which the granting of the said tariff reduction may be suspended until the end of the period in question.
Tariff Chapter	The HS is divided into a number of Tariff Chapters which are itself grouped in Tariff Sections. The Tariff Chapter is classified into two digits. [Tariff Classification]

Tariff Classification of Goods	Determination of the tariff subheading in a tariff nomenclature under which particular goods should be classified. [Tariff Classification]
Tariff Cliff	*See Water in the Tariff.* *See Tariff Overhang.* *See Binding Overhang Principle.* [Types of Duties]
Tariff Concession	Removes the duty on certain goods to assist a business (company) in reducing the costs for imported goods, i.e., where suitable alternative goods are not domestically produced or manufactured. A tariff concession removes the tariff duty that would otherwise be payable under the Tariff for certain goods. These may be goods used for social, humanitarian or industry assistance purposes. *See Concession.*
Tariff Description	Description of a good offered in accordance with the terminology used in the tariff nomenclature [Tariff Classification]
Tariff Engineering	It is possible for importers and their intermediaries to design, assemble, or disassemble a good to take advantage of lower rates of duty. The importer or the manufacturer will consider the rates of customs duties on specific materials and stages of assembly and design the goods to be customs duty optimal.
Tariff Equivalent	The estimation of the extent of the protective effect of an NTB. The rate of duty (tariff) would have the exact same effect on imports as the NTB.
Tariff Escalation	The rate of duty (tariff) increases as a good becomes more processed. The escalation discourages the import of more varieties of processed goods as it offers domestic producers with increased levels of protection. It also discourages the development of production activity in the countries where the raw materials originate. [Types of Duties]
Tariff Heading	It is a four-digit HS commodity code. [Tariff Classification]
Tariff Nomenclature	The classification and coding system introduced by a Customs Authority for the purpose of classifying a good. The WCO's Nomenclature of the Harmonized Commodity Description and Coding System, simply known as the HS

	Nomenclature, comprises the GRI, Section Notes, Chapter Notes, and a list of Headings and Subheadings. *See Nomenclature.* [Tariff Classification]
Tariff Overhang	The difference between the '*Bound Duties*' and the '*Applied Duties*'. *See Binding Overhang Principle.* *See Tariff Cliff.* *See Tariff Water.* *See Water in the Tariff.* [Types of Duties]
Tariff Peak	It is a tariff that has a particularly high rate of duty. The WB applies two measures to identify tariff peaks: an '*International Peak*', which refers to duties which are higher than 15%, and a '*National Peak*', which refers to duties which are over three times the average rate of duty. *See International Peak.* *See National Peak.* [Types of Duties]
Tariff Quota	Also known as '*Tariff Rate Quota*' or '*TRQ*', it is an import regime which provides for goods that fall within a quota to be imported at a lower rate of duty, while goods that fall outside a quota have a higher rate of duty applying to them. *See Tariff Rate Quota (TRQ).* [Types of Duties]
Tariff Rate Quota	Known as TRQ or Autonomous Tariff Quotas (ATQ), it is a measure under which a good is subject to an MFN tariff. Still, only a certain quantity, referred to as the '*Quota*', is admitted into a country at a lower rate of duty, sometimes even at a rate of 0%. TRQ tends to be applied mainly to the agricultural trade and then tends to be seasonal. *See Autonomous Tariff Quotas (ATQ).* [Types of Duties]
Tariff Regime	A country's set of tariff rates, general and preferential, for goods being imported into the country, or exported from the country.
Tariff Section	The HS Code divides its Tariff Chapters into 21 Sections internationally, with countries being able to add their National Tariff Sections. [Tariff Classification]
Tariff Schedule	Is the list of a country's tariffs (rates of duty) on goods which are organised according to the Customs Tariff.

Tariff Shift Rule	Requires that there is a change in the HS classification (commodity code) of each of the non-originating inputs or components to the HS classification code (commodity code) of the final product. *See Change of Tariff Classification Rule.* *See Specified Processed Rule.* [Origin]
Tariff Shopping	An informal term which is used when a business considers various rates of customs duties (import taxes) in trade agreements and trade preferences to establish the most preferential rate for their exports.
Tariff Subheading	It is a six-digit code (commodity code or HS code) when it is reference internationally, and an eight-digit code or more when it is country specific. [Tariff Classification]
Tariff Suspension	The payment of the import duties is suspended on goods which are used in the production of goods. This provision is also known as a '*Manufacturing Rebate*' or a '*Rebate*'. *See Manufacturing Rebate.* *See Rebate.* [The Lesson]
Tariff Water	Also known as '*Water in the Tariff*' and the '*Tariff Overhang*', it is simply the difference between '*Bound Rates*' and '*Applied Rates*'. *See Applied Rates.* *See Bound Rates.* *See Tariff Overhang.* *See Water in the Tariff.* [Types of Duties]
Tariffication	The procedure mainly relates to agricultural market-access provisions by which NTMs are converted into tariff equivalents. As part of the WTO's Uruguay Round Market Access for agricultural products, all NTM measures were '*tariffied*' by Members before a tariff reduction was made. *See NTMs.* *See Tariffied.* *See Trade Equivalents.* *See Tariffication.* [Types of Duties]
Tariffied	*See Tariffication.* [Types of Duties]
Tax	The OECD defines it as compulsory, unrequited payments to the government, central (national), regional, or local. [Types of Duties]

Technical Barriers to Trade	Known as TBT, these are measures that pertain to the technical specification of the goods or a production process and the conformity assessment systems thereof. Trade-restrictive effects arise due to the application of technical regulations or standards such as certification requirements, labelling, origin marking, packaging, and testing; health and safety regulations, SPS; and marketing standards. *See Non-tariff Measures.* [Technical Barrier to Trade]
Technical Measures	It is an NTM subgroup of Import-Related Measures, the others being '*Export-Related Measures*' and '*Non-Technical Measures*'. *See Non-tariff Measures.* [Non-tariff Measures]
Technical Rules	*See Specified Rules.* *See Specified Product.* *See Process Rules.* [Rules of Origin]
Technical Tariffs	The tariff rate depends on the input content, such as sugar or alcohol. [Types of Duties]
Temporary Admission	The Customs procedure under which certain goods can be brought into a Customs territory conditionally relieved totally or partially from payment of import duties and taxes. Such goods must be imported for a specific purpose and must be intended for re-exportation within a specified period and without having undergone any change except normal depreciation due to the use made of them. [Specific Use SCP]
Temporary Storage	Also known as TS, it is a Customs procedure, not an SCP, under which imported goods are temporarily stored under Customs control before they are placed under an SCP, such as a Transit, or released to free circulation (house use), or exported. By placing the goods under this Customs procedure, the full customs declaration, the payment of duties, and VAT can be delayed, normally for only a specified time. Covered in Specific Annex A, Chapter 2 of the RKC. [Special Customs Procedures: Storage]
Third Party	Any person who deals directly with a Customs Authority, for or on behalf of another person, in respect of the importation, exportation, movement, or storage of goods Covered in General Annex, Chapter 2 of the RKC.

Tolerance Rule	Permits a specified percentage, normally between 10% and 15% of the value or volume of the final good, to be non-originating without the good losing its originating status. It is also possible that a trade agreement or preference might specify a specific percentage. An added specification could be stipulating a negative list of components that would be excluded from the *de minimis* or tolerance rule. The provision is a relaxation of the rules of origin under certain conditions. It allows a small amount of non-originating materials to be used in the production of the good without affecting its originating status. The provision acts as the relaxation of the RoO, and the threshold is usually set at around 5% to 15%. *See De Minimis* Rule [Origin]
TIR Carnet	The Transports Internationaux Routiers or International Road Transports Carnet simplifies the administrative formalities of transiting commercial goods which are carried by international road transport. [Specific Use – Temporary Admission]
Tolls	Imposed on the movement of the goods themselves, rather than on the goods being traded. [Types of Duties]
Trade Blocs	A '*bloc*' means an alliance. Is it the collective name for the various forms of economic integration, which, depending on the level of integration, ultimately strives for full economic and commercial integration. *See Economic Integration.* *See Trade Expansion.* *See Trade Integration.* *See Trade Deflection.* *See Trade Diversion.* [Trade Bloc]
Trade Compliance	Encompasses all the processes, rules, regulations, and laws that govern the treatment of goods entering and exiting a country. *See Customs Compliance.*
Trade Creation	Also known as '*Trade Expansion*' and '*Trade Integration*', it results when the liberalisation of tariffs and trade barriers between the members displaces their respective less efficient domestic production, which previously benefited from protective measures.

	See Trade Expansion. *See Trade Integration.* [Trade Blocs]
Trade deflection	*See Trade Diversion.* [Trade Blocs]
Trade diversion	Also known as '*Trade Deflection*', it results when the trade reform discriminates between the members and a less efficient source (higher cost) displaces a more efficient source (lower cost). This can occur when tariffs and trade barriers are not removed in the same measure between the members. *See Trade Deflection.* [Trade Blocs]
Trade Expansion	Also known as '*Trade Creation*' and '*Trade Integration*', it refers to the increase in internal trade within the bloc due to the rates of duty (tariffs) being reduced and NTBs being removed between member countries. This positive effect leads to a more efficient allocation of factors of production within the agreement area, in line with the different members' comparative advantages. *See Trade Creation.* *See Trade Integration.* *See Comparative Advantage.* *See Factors of Production.* [Trade Blocs]
Trade Facilitation	The simplification and harmonisation of international trade procedures, including activities, practices, and formalities involved in collecting, presenting, communicating, and processing data required for the movement of goods in international trade. [The Lesson]
Trade Integration	Process of reducing barriers to trade and increasing participation in the international economy through trade. [Trade Blocs]
Trade Multilateralism	Refers to a system of international trade governed by agreed-upon rules negotiated by all participating countries, rather than individual governments dictating terms. This system, often associated with the WTO and its predecessor, GATT, aims to create a level playing field and foster a more open and predictable global trading environment.
Trade-Related Investment Measures	The WTO Agreement on Trade-Related Investment Measures, known as the TRIMs Agreement, deals with investment measures related to trade in goods. [Non-tariff Measures]

Trade Remedies	The trade remedies are anti-dumping, countervailing, and safeguards. Dumping and countervailing remedies are called '*Unfair Trade Remedies*', while safeguards are called '*Fair Trade Remedies*' and '*Protective Measures*'. The latter is incorrect. Unfair Trade Remedies are both '*Protective Measures*' and '*Corrective Measures*'. *See Fair Trade Remedies.* *See Unfair Trade Remedies.* *See Corrective Measures.* *See Protective Measures.* [Trade Remedies]
Trans-shipment	*See Transhipment.* *See Transshipment.* [Special Customs Procedures: Transit]
Transaction-Based Screening	Also known as '*Transaction Screening*', it means screening only the relevant business partners and clients for suspicious activity and only doing so before each business transaction and/or business opportunity. It allows for considered decisions on the level of risk associated between the payment beneficiaries and originators. It is one of the three types of '*Screening*', the others being '*Client Screening*', '*Party-Based Screening*', and '*Hybrid Screening*'. *See Client Screening.* *See Hybrid Screening.* *See Party-Based Screening.* *See Transaction Screening.* [Screening]
Transaction Screening	Also known as '*Transaction-Based Screening*', it means screening only the relevant business partners and clients for suspicious activity and only doing so prior to each business transaction and/or business opportunity. It allows for considered decisions on the level of risk associated between the payment beneficiaries and originators. It is one of the three types of 'Screening', the others being 'Client Screening', '*Party-Based Screening*', and '*Hybrid Screening*'. *See Client Screening.* *See Hybrid Screening.* *See Party-Based Screening.* *See Transaction-Based Screening.* [Screening]

Transaction Value	The Primary Method, also known as Method 1, for determining the customs value as defined in the WTO Customs Valuation Agreement (CVA). It is based on *'the price actually paid or payable'* for the goods when sold for export to the country of importation (Article 1 of the CVA), adjusted in accordance with the provisions of Article 8 of the CVA. [Customs Valuation]
Transfer Pricing	Also known by its acronym as TP, it is concerned with the terms and conditions surrounding transactions within a multinational company (MNC). It concerns the prices charged between associated enterprises established in different countries for their intercompany transactions, such as the transfer of goods and services. [Customs Valuation]
Transit	*See Customs Transit.* *See Transhipment.* [Special Customs Procedures: Transit]
Transports Internationaux Routiers	Also known as International Road Transports or TIR Carnet, serves to simplify the administrative formalities of transiting commercial goods carried by international road transport. [Special Customs Procedures: Temporary Admission]
Transhipment	Also known as *'transshipment'* or *'trans-shipment'*, the Customs procedure under which goods are transferred under Customs control from the importing means of transport to the exporting means of transport within the area of one Customs office which is the office of both importation and exportation. *See Transshipment.* *See Trans-shipment.* [Special Customs Procedures: Transit]
Transshipment	*See Trans-shipment.* *See Transhipment.* [Special Customs Procedures: Transit]
Trigger Price	*See Maximum Price System.* *See Minimum Price System.* [Types of Duties]
Unassembled Goods	Also known as *'Disassembled Goods'*, it is covered in GRI 2(a) Part 2, which describes how to classify the good. GRI 2(a) Part 1 describes how to classify *'Incomplete Goods'* and *'Unfinished Goods'*. [Tariff Classification]
UNCTAD	It is a body of the UN that aims to develop opportunities, investments and trade in developing countries. [Organisations]

Unfair trade Remedy	There are two types of unfair trade remedies: dumping and countervailing. The remedy, normally in the form of a duty, is imposed on the imported good in order to offset dumping or a subsidy, that is, to bring the price of the imported good in line with the '*normal value*' of that good in its domestic market. *See Dumping.* *See Countervailing (Anti-Subsidy).* [Trade Remedies]
Unfinished Goods	Also known as '*Incomplete Goods*', it is covered in GRI 2(a) Part 1, which describes how to classify the good. GRI 2(b) Part 2 describes how to classify unassembled goods or disassembled goods. [Origin]
Unilateral Trade Agreement	A non-reciprocal agreement, also called '*one-sided*', where a country lowers or removes trade restrictions and barriers to trade for the imports of another country or countries. The preferential arrangement is normally extended by a developed country to a developing country, an example of which is the GSP. The objective of such an agreement is to provide the developing country or countries with increased market access to the developing country's market and to increase its exports, aiding its economic growth. *See Bilateral Trade Agreement* *See Multilateral Trade Agreement.* [Trade Blocs]
Valorisation	It is the act or process of giving or assigning a customs valuation. In the context of customs, '*valorisation*' refers to the process of determining the monetary value of goods for customs purposes. This value is crucial for calculating duties, taxes, and other charges levied on imported or exported goods. [Customs Valuation]
Value-Added Rule	*See Value Content Rule.* [Origin]
Value Added Tax	An indirect tax is a general, broadly based consumption tax assessed on the value added to goods and services. *See VAT.* [Types of Duties] [Customs Valuation]

Value Content Rule	The origin of the good is based on the value thresholds – local content or regional content. The value-added criterion can be expressed in two ways: a maximum allowance for non-originating materials or a minimum requirement for domestic content. *See Ad Valorem Rule.* *See Value-Added Rule.* *See Percentage Rule.* [Origin]
Valuation	*See Customs Valuation.* [Trade Remedies]
Variable Import Levy	Tariff regime entails an automatic and continuous variation in duty levels through a scheme or formula; duty levels generally vary in response to international price developments, thus potentially impeding the transmission of international prices to the domestic market. [Types of Duties]
Variable Levies	A customs duty rate which varies in response to domestic price criteria. [Types of Duties]
Variable Tariff Formula	It accounts for international price movements, which result in duties being adjusted, normally without prior publication. The formula operates on the premise that the world reference price, subtracting the transport cost to a country, should be on par with the country's domestic price. [Types of Duties]
Veblen Good	It is a type of luxury good, named after American economist Thorstein Veblen, for which the demand increases as the price increases, in apparent contradiction of the law of demand. [Types of duties/Luxury taxes]
Vis Major	A Latin term meaning '*superior force*'. It refers to an event that is both natural and unavoidable. It is synonymous with an '*act of God*', which describes an event that cannot be prevented by human diligence. [*See* Force Majeure]
Voluntary Export Restraint	Better known as VER, it is an informal agreement between an exporter and an importer, whereby the former agrees to limit exports of a specified good to avoid dislocation of the industry and possible imposition of mandatory restrictions by the importing country. The restraint agreement may be concluded at either the industry or government level. [Trade Remedies]

Warehouse	Imported or domestically manufactured goods are stored under Customs control in a designated place without the payment of import duties and taxes. *See Bonded Warehouse.* [SCP: Warehousing]
Water in the Tariff	The difference, or gap, between the '*bound tariff*' and the '*applied tariff*' of MFN is called the '*water in the tariff*' or the 'tariff overhang'. Economists call it the '*policy space*', as the government could quickly increase the tariff rate from the applied rate to the bound rate. Economists contend that the '*tariff overhang*' makes a country's trade policies less predictable. *See Applied tariff.* *See Bound tariff.* *See Tariff Overhang.* *See Tariff Cliff.* *See Binding Overhang Principle.* [Types of Duties]
Wholly Obtained Goods	As the name suggests, these are exclusively produced, or originate, in a country, and they do not contain or incorporate any material from another country(ies) [Origin]
World Customs Organization	Better known as the WCO, established as the CCC, it is an independent intergovernmental body whose mission is to enhance the effectiveness and efficiency of Customs administrations. As the global centre of Customs expertise, it is the only international organisation with competence in Customs matters. It can rightly call itself the voice of the international Customs community. *See Customs Co-operation Council.* [Organisations]
World Free Zones Organization	The World FZO is a global not-for-profit organisation that provides one authoritative, collective voice representing the interests of FZs around the world. [Organisations]
World Trade Organization	Better known as the WTO, it is the only global international organisation dealing with the rules of trade between nations. At its heart are the WTO agreements, negotiated and signed by the bulk of the world's trading nations and ratified in their parliaments. The goal is to ensure that trade flows as smoothly, predictably and freely as possible. [Organisations]

WTO Customs Valuation Agreement	The Agreement on Implementation of Article VII of the GATT 1994, commonly known as the Customs Valuation Agreement, sets out the methodology and requirements for determining the customs value for imported goods subject to *ad valorem* duties. [Agreements]

CHAPTER 23

International Customs and Trade Organisations, Committees, Agreements, and Conventions

§23.01 THE MORE IMPORTANT INTERNATIONAL ORGANISATIONS

AIT	Alliance Internationale de Tourisme
ASAPRA	International Association of Professional Customs Agents
ASYCUDA	Automated System for Customs Data [*see* UNCTAD]
CCC	Customs Cooperation Council [*see* WCO]
CIT	International Rail Transport Committee
CITES	Convention on International Trade in Endangered Species of Wild Fauna and Flora
ECOSOC	United Nations Economic and Social Council
FIATA	International Federation of Freight Forwarders Association
GATT	General Agreement on Tariffs and Trade [*see* WTO]
GEA	Global Express Association
IAPH	International Association of Ports and Harbors
IATA	International Air Transport Association
IBRD	International Bank for Reconstruction and Development [*see* WBG*]
ICAO	International Civil Aviation Organization
ICC	International Chamber of Commerce
IFCBA	International Federation of Customs Brokers Associations

IFIA	International Federation of Inspection Agencies (IFIA) [*see* TIC Council]
IMF	International Monetary Fund*
IMO	International Maritime Organization
INCU	International Network of Customs Universities
INTERPOL	International Criminal Police Organization
IRU	International Road Transport Union
ISO	International Organization for Standardization
ITC	International Trade Centre
ITO	International Trade Organization [*see* GATT and WTO*]
LN	League of Nations [*see* UN]
OCTI	Central Office for International Carriage by Rail [*see* OTIF]
OECD	Organisation for Economic Co-operation and Development
OTIF	Intergovernmental Organization for International Carriage by Rail [*see* OCTI]
TIACA	International Air Cargo Association
TIC Council	Testing, Inspection, and Certification [*see* IFIA]
UIC	International Union of Railways
UN	United Nations [*see* LN]
UNECE	United Nations Economic Commission for Europe
UNESCO	United Nations Educational Scientific and Cultural Organization
UNCITRAL	United Nations Commission on International Trade Law
UNCTAD	United Nations Conference on Trade and Development
UPU	Universal Postal Union
WBG	World Bank Group [*see* IBRD*]
WCO	World Customs Organization [*see* CCC]
WFPIA	World Federation of Pipe Line Industry Associations
WHO	World Health Organization
WIPO	World Intellectual Property Organization
WTO	World Trade Organization [*see* GATT*]
WFZO	World Free Zones Organization

* *The Bretton Woods Trilogy – IMF, WBG (IBRD) and WTO (ITO/GATT).*

Alliance Internationale de Tourisme (AIT)

'Represent the interests of national automobile associations and touring clubs.'

Website: *https://www.ait-touringalliance.com/*

Established: 4 August 1898
Headquarters: Geneva, Switzerland

The AIT is an international federation of motoring organisations established at the Casino Bourgeois in Luxembourg City in 1898 as a non-profit, non-governmental organisation (NGO) representing the interests of national associations and federations. On 30 May 1919, it changed its name, Ligue Internationale des Associations Touristes (LIAT), to the Alliance Internationale de Tourisme.

After a century of providing a wide variety of products and services to its members, the AIT today deals primarily with international documents, in particular, the sale of the CPD Carnet to its constituent member clubs and the representation of interests of road users as well as advisory opinions in the legislative process regarding transport regulations and road safety issues.

International Association of Professional Customs Agents (ASAPRA)

'To promote and defend the importance of Customs and Customs Brokers as assistants to the public customs function.'

Website: *https://asapra.com/*
Established: 27 November 1969
Headquarters: Montevideo, Uruguay

The objective is to promote the continuous and sustained improvement of customs practices, aligning them with international standards and norms, in collaboration with international organisations such as the WCO, the WTO, and UNCTAD, as well as other private sector organisations. In this way, the aim is to achieve operational excellence that benefits trade and security at a global level, adapting to the challenges and changes of the international landscape, and ensuring effective integration of efforts among the various involved actors.

> The '*WCO Customs Brokers Guidelines*' provide reference guidance to Members and stakeholders in establishing/adjusting their Customs brokers' regime in line with the RKC and the WTO Agreement on TFA. The Guidelines will assist Members in the accession to, and implementation of, the relevant provisions of the RKC and the WTO TFA. The Guidelines also explore various potential opportunities for enhancing cooperation between Customs and Customs brokers, in the context of new and emerging developments in the international supply chain.

> The '*WCO Study Report on Customs Brokers*' document provides a general background and overview of Customs brokers' role in the international supply

chain together with some suggested policy and organisational considerations on Customs broker regimes and a model checklist for licensing/regulating brokers.

Automated System for Customs Data (ASYCUDA) [Customs Automation]

'The UNCTAD ASYCUDA is an integrated customs management system for international trade and transport operations in a modern automated environment.'

Website: *https://asycuda.org/en/*
https://unctad.org/topic/transport-and-trade-logistics/customs-automation-ASYCUDA
Headquarters: Geneva, Switzerland
Established: 1981

The ASYCUDA software, developed by UNCTAD, considers the international codes and standards developed by ISO, the WCO's Data Model, and the UN.

Through its ASYCUDA programme, UNCTAD aims at:

- modernising customs operations and helping to improve revenue collection;
- facilitating trade efficiency and competitiveness by substantially reducing transaction time and costs;
- improving security by streamlining cargo control procedures, transit of goods and clearance of goods;
- helping fight corruption by enhancing the transparency of transactions;
- promoting sustainable development by reducing paper use through electronic transactions and documents.

Customs Co-operation Council (CCC) [*See* WCO]

'Borders Divide, Customs Connects.'

Established: 26 January 1953
Headquarters: Brussels, Belgium

The CCC, known as the WCO, was established as an independent intergovernmental body whose mission is to enhance the effectiveness and efficiency of Customs administrations. It is particularly noted for its expertise in the development of international standards, simplification and harmonisation of Customs procedures, trade security, trade facilitation, Customs anti-fraud and compliance, HS commodity nomenclature, RoO, Customs Valuation, and capacity building.

International Rail Transport Committee (CIT)

'To develop and maintain the international rail transport conventions.'

Website: *https://www.cit-rail.org/*
Established: 1902
Headquarters: Bern, Switzerland

The CIT is an association of some 216 railway undertakings and shipping companies which provide international passenger and/or freight services. A total of 130 organisations are members in their own right, and 80 organisations are linked indirectly by being members of CIT associate members.

Convention on International Trade in Endangered Species of Wild Fauna and Flora (CITES)

'Represent the interests of national automobile associations and touring clubs.'

Website: *https://cites.org/eng*
Established: 3 March 1973
Headquarters: Geneva, Switzerland

CITES is a multilateral treaty to protect endangered plants and animals from the threats of international trade. It was drafted due to a resolution adopted in 1963 at a meeting of members of the International Union for Conservation of Nature (IUCN). The Convention was signed in 1973 and CITES entered into force on 1 July 1975.

> The '*WCO-Interpol Customs – Police Cooperation Handbook*' aims to foster increased cooperation between the two types of agencies at the national level. While this document highlights the need for customs - police cooperation - while, it also offers professional insight on how to strengthen the collaboration between these institutions that are so important to a country's national security.

United Nations Economic and Social Council (ECOSOC)

'To promote a sustainable world.'

Website: *https://ecosoc.un.org/*
Established: 26 June 1945
Headquarters: Geneva, Switzerland

ECOSOC is a principal organ of the UN responsible for coordinating the economic, social, and related work of the organisation and its affiliated agencies. It acts as a central forum for discussing and formulating policy recommendations on international economic and social issues.

ECOSOC is one of the six principal organs of the UN, responsible for coordinating the economic and social fields of the organisation, specifically in regard to the 15 specialised agencies, the eight functional commissions, and the five regional commissions under its jurisdiction.

International Federation of Freight Forwarders Associations (FIATA)

'The global voice of freight logistics.'

Website: *https://fiata.org/*
Established: 31 May 1926
Headquarters: Geneva, Switzerland

FIATA is the leading non-governmental organisation (NGO) in the field of transportation and logistics and is best placed to represent the unique position of the forwarder in the global supply chain. Its members' expertise touches on all aspects of international transport and logistics and is fostered through an autonomous training programme deployed in almost hundred countries.

FIATA actively pursues its mandate to define, craft and promote the role of the international forwarder and logistics service provider in international air cargo with strong efforts to improve the professional standards of forwarders in air cargo regarding facilitation, safety and security.

> Multimodal Transport Institute (MTI)
>
> The MTI's purpose is to keep freight forwarders advised of legislative developments and their implementation where it may impact their activities. MTI represents the global freight forwarding industry to international organisations and keeps the freight forwarding industry up to date concerning ongoing talks with and the decisions of these bodies, e.g., ICC, UN, UIC, IRU. MTI is also involved in policy making.

General Agreement on Tariffs and Trade (GATT) [*see* WTO]

'Nothing is agreed until everything is agreed.'

Established: 30 October 1947
Headquarters: Paris, France

GATT, which was never institutionalised, was signed on 30 October 1947 by 23 countries and was a legal agreement minimising barriers to international trade by eliminating or reducing quotas, tariffs, and subsidies while preserving significant regulations. The GATT was intended to boost economic recovery after WWII through reconstructing and liberalising global trade.

GATT came into effect on 1 January 1948. Since that beginning, it has been refined, eventually leading to the creation of the WTO on 1 January 1995, which absorbed and extended it. By this time, 125 nations were signatories to its agreements, which covered about 90% of global trade.

Global Express Association (GEA)

'Connecting Businesses Globally.'

Website: *https://global-express.org/*
Established: 1983
Headquarters: Geneva, Switzerland

The GEA represents the international express delivery companies that serve over 215 countries, carrying over 30 million packages each day, all of them guaranteed to be delivered within specified time frames. This guarantee makes express delivery unique in the transportation industry and enable its customers to operate over broad territories with a high degree of confidence.

The *'WCO Immediate Release Guidelines'* aim to assist both Customs and trade with expediting the clearance of large number of small or negligible value goods across borders that were primarily being carried by courier and express mail services. These Guidelines operated on the principle of information being provided by the operator to Customs in advance of the arrival of the goods. The Guidelines also provided categorisation of goods. It also identified a set of data that was to be provided for grant of release of goods under these categories, as well as procedures to be followed, including the conclusion of MoUs between the Customs and trade for the implementation of these Guidelines and the procedures contained in them.

The Guidelines were further updated to provide specific guidance to both Customs and Trade on expediting the release/clearance of increasing volumes of low-value and small E-Commerce shipments/parcels. The Guidelines also provide examples of Members' practices and reference other relevant international standards and tools.

International Association of Ports and Harbors (IAPH)

'United Ports of the World.'

Website: *https://www.iaphworldports.org/*
Established: November 1955
Headquarters: Tokyo, Japan

The IAPH strives to promote the development of the international port and maritime industry by fostering cooperation among members to build a more cohesive partnership among the world's ports and harbours, thereby promoting peace and the welfare of humankind.

The IAPH and the WCO signed a memorandum of understanding (MoU) in 1987.

> The WCO-IAPH's *'Customs and Ports Authorities Cooperation Guidelines'* outline best practices between Customs and Port Authorities from advanced, emerging and developing countries over the last decades. Existing instruments such as the SAFE Framework of Standards (SAFE FOS) have been leveraged to design and implement the regulation of Customs and port digital systems, and both port and Customs authorities have amended Port Acts and Customs Acts to comply with data harmonisation requirements to facilitate trade.
>
> The Guidelines underscore the importance of understanding business processes and systems to drive interoperability and foster resilience through emerging technologies.

International Air Transport Association (IATA)

'To represent, lead, and serve the airline industry.'

Website: *https://www.iata.org/*
Established: 19 April 1945
Headquarters: Quebec, Canada

IATA improves the understanding of the air transport industry among decision-makers and increases awareness of the benefits that aviation brings to national and global economies. Advocating for the interests of airlines across the globe, we challenge unreasonable rules and charges, hold regulators and governments to account, and strive for sensible regulation.

It has developed global commercial standards upon which the air transport industry is built. It aims to assist airlines by simplifying processes and increasing passenger convenience while reducing costs and improving efficiency.

IATA helps airlines to operate safely, securely, efficiently, and economically under clearly defined rules. Professional support is provided to all industry stakeholders with a wide range of products and expert services.

IATA and the WCO signed two MoUs on 23 June 1986 and 20 June 1988.

> The *'WCO-IATA- ICAO Guidelines on Advance Passenger Information (API)'* establish a best practice to which Border Control Agencies, aircraft operators, and other passenger service operators implementing and operating API systems should adhere to the greatest extent practicable. With these Guidelines, the WCO, IATA, and ICAO envision API systems and practices that are developed in

a consistent and orderly manner, based on jointly agreed standards and principles to facilitate the development of API programmes around the globe.

Although these Guidelines focus on the acquisition of API from aircraft operators, they may also be considered in relation to passenger data for other transportation modes, such as cruise ships or international rail services. This document does not cover the collection and use of PNR data by Border Control Agencies.

The Passenger Name Record (PNR) is explored in other WCO/IATA/ICAO instruments.

International Bank for Reconstruction and Development Bank (IBRD) [*see* WBG]

'Ending extreme poverty and boosting shared prosperity.'

Website: *https://www.worldbank.org/*
Established: 22 July 1944, Bretton Woods, New Hampshire, United States of America
Headquarters: Washington, D.C., United States of America

The World Bank Group (WBG) is a family of five international organisations that make leveraged loans to developing countries. It is the world's largest and best-known development bank and an observer at the UN Development Group. The IBRD's stated mission is to achieve the twin goals of ending extreme poverty and building shared prosperity. Its five organisations are the IBRD, the International Development Association (IDA), the International Finance Corporation (IFC), the Multilateral Investment Guarantee Agency (MIGA) and the International Centre for Settlement of Investment Disputes (ICSID). The first two are sometimes collectively referred to as the World Bank.

International Civil Aviation Organization (ICAO)

'Safe Skies. Sustainable Future.'

Website: *https://www.icao.int/*
Established: 4 April 1947
Headquarters: Montreal, Quebec, Canada

The Convention on International Civil Aviation (ICA), also known as the Chicago Convention, in Chicago, was signed by 52 countries on 7 December 1944. The Provisional International Civil Aviation Organization (PICAO) was to be established and began operating on 6 June 1945, replacing ICAN. The PICAO was disestablished on 4 April 1947 and replaced by ICAO, which began its operations. In October 1947, ICAO became an agency of the UN under its Economic and Social Council (ECOSOC).

The ICAO is a UN agency which helps 193 countries to cooperate together and share their skies to their mutual benefit.

The ICAO's vision is to achieve the sustainable growth of the global civil aviation system.

The ICAO's mission is to serve as the global forum of States for international civil aviation. ICAO develops policies and standards, undertakes compliance audits, performs studies and analyses, provides assistance and builds aviation capacity through many other activities and the cooperation of its Member States and stakeholders.

Since it was established the ICAO's support and coordination has helped countries to diplomatically and technically realise a uniquely rapid and dependable network of global air mobility, connecting families, cultures, and businesses all over the world, and promoting sustainable growth and socio-economic prosperity wherever aircraft fly.

The '*Joint WCO-ICAO Guiding Principles for Pre-Loading Advance Cargo Information (PLACI)*' introduce the principal factors of the international air supply chain, with an emphasis on air cargo security and facilitation from both Civil Aviation and Customs perspectives.

The Joint Brochure provides basic information to all those involved in the air supply chain who are interested in understanding the various security and facilitation measures implemented by ICAO and WCO Members. It also identifies the roles and responsibilities of various entities and highlights how they can work together effectively to secure air cargo and mail.

The '*WCO-ICAO Moving Air Cargo Globally Air Cargo and Mail Secure Supply Chain and Facilitation*' serves to help to support the implementation of robust and harmonised standards worldwide, while fostering the improved air transport connectivity which will be so critical to the future sustainability of societies and economies everywhere.

International Chamber of Commerce (ICC)

'The merchants of peace.'

Website: *https://iccwbo.org/* and *https://iccwbo.org/world-chambers-federation/*
Established: 1919 [First Chamber in August 1599 in Marseille, France]
Headquarters: Paris, France

The ICC is the world's premier business organisation, enabling businesses to secure peace, prosperity, and opportunity for all. It is the institutional representative of over 45 million companies in over hundred countries with a mission to make business work for everyone, every day, everywhere. Through a unique mix of advocacy, solutions and standard setting, we promote international trade, responsible business conduct, a global approach to regulation, and market-leading dispute resolution services. Its members include many of the world's leading companies, Small and Micro Enterprises (SMEs), business associations and local chambers of commerce.

The ICC represents business interests at the highest levels of intergovernmental decision-making, whether at the WTO, the UN or the G20 – ensuring the voice of business is heard. This capacity to bridge the public and private sectors sets it apart as a unique institution, responding to the needs of any stakeholder involved in international commerce.

The ICC and the WCO signed an MoU on 19 June 1996.

Incoterms®: Launched in 1936. Help users select the appropriate Incoterms® rule for their sale transaction and incorporates expanded explanatory notes for users at the start of each Incoterms® rule.
ICC Genesis: Launched in 2024, ICC Genesis is a reliable verifying tool, useful not only to exporters for their origin statement but also to importers and customs authorities, working together to reduce fraud risks, costs and to facilitate smoother customs checks.

The *ICC World Chambers Federation (WCF)* is a non-political, non-governmental body providing a platform for chamber leaders to connect, inspire and strengthen links among chambers; it also helps individual chambers become more productive.

The WCF aims to create a better environment for business and Micro, Small, and Medium-sized Enterprises (MSMEs), and driving prosperity and opportunity for all.

Within the WCF, the *World ATA Carnet Council (WATAC)* runs the ATA system and its international guaranteeing chain. The WATAC consists of representatives from the countries and territories where ATA Carnets are issued and accepted.

International Federation of Customs Brokers Associations (IFCBA)

Website: *https://ifcba.org/*
Established: November 1990
Headquarters: Ottawa, Ontario, Canada

The IFCBA works to bring about improvements in Customs policies and practices on a global basis. These improvements benefit both customs brokers and their clients. As the only global organisation dedicated to representing customs brokers, the IFCBA promotes the value and use of customs brokers worldwide while supporting their continued role at the core of international trade.

The IFCBA has partnered with the WCO and national Customs administrations to deliver capacity-building opportunities in trade security, facilitation, and stakeholder engagement for the public and private sectors while providing specialised knowledge and expertise in customs brokerage regulation and education.

The IFCBA and the WCO signed an MoU on 25 June 2010.

> The '*WCO Customs Brokers Guidelines*' provide reference guidance to Members and stakeholders in establishing/adjusting their Customs brokers' regime in line with the RKC and the WTO Agreement on TFA. The Guidelines will assist Members in the accession to, and implementation of, the relevant provisions of the RKC and the WTO TFA. The Guidelines also explore various potential opportunities for enhancing cooperation between Customs and Customs brokers, in the context of new and emerging developments in the international supply chain.

> The '*WCO Study Report on Customs Brokers*' document provides a general background and overview of Customs brokers' role in the international supply chain together with some suggested policy and organisational considerations on Customs broker regimes and a model checklist for licensing/regulating brokers.

International Monetary Fund (IMF)

'Working to foster global monetary cooperation, secure financial stability, facilitate international trade, promote high employment and sustainable economic growth, and reduce poverty around the world.'

Website: *https://www.imf.org*
Established: 22 July 1944 [Bretton Woods, New Hampshire, United States of America.]
Headquarters: Washington, D.C., United States of America

The IMF is an international financial institution consisting of 190 countries. Its mission is to foster global monetary cooperation, secure financial stability, facilitate international trade, promote high employment and sustainable economic growth, and reduce poverty around the world.

> The WCO and the IMF collaborate on the International Survey of Customs Administration (ISOCA). This joint initiative aims to collect data on Customs

administrations globally, encompassing various aspects like revenue, enforcement, and trade facilitation. The data gathered through ISOCA is used for strategic planning, performance benchmarking, and identifying areas for technical assistance.

International Maritime Organization (IMO)

'A specialised agency of the United Nations responsible for regulating shipping.'

Website: *https://www.imo.org/*
Established: 17 March 1958
Headquarters: London, United Kingdom

As a specialised agency of the UN, the IMO is the global standard-setting authority for the safety, security and environmental performance of international shipping. Its main role is to create a regulatory framework for the shipping industry that is fair, effective, universally adopted, and universally implemented.

The IMO and the WCO signed an MoU on 23 July 2002.

The '*WCO Handbook Customs Convention on Containers, 1972*' deals with the Convention which provides for the temporary importation of containers, free of import duties and taxes, subject to re-exportation within three months and without the production of customs documents or security.

The Convention also provides for the approval of containers under customs seal (these approval provisions are identical to those in the Convention on the International Transport of Goods Under Cover of TIR Carnets – the TIR Convention, 1975).

The WCO administers this Convention on behalf of the UN/ECE.

International Network of Customs Universities (INCU)

'Promoting the Academic Standing of the Customs Profession.'

Website: *https://incu.org/*
Established: July 2005
Headquarters: Barton, Australian Capital Territory (ACT), Australia

INCU is a not-for-profit international association established to provide the WCO and other organisations with a single point of contact with universities and research institutes that are active in the field of customs research, education and training.

INCU was established to:

- promote the academic standing of the Customs profession;

- promote academic excellence in Customs matters;
- support research in Customs matters;
- organise academic conferences;
- generate greater public awareness of the Customs profession;
- promote the collective interests of its Members;
- provide the WCO and other organisations with a single point of contact with universities and research institutes that are active in the field of customs research, education and training; and
- provide a global resource for governments and the private sector, as well as an educational source for students wishing to further their knowledge in the field of customs, international trade, and logistics.

INCU is also designed to provide a global resource for governments and the private sector, as well as an educational source for students wishing to further their knowledge in the fields of customs management and administration and international trade and logistics management.

INCU provides a mechanism for progressively establishing a knowledge base on various important aspects of Customs and allows a free exchange of ideas and best practices that will not only assist countries undertaking reform processes but will also serve to build closer links between government, academia and the private sector.

INCU and the WCO signed an MoU on 30 September 2009.

The INCU Management Committee works in close cooperation with the WCO Capacity Building Directorate and WCO Research Unit to promote the academic standing of the Customs profession.

The primary areas of cooperation between the INCU and WCO are: PICARD Programme; INCU Network; World Customs Journal; Customs Research Database; Professional Standards; Recognition of University Curricula, and the Columbus Programme.

International Criminal Police Organization (INTERPOL)

'Stay safe and prevent crimes.'

Website: *https://www.interpol.int/*
Established: 7 September 1923
Headquarters: Lyon, France

INTERPOL is an international organisation that facilitates worldwide police cooperation and crime control. It is the world's largest international police organisation.

INTERPOL is unique. It is the only organisation with the mandate and technical infrastructure to share police information globally

INTERPOL and the WCO signed an MoU in 1998.

The '*WCO-Interpol Customs – Police Cooperation Handbook*' aims to foster increased cooperation between the two types of agencies at the national level. While this document highlights the need for customs - police cooperation - on the one hand, it also offers professional insight on how to strengthen the collaboration between these institutions that are so important to a country's national security.

International Road Transport Union (IRU)

'Working together for a better future.'

Website: *https://www.iru.org/*
Established: 12 March 1948
Headquarters: Geneva, Switzerland

The IRU, the '*World Road Transport Organisation*', represents the entire road transport industry worldwide through its national associations. It speaks for the operators of coaches, taxis, and trucks, as well as large transport fleets and driver-owners. In all international bodies that make decisions affecting road transport, it acts as the industry's advocate.

The IRU improves road transport's safety record and environmental performance and ensures people's and goods' mobility. Among its practical services to the industry, IRU is also an international guarantor of the TIR Carnet System, under which trucks are sealed by customs upon departure and can cross several borders without further checks until they reach their destinations.

The IRU and the WCO signed an MoU on 21 September 1987.

The main objective of the '*WCO Transit Guidelines*' is to render practical support to WCO Members in implementing efficient and effective transit regimes in their territories.

The '*WCO Compendium of Best Practices in the Area of Transit*' contains good practices that illustrate in practical terms how various WCO Members are implementing the guiding principles for efficient transit regimes as outlined in the '*WCO Transit Guidelines*'. It is aimed at supporting Members and partner international organisations in their efforts to improve transit effectiveness and efficiency and to implement relevant international and regional agreements in a harmonised manner.

> The '*WCO Transit Handbook*' deals with various aspects of the operation of Customs transit procedures and is accordingly intended to serve as a practical guide to assist WCO Members to develop a functional and effective transit system which may contribute to the enhancement of economic competitiveness and secure their revenue.
>
> In particular, this Handbook helps developing and least-developed Members to assess the effectiveness of their transit schemes and identify any further improvements needed.

International Organization for Standardization (ISO)

'International standards development.'

Website: *https://www.iso.org/*
Established: 23 February 1947
Headquarters: Geneva, Switzerland

The ISO brings global experts together to agree on the best way of doing things – for anything from making a product to managing a process. As one of the oldest non-governmental international organisations, ISO has enabled trade and cooperation between people and companies worldwide. The International Standards published by ISO serve to make lives easier, safer and better.

International Trade Centre (ITC)

'Trade impact for good.'

Website: *https://intracen.org/*
Established: 19 March 1964
Headquarters: Geneva, Switzerland

The ITC is a multilateral agency with a joint mandate with the WTO, formerly GATT, and the UN through the United Nations Conference on Trade and Development (UNCTAD). The ITC serves as a focal point for technical cooperation in trade promotion of developing countries.

The WCO established a working relationship with the ITC, whose main objective is to promote national developments through international trade, emphasising the relationship between exports and the private sector. The ITC organises symposiums that gather participants from legal, academic, and business backgrounds. By participating in these symposiums, the WCO promoted the RKC and other WCO instruments to the participants.

The ITC has produced information that is available on its website, through which the status of countries' accession to key international trade-related treaties is visually grasped. The ITC has agreed to cover data relating to the RKC and other key WCO instruments on its website.

The WCO and the ITC jointly launched the '*Rules of Origin Facilitator*', which is available online at *www.findrulesoforigin.org*.

The Facilitator contains information on trade agreements and applicable tariff rates at the detailed product level. The database includes the product-specific RoO as well as provisions on origin certification. Necessary documentation, such as CoO, is also provided.

International Trade Organization (ITO) [*see* GATT/WTO]

The ITO was supposed to be one of the Bretton Woods trilogies of institutions but was only institutionalised through the creation of the WTO.

The ITO was the proposed name for an international institution for the regulation of trade. Led by the US in collaboration with allies, the effort to form the organisation from 1945 to 1948, with the successful passing of the Havana Charter, eventually failed due to lack of approval by the US Congress. Until the creation of the WTO on 1 January 1995, international trade was managed through the GATT.

League of Nations (LN)

Established: 10 January 1920
Headquarters: Geneva, Switzerland

'Promote international co-operation and to achieve international peace and security.'

The LN was an international organisation, the first worldwide intergovernmental organisation whose principal mission was to maintain world peace; it was created after the First World War (WWI) to provide a forum for resolving international disputes. The main organisation ceased operations on 18 April 1946, when many of its components were relocated into the new UN. As the template for modern global governance, the League profoundly shaped the modern world.

Central Office for International Carriage by Rail (OCTI)

Established in 1893, OCTI is the predecessor of the Intergovernmental Organization for International Carriage by Rail (OTIF), which was established on 1 May 1985.

Organisation for Economic Co-operation and Development (OECD)

'Better policies for better lives.'

Website: *https://www.oecd.org/*
Established: 30 September 1961
Headquarters: Paris, France

The OECD is an international organisation that works to build better policies for better lives. Its goal is to shape policies that foster prosperity, equality, opportunity and well-being for all.

Together with governments, policymakers, and citizens, it works to establish evidence-based international standards and find solutions to a range of social, economic, and environmental challenges. From improving economic performance and creating jobs to fostering strong education and fighting international tax evasion, we provide a unique forum and knowledge hub for data and analysis, exchange of experiences, best-practice sharing, and advice on public policies and international standard setting.

> The WCO and the OECD held two joint '*Conferences on Transfer Pricing and Customs Valuation*' in Brussels, Belgium in 2006 and 2007.

Intergovernmental Organization for International Carriage by Rail (OTIF) [*see* OCTI]

'To promote, improve and facilitate international traffic by rail.'

Website: *https://otif.org/*
Established: 1 May 1985
Headquarters: Bern, Switzerland

The OTIF replaced the Central Office for International Carriage by Rail (OCTI) which was established in 1893.

The OTIF has three major areas of activity: technical interoperability, dangerous goods and railway contract law.

The OTIF develops uniform legal regimes for:

- contracts of carriage of passengers and goods;
- ancillaries to the contract of carriage, such as the contract of use of wagons or infrastructure;
- rules for the transport of dangerous goods;
- technical provisions and the procedure for the technical approval of rolling stock.

The OTIF provides its Member States with the legal and technical means to facilitate international traffic by rail, to develop this traffic on their territory and to connect to the railway networks of other Member States. It therefore supplies the means to promote real legal and technical interoperability.

> The '*WCO Railway Guidance*' aims to promote Customs procedures in railway transportation; simplify and harmonise Customs regulations and procedures

applicable to railway transportation; encourage the use of advanced technologies; and strengthen Customs-to-Customs and Customs-to-Business cooperation, etc.

International Air Cargo Association (TIACA)

'A safe, profitable and united air cargo industry that embraces modern technologies and practices to sustainably and fairly serve trade and social development worldwide.'

Website: *https://tiaca.org/*
Established: 1990
Headquarters: Miami, Florida, United States of America

The TIACA is the only worldwide organisation that brings together all the links in the air logistics chain. Its mission is to advance the interests of the air cargo industry and strengthen its contribution to world trade expansion.

The TIACA supports, assists and advocates for the progressive liberalisation of the global market and easier, enhanced trade between developing and developed economies.

The TIACIA and the WCO signed an MoU on 25 June 2010.

International Federation of Inspection Agencies (IFIA) [*see* TIC Council]

Presently known as the TIC Council.

TIC Council (Previously International Federation of Inspection Agencies or IFIA)

'To be recognised and trusted globally as the voice of the independent testing, inspection and certification industry, and to stand for best practice and the highest standards in safety, quality, health, ethics and sustainability.'

Website: *https://www.tic-council.org/*
Established: 1982/10 March 2019
Headquarters: Brussels, Belgium

The Testing, Inspection, and Certification (TIC) Council was formed following the merger of IFIA and the International Confederation of Inspection and Certification Organisations (CEOC International). The TIC Council represents more than 90 leading international companies and organisations in the TIC industry.

International Union of Railways (UIC)

'Promote rail transport at world level.'

Website: *https://uic.org/*
Established: 17 October 1922
Headquarters: Paris, France

The acronym UIC is derived from the French expansion Union Internationale des Chemins de fer.

The overall objective for UIC is to enable it to effectively fulfil its mission; three levels have been defined for international cooperation activities:

- Strategic level: Coordination with and between the six UIC Regions created as part of the new Governance (activities steered by the UIC Regional Assemblies for Africa, Asia, North America, South America, Europe and the Middle-East).
- Technical/Professional Cooperation Level (structured around the following railway activities): Passenger, Freight, Rail System – including infrastructure, rolling stock, operations – and Fundamental Values including cross-sector activities such as Sustainable Development, Research Coordination, Safety, Security, Expertise Development. Strategic priorities for technical cooperation activities are set out by forums and platforms composed of member representatives.
- Support Services Level: Finance, Human Resources, Legal, Communications and Institutional Relations.

> The '*WCO Railway Guidance*' aims to promote Customs procedures in railway transportation; simplify and harmonise Customs regulations and procedures applicable to railway transportation; encourage the use of advanced technologies; and strengthen Customs-to-Customs and Customs-to-Business cooperation, etc.

United Nations (UN) [*see* League of Nations (LN)]

'Peace, dignity and equality on a healthy planet.'

Website: *https://www.un.org/en/*
Established: 24 October 1945
Headquarters: New York, NY, United States of America

The UN's work is guided by the purposes and principles contained in its founding Charter. It has evolved over the years to keep pace with a rapidly changing world. But one thing has stayed the same: it remains the one place on Earth where all the world's nations can gather together, discuss common problems, and find shared solutions that benefit all of humanity.

United Nations Economic Commission for Europe (UNECE)

'To promote the progressive harmonization and unification of international trade law'.

Website: *https://unece.org/*
Established: 28 March 1947

Headquarters: Geneva, Switzerland

The United Nations Economic Commission for Europe (UNECE) was set up by the Economic and Social Council (ECOSOC), the United Nations' (UN's) central platform for reflection, debate, and innovative thinking on sustainable development.

The ENECE serves as the focal point within the UN system for the development of norms, standards, policy recommendations, and conventions to facilitate of international trade.

United Nations Educational, Scientific and Cultural Organization (UNESCO)

'Building peace in the minds of men and women.'

Website: *https://www.unesco.org/*
Established: 16 November 1945
Headquarters: Paris, France

UNESCO is a specialised agency of the UN with the aim of promoting world peace and security through international cooperation in education, arts, sciences and culture.

The WCO and UNESCO cooperate to combat illicit trafficking in cultural property. The two Organisations have signed an MoU and have jointly developed a '*Model Export Certificate for Cultural Objects*' and explanatory notes to the model.

United Nations Commission on International Trade Law (UNCITRAL)

'To promote the progressive harmonization and unification of international trade law.'

Website: *https://uncitral.un.org/*
Established: 17 December 1966
Headquarters: Vienna, Austria

UNCITRAL is the core legal body of the UN system in the field of international trade law. It is a legal body with universal membership, specialising in commercial law reform worldwide for over 50 years. UNCITRAL's business is the modernisation and harmonisation of rules on international business.

United Nations Conference on Trade and Development (UNCTAD)

'Maximize the trade, investment and development opportunities of developing countries and assist them in their efforts to integrate into the world economy on an equitable basis.'

Website: *https://unctad.org/*
Established: 30 December 1964

Headquarters: Geneva, Switzerland

UNCTAD supports developing countries in accessing the benefits of a globalised economy more fairly and effectively. And it helps equip developing countries to deal with the potential drawbacks of greater economic integration. To do this, it provides analysis, facilitates consensus-building, and offers technical assistance. This helps developing countries to use trade, investment, finance, and technology as vehicles for inclusive and sustainable development.

The WCO and UNCTAD, on 4 October 2022, signed an MoU, updating the MoU between the two organisations dating back to 2013.

The MoU aims to support Customs modernisation by enabling interoperability between the UNCTAD's ASYCUDA and the WCO Cargo Targeting System (CTS), National Customs Enforcement Network (nCeN) and Time Release Study (TRS). UNCTAD and the WCO are committed to enhancing Customs' capability in managing risks by utilising information and technology while streamlining and simplifying data collection and eliminating redundancies.

UNCTAD and the WCO agreed to collaborate further to accelerate harmonised supply chain digitalisation through the implementation of international standards for data exchange, such as the WCO Data Model.

Universal Postal Union (UPU)

'One world. One postal network.'

Website: *https://www.upu.int/*
Established: 9 October 1874
Headquarters: Berne, Switzerland

The UPU established date marks the signing of the Treaty of Berne, which officially created the General Postal Union (later renamed the UPU in 1878). It operated independently before being incorporated into the UN in 1948.

The UPU's origins can be traced back to a Paris Postal Conference in June 1863. Following the Paris Conference, a second conference was convened in Berne, Switzerland, and the Treaty of Berne was signed. This treaty established the principles of universal transmission of mail and uniform postal rates. The agreement officially came into effect on 1 July 1875.

With its 192 member countries, the UPU is the primary forum for cooperation between postal sector players.

The '*WCO–UPU Postal Customs Guide*' is a joint WCO–UPU tool for Posts and for Customs administration staff dealing with Customs clearance of postal items.

The Guide is also intended to form a common basis for dialogue and discussion at the national level between the designated operators of the Universal Postal Union (UPU) member countries and WCO Member Customs administrations.

The World Bank Group (WBG) [*see* IBRD]

'Ending extreme poverty and boosting shared prosperity.'

Website: *https://www.worldbank.org/*
Established: 22 July 1944, Bretton Woods, New Hampshire, United States of America
Headquarters: Washington, D.C., United States of America

The WBG is a family of five international organisations that make leveraged loans to developing countries. It is the world's largest and best-known development bank and an observer at the UN Development Group.

The WBG's stated mission is to achieve the twin goals of ending extreme poverty and building shared prosperity. Its five organisations are the IBRD, the IDA, the IFC, the MIGA and the ICSID. The first two are sometimes collectively referred to as the WB.

The WCO and the WBG collaborate on various initiatives related to trade facilitation and customs modernisation, particularly in developing countries. This includes the Trade Facilitation in Middle Income Countries (TFMICs) programme.

It also collaborates on:

Trade Facilitation:
- The WCO and WBG jointly implement the TFMICs programme to reduce the time and cost of trade for middle-income countries.
- This programme helps countries meet the requirements of the WTO TFA.
- The TFMICs programme is supported by the UK Foreign, Commonwealth, and Development Office (FCDO) Prosperity Fund.

Customs Modernisation:
- The WCO and WBG work together on customs reform initiatives in developing countries.
- These reforms aim to improve efficiency and security and reduce corruption in customs administrations.
- The WBG's '*Doing Business*' project considers Customs Procedures as a key factor in a country's overall business environment.

Trade Data and Analysis:
- The WCO has developed the HS, a hierarchical classification of products used for trade statistics.

- The WBG utilises this data to analyse trade flows and patterns.
- The WCO and WBG also collaborate on projects related to trade data collection and analysis using blockchain technology.

Other Areas of Cooperation:
- The WCO and WBG have discussed cooperation on various issues, including the impact of customs modernisation programmes on the '*Doing Business*' rankings.
- They also collaborate on efforts to address illicit trade, particularly with the support of the OECD.

World Customs Organization (WCO) [*See* CCC.]

'Borders Divide, Customs Connects.'

Website: *https://www.wcoomd.org/*
Established: 26 January 1953 [The CCC was renamed the World Customs Organization on 22 June 1994.]
Headquarters: Brussels, Belgium

The WCO, established as the CCC, is an independent intergovernmental body whose mission is to enhance the effectiveness and efficiency of Customs administrations. With its members collectively representing approximately 98% of world trade, the WCO is the only international organisation with competence in Customs matters and can rightly call itself the voice of the international Customs community.

As the only international organisation devoted exclusively to Customs matters, the WCO is recognised as the voice of the Customs community. It is noted for its expertise in the development of international standards, simplification and harmonisation of Customs procedures, trade security, trade facilitation, Customs anti-fraud and compliance, HS commodity nomenclature, RoO, Customs Valuation, and capacity building.

Customs Day is celebrated annually on 26 January. The day was chosen as it coincides with the date on which the CCC held its inaugural session in 1953.

The WCO signed an MoU with:

- IAPH in 1987.
- IATA on 23 June 1986 and on 20 June 1988.
- ICC on 19 June 1996.
- IFCBA on 25 June 2010.
- IMO on 23 July 2002.
- INCU on 30 September 2009.
- INTERPOL in 1998.
- TIACIA on 25 June 2010.

- WHO on 21 September 1987.

World Federation of Pipe Line Industry Associations (WFPIA)

'Encourages interest from other associations in order to expand and provide to the industry the very latest technology in all disciplines associated with the international pipeline industry both on and offshore.'

Website: *https://www.iploca.com/*
Established: 20 June 1966
Headquarters: Geneva, Switzerland

The WFPIA provides a platform for collaboration among the associations related in one way or another to the onshore and offshore construction of international and regional oil, gas, water and slurry pipelines.

World Health Organization (WHO)

'We champion health and a better future for all.'

Website: *https://www.who.int/*
Established: 7 April 1948
Headquarters: Geneva, Switzerland

The WHO is the UN agency that connects nations, partners, and people to promote health, keep the world safe, and serve the vulnerable so that everyone, everywhere, can attain the highest level of health.

The WHO and the WCO work together on issues such as counterfeiting pharmaceuticals. The WCO is an active member of the International Medical Products Anti-Counterfeiting Taskforce (IMPACT) project coordinated by the WHO.

The WHO and the WCO signed an MoU in July 2002.

World Intellectual Property Organization (WIPO)

'To lead the development of a balanced and effective international intellectual property system that enables innovation and creativity for the benefit of all.'

Website: *https://www.wipo.int/*
Established: 14 July 1967
Headquarters: Geneva, Switzerland

The origins of WIPO go back to 1883 when the Paris Convention for the Protection of Industrial Property and to 1886 when the Berne Convention for the Protection of Literary and Artistic Works established an '*International Bureau*'. The two bureaus were united in 1893 and, in 1970, were replaced by the WIPO by virtue of the WIPO Convention.

The WIPO is a specialised agency of the UN which aims to develop a balanced and accessible international intellectual property system. The WCO and WIPO closely cooperate to promote the effective use and protection of IP worldwide.

The WIPO's activities include hosting forums to discuss and shape international IP rules and policies, providing global services that register and protect IP in different countries, resolving transboundary IP disputes, helping connect IP systems through uniform standards and infrastructure, and serving as a general reference database on all IP matters; this includes providing reports and statistics on the state of IP protection or innovation both globally and in specific countries.

'*World Intellectual Property Day*' is celebrated annually on 26 April. The day was chosen as it coincides with the date on which the Convention Establishing the WIPO entered into force in 1970. The Convention was signed in Stockholm, Sweden, on 14 July 1967 and entered into force on 26 April 1970.

> The WCO and WIPO have a close working relationship, particularly in addressing intellectual property enforcement at borders and combating counterfeiting and piracy. The WCO provides the Customs infrastructure and expertise to enforce IP rights at borders, while WIPO provides the technical and legal framework for IP protection.
>
> The two organisations collaborate on initiatives such as the '*Global Congress on Combating Counterfeiting and Piracy*' and joint training sessions to enhance IP enforcement at the international level.

World Trade Organization (WTO)

'*Full Participation, Inclusiveness, and Transparency.*

Website: *https://www.wto.org/*
Established: 1 January 1995
Headquarters: Geneva, Switzerland

The WTO is the only international organisation dealing with the global rules of trade. Its primary function is to ensure that trade flows as smoothly, predictably and freely as possible. The overall objective of the WTO is to help its members use trade as a means to raise living standards, create jobs and improve people's lives. The WTO operates the global system of trade rules and helps developing countries build their trade capacity. It also provides a forum for its members to negotiate trade agreements and resolve the trade problems they face with each other. The WTO focuses on trade rules, which include trade in goods, trade-related aspects of intellectual property rights (IRP), trade in services and other trade-related agreements.

The WTO provides a framework for negotiating trade agreements between the WTO Members. It also provides a dispute settlement mechanism to enforce the agreements and help Member countries adhere to the agreements of the WTO.

Members of the WTO must resolve any trade conflicts under the dispute settlement mechanism to discourage/stop Members from taking a unilateral retaliatory measure against any other member.

Agreement Establishing the WTO		
GATT	*GATS*	*TRIPS*
Goods	Services	Intellectual Property
DISPUTE SETTLEMENT		
TRADE POLICY REVIEWS		

The WCO and WTO have a strong and mutually beneficial relationship, working together to facilitate global trade and ensure smooth customs procedures. The WTO sets the legal framework for trade, while the WCO provides the technical expertise and practical implementation of those frameworks.

World Free Zones Organization (WFZO)

'Where Innovation Meets Trade.'

Website: *https://www.worldfzo.org/*
Established: 19 May 2014
Headquarters: Dubai, United Arab Emirates (UAE)

The WFZO is a global not-for-profit organisation that provides one authoritative, collective voice representing the interests of free zones around the world.

The WFZO's objectives are the following:

- Bring together FZ; regional, national, subnational and local FZ associations; consultants and advisors to FZ; FZ users; interested governmental organisations; and international trade-related organisations for knowledge exchange, education and training, networking and business development.
- Provide a forum for FZ around the world to learn, grow and prosper through unrivalled access to exclusive in-depth research and insights.
- Create '*best in class*' standards for FZ that enhance the economic ecosystem both globally and in local markets, as well as guidelines for the establishment and administration of FZ.
- Gather, create, expand and disseminate the knowledge of, and about, FZ internationally.
- Improve the perception of FZ globally and position them as areas that make valuable contributions to the local economy and promote sustainable business.

- Provide specialised operational, administrative, educational and networking services to Members, Partners and Observers through trainings as well as physical and electronic resources.
- Support and advise new FZ internationally as they develop.
- Become the global through leader on FZ and issues relating to them.

The WCO's '*Practical Guidance on Free Zones*' aims at providing practical guidance, and WCO Members' best practice, to help Customs enhance the Customs procedures/control to be globally applied in FZ, while effectively supporting the healthy development and competitiveness of FZ.

The Guidance consists of eight core elements, with practical guidance and associated best practice by WCO Members. The core elements are as follows:

- Territoriality aspect of FZ.
- Full Customs involvement in FZ.
- Customs involvement in the company approval process and AEO concept.
- Reporting to Customs and the use of data and IT systems.
- Customs audit in FZ.
- Customs control and surveillance: authority to seize illegal goods in FZ.
- On-site checks inside FZ; and use of technology for inspections in FZ.
- Cooperation.

The material contained in the Guidance will provide Custom administrations with information to assist in the possible development and updating of FZ.

§23.02 THE MORE IMPORTANT WCO AND WTO CUSTOMS AND TRADE COMMITTEES

CCV	GATT/WTO Committee on Customs Valuation
CRO	WCO Committee on Rules of Origin
CRTA	WTO Committee on Regional Trade Agreements
CTG	WTO Council for Trade in Goods
HSC	WCO Harmonized System Committee
PSCG	Private Sector Consultative Group
RSC	WCO Harmonized System Review Subcommittee
SSC	WCO Scientific Subcommittee
TCCV	WCO Technical Committee on Customs Valuation
TCRO	WCO Technical Committee on Rule of Origin
TDC	WTO Committee on Trade and Development
TFC	WTO Trade Facilitation Committee

Tariff Classification

WCO Harmonized System Committee (HSC)

The HSC interprets and maintains the HS and the HS legal texts to secure uniform classification of goods, including settlement of classification disputes between contracting parties and amends the HS legal texts to reflect developments in technology and changes in trade patterns.

There are three Subcommittees:

- HS Working Party (Pre-Sessional).
- HS Review Subcommittee.
- Scientific Subcommittee.

WCO Harmonized System Working Party

The purpose and scope of the Working Party is to draft the texts of possible amendments to the HS Nomenclature, EN and Compendium of Classification Opinions before their final adoption by the HS Committee.

WCO Harmonized System Review Subcommittee (RSC)

The RSC is responsible for periodically reviewing the HS and proposing amendments to the legal text that reflect changes in technology and tariff classification patterns of international trade.

The purpose and scope of the Subcommittee is to:

- pursue a review of the HS under the general guidance of the HS Committee;
- propose to the Committee such amendments to the HS as may be considered desirable, having regard, in particular, to the needs of users and changes in technology or patterns of international trade; and
- prepare, to the extent appropriate, any consequential amendments to the EN and the Compendium of Classification Opinions for consideration by the Committee.

WCO Scientific Subcommittee (SSC)

The HSC is often assisted in its technical work by the SSC, an advisory body of the WCO, for questions involving chemical or other technical or scientific matters.

The purpose and scope of the Scientific Subcommittee is to:

- assist the HS Committee and the Review Subcommittee in their technical work, in particular with regard to questions involving the classification of chemical products;
- assist the Council and its Committees and Subcommittees in their work related to all scientific and engineering aspects of Customs administration, operation and procedures; and

- serve as a forum for the exchange of views by the Customs laboratory services of Council Members on Customs-related scientific and engineering developments and best practices.

Origin

WCO Technical Committee on Rules of Origin (TCRO)

The TCRO is a WTO body but operates under the auspices of the WCO. Its two major mandates are to undertake the technical exercise of the work programme for harmonising non-preferential RoO and to assume its permanent responsibilities, such as examining specific technical problems.

WTO Committee on Rules of Origin (CRO)

The TCRO was established in 1995 by the WTO Agreement on RoO and has, since then, carried out the main work of harmonising non-preferential RoO. After establishing the overall framework of the Harmonised Rules of Origin (HRO) and completing all necessary technical work, the TCRO in June 1999 transmitted almost five hundred outstanding issues for discussion and decision in the WTO CRO. On the basis of these invaluable inputs from TCRO, the CRO has been working hard to complete the remaining work.

Customs Valuation

WCO Technical Committee on Customs Valuation (TCCV)

The TCCV was established to ensure, at the technical level, uniformity in the interpretation and application of the WTO Customs Valuation Agreement.

The Agreement also establishes a TCCV under the auspices of the WCO to ensure, at the technical level, uniformity in the interpretation and application of the Agreement. The responsibilities of the Technical Committee include advising on specific technical matters as requested by Members or by a panel in a dispute.

GATT/WTO Committee on Customs Valuation (CCV)

The WCO TCCV was established in 1980 by the Tokyo Round Agreement on Customs Valuation. Since then, the TCCV and the GATT/WTO Committee on CCV have maintained an excellent relationship. The '*WCO Compendium of Customs Valuation*' contains advisory opinions, commentaries, ENs and case studies adopted by the TCCV, which provide very useful guidelines for addressing various technical questions on customs valuation.

The Agreement established a Committee on Customs Valuation composed of representatives from each of the Members to afford Members the opportunity to consult on matters relating to the administration of the customs valuation system by any Member or the furtherance of the objectives of the Valuation Agreement.

Trade Blocs

WTO Committee on Regional Trade Agreements (CRTA)

The CRTA considers individual regional agreements and is mandated to hold discussions on the systemic implications of the agreements for the multilateral trading system.

Private Sector

Private Sector Consultative Group (PSCG)

The PSCG informs and advises the WCO Secretary General, the Policy Commission, and WCO Members on Customs and international trade matters from the perspective of the private sector, in addition to issues related to the implementation of the SAFE Framework of Standards to **S**ecure **a**nd **F**acilitate Global Trad**e**, simply known as the SAFE Framework.

WTO Committee on Trade Facilitation (FTC)

The TFC provides WTO members the opportunity to consult on any matters relating to the operation of the TFA or the furtherance of its objectives. Established under Article 23.1 of the TFA, the TF Committee reaches its decisions by consensus. It reports to the Council for Trade in Goods (CTG) and provides records of its work in its annual reports to the CTG.

WTO Committee on Trade and Development (TDC)

The TDC has a wide-ranging mandate. Among the broad areas of topics it has tackled as priorities are: how provisions favouring developing countries are being implemented, guidelines for technical cooperation, increased participation of developing countries in the trading system, and the position of least-developed countries.

The WTO Member countries also have to inform the WTO about special programmes involving trade concessions for products from developing countries and regional arrangements among developing countries. The TDC handles notifications of:

- GSP programmes, in which developed countries lower their trade barriers preferentially for products from developing countries;
- Preferential Arrangements among developing countries such as MERCOSUR (the Southern Common Market in Latin America), the Common Market for Eastern and Southern Africa (COMESA), and the ASEAN Free Trade Area (AFTA).

WTO Council for Trade in Goods (CTG)

It is one of the top subsidiary bodies of the WTO and reports directly to the General Council. The CTG oversees the implementation of all agreements relating to trade in goods, including the GATT 1994.

The following 14 WTO bodies report to the CTG:

- Committee on Agriculture
- Committee on Anti-Dumping Practices
- Committee on Customs Valuation
- Committee on Import Licensing
- Committee on Market Access
- Committee on Rules of Origin
- Committee on Safeguards
- Committee on Sanitary and Phytosanitary Measures
- Committee on Subsidies and Countervailing Measures
- Committee on Technical Barriers to Trade
- Committee on Trade Facilitation
- Committee on Trade-Related Investment Measures
- Committee of Participants on the Expansion of Trade in Information Technology Products
- Working Party on State Trading Enterprises

WCO Working Bodies

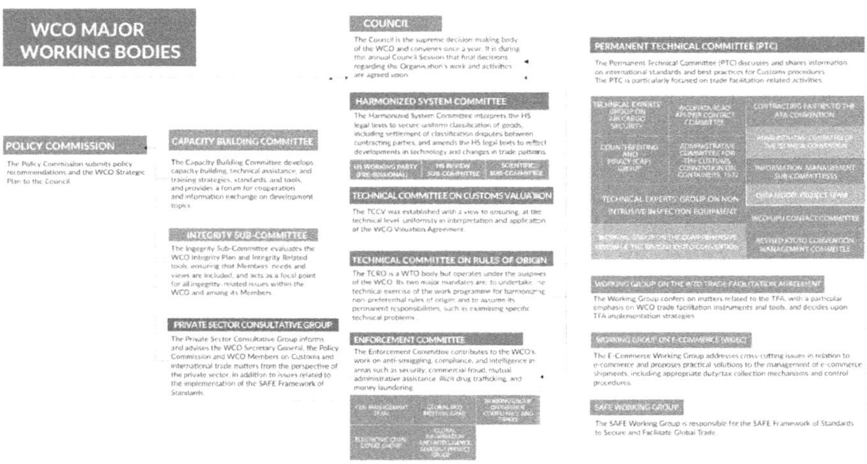

Source: WCO.

WTO Organisational Chart

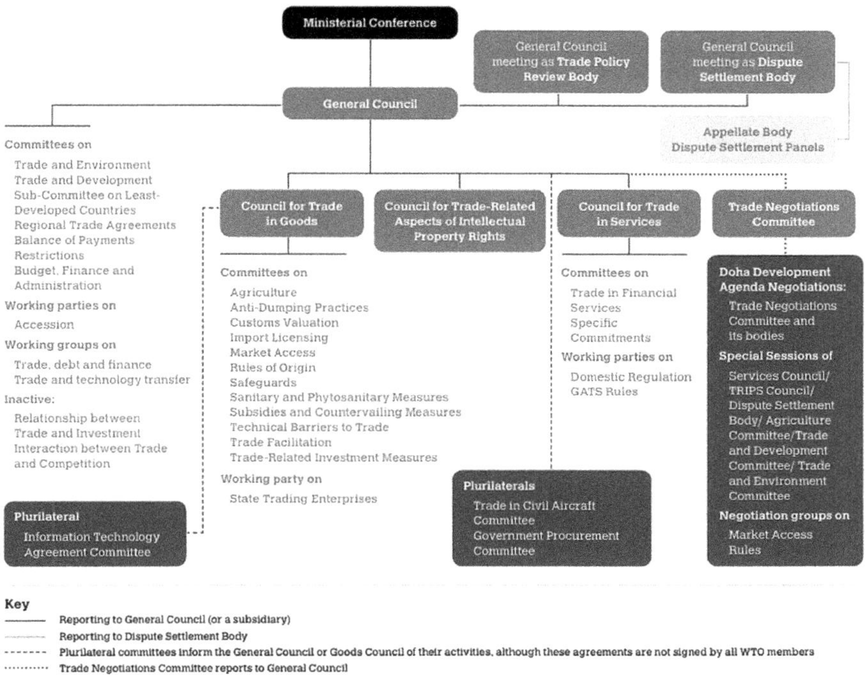

Source: WTO.

§23.03 AGREEMENTS AND CONVENTIONS

The more essential Agreements and Conventions

WCO Agreements

Agreements Sponsored or Administered by the WCO

- WTO Agreement on Rules of Origin (RoO)
- WTO Agreement on Valuation (Article VII of the GATT 1994).

WTO Agreements

Agreements Administered by the WTO

- Agreement on Implementation of Article VI of the GATT 1994 (Anti-dumping)

- Agreement on Implementation of Article VII of the GATT 1994 (Customs Valuation) (ACV)
- Agreement on Import Licensing Procedures
- Agreement on Preshipment Inspection (PSI)
- Agreement on Regional Trade Agreements (RTA) (Article XXIV of the GATT 1994)
- Agreement on Rules of Origin (RoO)
- Agreement on Safeguards (SG)
- Agreement on Subsidies and Countervailing Measures (SCM)
- Agreement on Technical Barriers to Trade (TBT)
- Agreement on Trade Facilitation (TFA)
- Agreement on the Application of Sanitary and Phytosanitary Measures (SPS)
- General Agreement on Tariffs and Trade 1947 (GATT 1947)
- General Agreement on Tariffs and Trade 1994 (GATT 1994)
- Understanding on the Interpretation of Article II:1(b) of the GATT 1994 (other duties and charges).

Agreements

- Montreal Protocol on Substances that Deplete the Ozone Layer
- United Nations (UN) Convention Against the Illicit Traffic in Narcotic Drugs and Psychotropic Substances.

WCO Conventions

Conventions Sponsored or Administered by the CCC

- Brussels Convention on Nomenclature for the Classification of Goods in Customs Tariffs (CCCN)
- Convention establishing a Customs Co-operation Council (CCC)
- Convention establishing the World Intellectual Property Organization (WIPO)
- Convention on Temporary Admission (TA) (Istanbul Convention)
- Convention on the Valuation of Goods for Customs Purposes (BDV)
- Customs Convention concerning Facilities for the Importation of Goods for Display or Use at Exhibitions, Fairs, Meetings or Similar Events
- Customs Convention concerning Welfare Material for Seafarers
- Customs Convention on Containers
- Customs Convention on Échantillons Commerciaux – Commercial Samples (ECS) Carnets for Commercial Samples
- Customs Convention on the ATA Carnet for the Temporary Admission of Goods (ATA Convention)
- Customs Convention on the International Transit of Goods (ITI Convention)
- Customs Convention on the International Transport of Goods under Cover of TIR (TIR Convention)

- Customs Convention on the Temporary Importation of Packings
- Customs Convention on the Temporary Importation of Pedagogic Material
- Customs Convention on the Temporary Importation of Professional Equipment
- Customs Convention on the Temporary Importation of Scientific Equipment
- International Convention on the Harmonized Commodity Description and Coding System (HS)
- International Convention on Mutual Administrative Assistance for the Prevention, Investigation and Repression of Customs Offences (Nairobi Convention)
- International Convention on Mutual Administrative Assistance in Customs Matters (Johannesburg Convention)
- International Convention on the Simplification and Harmonization of Customs Procedures (Kyoto Convention)
- International Convention on the Simplification and Harmonization of Customs Procedures (Kyoto Convention) as amended – Revised Kyoto Convention (RKC).

Conventions

- Basel Convention in the Control of Transboundary Movements of Hazardous Waste and the Disposal
- Convention on International Civil Aviation (ICA), known as the Chicago Convention
- Convention on International Trade in Endangered Species of Wild Fauna and Flora (CITES)
- Vienna Convention for the Protection of the Ozone Layer (Montreal Protocol)
- Montreal Protocol on Substances that Deplete the Ozone Layer
- United Nations (UN) Convention Against the Illicit Traffic in Narcotic Drugs and Psychotropic Substances.

CHAPTER 24
Selected Resources

This practical reference to selected Customs and Excises resources should not be construed as a comprehensive list. These are particularly worthwhile and valued resources that should stand you in good stead and further enrich your Customs and Excises journey of discovery.

Caveat lector: The terms and the terminology used in these resources should under no circumstances be accepted for their linguistic appearance and meaning. It should be understood for its true meaning in Customs and Excises.

All links were accessed on 10 March 2025.

Section I The Cornerstones, Remedies, Duties, Taxes, and Levies

Chapter 2 Codification – Tariff Classification

Harmonised System Convention: https://www.wcoomd.org/en/topics/nomenclature/instrument-and-tools/hs_convention.aspx

Nomenclature and Classification of Goods: https://www.wcoomd.org/en/topics/nomenclature.aspx

Tariff Classification and Duty Rates: www.wcoomd.org/en/topics/nomenclature/resources/hs_tariff_classification.aspx

Tools to Assist with the Classification in the Harmonised System: https://www.wcoomd.org/en/topics/nomenclature/resources/hs_tariff_classification.aspx

Customs Rulings Online Search System (CROSS): https://rulings.cbp.gov/home

Alphabetical index: https://www.wcotradetools.org/en/harmonized-system/alphabetical-index/en/2022/b

Chapter 3 Origination – Origin

Agreement on Rules of Origin: https://www.wto.org/english/docs_e/legal_e/22-roo_e.htm, http://www.wcoomd.org/en/topics/origin/instrument-and-tools/wto-agreement-on-rules-of-origin.aspx, https://www.wcoomd.org/-/media/wco/public/global/pdf/topics/origin/overview/wto-agreement.pdf?db=web, https://www.wto.org/english/docs_e/legal_e/22-roo_e.htm

Rules of Origin Gateway: https://www.wto.org/english/tratop_e/roi_e/roi_e.htm

Origin: https://www.wcoomd.org/en/topics/origin.aspx

Rules of Origin [revised Kyoto Convention]: https://www.wcoomd.org/en/topics/facilitation/instrument-and-tools/conventions/pf_revised_kyoto_conv/kyoto_new/spank.aspx

WCO Origin Compendium: https://www.wcoomd.org/-/media/wco/public/global/pdf/topics/origin/instruments-and-tools/guidelines/origin_compendium.pdf?db=web

WCO Rules of Origin Handbook: https://www.wcoomd.org/~/media/wco/public/global/pdf/topics/origin/overview/origin-handbook/rules-of-origin-handbook.pdf

Rule of Origin Facilitator [Find the Rules of Origin]: https://findrulesoforigin.org/

WCO Comparative Study on Preferential Rules of Origin: https://www.wcoomd.org/-/media/wco/public/global/pdf/topics/origin/instruments-and-tools/reference-material/170130-b_comparative-study-on-pref_roo_master-file_final-20_06_2017.pdf?db=web

Geographical indications [WTO – TRIPS]: https://www.wto.org/english/tratop_e/trips_e/gi_background_e.htm

TRIPS – Trade-Related Aspects of Intellectual Property Rights: https://www.wto.org/english/tratop_e/trips_e/trips_e.htm

Market Access Map: https://www.macmap.org/

- Access a market.
- Compare a market.
- Analyse markets.
- Download data

Regional Trade Database: http://rtais.wto.org/UI/PublicMaintainRTAHome.aspx

Generalized System of Preferences UNCTAD Handbook on the Rules of Origin of the EU: https://unctad.org/system/files/official-document/itcdtsbmisc25rev3add1_en.pdf, https://www.wipo.int/geo_indications/en/

Generalized System of Preferences UNCTAD Website: https://unctad.org/topic/trade-agreements/generalized-system-of-preferences

Chapter 4 Valorisation – Customs Valuation

Customs Valuation Agreement: https://www.wto.org/english/docs_e/legal_e/20-val_01_e.htm

Customs Valuation Gateway: https://www.wto.org/english/tratop_e/cusval_e/cusval_e.htm

WCO Customs Valuation Compendium: https://www.wcoomd.org/en/topics/valuation/instruments-and-tools/val_customs_compendium.aspx

CBP Customs Valuation Encyclopaedia [United States of America]: https://www.cbp.gov/sites/default/files/assets/documents/2016-Jul/Valuation%20Encyclopedia%20Dec%202015%20final.pdf

Compendium Of Customs Valuation Texts – 2024 [European Union]: https://taxation-customs.ec.europa.eu/system/files/2022-07/2022%20EU%20Valuation%20Compendium%20EN.pdf

WCO Guide to Customs Valuation and Transfer Pricing: https://www.wcoomd.org/-/media/wco/public/global/pdf/topics/key-issues/revenue-package/wco-guide-to-customs-valuation-and-transfer-pricing.pdf?db=web

The Convergence Between Customs, VAT, and Transfer Pricing in a Global Supply Chain: https://www.erasmusfiscalstudies.nl/upload/Paper%20Sara%20Claeys.pdf

Chapter 5 Trade Remedies – Dumping, Countervailing and Safeguards

WTO Anti-Dumping Agreement: https://www.wto.org/english/docs_e/legal_e/19-adp_01_e.htm

WTO Subsidies and Countervailing Measures Agreement: https://www.wto.org/english/docs_e/legal_e/24-scm_01_e.htm

WTO Agreement on Safeguards: https://www.wto.org/english/docs_e/legal_e/25-safeg_e.htm

Chapter 6 Excises, and Excise Duties

As a domestic duty, consider your Customs and Excises Authority's Guidance.

The Economics of Excise Taxation: https://www.researchgate.net/publication/254391989_The_Economics_of_Excise_Taxation

Chapter 7 Types of Duties, Taxes, and Levies

Importation: https://www.wcoomd.org/en/topics/facilitation/instrument-and-tools/conventions/pf_revised_kyoto_conv/kyoto_new/spanb.aspx

- Clearance for home use.
- Re-importation in the same state.
- Relief from import duties and taxes.

Arrival of Goods in a Customs Territory: https://www.wcoomd.org/en/topics/facilitation/instrument-and-tools/conventions/pf_revised_kyoto_conv/kyoto_new/spana.aspx, https://www.wcoomd.org/en/topics/facilitation/instrument-and-tools.aspx!

- Formalities prior to the lodgement of the Goods declaration

Exportation: https://www.wcoomd.org/en/topics/facilitation/instrument-and-tools/conventions/pf_revised_kyoto_conv/kyoto_new/spanc.aspx!

- Outright exportation

Tariff

WTO World Tariff Profiles: https://www.wto.org/english/res_e/reser_e/tariff_profiles_e.htm

WTO Tariff: https://www.wto.org/english/tratop_e/tariffs_e/tariffs_e.htm

WTO Get Tariff: https://www.wto.org/english/tratop_e/tariffs_e/tariff_data_e.htm

WTO Tariff Download Facility – MFN applied tariffs and, bound tariffs, and RTAs: http://tdf.wto.org/

Integrated Database (IDB) – Tariffs Applied: https://www.wto.org/english/tratop_e/tariffs_e/idb_e.htm

Consolidated Tariff Schedules (CTS) – Maximum Tariffs: https://www.wto.org/english/tratop_e/tariffs_e/cts_e.htm#:~:text=The%20Consolidated%20Tariff%20Schedules%20(CTS, accessed%20outside%20of%20the%20WTO

United Nations Comtrade Database: https://comtradeplus.un.org

Tariff Analysis Online (TAO): https://ttd.wto.org/en

Schedules of Concessions: https://www.wto.org/english/tratop_e/schedules_e/goods_schedules_e.htm

Goods – Commercial: https://www.wto.org/english/tratop_e/tariffs_e/tariffs_e.htm

Goods – Agriculture: https://www.wto.org/english/thewto_e/whatis_e/tif_e/agrm2_e.htm

Pharmaceutical Agreement: https://www.wto.org/english/tratop_e/pharma_ag_e/pharma_agreement_e.htm

Section II Special Customs Procedures – Regimes

Chapter 8 Processing – Inward Processing and Outward Processing

RKC – Specific Annex F: https://www.wcoomd.org/en/topics/facilitation/instrument-and-tools/conventions/pf_revised_kyoto_conv/kyoto_new/spanf.aspx

- Inward Processing (known as IP).
- Outward Processing (known as OP).
- Drawback.
- Processing of goods for home use.

The RKC Guidelines to Specific Annex F, Chapter 1 Inward Processing: https://www.wcoomd.org/~/media/wco/public/global/pdf/topics/wto-atf/dev/rkc-guidelines-sa-f-1.pdf?la=en

The RKC Guidelines to Specific Annex F, Chapter 2 Outward Processing: https://www.wcoomd.org/-/media/wco/public/global/pdf/topics/wto-atf/dev/rkc-guidelines-sa-f-2.pdf?la=en

Chapter 9 Storage – Customs Warehousing and Free Zones

RKC – Specific Annex D: https://www.wcoomd.org/en/topics/facilitation/instrument-and-tools/conventions/pf_revised_kyoto_conv/kyoto_new/spand.aspx

Chapter 10 Specific Use – Temporary Admission and End Use

RKC – Specific Annex G: https://www.wcoomd.org/en/topics/facilitation/instrument-and-tools/conventions/pf_revised_kyoto_conv/kyoto_new/spang.aspx

Convention on Temporary Admission [Istanbul Convention]: https://www.wcoomd.org/en/about-us/legal-instruments/~/media/2D53E23AA1A64EF68B9AC708C6281DC8.ashx

WCO ATA Handbook: https://www.wcoomd.org/-/media/wco/public/global/pdf/topics/facilitation/instruments-and-tools/conventions/ata/manuel_ata_en.pdf?la = en

ATA Convention: https://www.wcoomd.org/-/media/wco/public/global/pdf/about-us/legal-instruments/conventions-and-agreements/ata/pf_ata_conv_text.pdf?la = en

CPD Carnet: https://unece.org/sites/default/files/2022-06/CPD_eCPD_Brochure.pdf

CPD – Administration [Alliance Internationale de Tourisme (AIT)]: www.ait-touringalliance.com/

TIR Carnet Convention: https://unece.org/transport/tir

Chapter 11 Transit – Customs Transit and Transhipment

RKC – Specific Annex E: https://www.wcoomd.org/en/topics/facilitation/instrument-and-tools/conventions/pf_revised_kyoto_conv/kyoto_new/spane.aspx

- Customs Transit.
- Transhipment.
- Carriage of Goods Coastwise.

WCO Transit Handbook: https://www.wcoomd.org/-/media/wco/public/global/pdf/topics/key-issues/ecp/2015/transit-handbook-for-upload-en.pdf?la = en

The WCO Transit Guidelines: https://www.wcoomd.org/-/media/wco/public/global/pdf/topics/facilitation/instruments-and-tools/tools/transit/transit-guidelines.pdf?la = en

The WCO Compendium – Best Practices in the Area of Transit: https://www.wcoomd.org/-/media/wco/public/global/pdf/topics/facilitation/instruments-and-tools/tools/transit/transit-compendium_2020_en.pdf?la = en

Bonded Customs Transit: https://unctad.org/system/files/official-document/TN17_BondedTransportRegimes.pdf

Chapter 12 Customs Debt and Customs Guarantee – Security

General Annex Guidelines Chapter 5 Security: https://www.wcoomd.org/-/media/wco/public/global/pdf/topics/wto-atf/dev/rkc-guidelins-ch5.pdf?la = en

Section III Trade Blocs – Economic Integration

Chapter 13 Trade Blocs – Economic Integration

WTO Regional Trade Agreements Gateway: https://www.wto.org/english/tratop_e/region_e/region_e.htm

Regional Trade Agreements (RTA) Database: https://www.wto.org/english/tratop_e/region_e/region_e.htm

Global Preferential Trade Agreements Database (GPTAD): https://wits.worldbank.org/gptad/database_landing.aspx

WCO Practical Guidance on Free Zones: https://www.wcoomd.org/-/media/wco/public/global/pdf/topics/facilitation/activities-and-programmes/free-zone/wco-fz-guidance_en.pdf?la=en

Deep Trade Agreements: https://datatopics.worldbank.org/dta/index.html

Section IV Non-tariff Measures And Trade Barriers

Chapter 14 Import Controls and Export Controls

WTO Import Licensing Gateway: https://www.wto.org/english/tratop_e/implic_e/implic_e.htm#:~:text=The%20Agreement%20on%20Import%20Licensing,why%20the%20licences%20are%20granted.

Strategic Trade and Export Control (STEC): https://www.unodc.org/unodc/en/ccp/activities/strategic-trade-and-export-control.html?testme

Chapter 15 and Chapter 16 Non-Tariff Measures – NTMs/Non-Tariff Barriers – NTBs

Non-Tariff Barriers (NTBs) and Non-Tariff Measures (NTMs): https://www.tradebarriers.org/

Quantitative Restrictions (QRs) Database: https://www.wto.org/english/tratop_e/markacc_e/qr_e.htm, https://qr.wto.org/en#/about

WTO Quantitative Restrictions Gateway: https://www.wto.org/english/tratop_e/markacc_e/qr_e.htm

Technical Barriers to Trade (TBT): https://www.wto.org/english/tratop_e/tbt_e/tbt_e.htm

WTO Preshipment Inspection (PSI) Gateway: https://www.wto.org/english/tratop_e/preship_e/preship_e.htm

Chapter 17 Prohibited Goods and Restricted Goods

Basel Convention on the Control of Transboundary Movements of Hazardous Wastes and their Disposals: https://www.basel.int/Portals/4/Basel%20Convention/docs/text/BaselConventionText-e.pdf

Section V International Commercial Terms®

Chapter 18 International Chamber of Commerce (ICC): https://iccwbo.org/business-solutions/incoterms-rules/, https://iccwbo.org/business-solutions/incoterms-rules/incoterms-2020/

Section VI Denied Party Screening and Sanctions Screening

Chapter 19 Denied Party Screening and Sanctions Screening

United Nations Security Council Consolidated List: https://www.un.org/securitycouncil/content/un-sc-consolidated-list, https://www.un.org/securitycouncil/sanctions/information

United Kingdom Sanctions List: https://www.gov.uk/government/publications/the-uk-sanctions-list

United States of America Sanctions List, Screening List, and Blocked: https://sanctionssearch.ofac.treas.gov/, https://ofac.treasury.gov/sanctions-programs-and-country-information, https://www.trade.gov/consolidated-screening-list, https://www.cbp.gov/trade/trade-community/programs-outreach/blocked-denied-debarred

European Union Sanctions and Related Resources: https://finance.ec.europa.eu/eu-and-world/sanctions-restrictive-measures/overview-sanctions-and-related-resources_en, https://www.sanctionsmap.eu/#/main, https://data.europa.eu/data/datasets/consolidated-list-of-persons-groups-and-entities-subject-to-eu-financial-sanctions?locale=en

The Financial Action Task Force (FATF): https://www.fatf-gafi.org/en/the-fatf/what-we-do.html

Section VII The Lesson's Roadmap, Timeline, Milestones, Elucidations of Trade Terms, Organisations, Agreements, Conventions, Resources, and In a Minute (I'm ™)

Chapter 20 The Lesson's Roadmap

Refer to the chapter.

Chapter 21 Customs and Excises Timeline and Milestones

Refer to the chapter.

Chapter 22 Acronyms and Elucidation of Trade Terms

Refer to the chapter.

Chapter 23 International Customs and Trade Organisations, Committees, Agreements, and Conventions

Alliance Internationale de Tourisme (AIT): https://www.ait-touringalliance.com/

International Association of Professional Customs Agents (ASAPRA): https://asapra.com/

Automated System for Customs Data (ASYCUDA) [Customs Automation]: https://asycuda.org/en/

Customs Co-operation Council (CCC) [*See* WCO.]: https://wcoomd.org

International Rail Transport Committee (CIT): https://www.cit-rail.org/

Convention on International Trade in Endangered Species of Wild Fauna and Flora (CITES): https://cites.org/eng

United Nations Economic and Social Council (ECOSOC): https://ecosoc.un.org/

International Federation of Freight Forwarders Associations (FIATA): https://fiata.org/

Global Express Association (GEA): https://global-express.org/

International Association of Ports and Harbors (IAPH): https://www.iaphworldports.org/

International Air Transport Association (IATA): https://www.iata.org/

International Bank for Reconstruction and Development Bank (IBRD): https://www.worldbank.org/

International Civil Aviation Organization (ICAO): https://www.icao.int/

International Chamber of Commerce (ICC): https://iccwbo.org/

International Federation of Customs Brokers Associations (IFCBA): https://ifcba.org/

International Monetary Fund (IMF): https://www imf.org

International Maritime Organization (IMO): https://www.imo.org/

International Network of Customs Universities (INCU): https://incu.org/

International Criminal Police Organization (INTERPOL): https://www.interpol.int/

International Road Transport Union (IRU): https://www.iru.org/

International Organization for Standardization (ISO): https://www.iso.org/

International Trade Centre (ITC): https://intracen.org/

Organisation for Economic Co-operation and Development (OECD): https://www.oecd.org/

Intergovernmental Organization for International Carriage by Rail (OTIF): https://otif.org/

International Air Cargo Association (TIACA): https://tiaca.org/

TIC Council (Previously International Federation of Inspection Agencies or IFIA): https://www.tic-council.org/

International Union of Railways (UIC): https://uic.org/

United Nations (UN): https://www.un.org/en/

United Nations Economic Commission for Europe (UNECE): https://unece.org/

United Nations Educational, Scientific and Cultural Organization (UNESCO): https://www.unesco.org/

United Nations Commission on International Trade Law (UNCITRAL): https://uncitral.un.org/

United Nations Conference on Trade and Development (UNCTAD): https://unctad.org/

Universal Postal Union (UPU): https://www.upu.int/

The World Bank Group (WBG): https://www.worldbank.org/

World Customs Organization (WCO) [*See* CCC.]: https://www.wcoomd.org/

World Federation of Pipe Line Industry Associations (WFPIA): https://www.iploca.com/

World Health Organization (WHO): https://www.who.int/

World Intellectual Property Organization (WIPO): https://www.wipo.int/

World Trade Organization (WTO): https://www.wto.org/

World Free Zones Organization (WFZO): https://www.worldfzo.org/

Chapter 24 Selected Resources

International Monetary Fund (IMF) – Customs Modernization Handbook: https://www.imf.org/en/Publications/Books/Issues/2022/06/15/Customs-Matters-Strengthening-Customs-Administration-in-a-Changing-World-512035

Revised Kyoto Convention (RKC): https://www.wcoomd.org/Topics/Facilitation/Instrument%20and%20Tools/Conventions/pf_revised_kyoto_conv/Kyoto_New, https://www.wcoomd.org/en/topics/facilitation/instrument-and-tools/conventions/pf_revised_kyoto_conv.aspx#: ~ :text = The%20revised%20Kyoto%20Convention%20promotes,Parties%20must%20accept%20without%20reservation

Trade Facilitation: https://www.oecd.org/trade/topics/trade-facilitation/, https://www.oecd.org/trade/topics/trade-facilitation/documents/trade-facilitation-indicators-methodology.pdf

Trade Facilitation Agreement: https://www.wto.org/english/docs_e/legal_e/tfa-nov14_e.htm

Trade Facilitation Implementation Guide: https://tfig.unece.org/

WCO Conventions and Agreements: https://www.wcoomd.org/en/about-us/legal-instruments/conventions.aspx

WCO SAFE Framework: https://www.wcoomd.org/-/media/wco/public/global/pdf/topics/facilitation/instruments-and-tools/tools/safe-package/safe-framework-of-standards.pdf

WCO SAFE Package: https://www.wcoomd.org/en/topics/facilitation/instrument-and-tools/frameworks-of-standards/safe_package.aspx

WTO Agreements: https://www.wto.org/english/docs_e/legal_e/ursum_e.htm#gAgreement

World Bank [International Bank for Reconstruction and Development Bank] Handbooks

Customs Modernization Handbook: https://documents1.worldbank.org/curated/en/850061468779087644/pdf/31477.pdf

Customs Modernization Initiatives Case Studies: https://documents1.worldbank.org/curated/en/147111468779373654/pdf/301120PAPER0Customs0case0studies.pdf

CHAPTER 25

Customs & Excises Series - In a Minute (I'am^{TM})

Have you ever pondered how many words in English you should be able to read in a minute, both for silent reading and for reading aloud? According to *ScienceDirect.com*, for silent reading, it is 238 words per minute, while for reading aloud, it is 183 words per minute.

With this in mind and unaware of anything similar, I have prepared a series of around 238 words each on Customs and Excises topics covered in this book. The series '*In a minute*', abbreviated to '*I'am*^{TM}', is most appropriate as '*I am*' is a declaration of existence.

The 'I'am^{TM}' 'Customs and Excise Series' topics.

§25.01 CARRIAGE OF GOODS COASTWISE I'AM^{TM}

The Customs procedure under which goods in free circulation (cleared for home consumption) and imported goods that have not been declared under the condition that they must be transported in a vessel other than the importing vessel in which they arrived in the Customs territory are loaded on board a vessel at a place in the Customs territory and are transported to another place in the same Customs territory where they are then unloaded. A Customs Authority will normally allow goods to be transported under this procedure on board a vessel carrying other goods at the same time, provided that the Customs Authority is satisfied that the goods can be identified and other requirements that the Customs Authority might impose will be met.

Special Annex E: Transit: Chapter 3: E3 Carriage of Goods Coastwise: RKC.

§25.02 CLEARANCE FOR HOME USE I'AM™

It simply means the Customs procedure which provides for imported goods to enter into free circulation (home consumption) in the Customs territory upon the payment of any duties, taxes, and levies and that all Customs formalities are completed. The goods can be disposed of once in 'free circulation' without any Customs Authority restriction.

Specific Annex B: Importation: Chapter 1: B1 Clearance for Home Use: RKC.

§25.03 CODIFICATION – TARIFF CLASSIFICATION I'AM™

The first of the three cornerstones of Customs and Excises, concerned with the nature of the goods, is the international standardise process of assigning a numerical code, a Commodity Code, also known as an HS code, to a good moving across an international border or manufactured in a country. The HS code identifies the duties, taxes, levies, trade restrictions (NTBs, NTMs, import control, export control, prohibited goods, restricted goods), non-preferential tariff treatment, whether the good qualifies for any preferential tariff treatment, and is used in the compilation of national and international trade statistics. Tariff classification is governed by '*The International Convention on the Harmonized Commodity Description and Coding System*', widely held as the true '*language of international trade*' or the '*numeric language of international trade*', which is arranged in a legal and logical structure and is supported by well-defined rules to achieve a uniform and consistent classification. The HS Nomenclature provides a uniform classification of goods, grouping them into 21 Sections on an international level and using digits to identify the Chapter (two digits), Heading (four digits), and Subheading (six digits). The first six digits are international, with any additional digits being country specific. As a rule of thumb, if an HS code contains the number '*9*' towards its end, such as '*19*', '*29*', '*90*', and '*99*', it tends to refer to '*Other*', which simply means that there is not a specific HS code for the classified good.

The International Convention on the Harmonized Commodity Description and Coding System.

§25.04 COUNTERVAILING – ANTI-SUBSIDY I'AM™

It is one of the three trade remedies and one of the two unfair trade remedies, meaning its purpose is to remedy unfair trade practices. Along with dumping, countervailing (anti-subsidy) is an unfair trade remedy, while safeguards is a fair trade remedy. Countervailing refers to the trade remedy imposed to offset the effects of subsidies provided by foreign governments to their domestic producers and exporters. A subsidy is a financial benefit granted by a government to a specific industry or company to encourage or support their activities, such as production or export. Similar to dumping, price discrimination is identified by comparing the prices in two international markets. The price difference is the comparison between the *'normal value'*, the price in the market of the export country, and the *'export price'*, the price in the market of the importing country. If there is a difference, this constitutes dumping and the margin of countervailing. For a domestic manufacturer to consider bringing a countervailing action to a Trade Remedy Authority, material injury would need to be substantiated. Once the '*D*' and the '*I*' have been substantiated, it requires the substantiation of the '*C*' - causality, or the causal link. In essence, the domestic manufacturer would have to substantiate that the material injury being suffered is a direct result of the dumping. If dumping occurs but the causal link is not established, no countervailing duty can be imposed. Countervailing duties are imposed, in addition to duties, taxes, and levies, against the exporting country.

The Agreement on Subsidies and Countervailing Measures.

§25.05 CUSTOMS AND EXCISES ABBREVIATIONS I'AM™

ACV, AD, ADA, AGOA, AIT, ARO, ATQ, ASYCUDA, ATA Carnet, ATQs, AVE, BC, BDV, BTA, BTN, C&F, CAPA, CCC, CCI, CCCN, CCV, CET, CIF, CIP, CITES, CO_2, CoO, CPD, Carnet, CPEI, CPT, CRO, CRTA, CTS, CU, CUP, CVA, CW, DAF, DAP, DAT, DCP, DDP, DDU, DES, DEQ, DIC, DPU, eATA, EC, ECS Carnet, EDI, EN, EOR, EPZ, Ex Quay, Ex Ship, EXW, FAN, FAS, FCA, FCI, FIA, FIATA, FOB, FOBA, FOR, FOT, FRC, FTA, FTZ, FZ, G20, GATS, GATT, GATT 1994, GIs, GPTAD, GRI, GSP, GST, HRO, HS, HSC, IAPH, IATA, IBRD, ICC, ICSID, IDA, IDB, IFC, IFCBA, IFIA, IMF, IMO, IMPACT, Incoterms®, INCU, INTERPOL, IOR, IP, IPR, IQTR, IRU, ISO, ITC, ITI, ITO, LIAT, LDCs, MFN, MIGA, MoU, MNC, NGO, NTBs, NTMs, OECD, OP, OQTR, PICARD, PSCG, PSI, PSST, PTA, QRs, R&D, REACH, RGR, RKC, RoO, RSC, RTA, SAFE Framework, SCP, SCM, SEZ, SITC, SMEs, SPS, SPUR, SSA, SSC, TA, TBT, TCRO, TCCV, TFA, TIACA, TIC, TIC Council, TIR Carnet, TNMM, TRIMS, TRIPS, TRQ, TS, TV, UN, UCC, UNCITRAL, UNCTAD, UNSD, VAT, VER, WATAC, WB, WBG, WCF, WCO, WHO, WIPO, WTO, WWI, and WWII.

Own compilation.

§25.06 CUSTOMS AND EXCISES BUZZWORDS I'AM™

Ad valorem duty, Authorised Economic Operator, ATA Carnet (Admission Temporaire/Temporary Admission), Certificate of Origin, Codification, Commodity

Code, Common Market, Countervailing, CPD Carnet (Carnet de Passages en Douane), Customs Procedure & Economic Impact (CPEI), Customs Authority, Customs Cooperation Council, Customs Debt, Customs Guarantee, Customs Procedure, Customs Transit, Customs Union, Customs Valuation, Customs Warehousing, Denied Party Screening, Direct representation, Drawback, Dumping, Duties, ECS Carnet (Echantillons Commerciaux/Commercial Samples), End Use, Export Control, Export Processing Zone, Excise, Excises, Fair Trade Remedies, Free Trade Agreement, Free Trade Zone, Free Zone, General Agreement on Tariffs and Trade (GATT), Harmonised Commodity Description and Coding System, HS Code, Import Control, Import Taxes, Incoterms®, Indirect Representation, International Bank for Reconstruction and Development, International Chamber of Commerce (ICC), International Monetary Fund (IMF), International Transit Operations, Inward Processing (IP), Levies, Monetary Union, National Transit Operations, Non-tariff Barriers (NTBs), Non-tariff Measures (NTMs), Origin Origination, Outward Processing (OP), Private Warehouse, Political Union, Public Warehouse, Pre-shipment Inspection (PSI), Prohibited Goods, Quantitative Restrictions (QR), Re-importation, Rebate, Refund, Restricted Goods, Restricted Party Screening, Returned Goods Relief (RGR), Revised Kyoto Convention (RKC), Rule of Origin, SAFE Framework of Standards, Safeguards, Sanctions Party Screening, Special Customs Procedures, Special Economic Zone, Specific Duty, Specific Use, Suspension, Tariff, Tariff Classification, Taxes, Temporary Admission, Temporary Storage, Trade Facilitation, Transfer Pricing (TP), Transhipment, TIR Carnet (Transports Internationaux Routiers or International Road Transports), Unfair Trade Remedies, Valorisation, Value Added Tax (VAT), World Bank, World Customs Organization (WCO), and World Trade Organization (WTO).

Own compilation.

§25.07 CUSTOMS DEBT AND CUSTOMS GUARANTEE/SECURITY I'AM™

Although it is not part of the RKC, a substantive case could be made for it to contain comprehensive rules, as customs debt law constitutes a central aspect of all national customs legislation. This could imply the next consequential step in harmonising customs processes and improving the transparency of customs rules with predictable enforcement, which is the essence of the RKC. The RKC does not define a '*customs debt*' nor a '*customs guarantee*'. It defines '*security*' as '*which ensures to the satisfaction of the Customs that an obligation to the Customs will be fulfilled*'. '*Security*' is described as '*general*' when it ensures *that* the obligations arising from several operations will be fulfilled. Customs debt means the obligation of a customs representative to pay the amount of import or export duty, which applies to specific goods under the country's Customs legislation. It refers to '*import duty*' and not '*customs duty*', and it does so as customs duty is one of the various duties, taxes, and levies that constitute an import duty. A customs debt on import is incurred when goods are placed under a SCP –

Processing, Storage, Specific Use, and Transit - PSST. The extent of the customs debt would depend on the procedure's coverage as to whether the import duty relief would be partial or full. Should the goods be released for free circulation, or in other words, cleared for domestic consumption, then the import duty liability will arise, and the import duty needs to be paid.

General Annex: Chapter 5: Security: RKC.

§25.08 CUSTOMS TRANSIT I'AM™

After the consideration of the nature of the goods (the cornerstones), the last of the four groups of CSPs concerned with the treatment of the goods is Transit, which distinguishes between Customs Transit and Transhipment. The RKC defines Customs Transit as the Customs procedure where goods are transported (moved) under Customs control from one Customs office to another with the temporary suspension of the duties, taxes, and levies. Unlike the other SCP - Processing, Storage, and Specific Use - Transit is not considered a CPEI. The RKC distinguishes two types of Customs Transit - National Transit operations, which should be National Customs Transit, referring to the transport of goods between departure Customs offices and destination Customs offices within the same country or territory, and International Customs Transit, referring to the transport of goods across one or more borders, also known as frontier, in accordance with a bilateral or multilateral agreement. Consequently, Customs clearance can take place at the point of destination rather than at the point of entry into the Customs territory or country. Since the goods being moved are not Customs cleared, a guarantee is required to secure all the duties, taxes, and levies liabilities that were temporarily suspended on the goods. In certain cases, other obligations arising from the operations under the procedure would need to be fulfilled. There is a link between '*Customs Transit*' and the '*ATA Carnet*' in that an ATA Carnet can be used as a transit document. So, too, the CPD Carnet, the E.C.S. Carnet and the TIR Carnet.

Specific Annex E: Transit: E1 Customs Transit: RKC.

§25.09 CUSTOMS WAREHOUSING I'AM™

After the consideration of the nature of the goods (the cornerstones), the second of the four groups of CSPs concerned with the treatment of the goods is Storage, which distinguishes between Customs Warehouses and FZ. The RKC defines the customs warehousing procedure as the Customs procedure under which imported goods are stored under Customs control in a designated place (a Customs warehouse) without payment of import duties, taxes, and levies. It is an SCP under which imported goods that arrive in a country are stored under Customs control in a designated warehouse for a period, which could be subject to limitation. During this time, the goods remain under the surveillance of a Customs Authority. These goods are not subject to import duties (the collective term that includes customs duty, excise duty, taxes, and levies or VAT), in which payment is delayed. If the warehouse is not designated as a customs and excise warehouse, then excise duties will become payable when the goods are received in the warehouse. There are also tax warehouses where excise goods are received, processed, produced, held, or stored. The import duties, taxes and levies will become payable after the goods are removed from the customs warehouse for domestic use, but not if the goods are re-exported or entered under another SCP. There are two types of customs warehouses: public and private. The storing of the goods is subject to a guarantee. A customs warehouse should not be confused with a Transit Shed, which is meant for short-term storage only, with charges generally accruing daily or weekly, making it a very expensive option if used over an extended period.

Specific Annex D: Customs Warehouses and Free Zones: D1 Customs Warehouses: RKC.

§25.10 DENIED PARTY SCREENING AND SANCTIONS SCREENING I'AM™

Although not traditionally associated with Customs and Excises, Denied Party Screening and Sanctions Screening have been included in this specialisation due to their general inclusion in the Trade Compliance function. The screening focus tends to be on the individuals and the entities involved in the cross-border transaction. Due to their classification, parties may be prohibited or restricted from doing business with government agencies. Companies and individuals are expected to undertake screening activities of all the business partners in their transactions, with such screening not being a once-off process but a continuous process, which tends to be supported with electronic solutions. It is essential that companies have documented processes and procedures to ensure compliance with national and international rules, regulations, and laws and to protect the company's interests. '*Denied Party Screening*', also known as '*Denied Trade Screening*' or '*Sanctions Party Screening*', is often used interchangeably with '*Restricted Party Screening*'. The differing terminology is not very helpful and confuses the layperson, who could be under the impression that each term is of different significance, while it is, in effect, one and the same. The only constant is that screening purports to detect, prevent and manage risk as part of export, trade and financial compliance. There are three types of screening – '*Client Screening*' or '*Party-Based Screening*'; '*Transaction Screening*' or '*Transaction-Based Screening*'; and '*Hybrid Screening*'. '*Sanctions Screening*' is broadly defined as a control employed by financial institutions to detect, prevent, and manage the disruption of financial crime and, in particular, sanctions risk.

No Agreements or Conventions.

§25.11 DUMPING I'AM™

It is one of the three trade remedies and one of the two unfair trade remedies, meaning its purpose is to remedy unfair trade practices. Along with countervailing (anti-subsidy), dumping is an unfair trade remedy, while safeguards is a fair trade remedy. The WTO aptly describes dumping, in general, as a situation of international price discrimination, where the price of a good when sold in the importing country is less than the price of that good in the market of the exporting country. So, dumping can simply be identified by comparing the prices in two international markets. The price difference is the comparison between the '*normal value*', the price in the market of the export country, and the '*export price*', the price in the market of the importing country. If there is a difference, this constitutes dumping and the margin of dumping. For a domestic manufacturer to consider bringing an anti-dumping action to a Trade Remedy Authority, it would need to substantiate material injury. Once the '*D*' and the '*I*' have been substantiated, it requires the substantiation of the '*C*' – causality, or the causal link. In essence, the domestic manufacturer would have to substantiate that the material injury being suffered is a direct result of the dumping. If dumping occurs but the causal link is not established, no anti-dumping duty can be imposed. Anti-dumping duties are imposed, in addition to duties, taxes, and levies, against not only a country but also the company(ies) in the exporting country.

The WTO Anti-Dumping Agreement. *The Agreement on Implementation of Article VI of the General Agreement on Tariffs and Trade 1994.*

§25.12 END USE I'AM™

After the consideration of the nature of the goods (the cornerstones), the third of the four groups of CSPs concerned with the treatment of the goods is Specific Use, which distinguishes between End Use and TA. Although there is no Specific Annex in the RKC for End Use, it is generally considered the ultimate specific use to which a manufactured good is put or restricted. Also known as '*Authorised Use*', it is a procedure that provides specified industries with a reduced or zero rate of customs duty on certain goods imported into a country, provided that it meets the defined criteria and is put to prescribed (specific) use, the final item that a good is integrated into, within a set time period. So, End Use refers to a good's final use or purpose. The provision generally does not apply to anti-dumping duty, excise duty, and VAT. Goods commonly identified in a country's Customs Tariff Schedule to be put to End Use include shipwork goods, helicopters, aeroplanes and other aircraft for civil use, hydrocarbon oil, marine propulsion engines, and military equipment. End Use can also be used where export regulations apply. For the authorisation of End Use, the Customs Authority will require a guarantee and assurances for the proper conduct of the operations.

Not in the RKC.

§25.13 EXCISES AND EXCISE DUTIES I'AM™

Excise duty differs from Customs duty in that Customs duty is supposed to only apply to goods imported into a country, while Excise duty applies to selected goods manufactured in a country. Consequently, '*Excise*' forms part of a country's national legislation rather than international legislation and agreement. Consequently, it is not within the ambit of the WTO. Nonetheless, the application of excise duty, which is now also imposed on goods imported into a country rather than only on domestic manufacture or consumption, is starting to blur the lines of its application. As for '*Excises*', although not adopted as a universal term, there is the odd reference to '*Excises*', which tends to be considered the plural form of '*Excise*'. Due to the general lack of an officially acceptable definition, '*Excises*' is considered the collective term for all forms of excise duties, excise taxes, and excise levies. The sole definition broadly defines it as '*the distinguishing features of excise taxation are selectivity in coverage, discrimination in intent, and some form of quantitative measurement in determining the tax liability*'. This definition further proposes the distinction of three systems: a limited excise system of between 10 to 15 commodity groups, an intermediate excise system of between 15 to 30 commodity groups, and an extended excise system comprising more than 30 commodity groups spanning almost the whole range of production activities in a particular country.

In domestic legislation. It is country competency.

§25.14 FREE ZONES I'AM™

After the consideration of the nature of the goods (the cornerstones), the second of the four groups of CSPs concerned with the treatment of the goods is Storage, which distinguishes between Free Zones and Customs Warehousing. Abbreviated to FZ, it is a customs enclave in a country, an enclosed area within a country's Customs territory where imported goods can be entered into or stored, moved, used, or processed for export outside of the country's Customs territory or released under another SCP such as IP, TA, or End Use. An FZ aims to reduce barriers to international trade by facilitating the transhipment and storage of goods. The RKC defines it as a part of the territory of a country where any goods introduced are generally regarded, insofar as import duties and taxes are concerned, as being outside the country's Customs territory. Should the goods be exported to the country's adjacent Customs territory, then the prevailing import duties, taxes, and levies must be accounted for. An FZ could also be used as a bonded warehouse for the storage of goods for the domestic market. An FZ tends to be located around international airports, seaports, and national frontiers, which offer many geographic advantages for trade and remove the hindrances caused by high tariffs or complex Customs regulations, examinations, and formalities. The IBRD, commonly known as the World Bank, identifies four major FZ – Free Port, FTZ, EPZ, and SEZ.

> Specific Annex D: Chapter 2: D2 Free Zones: RKC.

§25.15 IMPORT CONTROLS AND EXPORT CONTROLS I'AM™

There is nothing mysterious or nuanced about Import Control and Export Control. Every country has it as part of its measures to protect and safeguard its citizens. The crucial role of import and export controls is essential to enforce health, environmental, security, safety, and technical standards arising from the country's domestic laws and its obligations under international agreements. International Agreements, in this context, generally refer to the Montreal Protocol on Substances that Deplete the Ozone Layer, the Basel Convention on the Control of Transboundary Movements of Hazardous Wastes and Their Disposal, and the UN Convention Against the Illicit Traffic in Narcotic Drugs and Psychotropic Substances. In international trade, the application of import and export control measures or restrictions is limited to those permitted (allowed) under the relevant WTO Agreements. There are essentially three types of Import Control and Export Control: Bans refer to instances where no imported goods and exported goods are permitted; Quotas, where the volume of imported goods and exported goods are restricted; and Surveillance is where the importation and exportation of goods are monitored and subject to licences or other specifications.

> In domestic legislation. It is country competency.

§25.16 INCOTERMS® I'AM™

International **Co**mmercial Terms, abbreviated to Incoterms®, for the 2020 iteration is a series of 11 pre-defined internationally recognised three-letter '*delivery terms*' (commercial terms), which are concerned with the point and, at the very least, the place of delivery. Incoterms® is a registered trademark of the ICC. Incoterms® does not constitute a complete contract. For it to have a legal effect, it has to be incorporated into the contract of sale between the buyer and the seller. As Incoterms® are *'delivery terms'*, they are not concerned with the transfer of the title of the goods. Its creation and introduction aligned with ICC's founders' conviction that the private sector is best qualified to set global standards for business. Incoterms® is concerned with dealing with three issues between the buyer and the seller – obligations, risks, and costs. Incoterms® is not concerned with the goods sold, nor its contract price; when title or ownership of the goods passes; the documentary requirements; the method of payment or when the payment is due; liability for the failure to provide the goods in conformity with the contract of sale; sanctions and prohibitions; the tariff, duties, levies, and taxes. There are seven Incoterms® that can be used for any mode of transport and four for sea, land or inland waterway transport, known as *'multimodal transport'*. There are four principal categories – E (Departure Term); F (Shipment Terms – Main Carriage Unpaid); C (Shipment Terms – Main Carriage Paid Terms); and D (Arrival Terms).

ICC Incoterms® 2020

§25.17 INWARD PROCESSING I'AM™

After the consideration of the nature of the goods (the cornerstones), the first of the four groups of CSPs concerned with the treatment of the goods is Processing, which distinguishes IP and OP. The RKC defines IP as a Customs procedure under which certain goods, typically components or primary inputs, are to be imported into a country, conditionally relieved from payment of import duties and taxes, on the basis that they would be manufactured, processed in a final good or end good, or repair and subsequent exportation. IP is limited to goods imported directly but can also be granted for goods already placed under another Customs procedure. In the instance of Prohibited Goods and Restricted Goods, goods entered under IP are not exempt from import and/or export prohibitions and restrictions. However, goods subject to QRs, tariff quotas or other quantitative import restrictions may be entered under IP. IP also tends to include a provision to sell goods in the domestic market, provided that all duties, levies, and taxes are brought into account. This is considered to be the discharge of the goods, which simply means that all conditions for the use of the IP have been complied with. Duties, levies, and taxes may be collected on any goods, including waste, deriving from the processing or manufacturing of goods admitted for IP that are not exported or treated in such a way as to render them commercially valueless.

Specific Annex F: Processing: F1 Inward Processing: RKC. Article 10.9: Inward and Outward Processing: WTO TFA.

§25.18 NON-TARIFF BARRIERS I'AM™

There is no clear definition of NTBs, which are frequently used interchangeably with NTM's subcomponents. To add complication, governments might legitimately employ measures other than tariffs as policy instruments, which might then be deemed as NTBs. NTBs are considered *'implicit barriers'* to trade. Even the WTO does not explicitly deal with NTBs. Under *'NTBs: red tape, etc. – A number of agreements deal with various bureaucratic or legal issues that could involve hindrances to trade.'* The WTO offers: Import Licensing; Rules for the valuation of goods at customs (customs valuation); PSI: further checks on imports; RoO: made in ... where?; and Investment measures. The only comprehensive reference to NTBs, which itself could be contested as to whether it is indeed NTBs or rather NTMs, is the website – *www.tradebarriers.org*, which defines NTBs as *'restrictions that result from prohibitions, conditions, or specific market requirements that make importation or exportation of products difficult and/or costly. NTBs also include unjustified and/or improper application of NTMs such as SPS measures and other TBT. NTB arise from different measures taken by governments and authorities in the form of government laws, regulations, policies, conditions, restrictions or specific requirements, and private sector business practices, or prohibitions that protect the domestic industries from foreign competition'*. The eight NTM categories: Government Participation in Trade and Restrictive Practices Tolerated by Governments; Customs and Administrative Entry Procedures; TBT; SPS Measures; Specific Limitations; Charges on Imports; Other Procedural Problems; and Transport, Clearing and Forwarding.

> In domestic legislation. It is country competency.

§25.19 NON-TARIFF MEASURES I'AM™

NTMs, similar to NTBs, are considered *'implicit barriers'*, which can potentially have an economic effect on international trade in goods. Although NTMS tend to be used interchangeably with NTBs, there is a difference. NTBs are subsets of NTMs and are considered measures that have potentially trade-inhibiting effects. Even though the primary aim of many NTMs is to protect public health or the environment, it negatively impacts compliance costs and procedural costs. Increased transparency of NTMs and, subsequently, a better understanding of NTMs can assist policymakers, trade negotiators, and researchers in zoning in on and deliberating on the reduction of international trade costs. In defining and categorising the NTMs, UNCTAD categorises NTMs into three groups: Import-Related Measures, Export-Related Measures, and Non-Technical Measures, which are further classified in 16 Chapters or Types: SPS measures; TBT; Pre-shipment Inspection and other formalities; Contingent trade-protective measures, Non-automatic licensing, quotas, prohibitions and quantity control, measures other than for SPS or TBT reasons; Price-control measures, including additional taxes and charges; Finance measures; Measures affecting competition; TRIMS; Distribution restrictions; Restrictions on post-sale services; Subsidies; Government procurement restrictions; IP; RoO; and Export-Related Measures. The first 15 Chapters cover import-related NTMs, which encompass the requirements imposed by a country on imported products, while the final Chapter covers export-related measures that encompass the requirements imposed by a country on exported products.

In domestic legislation. It is country competency.

§25.20 ORIGINATION – ORIGIN I'AM™

The second of the three cornerstones of Customs and Excises, concerned with the nature of the goods, is the criteria used to establish a good's 'economic nationality' – its national source. Its importance is due to duties, levies, taxes, trade restrictions (trade quotas), trade remedies (anti-dumping, countervailing, and safeguards), non-preferential tariff treatment, preferential tariff treatment, and trade policy measures depending on the source of the imported good. The RoO provisions are contained in trade agreements and trade preferences, while the WTO Agreement on RoO aims to harmonise non-preferential RoO and ensure that such rules do not themselves create unnecessary obstacles to trade. The lack of harmony is challenging as more and more FTAs are concluded, creating the spaghetti bowl effect. For preferential RoO criteria for '*in-country goods*', the criteria is twofold – wholly obtained goods, or sufficient worked or processed (substantial transformation) – the latter which is further divided into the *ad valorem* rule (value-added rule, value content rule, or percentage rule); tariff shift rule (change of the tariff classification rule, or specified process rule); and specific rules (specified good or process, or technical rules). For '*out-country goods*', the consideration of the type of cumulation – combining materials without losing originating status (bilateral cumulation, diagonal cumulation, regional cumulation, full cumulation, extended cumulation, multilateral cumulation, and multilateral extended cumulation). The exceptions to the sufficiently worked (*substantial transformation criterion*) are full cumulation, *de minimis*, and non-qualifying operations.

The WTO Agreement on Rules of Origin.

§25.21 OUTWARD PROCESSING I'AM™

After the consideration of the nature of the goods (the cornerstones), the first of the four groups of CSPs concerned with the treatment of the goods is Processing, which distinguishes OP and IP. The RKC defines OP as the Customs procedure under which goods in free circulation in a country may be temporarily exported for manufacturing, processing, or repair abroad and then re-imported with total or partial exemption from import duties and taxes. The Customs procedure's basic premise is to provide for goods (primary and/or secondary) which are in free circulation in a country (territory) to be temporarily exported for manufacturing, processing or repair overseas (abroad) and then re-imported with total or partial exemption from import duties and taxes. On the return of the final good to the country, the Customs Authority would consider the value added abroad and accordingly only impose duties, taxes, and levies on the value-added component. OP provides for businesses to take advantage of the benefits that provide them a competitive advantage, such as lower labour costs or specific technical expertise which is not available domestically. OP is subject to an authorisation from a Customs Authority, which will specify the period within which the OP is to be discharged and the guarantee that needs to be provided. Such an authorisation must also provide for the possibility of the return for export of an inclusion of '*equivalent goods*', the raw materials used in its manufacture.

> Specific Annex F: Processing: Chapter 2: F2 Outward processing: RKC.
> Article 10.9: Inward and Outward Processing: WTO TFA.

§25.22 PROCESSING OF GOODS FOR HOME USE I'AM™

A '*rebate*' is a Customs provision that provides for the suspension (full or partial) of the payment of the duties, taxes, and levies, provided that the imported components are used in the manufacture of specified goods, which can then be sold on the domestic market. The RKC calls it '*processing of goods for home use*' as the Customs procedure under which imported goods may be manufactured, processed or worked before clearance for home use and under Customs control, to such an extent that the amount of the duties, taxes, and levies applicable to the goods thus obtained is lower than that which would apply to the imported goods. [Read more: Rebate, Drawback and Refund I'am™.]

> Specific Annex F: Processing: Chapter 4: F4 Processing of Goods for Home Use: RKC.

§25.23 PROHIBITED AND RESTRICTED GOODS I'AM™

All countries have a '*Prohibited Goods and Restricted Goods List*' of some kind, which tends to be published by a Customs Authority. The two terms '*prohibited*' and '*restricted*' are distinctly different. '*Prohibited goods*' are goods whose importation or exportation is forbidden or completely banned by law or authority due to a possible health threat, environmental danger, protection of endangered species of flora and fauna (Convention on International Trade in Endangered Species or CITES), security, dangerous chemicals (Authorisation and Restriction of Chemicals or REACH), the Basel Convention on hazardous waste, counterfeit or pirated goods, to name but a few. In essence, prohibited goods are never allowed to enter or exit a country under any circumstances. *'Restricted goods'*, also known as *'controlled goods'*, are goods whose importation or exportation is limited or restrained and are only possible should specific conditions be met or complied with. The control of these goods could, in its interpretation and administration, be regarded as NTBs, which implies that restriction diverts from its original intent to a protectionist measure. Restricted goods are allowed to enter or exit a country only in certain circumstances or under certain conditions, for example, when producing a permit, certificate, or letter of authority from the relevant government department, institution, or body. A Customs Authority normally administers certain prohibitions or restrictions on behalf of government departments, institutions, or bodies. In essence, restricted goods tend to require permits, certificates or authorisations for their importation or exportation

In national (domestic) legislation. It is country competency.

§25.24 RE-IMPORTATION IN THE SAME STATE I'AM™

The Customs procedure under which goods which were exported may be taken into home use (free circulation) free of duties, taxes, and levies provided they have not undergone any manufacturing, processing or repairs abroad (overseas) and provided that any sums chargeable as a result of repayment or remission of or conditional relief from duties, taxes, and levies or of any subsidies or other amounts granted in connection with exportation must be paid. Goods eligible for re-importation in the same state can be goods in free circulation or compensating products. *'Compensation Products'* are products resulting from the manufacturing, processing or repair of the goods for which the use of the IP procedure is authorised. The goods can be disposed of once in *'free circulation'* without any Customs Authority restriction.

Specific Annex B: Importation: Chapter 2: B2 Re-Importation in the Same State

§25.25 REBATE, DRAWBACK, AND REFUND I'AM™

The terminology of *'drawback'*, *'rebate'*, and *'refund'* is still in use in several countries. A *'rebate'* is a Customs provision that provides for the suspension (full or partial) of the payment of the duties, taxes, and levies, provided that the imported components are used in the manufacture of specified goods, which can then be sold on the domestic market. The RKC calls it *'processing of goods for home use'* as the Customs procedure under which imported goods may be manufactured, processed or worked before clearance for home use and under Customs control, to such an extent that the amount of the duties, taxes, and levies applicable to the goods thus obtained is lower than that which would apply to the imported goods. A *'drawback'* Customs provision that provides for the repayment of the duty, tax, and levy that were paid on imported components that were used in the manufacture of goods that were then exported. It is similar to IP. The RKC defines *'drawback'* as the amount of import duties and taxes repaid under the drawback procedure. The drawback procedure means the Customs procedure, which, when goods are exported, provides for a repayment (total or partial) for the duties, taxes, and levies imposed on the goods or materials contained in them or consumed in their production. The *'refund'* is not a Customs provision; it allows for the repayment of the duties, taxes, and levies that were paid for which the importer was not liable.

Specific Annex F: Processing: Chapter 3: F3 Drawback: RKC.
Specific Annex F: Processing: Chapter 4: F4 Processing of Goods for Home Use: RKC.

§25.26 RELIEF CONSIGNMENTS I'AM™

It simply means goods, including vehicles and other means of transport, foodstuffs, medicaments, clothing, blankets, tents, prefabricated houses, water purifying and water storage items, or other goods of prime necessity, forwarded as aid to those affected by disaster; and all equipment, vehicles and other means of transport, specially trained animals, provisions, supplies, personal effects and other goods for disaster relief personnel to perform their duties and to support them in living and working in the territory of the disaster throughout their mission. It requires that the Customs clearance of relief consignments for export, import, TA, and Transit must be carried out as a matter of priority and that any economic import and export prohibitions or restrictions and any duties, levies, or taxes that are typically payable should be waived.

Specific Annex J: Special Procedures: Chapter 5: J5 Relief consignments: RKC.

§25.27 RETURNED GOODS RELIEF – REJECTED GOODS I'AM™

Also known as RGR, it is not covered in the RKC, although it is referenced in the WTO FTA. RGR is a Customs procedure that provides for goods that were previously exported from a country (or territory) to be re-imported into that same country (or territory), normally within a specified period of the original export, without incurring additional duties, taxes (such as VAT) or levies, provided certain conditions are met. Goods under RGR cannot be processed or repaired in any way unless the work carried out on the goods is routine maintenance. Typically, proof is required that the goods have not been altered. Although not referenced by name, the WTO FTA covers *'rejected goods'*, which addresses the re-export or return of rejected goods, which can be seen as a form of RGR where goods are returned to their original country (territory) due to non-compliance or rejection. Where goods presented for import are rejected by a Customs Authority because of their failure to meet prescribed SPS regulations or technical regulations, the Customs Authority will allow the importer to re-consign or return the rejected goods to the exporter.

> Article 10: Formalities Connected with Importation, Exportation and Transit: 8.1 and 8.2 Rejected Goods: WTO TFA.

§25.28 SAFEGUARDS I'AM^{TM}

It is one of the three trade remedies and the only fair trade remedy, meaning its purpose is to remedy fair trade practices. The unfair trade remedy practices are dumping and countervailing (anti-subsidy). Safeguards is considered a *'safety value'* – an *'emergency measure'*, or *'emergency protection'*. It allows a country to act against a surge of imports if the domestic manufacturing industry is experiencing a material injury or the threat of material injury. The WTO permits it because a country cannot exceed its binding rates and thus cannot increase its customs duty rates of an affected good. A *'surge of imports'* is regarded as a *'real increase'* in imports, also known as an *'absolute increase*', or it can be an increase in the imports' share of a shrinking market, or even if the import quantity has not increased, in other words, a *'relative increase'*. Unlike the unfair trade remedies, a safeguard measure is not imposed to address fair trade. Consequently, this type of potential action is considered a very politically sensitive matter. As a first step, the country whose industry is experiencing *'serious injury'* tends to engage in diplomacy by attempting to persuade the exporting country's exporter to consider Voluntary Export Restraint (VER). *'Serious injury'* is defined as *'the significant overall impairment in the position of a domestic industry'*. A safeguard measure, or simply a safeguard, is expected to offer adequate trade compensation to the adversely affected industry.

> The WTO Agreement on Safeguards (Article XIX of GATT 1994).

§25.29 TEMPORARY ADMISSION I'AM^{TM}

After the consideration of the nature of the goods (the cornerstones), the third of the four groups of CSPs concerned with the treatment of the goods is Specific Use, which distinguishes between TA and End Use. TA allows for certain goods to be brought into a Customs territory conditionally relieved totally or partially from payment of duties, taxes, and levies. These goods must be imported for a specific purpose. They must be intended for re-exportation within a specified period without having undergone any change except normal depreciation due to their use. Goods are not intended to undergo any change and must be re-exported within the specified period. The RKC recommends that a provision be made to permit TA goods to be re-exported in one or more consignments. TA is typically used for goods that are imported to be exhibited at a trade fair, typically commercial samples, or as part of a music or stage show, or professional equipment, provided that all customs requirements and formalities are met and a guarantee is provided. This can be facilitated through a Carnet, pronounced kar-nay, which is a customs document, of which the most well known are the ATA (Admission Temporaire or Temporary Admission); E.C.S. (Echantillons Commerciaux - Commercial Samples); the CPD (Carnet de Passages en Douane) Carnet for a motor vehicle, other valuable equipment or baggage; and the TIR (Transports Internationaux Routiers or International Road Transports) Carnet.

> Specific Annex G: Temporary Admission: Chapter 1: G1 Temporary Admission: RKC.

§25.30 TEMPORARY STORAGE I'AM™

Contrary to its name, it is not part of the CSP's TA (specific use) and CW (temporary). Still, it is also covered in the RKC. It is a Customs procedure under which imported goods are temporarily stored under a Customs Authority's control and authorisation before they are placed under an SCP, such as a Transit, released to free circulation or exported. By placing the goods under TS, the full customs declaration, the payment of duties, taxes, and levies can be delayed, but only for a specified time. The RKC's recommended practice is that it should be allowed for all goods irrespective of quantity, CoO or country from which they arrived. It further recommends that goods that constitute a hazard will likely affect other goods or require special installations. The goods should be admitted only into temporary stores specially equipped and be designated by the competent Customs Authority to receive them. On the duration of TS, the RKC recommends that where national legislation lays down a time limit, it should be sufficient to enable the importer to complete the necessary formalities to place the goods under another Customs procedure. As for goods that are deteriorated, spoiled or damaged by accident or force majeure before leaving TS, they should be allowed to be cleared as if they had been imported in their deteriorated, spoiled or damaged state, provided that such deterioration, spoilage or damage is duly established to the satisfaction of the Customs Authority.

Specific Annex A: Arrival of goods in a Customs territory: Chapter 2: A2 Temporary Storage of goods: RKC.

§25.31 TRADE BLOCS I'AM™

Its spelling *'bloc'*, not *'block'*, is because it constitutes a group of countries that have an alliance, united by a common or aligned interest, striving to achieve a specific purpose. A *'trade bloc'* is a type of intergovernmental agreement whose core preoccupation is the elimination of tariffs and trade-restrictive measures between contracting parties or member countries. In international economics, trade blocs are viewed as forms of economic integration that progress towards ultimate full economic and commercial integration. Some consider trade blocs as building blocks, while others view them as stumbling blocks. In the formation of trade blocs, there are five forms or stages of economic integration – free movement of goods, common external tariff, free movement of factor endowments, common economic policies, and a common political environment. There are seven trade blocs: free FTZ, PTA, FTA, CU, customs union, common market or single market, economic union, and political union. The first three are termed *'shallow integration stages'*, while the remaining four are termed *'deep integration stages'*. With countries becoming signatories to multiple trade agreements and trade preferences, the overlap, confusion, and challenge in the application of the RoO provisions have been termed the *'spaghetti bowl'*. *'Tax-free shops'*, found at airports and seaports, do not constitute a stage of economic integration. The WCO has expressed its concern where these shops are established at land frontiers (road or rail).

Article XXIV of the GATT 1994 (Regional Trade Agreements): WTO.

§25.32 TRANSHIPMENT I'AM™

Transhipment, also known as *'transshipment'* or *'trans-shipment'*, is defined by the RKC as the Customs procedure under which goods are transferred under Customs control from the importing means of transport to the exporting means of transport within the area of one Customs office, which is the office of both importation and exportation. Transhipment applies to all modes of transport, also known as multimodal transport. The goods admitted to transhipment are not subject to the payment of duties, taxes, and levies, provided the conditions laid down by the Customs Authority are complied with. The RKC further stipulates that transhipment should not be refused solely on the grounds of the CoO of the goods, the country from which they arrived or their country of destination. Since the goods being moved are not Customs cleared, a guarantee is required to secure all the duties, taxes, and levies that were temporarily suspended on the goods. Under certain tariff and trade preference agreements, the RoO provisions could have a requirement known as a '*direct consignment rule*', also known as the '*direct shipment rule*', which effectively prohibits or disqualifies goods that are more under the transhipment procedure. Certain agreements replace the '*direct shipment rule*' with a '*non-manipulation rule*' for which transhipment goods could qualify. The requirement is simply that the goods may not be further processed during transportation, for which a Customs Authority could require documentary evidence of non-manipulation on importation.

Specific Annex E: Transit: Chapter 2: E2 Transhipment: RKC.

§25.33 TYPES OF DUTIES, TAXES AND LEVIES I'AM™

The interchangeable and indiscriminate use of terminology is no more evident than when considering duty, tax, levy, and tariff. An added challenge is also to consider the context in which the terminology is used, be it as a verb or a noun. The interest (financial interest) is in the movement of the goods, entering and leaving a Customs Authority's country or territory. It is said that a Customs Authority can levy a tax (a tax could also be a duty) or impose a levy or a duty. One might despair that '*a duty is a tax that you levy*'. Then, not only can a duty, a tax, or a levy be imposed but so too can a surcharge and a toll. To complicate matters further, customs and excise duties are classified as '*indirect taxes*'. Add to this that a '*tariff*' is often confused with duty, which could mean the duty liability or the rate of duty, depending on the context of use. A '*tariff*' has a trilogy of meanings. It could first be a list or a schedule that depicts the rates of duty payable on the importation or the exportation of the good. Second, it could refer to the actual duty being levied on the importation or the exportation of the good. Third, it could be the law that provides for the schedules of the tariff and customs provisions to mitigate the rate of customs duty. So it could, depending on the context, be the list or schedule, duty, and law. In essence, a '*duty*' is imposed on an activity which would not have been imposed in its absence. A '*tax*' is imposed on a range of activities that generate revenue, while a '*levy*' tends to be an obligatory payment to the government.

General Annex: Chapter 4 Duties and Taxes: RKC.

§25.34 VALORISATION – CUSTOMS VALUATION I'AM™

The third of the three cornerstones of Customs and Excises, concerned with the nature of the goods, is the process of determining the '*economic value*' of an imported good for calculating the duties, taxes, and levies. Customs valuation forms the basis of the assessment of a good which is liable for an *ad valorem* duty, taxes, or levies applied to the value of the good. It does not apply when a specific duty is imposed as it relates to the basis of customs valuation being a quantitative measure – quantity, weight, units, etc. There are two bases for customs valuation – FOB and CIF, which should never be confused with its Incoterms® *'delivery terms'* namesakes. Customs valuation intends to achieve two principal objectives: a fiscal objective – to ensure the precise levying of customs duties, taxes, and levies – and an economic objective – to promote international trade. In alignment with the objectives, it is imperative for any business engaged in international trade to establish the value of their goods – the *'price actually paid or payable'*. This is the real price paid (positive notion) and not the normal price. The WTO specifies six methods – the primary method (Transaction Value) and five secondary methods (alternative methods or replacement valuation methods – TV of Identical Goods, TV of Similar Goods, Deductive Method, Computed Method, Fallback Method) which need to be employed, in hierarchical order, to establish the value on which customs duties, levies, and taxes (including import VAT) needs to be paid.

The Agreement on Implementation of Article VII of the GATT 1994 (The Valuation Agreement): WTO.

Index

C

E

N

O

S

T

U

www.ingramcontent.com/pod-product-compliance
Ingram Content Group UK Ltd.
Pitfield, Milton Keynes, MK11 3LW, UK
UKHW020229290926
15470UKWH00002B/436